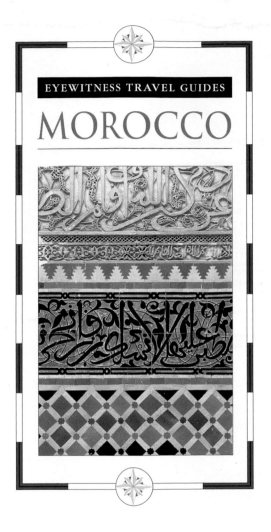

EYEWITNESS TRAVEL GUIDES

MOROCCO

TANGIER
Tetouan
Al-Hoceima
Larache · Melilla

NORTHERN
ATLANTIC COAST

MEDITERRANEAN COAST
& THE RIF

RABAT
ASABLANCA

MEKNÈS
& VOLUBILIS

FÈS
· Taza

MIDDLE ATLAS

HIGH ATLAS

-Jadida

Beni Mellal ·
Midelt
Figuig ·

ARRAKECH
· Er-Rachidia

· Asni

OUARZAZATE
& THE SOUTHERN OASES
Ouarzazate

· Zagora

TANGIER
Pages 128–141

**MEDITERRANEAN
COAST & THE RIF**
Pages 142–161

**MEKNÈS &
VOLUBILIS**
Pages 184–205

MIDDLE ATLAS
Pages 206–221

FÈS
Pages 162—183

HIGH ATLAS
Pages 244–259

**OUARZAZATE &
SOUTHERN OASES**
Pages 260–281

0 km   200

0 miles   200

DK EYEWITNESS TRAVEL GUIDES

MOROCCO

DORLING KINDERSLEY
LONDON • NEW YORK • MUNICH
MELBOURNE • DELHI
www.dk.com

DK

LONDON, NEW YORK,
MELBOURNE, MUNICH AND DELHI
www.dk.com

Produced by Hachette Tourisme, Paris, France

EDITORIAL DIRECTOR Catherine Marquet
PROJECT EDITORS Hélène Gédouin-Hines,
Catherine Laussucq, Paulina Nourissier
ART DIRECTOR Guylaine Moi
DESIGNERS Maogani
CARTOGRAPHY Fabrice Le Goff

CONTRIBUTORS
Rachida Alaoui, Jean Brignon, Nathalie Campodonico,
Fabien Cazenave, Gaëtan du Chatenet, Alain Chenal,
Emmanuelle Honorin, Maati Kabbal,
Mohamed Métalsi, Marie-Pascale Rauzier

Dorling Kindersley Limited
PUBLISHING MANAGER Jane Ewart
MANAGING EDITOR Anna Streiffert
ENGLISH TRANSLATION & EDITOR Lucilla Watson
CONSULTANT Christine Osborne
DTP Jason Little, Conrad van Dyke
PRODUCTION Sarah Dodd

Printed and bound in China
by Toppan Printing Co. (Shenzhen Ltd)

First published in Great Britain in 2002
by Dorling Kindersley Limited
80 Strand, London WC2R 0RL

Reprinted with revisions 2004

**The information in every
Dorling Kindersley Travel Guide is checked regularly.**
Every effort has been made to ensure that this book is as up-to-date
as possible at the time of going to press. Some details, however,
such as telephone numbers, opening hours, prices, gallery hanging
arrangements and travel information are liable to change. The
publishers cannot accept responsibility for any consequences arising
from the use of this book, nor for any material on third party
websites, and cannot guarantee that any website address in this
book will be a suitable source of travel information. We value the
views and suggestions of our readers very highly. Please write to:
Publisher, DK Eyewitness Travel Guides,
Dorling Kindersley, 80 Strand, London WC2R 0RL, Great Britain.

◁ **The kasbah at Aït Benhaddou, near Ouarzazate**

The Dadès valley *(see pp272–3)*

CONTENTS

**Detail of the mosque
at Tin Mal** *(see p252)*

Rose petals gathered for making
rosewater

Olives from the Dadès Valley

SURVIVAL GUIDE

An illuminated manuscript

TRAVELLERS'
NEEDS

Dish from the Fès region

The Mausoleum of
Moulay Ismaïl at Meknès *(pp194–5)*

HOW TO USE THIS GUIDE

THIS GUIDE HELPS you get the most from your visit to Morocco, providing expert recommendations and detailed practical information. *Introducing Morocco* maps the country and sets it in its historical and cultural context. The 13 sections comprising *Morocco Region by Region*, six of which focus on the country's major towns, describe important sights, using photographs, maps and illustrations. Restaurants and hotel recommendations, and information about hiking, trekking and other outdoor activities, can be found in *Travellers' Needs*. The *Survival Guide* contains practical tips on everything from visiting mosques to transport around the country.

MAJOR CITIES
In this guide, Morocco is described in 13 sections, three of which concentrate on Morocco's historic imperial cities – Fès, Meknès and Marrakech – and three on the country's major modern cities – Rabat, the capital, Casablanca and Tangier. A section is devoted to each city, except for Meknès. Each city's major sights are described in detail.

A country map shows the city's location in Morocco.

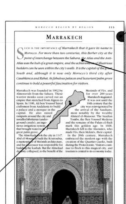

Coloured thumb tabs indentify the various towns and regions of Morocco.

1 Introduction
Each town's geographical setting and economic life are described, as well as its historical development and features of interest to the visitor.

2 City Map
For easy reference, the sights are numbered and located on a map. The main streets, bus stations and railway stations, parking areas and tourist offices are also shown.

Sights at a Glance lists the chapter's sights by category: mosques and churches, historic buildings, museums, parks and historic districts.

A locator map shows the central area of each city.

3 Detailed Information
All the sights in each city are described individually. Addresses, telephone numbers, opening hours, admission charges and information on how to get there are given for each sight. The key to symbols is shown on the back flap.

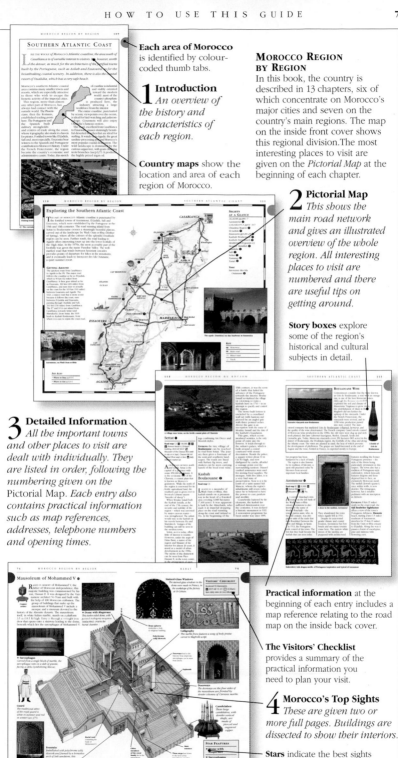

Each area of Morocco is identified by colour-coded thumb tabs.

1 Introduction
An overview of the history and characteristics of each region.

Country maps show the location and area of each region of Morocco.

MOROCCO REGION BY REGION
In this book, the country is described in 13 chapters, six of which concentrate on Morocco's major cities and seven on the country's main regions. The map on the inside front cover shows this regional division. The most interesting places to visit are given on the *Pictorial Map* at the beginning of each chapter.

2 Pictorial Map
This shows the main road network and gives an illustrated overview of the whole region. All interesting places to visit are numbered and there are useful tips on getting around.

Story boxes explore some of the region's historical and cultural subjects in detail.

3 Detailed Information
All the important towns and other places to visit are dealt with individually. They are listed in order, following the numbering given on the Pictorial Map. Each entry also contains practical information such as map references, addresses, telephone numbers and opening times.

Practical information at the beginning of each entry includes a map reference relating to the road map on the inside back cover.

The Visitors' Checklist provides a summary of the practical information you need to plan your visit.

4 Morocco's Top Sights
These are given two or more full pages. Buildings are dissected to show their interiors.

Stars indicate the best sights and important features.

INTRODUCING MOROCCO

Putting Morocco on the Map

Morocco has many faces. It is situated on the African continent and has traces of African heritage. But its climate and varied topography, its historical association with Andalusian Spain, and its wish to join the European Union give it a European facet. In the distant past it belonged to the indigenous Berbers. To the Arabs and Muslims who have held Morocco since the 7th century, it is known as Maghreb el-Aqsa – the westernmost country of the Muslim world. Morocco has 28,750,000 inhabitants, almost 40 per cent of whom are under 15 years old. The population is unevenly distributed over the country's 710,850 sq km (274,388 sq miles), being concentrated along the Atlantic coast and in the Rif and the High Atlas mountains.

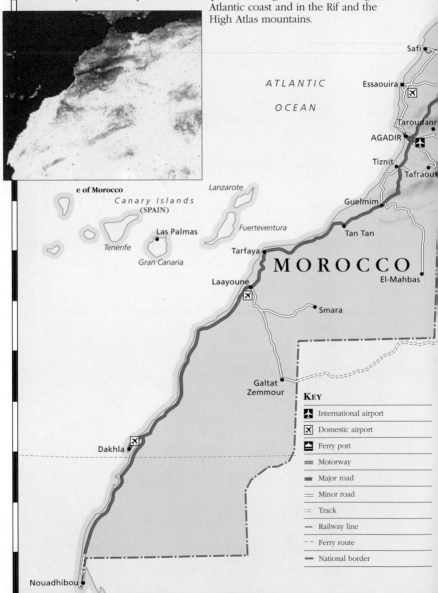

ATLANTIC

OCEAN

Safi

Essaouira

Taroudann

AGADIR

Tiznit

Tafraou

e of Morocco

Lanzarote

Canary Islands
(SPAIN)

Guelmim

Tan Tan

Fuerteventura

Las Palmas

Tarfaya

MOROCCO

Tenerife

Gran Canaria

Laayoune

El-Mahbas

Smara

Galtat
Zemmour

KEY

✈	International airport
✕	Domestic airport
⛴	Ferry port
▬	Motorway
▬	Major road
═	Minor road
∷	Track
—	Railway line
--	Ferry route
—	National border

Dakhla

Nouadhibou

◁ *Moroccan Festival*, a painting by André Suréda (1872–1930)

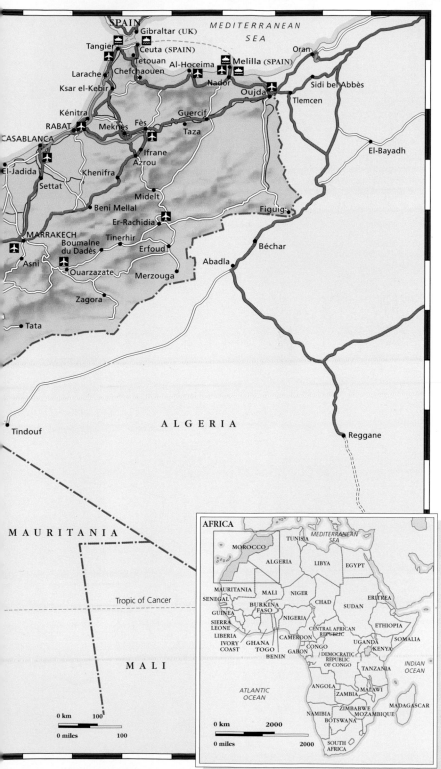

A PORTRAIT OF MOROCCO

*M*OROCCO IS *like a tree whose roots lie in Africa but whose leaves breathe in European air. This is the metaphor that King Hassan II (1929–99) used to describe a country that is both profoundly traditional and strongly drawn to the modern world. It is this double-sided, seemingly contradictory disposition that gives Morocco its cultural richness.*

Morocco is a country that is unique in the Muslim world. Its richly diverse culture has been shaped by 3,000 years of history, by ethnic groups whose roots go far back in time, and also by its geographical location, with the Atlantic Ocean to the west, sub-Saharan Africa to the south, Europe to the north and the Mediterranean countries to the east.

Moroccan girl in the traditional costume of the Atlas

The Moroccan people are torn between the lure of modernity on the one hand and a profound desire for

Islamic reform on the other. With events such as the death in 1999 of Morocco's sovereign, Hassan II, and the enthronement of his son and successor, Mohammed VI, as well as the establishment of a left-wing coalition government and the problems that that government faces regarding the economy and freedom of the press, Morocco today stands on the threshold of a challenging new phase in its history.

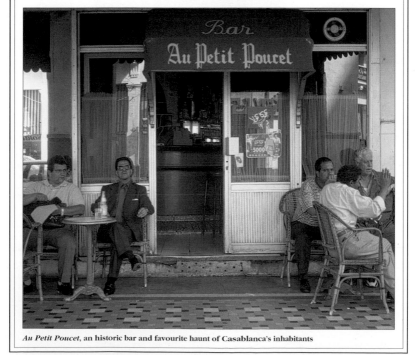

Au Petit Poucet, an historic bar and favourite haunt of Casablanca's inhabitants

◁ *A woman from Essaouira, dressed in the traditional white* haik

Members of a Gnaoua brotherhood

AN EVOLVING SOCIETY

Since the 1950s, Morocco has undergone profound social change. Traditional tribal cohesion
has been replaced by
the European-style
nuclear   family,
polygamy has be-
come distinctly rare,
a money-based econo-
my is now the norm,
and the notion of indi-
viduality has emerged.
These   changes   have
been accompanied by a
growth in the urban popu-
lation and by the rise of a
bi-cultural elite, with a traditional background and   a
European outlook. With an
unusually large percentage of
young people, Moroccan society is un-
mistakably breaking away from the

Water-seller
in Marrakech

past. However, Morocco still faces the
challenge of resolving the difficulties
that sharp contradictions in its social,
political and economic life present.

Since gaining independence from
France in 1956, Morocco has made
attempts to tackle three major scourges:
illiteracy, unemployment and poverty.
Although the country assigns 26.3 per
cent of its budget to education, the
literacy rate (55 per cent) remains one
of the lowest in the world. Education
no longer guarantees work and more
than 200,000 high-school graduates are
unemployed. Neither is university
education, now under the control of
Islamic fundamentalists, any longer a
passport to success.

BERBER CULTURE

With its mixed Berber and Arab
population, Morocco has,
however, successfully maintained ethnic and cultural
stability and equality between
the Berber and Arabic languages. Although Tamazight,
the Berber language, is not
spoken or taught in schools,
it is one of the languages
heard on Moroccan radio
and television. The move-
ment to promote Berber language and
culture through the medium of news-

Filming at the Atlas Studios at Ouarzazate

Traditional agricultural labour in the Ourika valley

the *mudawwana* – a statute of 1957 that dominates the lives of Moroccans and prevents women from being treated as fully-fledged adults. Moves to raise the status of women made in March 1999 were met by opposition and incited the wrath of the Minister of Religious Affairs, the *ulemas* (councils) and Parliament's Islamic deputies. At the present time, the desire for progress and modernization on the part of Morocco's new king and his government has met with resistance from religious bodies of all denominations.

papers, concerts and other cultural events is dynamic, as are efforts to encourage the wider use of the language and to nurture respect for the rich Berber culture.

Pilot projects, such as the construction of mosques, wells, roads and schools, have been undertaken in the southern Souss region, funded by money sent back by Berbers of southern Morocco working abroad.

THE STATUS OF WOMEN

Women today work in all sectors – as political delegates and ambassadors, airline pilots, company directors and royal advisers; they are also Olympic champions, writers, publishers, active militants and journalists. Thus they have a secure place in Moroccan society.

In the space of 30 years, the status and position of women has radically changed. The constitution of 10 March 1972, which granted women the right to vote and to be elected, was the first of these changes. In 1994, 77 women were elected to the Chamber of Representatives. However, the highly militant feminist associations are still not entirely satisfied. They demand the abolition of

POLITICAL CHANGE

Until the death of Hassan II in 1999, Morocco was ruled by a distant and autocratic king.

Westernized young girls in Casablanca

The effect of the attempted coups d'état of 1971 and 1972 was to encourage the Moroccan authorities to control the wheels of government even more tightly. Driss Basri, then Minister of the Interior, was responsible for this clamp-down.

Berber women in the traditional costume of the Rif

The Rose Festival in El-Kelaa M'Gouna

At the end of his reign, Hassan II began to relax his authoritarian grip on power by involving the left wing in the country's government. In February 1998, a government of national unity, led by the Socialist leader Abderrahmane Youssoufi, was formed, although in the years since, its success is deemed to have been limited.

Since 1999, Mohammed VI has ushered in a new style of government. Underlying his political approach are a willingness to listen more closely to his people and a commitment to countering Islamic radicals. He also won popular support for sacking Driss Basri, Minister of the Interior. Brushing aside protocol, he has publicly presented his new wife and has ordered the setting-up of royal commissions to look into economic development, the problem of the southern Sahara, employment and education.

Berber
cameraman

For the September 2002 parliamentary election, Morocco had more than 20 parties, many of which had been specially formed. This led to the success of the Islamic Party of Justice and Development (PJD), the third political party in the country after the Socialist Party (USFP) and the Istiqual Party, the principal opposition party to the coalition government. The terrorist bombs of May 2003 in Casablanca, which killed 43 people, have made the country unstable and seem to question the development of a process of democratisation that was started by Mohammed VI.

A VARIED ECONOMY

Morocco's geographical location, at the nexus between Africa and Europe, brings it considerable economic advantage, especially in the fields of tourism, agriculture and the textile industry. Moreover, the extensive oil-fields that have recently been discovered in Morocco are large enough to supply the country's domestic needs for 35 years. Fishing and hydroelectric power are Morocco's other two natural resources. The economy also benefits from the influx of funds sent back by

Schoolchildren in the Dadès valley

influx of funds sent back by Moroccans working abroad. Some US $2,000 million are sent back to Morocco each year.

The arrival of multinational companies has transformed telecommunications and has led to an explosion in the use of mobile phones. The number of computers has also risen.

Nevertheless, the Moroccan economy is handicapped in several ways: agriculture is dependent on rainfall, the education system is inadequate, energy costs are prohibitively high, and sparse investment is made in the population. In 1999, the number of people living in poverty stood at 5 million. Every year, almost 460,000 rural emigrants swell the poor ghettos in the towns and cities. For a number of reasons, the economic reforms introduced by the government of national unity have not had the anticipated effect. Morocco is being encouraged by the World Bank to liberalize its economy, boost exports and devalue its currency.

The country has a positive image in Europe, and relations are being consolidated. Free trade between Morocco and the EU is projected for 2010. The

A spice and medicinal plant seller in one of the souks of Marrakech

arrangement depends on Morocco putting in place a solid financial and technological infrastructure.

The country is in need of modernization, although the evolution of true democracy is likely to be slow. This is a key policy, however, since the slow progress of reforms is encouraging young people to emigrate. Whether Mohammed VI will succeed in controlling Islamic radicals, invigorating his country's economy, and abolishing illiteracy remains to be seen. An entire nation looks towards its new king.

The picturesque Place Jemaa el-Fna in Marrakech

The Landscape and Wildlife of Morocco

WITH A MOUNTAIN range exceeding a height of 4,000 m (13,130 ft) and a coastline stretching from the Mediterranean to the Atlantic, Morocco has a varied topography. In environments ranging from arid scrublands to cedar forests and high mountains, plant life comprises over 4,000 species adapted to extreme conditions. The coast is visited by migratory birds while the mountains are the habitat of Barbary sheep and birds of prey, including the lammergeier *(see p219)*.

Eleonar's falcon

The argan, a tree growing only in southwestern Morocco *(see p127)*

MOUNTAIN FORESTS & HIGH STEPPES

Forests grow in the Rif, the Middle Atlas and the western High Atlas, at altitudes of 1,400–2,500 m (4,600–8,200 ft), where annual rainfall is 650 mm–2,000 mm (25–78 in). The varied vegetation here includes Atlas cedar, maritime pine and holm-oak. The high steppes, covered with low, thorny vegetation, are found at altitudes over 2,700 m (8,860 ft) in the High Atlas *(see p218–19).*

The golden eagle is seen mostly in the mountains, where it preys on jackals, bustards and small mammals.

The kite builds its nest on rocky outcrops. It is a scavenger but sometimes also kills its prey by knocking it off high rocks with a strong flap of its wing.

ARID COASTAL REGIONS & DESERT

The rocky coastal lowlands between Safi and Agadir has an annual rainfall ranging from 40 to 150 mm (1.5 to 6 in). Vegetation, which is adapted to saline conditions, consists of sparse shrubs, mostly acacia. Further south is the desert with *ergs* (sand dunes) and the stony *hammada*.

The bald ibis, almost extinct, is found in the Souss Massa National Park (see p292), *a fertile exception to the arid littoral.*

The Barbary squirrel, whose favourite food is argan nuts, inhabits the arid lowlands of southwestern Morocco.

The great cormorant nests on sea cliffs between Agadir, in the north, and the Arguin sand banks of Mauritania.

THE MACAQUE OR BARBARY APE

The macaque is North Africa's only monkey. Three-quarters of the population lives in the cedar forests of the Middle Atlas, up to an altitude of 2,000 m (6,565 ft). Macaques are also found in the Rif, the High Atlas and on the Rock of Gibraltar. The animals live in colonies of 10 to 30 individuals, consisting of adults and young monkeys of both sexes. In summer, they feed on caterpillars, acorns, mushrooms and asphodel bulbs. In winter, their diet consists of grasses, cedar leaves and sometimes bark.

The macaque, a tail-less monkey of North Africa

SCRUB & STEPPE
Southeastern Morocco consists of steppes covered in esparto grass and artemisia. On the high plateaux, on the southern slopes of the High Atlas and on part of the Anti-Atlas annual rainfall ranges from 100 mm to 300 mm (4 in to 12 in) and snow is rare. Trees include Atlas pistachio, juniper and ash.

DRY WOODLAND
Almost all the low-lying and middle-altitude regions on the northern side of the Atlas are covered by dry woodland. Annual rainfall here ranges from 350 mm to 800 mm (14 in to 31 in) and snowfall is occasional. Trees include holm-oak, cork oak (pictured above) and kermes oak, olive, Barbary thuya, and Aleppo and maritime pine.

The Numidian crane nests on Morocco's high plateaux in summer.

The Houbara bustard *lives in the semi-desert plains of the south.*

Dorca's gazelle inhabits the semi-desert regions of the south and east. It feeds on grasses and acacia shoots.

The golden jackal *is found throughout North Africa and in the Sahara. It can survive for long periods without water.*

The booted eagle *lives in the forests of the north and the Atlas Mountains. It makes its nests in tall trees.*

The Urban Architecture of Morocco

T HE HISTORY OF urban architecture in Morocco goes back more than 1,000 years. The Karaouiyine Mosque in Fès was built in 857 by the first Idrissid rulers of Morocco *(see p46)*, who founded the city. From the age of the Idrissids until the 20th century, a succession of many different architectural styles has produced a rich architectural heritage. The artistic conventions and styles of each period shed light on the secular and religious life of the rulers and people who lived in those times.

Karaouiyine Mosque *(see pp176–7)*, **the earliest Idrissid building**

THE ALMORAVIDS (11TH–12TH C.)

It was under the Almoravids that the Moorish style developed in Morocco, which was then the centre of an Ibero-Maghrebian empire. Andalusian elements included the horseshoe arch and the lobed arch, Kufic script, which was often used in conjunction with floral decoration, the scrolling acanthus-leaf motif and the use of decorative plasterwork.

The exterior of the 12th-century Koubba Ba'Adiyn dome

The interior of the Koubba Ba'Adiyn *(see p231) is made up of interlaced pointed arches and radiating rosettes.*

THE ALMOHADS (12TH–13TH C.)

The Almohads, under whom the Ibero-Maghrebian empire reached its apogee, established an architectural style that later dynasties were to emulate. The Koutoubia Mosque in Marrakech, the Mosque of Hassan II in Rabat and grand monumental gateways each exemplify this style.

The Koutoubia minaret

The carved decoration of the Koutoubia minaret (see pp236–7) consists of an interlacing geometric pattern.

THE MERINIDS (13TH–15TH C.)

The Merinids used the same building techniques and mostly the same architectural forms as those of the preceding period. They were, however, the greatest builders of *medersas (see pp172–3)*, those peculiarly Moroccan masterpieces of architecture. They also displayed a remarkable aptitude for exquisite architectural ornamentation.

The inner façade of the Bou Inania Medersa *displays a wide range of techniques, ornamental styles and materials.*

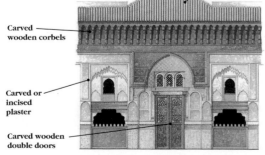

Pyramidal roof of green tiles

Carved wooden corbels

Carved or incised plaster

Carved wooden double doors

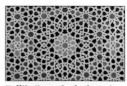

Zellij *tilework* *of coloured terracotta squares in the Bou Inania Medersa in Fès depicts complex geometric patterns.*

The Saadians (16th–17th C.)

Morocco's Saadian rulers gave the country two master-pieces: the Palais el-Badi *(see p235)* and the Saadian Tombs, both in Marrakech *(see p238)*. These embody the Andalusian traditions that had taken root in Morocco.

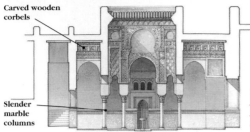

Carved wooden corbels

Slender marble columns

Decorative plasterwork, *with a lattice of floral and geometric motifs, covers the upper walls of the mausoleum.*

The royal mausoleum, *in Marrakech, is a magnificent building. It was completed in the 16th century by the sultan Ahmed el-Mansour.*

The Alaouites (17th C.–present day)

The two great builders of the Alaouite period were Moulay Ismaïl, who made Meknès the royal city, and Sidi Mohammed ben Abdellah, who founded Essaouira *(see pp120–25).*

The Mausoleum of Moulay Ismaïl (see pp194–5) *is designed in a style similar to that of the Saadian Tombs.*

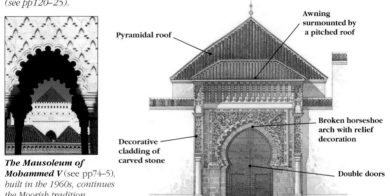

Pyramidal roof

Awning surmounted by a pitched roof

Decorative cladding of carved stone

Broken horseshoe arch with relief decoration

Double doors

The Mausoleum of Mohammed V (see pp74–5), *built in the 1960s, continues the Moorish tradition.*

The Modern Era

During the French Protectorate, in the early 20th century, Nouvelles Villes (modern towns) were built outside the medinas, whose traditional layout *(see pp22–3)* thus was spared from development. A Neo-Moorish style evolved in many towns, while Art Deco was predominant in the city of Casablanca *(see p101).*

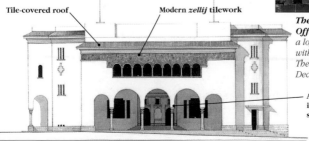

Tile-covered roof

Modern *zellij* tilework

The Casablanca Post Office *(1918–20) has a loggia decorated with zellij tilework. The interior is in Art Deco style.*

Arched entrance in the Moorish style

Medinas

MOROCCO'S MEDINAS almost all have the same layout. The typical medina (meaning "town" in Arabic) consists of a densely packed urban conglomeration enclosed within defensive walls set with lookout towers. The tangle of narrow winding streets and countless alleyways turns the layout of a medina into a labyrinth. The centre of the medina is cut through by wide avenues running between the main gateways and by other main streets, which, as a defensive measure, are either angled or closed off by houses or projecting walls.

Minaret in the medina

Hundreds of narrow streets wind through the medina. Some are no more than 50 cm (20 in) wide.

The monumental gateway, a fortified entrance flanked by projecting crenellated towers, leads into the medina. Bab el-Chorfa in Fès is a particularly splendid example.

Roof-terrace

THE LAYOUT OF A MEDINA

Despite their apparent chaos, medinas are laid out according to certain set considerations. The mosque is always located at the heart. Other features include the separation of different religious and ethnic groups, the distinction between home and the workplace, and the location of activities according to a social and commercial hierarchy. Every medina is laid out according to these factors.

Street partly blocked by a house

Lookout tower

Open-air souks, like the basket souk in Marrakech, are markets where specialist crafts and other products are sold. Souks are also the regular meeting places of city people and visiting country-dwellers.

QUARTERS

The quarters of a medina are no more than loosely defined areas. A quarter, or *hawma*, is really just a communal space consisting of several small streets and alleyways, and it is the focus of the inhabitants' material and spiritual life. Each quarter has a communal oven, a hammam (steam bath), a Koranic school, and a grocer's shop, which is always located in one of the smaller streets. The shop sells such basic necessities as vegetables, fruit, oil, coal, sugar, spices and other foods. There are no shops selling luxury goods in quarters like these.

A grocer's shop in a quarter of Fès

The grand mospue mosque is the central point of the city.

The patio, or riad, *like this one in Essaouira, is the focal point of a building. The rooms are arranged around the courtyard, which often contains a fountain.*

Sturdy defensive walls protect the medina.

The souk for valuable items is located next to the mosque.

Craftsmen, like the tanners of Fès, work together in parts of the medina known as souk, kissaria or fondouk. Their location, from the centre to the periphery, depends on the craft's rarity and its pollution level.

Workshops in the souks, *like the dyers' souk in Marrakech, shown here, are often tiny. The craftsman has only just enough space to make and sell his products.*

Moroccan Crafts

Chichaoua carpet detail

THE CUSTOM of producing utilitarian objects that are visually pleasing and enlivened with decoration is a deeply rooted tradition among Moroccan craftsmen. They inject beauty into the humblest of materials, from leather, wood and clay, to copper and wool. The importance given to decoration is often so great that it sometimes takes precedence over the object to which it is applied. The endless interplay of arabesques, interlacing patterns, beguiling floral motifs and intricate inscriptions are an integral part of traditional Moroccan life.

Perfume bottle

Sheepskin binding for the Koran, with geometric decoration

LEATHERWORK

Leatherworking has always been a major industry in Morocco, particularly in Fès, Meknès, Rabat, Salé and Marrakech. The leatherworkers and tanners of Marrakech and Fès, whose numerous workshops fill the picturesque quarters of the medina, are those with the most illustrious reputation.

Tanners first clean the hide – either sheepskin or goatskin – and then dye it red, yellow or orange. Gold-leaf decoration may also be applied. The leatherworkers then fashion the material into utilitarian or decorative objects such as pouffes, handbags, *babouches* (slippers) and desk sets.

Sheepskin binding for the Koran with gold-leaf decoration

WOODWORK

The traditional craft of woodworking is centred mostly in Essaouira, Fès, Meknès, Salé, Marrakech and Tetouan. The many different kinds of wood used by Moroccan woodworkers and cabinet-makers come from the forests of the Atlas and the Rif. Cedar and walnut are used mostly by cabinet-makers, who are highly skilled makers of carved or studded doors, and also in the construction of wooden ceilings. Ebony and citrus wood are used for marquetry and veneering. Thuya, with its beautiful rosewood hue, can be made into elegant furniture and decorative objects.

Painted wooden bread box from Meknès (early 19th century)

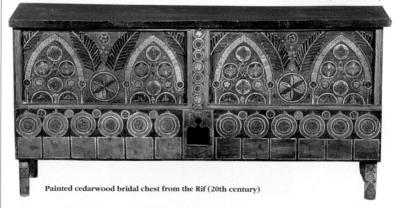

Painted cedarwood bridal chest from the Rif (20th century)

CARPETS

Carpets are a ubiquitous part of the furnishings of the Moroccan home *(see p340)*. City-made carpets, woven mostly in Rabat and Médiouna, are characterized by bright colours and a pattern consisting of a rectangular field on a red background, framed by bands of edging and with geometric motifs. Symmetry is a central feature of carpets made in Rabat. Village carpets, which are either woven or knotted, are produced in the Middle and High Atlas, in Marrakech and in Haouz. They have more imaginative patterns, such as animal, plant and architectural motifs, which the weavers (mostly women) themselves devise. Weaving and knotting techniques vary according to region, and the various types of village carpets are referred to by their place of origin, such as Middle Atlas, High Atlas, Haouz or Marrakech.

Sahraoui woman weaving a carpet

A knotted carpet from Rabat

POTTERY

Glazed pottery dish from Fès (19th century)

Decorated pottery is an integral part of everyday domestic life. Jugs, dishes and bowls are seen in every Moroccan kitchen and living room. Fès, one of the most important centres of pottery production, is renowned for its pottery – blue and white and multi-coloured on a white base. Safi, whose potting industry is more recent, produces pieces characterized by shimmering colours. Local tradition dictates shape, colour, glaze and type of decoration. Meknès and Salé are two other important centres of pottery manufacture.

Pottery oil jar

Ceramic honey jar with floral decoration

COPPER AND BRASS

Copper and brass are metals that lend themselves to being cut, hammered, embossed, inlaid and engraved. The repertoire of the Moroccan coppersmith ranges from the humblest domestic objects to the most ostentatious, such as inlaid or panelled doors, trays and chandeliers. This craft reveals a highly developed skill and a love of intricate detail, and follows an ancient tradition.

Brass door with geometric and other decorative motifs

Copper jug from Meknès (19th century)

Moroccan Music

MOROCCO'S RICH musical tradition reflects the country's cultural and geographical diversity. In towns and cities, the Arab musical tradition comprises Moorish music *(al-ala)*, religious popular music (which may be ceremonial or therapeutic), secular music, such as *melhoun*, *sama* and *daqqa*, and Judeo-Arabic music, as well as many other types besides. In rural areas, Berber music, which includes songs and dances, such as the *ahouach*, the *ahidous* and the *rwayes*, is connected to the cycle of the seasons, to work in the fields and to religious and secular ceremonies. Modern popular music, *chaabi*, which is broadcast by national television and radio, fuses and explores new genres that combine the traditional and the modern.

Oud player

The ahouach *is a kind of musical poetry sung by the Berbers of the High Atlas. They accompany themselves with a bendir, a strung tambourine.*

Taarija

Rattles

The guedra *is a dance of the western Sahara, usually performed by women on their knees.*

The taarija *is a clay tam-tam that is used in popular music. It is made in different sizes.*

Rattles, *known as* garagab, *are iron castanets that are used by the Gnaoua people and by musicians who play* daqqa *music.*

Tbila *are pairs of drums made from a skin stretched over a pottery vessel and secured with thongs. They are shown here with* guembri, *a type of oud used in folk music.*

The ghayta, *a conical wind instrument made of apricot wood, is similar to an oboe.*

*The **gasba** is a kind of reed flute. It is played in several regions of Morocco, most pariculary by the Jilala brotherhood, devotees of Moulay Abdelkader Jilal.*

***Small shops** where musical instruments are made and sold have hardly changed since the Middle Ages. They sell a very wide range of traditional instruments.*

Bendir

Choukara
(money bag)

*The **bendir** is an instrument consisting of a goatskin stretched over a wooden frame. Two strings tied crosswise within produce the sound.*

THE *DAQQA* OF MARRAKECH

This type of music is performed by a group of men and consists of different rhythms accompanied by singing. The *daqqa* is performed once a year at the Achoura Festival in Marrakech and Taroudannt.

THE GNAOUA

The Gnaoua are musicians descended from black brotherhoods of slaves transported from Mali, Guinea and Ghana to act as guards to the sultans Moulay Ismaïl (1672–1727) in Meknès and Moulay Abdallah (1757–90) in Essaouira. They venerated Bilal, the black Christian slave set free by the Prophet Mohammed for having cured his daughter Fatima of an illness by his singing. Emulating Bilal, these musicians and "doctors" combine music and curing, fusing African tradition and the cult of saints of Islamic folklore. Their rituals, known as *lila* and performed at night, consist of trance ceremonies during which, through feverish ritual chants and dances, they call up African spirits *(mlouk)*, Muslim saints, legendary figures and ancestors.

Group of Gnaoua singers and dancers

Literature and Cinema

MODERN MOROCCAN LITERATURE came to the fore in the 1950s at the same time as socio-political upheaval shook Morocco. Among the causes of this upheaval were the rise of major towns and cities, the launch of an education programme, with the establishment of modern schools alongside traditional Koranic schools, and the polarization of a proletariat and a social elite. It was in this fresh context that the Moroccan novel, written either in Arabic or in French, developed.

Paperback edition of Tahar ben Jelloun's *Les Yeux Baissés*

THE AUTOBIOGRAPHICAL NOVEL

RESPONSIBILITY FOR sounding the death knell of a literary tradition that had become hidebound by tradition, hemmed in by an ethnographic and folkloric approach, lies with two writers: Driss Chraïbi, writing in French, with *Le Passé Simple (The Simple Past*, 1954), and Abdelmajid Benjelloun, writing in Arabic, with *De l'Enfance* (1957). In a society so fundamentally Muslim as that of Morocco, writing in the first person in a work of literature was nothing less than shocking.

These two autobiographies were to open the gates of literary freedom, no longer circumscribed by a feudal and patriarchal ethic. In the 1960s Moroccan literature began to take a radical new direction. What emerged was a genre of writing in the French deconstructionist mould. The periodicals *Souffles* and *Lamalif* (which were banned by the authorities) took a new editorial and political lead. They, and such organizations as the Union des Ecrivains, gave Moroccan literature a new vitality. Writers and intellectuals, who had been submissive for so long, could at last express their vision. Among these writers are Tahar Ben Jelloun (*L'Enfant de Sable/The Sand Child,* 1988, and *Les Yeux Baissés/ With Downcast Eyes*, 1992), Abdelkebir Khatibi *(Amour Bilingue/ Love in Two Languages*, 1983), Mohammed Choukri (the two-volume

Driss Chraïbi

autobiography *For Bread Alone*, 1987, and *Streetwise*, 1996 – translated from the Arabic) and Mohammed Berrada *(The Game of Forgetting*, 1996, also from the Arabic). Other authors in the same genre, dealing with themes of past experiences, of language, of the body, of history and of experiences related in the first person are Mohammed Khair Eddine, Abdellatif Laabi, Mostapha Nissabouri, Edmond Amran El-Maleh, Ahmed El-Majjati, Mohammed Zafzaf and Mohammed Bennis.

NEW GENERATION, NEW HOPES

NOW THAT Moroccan writers have all but won their fight, literature in Morocco today, in Arabic as in French, is seeking fresh inspiration and impetus. The lead weight that stifled Moroccan culture up to relatively recent times is gradually lifting.

Through such literary genres as the novel, poetry, criticism and the essay, writers are exploring new avenues. Their aim is to throw off the censorship that is still imposed on, as well as by, writers of the first and second generations to have emerged since the 1960s. Thus, the poetry and novels of Fouad Laroui, Mahi

Mohammed Choukri, whose books have been widely translated

MOROCCAN CINEMA

Moroccan cinema, currently in the process of emerging from a long dark night, has produced some fine films, and its young directors have won popular acclaim both in Morocco and in Europe. Among them are Nour Eddine Lakhmari (maker of *Brèves Notes* and *Le Dernier Spectacle)*, Faouzi Bensaïdi *(La Falaise* and *Le Mur)*, Ahmed Boulane *(Ali Rabiaa et les Autres)*, Myriam Bakir *(Samia)* and Nabil Ayouch *(Le Vendeur de Silence, Mektoub* and *Ali Zaoua, Prince de la Rue)*. Some were born and live outside Morocco, which has allowed them to gain experience of Western

Ali Zaoua, Prince de la Rue, a film by Nabil Ayouch, portrays the fate of street urchins

cinema before turning their attention to their native country, sometimes seeing it through fresh eyes. Themes of solitude are treated alongside the question of the plight of street children, as in Nabil Ayouch's *Ali Zaoua* (released in English in 2002). These young film-makers draw on the harsh realities of life in Morocco for the raw subjects of their work.

Binebine and Salah El-Ouadie, tackle head on such thorny subjects as corruption, nepotism, violence and imprisonment. Like a society that is in the process of rising from the ashes, Moroccan writing has conquered fear to pinpoint

such as Mohammed Choukri, Tahar Ben Jelloun and Driss Chraïbi who have managed to have their work published in Europe have become much more widely known.

In the 1960s, the imminent demise of Moroccan literature was predicted. However, the work of Fouad Laroui, Mahi Binebine and Rajae Benchemsi strongly demonstrates the new impetus with which they have revitalized their country's literary tradition.

Marocaines en Mâle-Vie by Rachida Saqi (1998)

Mahi Binebine, a writer who has reinvigorated Moroccan literature

and describe certain social nightmares. In *Cannibales* by Mahi Binebine, for example, would-be exiles attempting to cross the Straits of Gibraltar drift aimlessly in makeshift boats.

About 600 titles are published in Morocco each year. However, most of them are rarely available outside the country, and even fewer are translated into English, so that much excellent writing remains unknown to a wider readership. Writers

WOMEN WRITERS

THE FEMALE LITERARY tradition in Morocco is a phenomenon that began to develop only in the 1980s, and Moroccan literature still has few women writers. The work of Khanata Bennouna and Malika El-Asimi is rooted in tradition and focuses on classical Arabic themes. One of the few female authors available in English is Leila Abouzeid. Her novel *Year of the Elephant – A Moroccan Woman's Journey towards Independence* (1989; written in Arabic in 1983) tells the story of a divorced and

ostracized Muslim woman who starts to question traditional cultural attitudes towards women and who becomes involved with the struggle for Moroccan Independence. Abouzeid's autobiographical *Return to Childhood* (1999, published in Arabic in 1993) deals with her childhood and is also a rich account of different gene-rations. Among other female writers are Rajae Benchemsi and Rachida Saqi, their novels also focussing on the situation and lives of Moroccan women today.

Rajae Benchemsi, whose work is published in French

The Islamic Faith in Morocco

MOROCCO'S OFFICIAL RELIGION is the orthodox, or Sunni, sect of Islam. It is based on the Koran and the Sunna, in which the words and deeds of the Prophet Mohammed are recorded. It is this religion, which was introduced to Morocco in the 7th century, that underpins both the country's law and its faith. Islam is also the unifying force in the daily life of every Moroccan, whose duty it is to respect the Five Pillars of Islam. These are *chahada* (profession of faith), *salat* (prayer), *zakat* (ritual almsgiving), Ramadan (fasting) and *hadj* (the pilgrimage to Mecca). The king of Morocco is both the country's secular and spiritual leader. On his accession to the throne in 1999, Mohammed VI strongly reaffirmed this double prerogative.

***Mohammed VI**, King of Morocco, at prayer. For 1,000 years, each Moroccan sovereign has borne the title "leader of the faithful".*

***Ritual ablutions** must be performed before prayers. The courtyards of mosques always contain fountains and basins, with hammams (steam-baths) nearby. The Islamic faith places great importance on personal cleanliness.*

Maghrebi calligraphy, characteristic of North Africa, is derived from the more austere Kufic script.

***Ceramic tiles** painted with religious motifs, carved plaster and carved wood are the three main elements in the decoration not only of mosques and medersas but also of traditional Muslim homes.*

KORAN IN MAGHREBI SCRIPT

The Koran, the holy pronouncements of Allah dictated to the Prophet Mohammed, is central to Islamic faith. Islamic calligraphy, a major art form in the Muslim world, is highly stylized and combines perfect legibility with visual harmony and colourful illumination.

***Dish with three mihrabs (niches)**
Calligraphy and religious symbols are two prominent themes in the traditional decorative arts of the Muslim world.*

FRIDAY PRAYERS

The five daily prayers *(salat)* form part of the five obligations, or "pillars", of Islam that are incumbent on Muslims. The faithful are required to come to the mosque for the midday prayers that are said every Friday. On this day devoted to Allah they also hear a sermon delivered by the *khotba*, or preacher. The gathering at Friday prayers also reinforces the sense of belonging that Muslims have in their community.

Muslims leaving a mosque

Muslim prayer beads consist of a string of 33 or 99 beads separated by markers. Muslims use the beads to recite the 99 names or attributes of Allah.

The chapters, or suras, of the Koran are separated by illuminations.

Daily prayer consists of a series of recitations and prostrations. Kneeling in rows, on a strictly egalitarian basis, the faithful face the direction of Mecca. This direction is called qibla, *and it is symbolized by the mihrab, a niche in the wall of the mosque. The imam, who leads the prayers, kneels in front.*

ISLAMIC FESTIVALS

The Muslim calendar is based on the lunar year, which is a little shorter than the solar year *(see p41)*. The ninth month, Ramadan, is a time of fasting. Aïd el-Fitr, or Aïd es Seghir, marks the end of Ramadan, and at Aïd el-Adha, or Aïd el-Kebir, a sheep is sacrificed in memory of the sacrifice of Abraham. Mouloud commemorates the birth of the Prophet Mohammed.

Cakes baked for Ramadan

Sacrificial sheep

The Berbers

Terracotta vessel

Two out of every three Moroccans are, in cultural and linguistic terms, Berber. Thought to be the descendants of people of mixed origins – including Oriental, Saharan and European – the Berbers settled in Morocco at different times, and they do not make up a homogeneous race. By finding refuge in mountainous regions, they survived several successive invasions – those of the civilizations of the Mediterranean basin, of the Arabs, then, much later, those of the French and the Spaniards. The Berbers still speak several dialects and maintain distinct cultural traditions. They are renowned for their trading activities and for the strength of their tribal and family ties.

*The **fouta** is a rectangular piece of fabric with red and white stripes. It is worn with a conical straw hat by women of the Rif.*

Young Berber girls *dress in bright colours and from an early age wear a headscarf knotted at the top of the head, as their mothers do.*

Veils of many colours cover the women of the Tiznit region.

Henna patterns, *which Berber women paint on themselves, give protection against supernatural forces. Besides keeping evil spirits away, they are supposed to purify and beautify the wearer. On feast days, women decorate their hands and their feet.*

Young girls do not wear veils. Only when they reach adulthood do girls cover their face.

The grand souk at the moussem of Imilchil *is both a social and a commercial gathering. It is an opportunity for Berbers from all over the Atlas Mountains to buy all that they need for the year ahead.*

*The **hendira**, a striped cape woven on a simple loom, is the typical overgarment worn by Berber women.*

The **jellaba**, *an ankle-length robe with long sleeves and a hood, is worn over a wide-sleeved shirt by Berber men of the Atlas mountains. The turban is also part of Berber men's traditional attire.*

Berber woman in feast-day dress

BERBER TRIBES

Although Berber tribal structure is complex, three groups, each with their own histories, can be identified. The Sanhaja, nomadic herdsmen originating from the south, inhabit the central and eastern High Atlas, the Middle Atlas and the Rif. They speak the dialects of the Tamazight group. The Masmouda, settled farmers, live mostly in the western High Atlas and the Anti-Atlas, and they speak the Chleuh dialect. It was a Masmoudian tribe that founded the Almohad empire in the 12th century.

The Zenets are hunters and herdsmen who came from the East and settled in eastern Morocco. They speak the dialect of the Znatiya group. They founded the Merinid dynasty in the 13th century.

The **situle**, *a copper vessel of distinctive shape, is used by the women of the Igherm region in the Anti-Atlas to fetch water.*

RELIGIOUS *MOUSSEMS*

For Berber women, religious *moussems* (*see pp38–41*) are occasions when they sometimes travel far from home. This is an opportunity for them to meet other women, to sing and dance, and to get away from their everyday chores.

This **amber and silver necklace**, *from the Taliouine region of the Anti-Atlas, is part of the attire traditionally worn on feast days.*

A **mule** *is a prized possession among the Berbers. It is used as a beast of burden, to carry such heavy loads as fodder, sacks of grain and containers of water.*

Horses of Morocco

Detail from an
ancient manuscript

Two thousand years ago, at the time of the Phoenician, Carthaginian and Roman invasions, the first horses to be used in Morocco were cross-bred with Mongolian stock. The Arab horse was introduced to Morocco by the Arab conquest in the 7th century and, used in war, it played an important part in the establishment of Islam here. Today, owning horses is considered to be a sign of wealth in rural areas. Horses are shown off at festivals, especially in the performance of fantasias (displays of horsemanship), and are also used in daily life.

Mokahlas, long ceremonial guns, have engraved butts inlaid with mother-of-pearl and ivory.

Tall embroidered leather boots and loose white short breeches are worn by riders in a fantasia.

Horse harness, brightly coloured and made of sumptuous materials, is made by skilled and specialized craftsmen. The severe bit allows the rider to stop abruptly and steer his mount deftly. The blinkers protect the horses' eyes from sand and smoke.

Studs

There are national studs in Meknès, El-Jadida, Marrakech, Oujda and Bouznika. Their purpose is to promote the breeding of horses and to produce horses for racing, for equestrian sports and for fantasias. In Morocco today there are 180,000 horses, 550,000 mules and 1 million donkeys. To encourage horse-breeding, stallions are made available to breeders free of charge to cover their mares. On average, 15,000 mares are put to a stallion and 5,000 foals are registered every year.

Thoroughbreds are used for racing. The racing season runs from September to May.

The Barb, a type of horse used by the Berbers before the arrival of the Arabs, is strong, compact and capable of covering long distances.

The fantasia saddle, with typically elaborate decoration, consists of a wooden framework sheathed in goatskin. It is covered in embroidered silk and rests on several layers of woven saddle-cloths decorated with pompoms. The high pommel and back restraint keep the rider securely in place.

Large stirrups made of sheet metal or leather are attached to the saddle by stirrup-leathers.

FANTASIAS

Fantasias are displays of horsemanship that are performed according to precise rules. Galloping at full speed down a course 200 m (650 ft) long, the riders whirl their guns in the air and, at a signal from their leader, fire them in unison.

Fantasia horses, which are at least four years old, are Barb or Arabian Barb stallions.

The mule, a robust beast of burden, is more widely used than the horse. Here, its owner perches on a pack-saddle made out of thick blankets.

At the moussem of Sidi Abdallah Amghar, in El-Jadida, horses are bathed in the sea at dawn. Later in the day, in the fierce August heat, they will perform the galloping charges of the fantasia.

The Arabian Barb, an agile and robust horse, was produced by crossbreeding Arabs and Barbs in the 7th century. It is a saddle horse particularly well suited to the fantasia.

The pure-bred Arab was introduced to Morocco in the 7th century. Its elegance and beauty, as well as its capacity for endurance, make it one of the world's best-loved horses.

Moroccan Dress and Jewellery

TRADITIONAL DRESS indicates the wearer's geographical origin and social status. Berber women wrap themselves in rectangular pieces of fabric, secured by a brooch and a belt, while the men wear a *jellaba* and a burnous against the cold. In towns, the elegant kaftan, a long garment with buttons down the front, has become standard formal wear for women, who increasingly often dress in the Western style. Jewellery has long been made by Jewish craftsmen. Berber jewellery is made of silver, sometimes with the addition of coral and amber; necklaces, bracelets and brooches may simply be decorative, or may be a status symbol or an heirloom. Gold, sometimes inlaid with precious stones, is the material of city-made jewellery.

Brooch

Zemmour women of the Middle Atlas wear a belt in the form of a long plaited and twisted cord decorated with pompoms.

Hoodless collar

In oases bordering the Sahara, women cover their head with a large black or white cotton shawl. On feast days, they bedeck themselves with all their jewellery.

The shape of the sleeves and of the neck-opening varies from one kaftan to the next.

Berber women, on feast days, don more elaborate headwear. The shape often indicates the wearer's status, either as a married woman or as an unmarried girl.

Silk brocade kaftan made in Fès in the 18th–19th century.

This golden diadem from Fès consists of hinged plates that are decoratively pierced and set with many precious stones.

In the High Atlas, capes worn by women identify their belonging to a particular tribe. Aït Haddiddou women are recognizable by their *hendira*, a cloak made of woollen cloth with blue, white, black and red stripes.

Cherbils, velvet slippers embroidered with gold thread, elegantly curved and with pointed toes, are an essential part of a woman's feast-day dress.

In rural areas, *older men still wear a voluminous* jellaba *with pointed hood. The garment is made of handwoven woollen cloth, which is either of one colour or with patterned stripes.*

For special occasions, *women may wear a gold or silver belt. Silver is most usually worked by being liquefied and poured into a mould, but it may also be beaten into sheets, cut to shape, and then incised or engraved.*

These musicians and dancers *from the Rif are wearing their festival costume. On their head they wear the traditional orange and white rezza.*

Gold lace

KAFTANS

The women's kaftan, an ankle-length, tunic-like garment, collarless and with wide sleeves, is always made of such fine fabric as silk, satin, velvet or brocade. It is often worn with a *mansourya,* a light, transparent overgarment made of silk that sets off the kaftan. The garments are secured at the waist by a wide belt embroidered with silk and gold thread.

Tiny buttons made of silk or gold thread are sewn down the front of the kaftan.

Cotton, silk and velvet kaftan, *made in Salé in the 19th century.*

This young bride *wears a kaftan and, over it, a luxuriant veil, which is traditional in Fès.*

Embroidery, *decorating kaftans, belts and jellabas, is an integral part of women's clothing. The patterns, such as geometric, floral and animal motifs, the colours and the materials used are different in every city.*

Coral, amber and shells, *combined with silver, are strung together to make attractive necklaces, which are worn proudly by Berber women.*

MOROCCO THROUGH THE YEAR

MUSLIM FEAST DAYS, agricultural festivals and *moussems* (pilgrimage-festivals) punctuate the Moroccan year. Because the Muslim calendar is lunar, the dates of religious festivals are never fixed. After the harvests of early summer and during the autumn, lively festivals at which the local produce is fêted are held in every region of the country.

Young girl dressed for the Feast of the Throne

More than 600 *moussems* take place each year in Morocco; besides the pilgrimage to the tomb of a saint, there is large regional souk, singing and dancing, and sometimes a fantasia. The month of Ramadan is still an important religious occasion; then, the inactivity of the daylight hours, when fasting is required, is followed by joyful night-time festivities.

SPRING

IF RAINFALL is not scarce, spring in Morocco is a remarkable season. In the space of a few days, the dry ochre earth becomes carpeted in flowers of every hue and the mountainsides are flushed with the pale green of new barley. The high peaks, however, are still covered in snow. In the Saharan south, spring is much like summer. It is already warm enough to swim in the Mediterranean and off the southern Atlantic coast.

MARCH

Amateur Theatre Festival, Casablanca.
Cotton Festival, Beni Mellal *(after the harvest)*.
Classic Car Rally *(10 days)*. The itinerary of this international rally for cars

dating from 1939 to 1997 crosses part of Morocco.
***Moussem* of Moulay Aissa ben Driss**, Aït-Attab (in the Beni Mellal region). Pilgrimage to the holy man's tomb.

APRIL

Candle Festival, Salé. At Achoura, 10 days after the Muslim New Year, boatmen come to place candelabras full of flaming candles at the the Marabout of Sidi Abdallah ben Hassoun.
Marathon des Sables *(8 days)*. Foot race run over 200 km (124 miles) in the Saharan south of Morocco.
***Moussem* of the Regraga** *(40 days)*. Pilgrimage that takes place in 44 stages, passing through the provinces of Essaouira and Safi, in honour of the Regraga – descendants of the Seven Holy Men of Berber history.

Rose Festival at El-Kelaa M'Gouna, near Ouarzazate

MAY

Rose Festival *(after the rose harvest)*, El-Kelaa M'Gouna (near Ouarzazate). Held in the town that is the capital of rose cultivation *(see p272)*, this festival features folk music and dance.
International Festival of Sacred Music *(1 week)*, Fès. Concerts every day. Jewish, Christian and Sufi religious music, gospel singing, Senegalese songs, and so on.
Aïcha Gazelles' Trophy *(1 week)*. An international event for women rally drivers, along tracks in the desert regions.
Harley-Davidson Raid *(15 days)*. Harley-Davidson motorbike rally through Spain and Morocco.
Crafts Festival, Ouarzazate.
***Moussem* of Moulay Abdallah ben Brahim**, Ouezzane. Pilgrimage held in honour of the holy man

The Candle Festival at Salé, which takes place at Achoura

**Cherry Festival in Sefrou,
at the foot of the Middle Atlas**

who came to the town in
1727 and then made it a
religious centre.

***Moussem* of Sidi
Mohammed Ma al-Aïnin**,
Tan Tan. This commercial
and religious festival is held
in honour of the founder of
the town of Smara, who was
a great hero of the French
Resistance. Events include a
performance of the *guedra*,
the famous dance of the
Guelmim region.

Oudaïa Jazz Festival
(4 days), Rabat. This jazz
festival is named after the
loyal Oudaïa, a well-known
tribe that is descended from
an Arab tribe, and that
Moulay Ismaïl entrusted
with watching over the
town *(see p68)*.

SUMMER

IN SUMMER the only parts of
the country that are spared
high temperatures are the
coasts, which are cooled by
sea breezes, and the Atlas
mountains. This is not the
best time to tour the inner
countryside or visit inland
towns and cities. In the
Saharan south, the sky
becomes leaden with the
heat, and elsewhere the
medinas are stifling. Despite
this, the start of summer is
marked by many festivals.

JUNE

National Folklore Festival
(10 days), Marrakech. At this
festival, in the Palais El-Badia,
troupes of dancers and
musicians from Morocco and
elsewhere bring Moroccan
folk traditions to life.

Gnaoua Festival *(4 days)*,
Essaouira. Gnaoua musicians
perform their distinctive
music *(see p27)*. Also other
traditional Moroccan music,
as well as visiting American
and European jazz groups.

Cherry Festival
*(2 days, after the cherry
harvest)*, Sefrou. Folk
performers take part in
this festival, which is held
in honour of Sefrou's
famous cherries.

Fig Festival *(after the fig
harvest)*, Bouhouda,
near Taounate.

***Moussem* of Sidi
el-Ghazi** *(last
Wednesday in June)*,
Guelmim. Sahraouis
gather to attend a
major camel market.
A fantasia is also
performed.

Sahraoui Festival,
Agadir. Camel
races, dancing and
music.

***Moussem* of Moulay
Bousselham**.
Religious festival, with
music and festivities.

JULY

***Moussem* of Moulay
Abdessalam ben Mchich**,
Tetouan. Thousands of
people, most of them from
local tribes, take part in this
great pilgrimage to the holy
man's tomb.

Feast of the Throne
(30 July). Major celebrations
marking the anniversary of
the accession to power of
Mohammed VI in 1999 take
place throughout the
country.

Music Festival, Tangier.

***Moussem* of Sidi
Mohammed Laghdal**, Tan
Tan. Religious pilgrimage.

AUGUST

Honey Festival *(between
15 and 20 August)*, Imouzzer
des Ida Outanane (north of
Agadir). Celebrations
marking the end of the
honey harvest, with folk
performances and an
exhibition of different kinds
of honey, one of the region's
major products.

***Moussem* of Moulay
Abdallah Amghar** *(1 week)*,
El-Jadida. Major pilgrim-
age with renowned
fantasias and other
entertainments.

**International
Cultural Festival**,
Asilah *(2 weeks)*.
Music, poetry and
painting competi-
tions, discussions
with artistes, and
other events,
including street
performances.

Festival of Folk Music,
Al-Hoceima.

***Moussem* of Setti
Fatma**. Pilgrimage
and souk in the
Ourika valley,
southeast of Marrakech.

**Performer at the
Gnaoua Festival**

***Moussem* of Dar Zhiroun**,
Rabat. Religious festival.

***Moussem* of Sidi Ahmed
(or Sidi Moussa)**, east of
Tiznit. Religious festival in
honour of the holy man and
Acrobats' Festival.

Apple Festival, Imouzzer
du Kandar, 38 km (24 miles)
south of Fès.

***Moussem* of Sidi Daoud**,
Ouarzazate. Religious
pilgrimage.

***Moussem* of Sidi Lahcen
ben Ahmed**, Sefrou. Festival
in honour of the town's
patron saint, who lived
during the 18th century.

***Moussem* of Sidi Yahya
ben Younes**,
Oujda.
Religious
festival in
honour of
St John the
Baptist, the
town's principal
saint, to whom
Muslims, Jews
and Christians
all pray.

Camel race at the Sahraoui Festival in Agadir

Moussem of Moulay Idriss II in Fès

AUTUMN

SEPTEMBER AND October are very pleasant months in which to explore the Atlas mountains, visit the imperial cities, or experience the vastness of the desert, where the heat is then bearable. In November, heavy rains can sometimes make the *wadis* burst their banks and render tracks impassable.

SEPTEMBER

Marriage Fair
(Towards end of September, 3 days), Imilchil. Tribal gathering of the Aït Haddidou at which betrothals are made. Peformances of folk song and dancing.

Tourism Fortnight, Marrakech.
Moussem **of Moulay Idriss Zerhoun**.
Pilgrimage to the tomb of Moulay Idriss, founder of the first dynasty, marked by major festivities.
Moussem **of Moulay Idriss II** *(1 week)*, Fès. Processions of craftsmen's guilds and of brotherhoods to the mausoleum of the city's founder.
Moussem **of Sidi Alla el-Hadj**, Chefchaouen. Religious festival held in the hills around the city.
Festival of Volubilis *(1 week)*, Meknès. Performances by musicians and dancers from Morocco, the Arab world, Europe and the United States.
Moussem **of Sidi Ahmed ben Mansour**, Moulay Bousselham. Religious festival.
Moussem **of Dar Zhira**, Tangier. Religious festival.
Jazz Festival, Tangier.

OCTOBER

Date Festival *(3 days after the date harvest in the groves of the Tafilalt)*, Erfoud. Many tribes from the Tafilalt gather and several varieties of dates are sold in the souks. Folk dancers and

musicians perform in the streets of Erfoud.
Apple Festival *(after the harvest)*, Midelt.
Horse Festival *(1 week)*, Tissa. Various breeds of horses compete and take part in shows, and many fantasias are performed.
International Contemporary Dance Festival, Casablanca.
Fantasia Festival *(4 days)*, Meknès. Teams of horsemen compete in fantasias.

Date Festival in Erfoud, taking place after the harvest

NOVEMBER

Moussem **of Mohammed Bou Nasri**, Tamegroute. Religious festival in memory of the great saint *(see p269)*.
International Music Festival, Ouarzazate.

Charging horsemen at a fantasia performed in Tissa

Almond trees in blossom in the Tafraoute region

WINTER

THE BEST TIME to explore Morocco's Saharan region is in the winter. The days are sunny and the sky is a deep blue but the nights are cold. On the coasts, the temperature remains mild. By contrast, the valleys of the High Atlas can receive heavy snowfalls and may be inaccessible. In February, the almond trees of the Tafraoute valley are covered in blossom. Few festivals take place in winter.

DECEMBER

Olive Tree Festival, Rhafsaï *(north of Fès)*. Agricultural festival.

JANUARY

Go-Kart 24-Hour Race, Marrakech.

FEBRUARY

Almond Blossom Festival, Tafraoute *(south of Agadir)*. Agricultural festival marking the short-lived but spectacular pink and white almond blossom.

PUBLIC HOLIDAYS

New Year's Day
(1 January)
Manifesto of Independence Day
(11 January)
Labour Day (1 May)
Feast of the Throne
(30 July)
Allegiance Day
(14 August)
King Mohammed VI's Birthday and **Youth Festival**
(21 August)
Day of the Green March
(6 November)
Independence Day,
return from exile of King Mohammed V
(18 November)

RELIGIOUS FESTIVALS

The dates of Muslim festivals are set according to the lunar calendar of the Hegira (the beginning of the Muslim era in 622). The Muslim year is 10 or 11 days shorter than that of the Gregorian calendar. Religious festivals also take place 11 days earlier each year in relation to the Western calendar. Guided by the phases of the moon, the religious authorities wait until the last moment before deciding on the exact date of each festival.
Moharem: Muslim New Year.
Achoura: traditional almsgiving *(zakat)* to the poor; presents are also given to children.
Mouloud (aïd al-wawlid): anniversary of the birth of the Prophet Mohammed. Many *moussems* also take place at the same time as Mouloud, and their dates are therefore different each year. Among the most important are the *moussem* of Moulay Brahim, near Marrakech, that of Moulay Abdessalam ben Mchich, in the north, the *moussem* of Sidi Mohammed ben Aïssa, of Sidi Ali ben Hamdouch, the Candle Festival in Salé and the *moussem* of Moulay Abdelkader Jilali.
Ramadan: practising Muslims fast for a month, eating only after sunset.
Aïd es-Seghir ("the small festival"), also known as Aïd el-Fitr: festival marking the end of the 30-day fast of Ramadan.
Aïd el-Kebir ("the grand festival"), also known as Aïd el-Adha: this festival, taking place 68 days after Aïd es-Seghir, commemorates the day when, by divine order, Abraham prepared to sacrifice his son Ismaïl, when Allah interceded by providing a ram in place of the child. Every household sacrifices a sheep and shares the meat at a family meal.

Souk in the High Atlas with sheep for sale just before Aïd el-Kebir

The Climate of Morocco

BORDERED BY the Atlantic and the Mediterranean, joined to the African continent by the Sahara, and diagonally bisected by the long mountain chain of the High and Middle Atlas, Morocco does not have a uniform climate. It is cooled by moist northwesterly winds and seared by hot, dry southeasterlies such as the *chergui*. In summer, conditions are those of a hot arid zone. In winter, which is very mild except in the mountains, conditions switch to those of a temperate coastal zone. Water is in relatively short supply everywhere and agriculture, involving about 40 per cent of the economically active population, is acutely dependent on adequate rainfall.

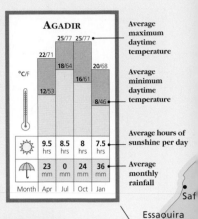

AGADIR

Month	Apr	Jul	Oct	Jan
Average maximum daytime temperature	22/71	25/77	25/77	20/68
Average minimum daytime temperature	12/53	18/64	16/61	8/46
Average hours of sunshine per day	9.5 hrs	8.5 hrs	8 hrs	7.5 hrs
Average monthly rainfall	23 mm	0 mm	24 mm	36 mm

°C/F

Landscape in the arid, mountainous Anti-Atlas region

Saf

Essaouira

Agadi

Tiznit

Tafraoute

Guelmim

Tan Tan

Laayoune

CLIMATE ZONES

Moist mountainous region: the Rif has the highest precipitation; rainfall is heaviest in the north and lightest in the south.

Atlantic region: mild winters and temperate summers; the dry season lengthens towards the south.

Eastern region: very light rainfall, shielded by the mountains; hot, dry summers.

Pre-Saharan and Saharan regions: rainfall becomes increasingly light and irregular; contrasts in temperature are more marked, with relatively cool winters and scorching summers.

Moist northwesterly winds.

Dry, hot southwesterly winds.

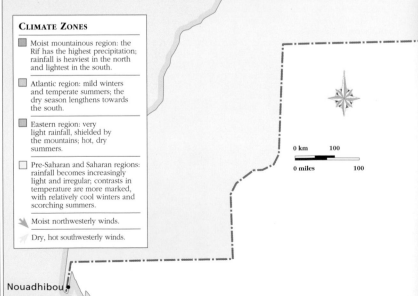

0 km   100

0 miles   100

Nouadhibou

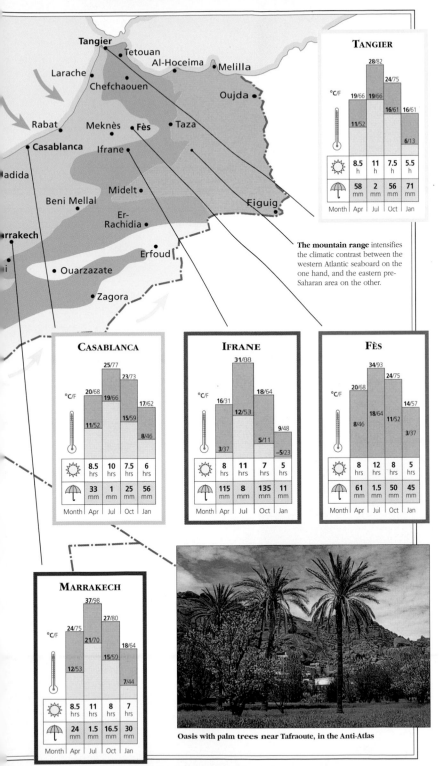

TANGIER

°C/F				
	19/66	28/82	24/75	
	11/52	19/66	16/61	16/61
				6/13

☼	8.5 h	11 h	7.5 h	5.5 h
☂	58 mm	2 mm	56 mm	71 mm
Month	Apr	Jul	Oct	Jan

The mountain range intensifies the climatic contrast between the western Atlantic seaboard on the one hand, and the eastern pre-Saharan area on the other.

CASABLANCA

°C/F				
	20/68	25/77	23/73	
	11/52	19/66	15/59	17/62
				8/46

☼	8.5 hrs	10 hrs	7.5 hrs	6 hrs
☂	33 mm	1 mm	25 mm	56 mm
Month	Apr	Jul	Oct	Jan

IFRANE

°C/F				
	16/31	31/88	18/64	
		12/53		9/48
	3/37		5/11	−5/23

☼	8 hrs	11 hrs	7 hrs	5 hrs
☂	115 mm	8 mm	135 mm	11 mm
Month	Apr	Jul	Oct	Jan

FÈS

°C/F				
	20/68	34/93	24/75	
	8/46		18/64	14/57
			11/52	3/37

☼	8 hrs	12 hrs	8 hrs	5 hrs
☂	61 mm	1.5 mm	50 mm	45 mm
Month	Apr	Jul	Oct	Jan

MARRAKECH

°C/F				
	24/75	37/98	27/80	
	12/53	21/70	15/59	18/64
				7/44

☼	8.5 hrs	11 hrs	8 hrs	7 hrs
☂	24 mm	1.5 mm	16.5 mm	30 mm
Month	Apr	Jul	Oct	Jan

Oasis with palm trees near Tafraoute, in the Anti-Atlas

THE HISTORY OF MOROCCO

Morocco is *an ancient kingdom. It came under the influence of Carthage and Rome, but its origins are Berber, Arab and African. Since the arrival of Islam in the 7th century, the country has been an independent power, and at times an empire. The only Arab country not to have fallen to the Ottomans, it entered the modern era under the Alaouite dynasty at the end of the colonial period.*

For 40,000 years Morocco has been a bridge between the East, Africa and Europe. Archaeological finds and rock engravings prove that it was settled in the remote past. but little is known of the first Berbers, who may have come from the east.

The Phoenicians, fearless navigators, established trading posts – such as Russaddir (Melilla) and Lixus (Larache) – along the Moroccan coast. They also introduced iron-working and the cultivation of vines.

In the 5th century BC, Hanno, a naval commander from Carthage (in modern Tunisia), set out to explore the Atlantic coast westwards, and soon the trading posts were taken over and developed by Carthage. Under their influence, the Berber tribes eventually joined forces and established the kingdom of Mauretania.

In 146 BC, having destroyed Carthage, the Romans extended their control westwards over the northern half of Morocco. Emperor Augustus made Tingis (Tangier) a Roman city. In 25 BC, the kingdom of Mauretania was entrusted to Juba II, king of Numidia. A Berber ruler who had been Romanized and educated, he married the daughter of Antony and Cleopatra. Ptolemy, Juba's son and heir, was murdered in AD 40 on the orders of Emperor Caligula. Emperor Claudius later annexed the kingdom, dividing it into Mauretania Caesariensis (west Algeria) and Mauretania Tingitana (Morocco). The Romans established few new towns here, but developed the existing ones, among them Tangier, Volubilis, Lixus, Banasa, Sala and Thamusida. The southern frontier lay at the level of Rabat. In the 3rd century, however, Christianity began to spread and Roman domination was severely diminished.

Juba II, the Romanized Berber ruler

The Vandals, whose king Genseric (428–77) conquered North Africa, followed by the Byzantines, maintained a lasting presence only at a few points along the Mediterranean coast. Religious unrest and local uprisings gradually extinguished the hold of all the ancient civilizations.

TIMELINE

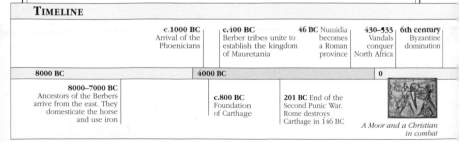

8000 BC	4000 BC	0

c.1000 BC Arrival of the Phoenicians

c.400 BC Berber tribes unite to establish the kingdom of Mauretania

46 BC Numidia becomes a Roman province

430–533 Vandals conquer North Africa

6th century Byzantine domination

8000–7000 BC Ancestors of the Berbers arrive from the east. They domesticate the horse and use iron

c.800 BC Foundation of Carthage

201 BC End of the Second Punic War. Rome destroys Carthage in 146 BC

A Moor and a Christian in combat

◁ *The Sultan Moulay Abderrahman Leaving Meknès, by Eugène Delacroix*

Pages from the Koran in the Maghrebi Kufic script of North Africa

ARRIVAL OF ISLAM

From the end of the 7th century, a new set of invaders, and with them a relatively new religion, began to make its mark on Morocco. The Arabs had started to expand their rule westwards, and in 681 there was a first attempt into Morocco. But the true conqueror of Morocco was Moussa ibn Nosaïr, who, active from 705, brought the territory from Tangier to the Draa valley under the control of the Ummayyad caliph in Damascus. With some resistance, Islam was introduced to the Berber population. Quickly rallying a mainly Berber army, Moussa then turned his attention to Europe, initiating the conquest of Spain in 711.

Reacting against their haughty Arab overlords, the Berbers of the Maghreb rebelled against them and, usually but not always, against Islam. Battles with troops sent from the East continued for more than 30 years, from 739 to 772. Petty kingdoms were formed and the western Maghreb kept the power of the caliphs at bay.

THE IDRISSID DYNASTY (789–926)

Meanwhile, Islam divided itself into two main sects: Sunni and Shia. In 786, the Sunnite Ummayad caliph crushed the Shi'ite Muslims. One of them, Idriss ibn Abdallah, escaped the massacre and was received in Morocco as a prestigious religious leader. In 789, the Aouraba, a Berber tribe in Volubilis, made him their leader. Idriss I carved out a small kingdom, and set about building a new city, Fès. He died soon afterwards, probably poisoned by an envoy of the caliph. His son, Idriss II (793–828), succeeded him and made Fès the Idrissid capital. The Idrissids are considered to be the founding dynasty and the first of Morocco's six ruling dynasties.

Fès soon became densely populated and a prestigious religious centre. At the death of Idriss II, the kingdom was divided between his two sons, then between their descendants. They were unable to prevent the simultaneous attacks of the two powerful rivals of the Abbassid caliph, the Shi'ites of Tunisia and Egypt, and the Ummayyad caliphs of Córdoba in Andalusia – Sunnis who for long fought over Fès and the allegiance of the Berber tribes.

THE ALMORAVIDS (1062–1147)

An unexpected push came from the south. A tribe of nomadic Sanhadja Berbers, based in present-day Mauritania and converts to Islam in the 9th century, were to give rise to a powerful new empire. The tribe's headman, Yahia ibn Ibrahim, invited a holy man to preach the Islamic faith to his people. A fortified camp, or *ribat*, was built on the

Fountain in the 9th-century Karaouiyine Mosque in Fès

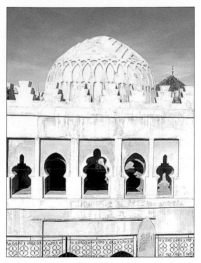

**Remains of the Koubba Ba'Adiyn in Marrakech,
built in 1106** *(see p231)*

the Faithful. Having founded Marrakech, which became Morocco's second capital, in 1062, he conquered the country as far north as Tangier and in 1082 as far east as Algiers.

In Al-Andalus (Andalusia), the fall of the Umayyad caliphate of Córdoba in 1031 led to the creation of *taifas,* small Muslim principalities. Alfonso VI, King of Castile and León, led the Christian Reconquest, taking Toledo in 1085. In response to a call for aid from the *taifas,* Youssef ibn Tachfin crossed the strait and routed Alfonso VI's forces at the Battle of Badajoz in 1086. He soon extended his empire as far north as Barcelona. In the south, Almoravid influence stretched to the Senegal and the Niger (1076).

The empire was unified by the orthodox, Sunni branch of Islam. On the death of Youssef ben Tachfine, his son Ali, whose mother was an Andalusian Christian, succeeded him. During his long reign (1107–43) the refined culture of Andalusia took hold in Morocco, although the empire itself was in decline. More Andalusian than Moroccan, the last Almoravids fled to Spain to escape a new rebellion from the south, that of the Almohads.

estuary of the Senegal river. In 1054, "the people of the *ribat*" (the al Mourabitoun, or Almoravids), fighters for a pure Islamic state, launched a holy war northward as far as the Atlas. The founder of the Almoravid empire was Youssef ibn Tachfin (1061–1107), who proclaimed himself Leader of

Carved wooden lintel from a mosque in Marrakech, dating from the 9th century

929 Abderrahman III establishes an independent caliphate in Córdoba

1062 Youssef ibn Tachfin founds Marrakech and starts to expand his Almoravid empire

1086 Spanish king Alfonso VI is defeated at Badajoz. The Reconquest is temporarily halted

960

1030

1100

1010 Berbers sack Abderrahman's palace at Medina Azahara, Córdoba

Zellij *tilework in the Palais du Glaoui, Marrakech*

1107–43 Andalusian culture takes root during the reign of Ali ben Youssef

Morocco and Al-Andalus

The philosopher Maïmonides

For almost eight centuries – from 711, when Tariq ibn Ziyad and his Berber forces crossed the Straits of Gibraltar to reach Spain, to the fall of the Nasrid kingdom of Granada in 1492 – the Iberian peninsula was partly under Muslim control. Muslim territory, known as Al-Andalus (the Land of the Vandals), was at times a melting pot of Muslims, Jews and Mozarabs (Christians adopting an Islamic lifestyle), philosophers, traders, scientists and poets. This gave birth to the most illustrious civilization of the late Middle Ages.

A love of gardens was one aspect of the cultured civilization of Al-Andalus

The Giralda, the clocktower of Seville Cathedral, added in the 16th century.

The minaret of the Great Mosque in Seville, transformed after the Christian Reconquest into the famous Giralda.

Irrigation

Under the Umayyad caliphs and their Berber successors, irrigation in Andalusia underwent a dramatic advance. The introduction of the noria, *a waterwheel for the mechanical extraction of water – shown here in a 13th-century manuscript – was to change, permanently, the method of water distribution in Spain.*

The minaret of the Koutoubia Mosque, in Marrakech, which was begun in 1162, was the model for those that the Almohads built later in Andalusia.

c.1184   1172–1198

Averroës

One of the greatest Islamic thinkers, and a protégé of the Almohad rulers, Averröes was born in Córdoba in 1126 and died in Marrakech in 1198 (see p231).

JUDAISM IN MOROCCO

Inscriptions in Hebrew dating from the Roman period show that there has been a Jewish community in Morocco since antiquity. It was involved chiefly in agriculture, stock-farming and trade. Judaism flourished thanks to the conversion of the Berber tribes and to the immigration of Jews fleeing from the east and from Spain. When Fès was founded, a Jewish community settled there, and scholars and rabbis travelled throughout the country. Although strictures imposed by the Almoravids and Almohads caused some Jews to emigrate, they flourished once again under the Merinids and Wattasids, who welcomed thousands of Jews expelled from Spain after 1492. The Alaouite sultans also protected them. Although their numbers are reduced, Jews hold certain influential positions in Morocco today.

Bronze Hanukkah lamp, 19th century

MINARETS

After the end of the independant Cordoban caliphate, Almoravids and Almohads directly controlled Al-Andalus, where their monumental architecture flourished. The architectural heritage of Al-Andalus, above all of religious architecture, is a clear expression of Andalusian culture. The striking similarity between the minarets of the three mosques built by the Almohads in Marrakech, Rabat and Seville demonstrates the unity of the Almohad architectural style.

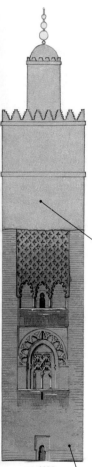

Reconstruction of the unfinished part of the Hassan Tower.

c. 1195

The Hassan Tower in Rabat, a colossal project and an over-ambitious undertaking, was never completed.

The Battle of Higueruela
This 15th-century fresco depicts an episode in the Reconquest, a centuries-long struggle between Muslim rulers and Christians for control of Spain.

King Boabdil's Farewell
Painted by the Orientalist Alfred Dehodencq (1822–82), this famous scene from Spanish history is redolent with nostalgia but is probably spurious. It depicts the fall of the last Moorish kingdom in Andalusia, that of the Nasrids of Granada, in 1492. Al-Andalus was to acquire a mythical aura in the minds of the Moorish communities who fled the Iberian peninsula during the Reconquest. In architecture, daily life, cuisine, music and vocabulary, Andalusian culture lives on in Moroccan towns and cities to this day.

THE ALMOHADS AND THE APOGEE OF THE WESTERN MUSLIM EMPIRE

In 1125, after a life devoted to study and to travelling in the Muslim world, Ibn Toumart, a Berber man of letters, settled in Tin Mal, a narrow valley in the High Atlas. A religious puritan driven by the doctrine of unity, he declared himself the *mahdi* (messiah) and, in opposition to the increasingly decadent Almoravids, began preaching moral reform. On his death, his successor Abd el-Moumen assumed the title of Leader of the Faithful. In 1146–7 he took control of the main cities of the Almoravid empire,

Mihrab of the mosque at Tin Mal, birthplace of the Almohads

including Marrakech, Fès and the great cities of Al-Andalus. Now the leader of the greatest empire that ever existed in the Muslim west, he went about centralizing it and reorganizing its army, administration and economy. He imposed taxes and land surveys, created a navy, founded universities and

Tiled panel depicting the Battle of Las Navas de Tolosa of 1212, at which the Almohads were defeated

enlisted the support of the great Arab dynasties. With such thinkers as Ibn Tufaïl and Averroës *(see p 231)*, intellectual life flourished. In 1162, Abd el-Moumen, founder of the Almohad dynasty, proclaimed himself caliph. The dynasty was at its peak during his reign, and that of his grandson Yacoub el-Mansour ("the Victorious", 1184–99).

But over the following decades the dynasty declined. The combined forces of the Spanish Christian princes inflicted a heavy defeat on Mohammed el-Nasser at the Battle of Las Navas de Tolosa. With the fall of Córdoba in 1236 and of Seville in 1248, the Muslims lost Spain, with only the small Nasrid kingdom of Granada surviving until 1492. The last Almohad sultans, who were reduced to the Maghreb, were challenged by dissidents: the Hafsids – Almohads who established their own dynasty (1228–1574) in Tunisia and western Algeria – and the Abdelwadid Berbers in Tlemcen in 1236.

In the south, the Almohads lost control of Saharan trade routes, while at the very heart of the kingdom, the Meri-

Carved wooden Merinid chest

nids, the Almohads' Berber allies of the high plateaux, defied their authority. The cycle described by the great Maghrebi historian Ibn Khaldoun *(see p181)*, in which over the centuries simple nomads wrench power from corrupt city-dwellers, and who are themselves overthrown, began again.

The age of the Almohads, a period of unequalled splendour, has left a lasting impression on Morocco: a form of Islam that is both spiritual and precisely defined, a *makhzen* (central

TIMELINE

	1130–63 Abd el-Moumen, the first Almohad caliph, conquers the Maghreb as far as Tripoli	**1212** Alfonso VIII of Castile defeats Mohammed el-Nasser at Las Navas de Tolosa		**1248–86** Abou Yahia, followed by Abou Yacoub Youssef, establishes the Merinid dynasty

1120	1180	1240	1300

| **1125** The *mahdi* Ibn Toumart settles in Tin Mal | **1195** Yacoub el-Mansour defeats the Castilians at Alarcos | **1212–69** Decline of the Almohad dynasty; gradual loss of territories in Al-Andalus | *Standard captured from the Muslims at the Battle of Las Navas de Tolosa* |

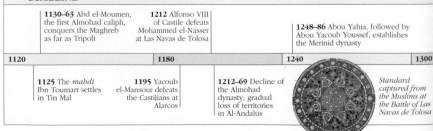

power) to control tribal self-determination, and a great urban Moorish civilization that is still in evidence.

THE MERINIDS (1248–1465)

Under the Merinids, Morocco was gradually reduced to the territory that it covers today. Unsuccessful on the battlefield, the Merinids were, however, inspired builders, and during their rule a brilliant urban civilization came into being. Led by Abou Yahia, these Zenet Berber nomads took control of the major cities and fertile plains from 1248, although it was not until 1269 that they conquered Marrakech, thus putting an end to the Almohad dynasty. Fès, which had been made capital by Abou Yacoub Youssef, experienced a new phase of expansion.

Despite some minor victories, the Merinids were unsuccessful in their attempts to reconquer territory on the Iberian peninsula. In 1415, the Portuguese, led by Henry the Navigator, took Ceuta. However, Abou el-Hassan (the "Black Sultan") managed to re-establish temporary order and unity in the Maghreb. He and his successor, Abou Inan, were great rulers and great builders. But crises of succession grad-

GEOGRAPHY

Geography was a favourite discipline with Arabs the early Middle Ages. Ibn Battuta (c. 1300–c.1370), who was born in Tangier and studied in Damascus, took the art of the *rihla* – encyclopedic travel writing – to its height. Towards the end of his life he dictated an entertaining account of his travels over almost 30 years. He visited the holy cities of Arabia, was a minister in the Maldives, a merchant in India and China, and explored Indonesia and the Persian Gulf. Having returned to the Maghreb, he travelled through the kingdoms of sub-Saharan Africa.

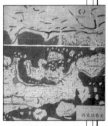

Map by the cartographer Al Idrissi (1099–1166), born in Ceuta, who put together one of the first geographic accounts of the known world

ually undermined their authority, and the Wattasids, another Zenet Berber dynasty, started taking over power from 1420 and ruled solely 1465–1549. With the 15th century began the slow decline of Moroccan power: fortune now favoured the Europeans.

Tapestry depicting the fall of Ceuta to the Portuguese in 1415

1331–49 The Merinid period reaches its peak under Abou el-Hassan		**1415** Henry the Navigator wins Ceuta for Portugal		*Tiled panel depicting the conquest of Ceuta*
1360		**1420**		**1480**
1349–58 Reign of Abou Inan, a great builder	**1420** The Merinids come under the control of the Wattasids	**1465** The Wattasids oust the Merinids permanently		**1497–1508** After the fall of Granada to the Christians, the Spanish move into northern Morocco

THE TWO SHORFA DYNASTIES

Since the time of Idriss I, the *shorfa* (the plural form of sherif) – Arabs of high social standing who are descendants of the Prophet Mohammed – have always played an important part in the social and political life of Morocco. Putting an end to Berber rule, they emerged

A gold dinar, proof of Saadian prosperity

from the south and governed Morocco from the 16th century to the present day. Because of their social origins, these two final dynasties, the Saadians and the Alaouites, are known as the Shorfa dynasties.

SAADIAN PROSPERITY (1525–1659)

At the beginning of the 16th century, the encroachment of Christian armies on Moroccan soil stimulated a vigorous renewal of religious fervour. From 1509, supporters of the movement of resistance against the Europeans found a leader in El-Kaïm, sherif of the Beni Saad, an Arab tribe from the Draa valley. Boldly leading the campaign for the reconquest of the Portuguese enclaves and for the seizure of power, they took control of the Souss, of Marrakech (1525), which was to become their capital, and of Fès (1548), ousting the last Wattasid sultans.

The Saadians stepped o to the stage of international relations; in 1577, France even appointed a Moroccan consul. To help counter the threat of the Turks, who had settled in Algiers, Mohammed ech-Cheikh requested the support of Madrid, whose attention was then focused on the Americas

Dom Sebastião, the young king killed in battle in Morocco in 1578

rather than the Maghreb. The Ottomans had Mohammed assassinated in 1557, but did conquer Morocco. The Saadians traded with Europe and drew up treaties with England and the Netherlands. From the Moriscos, the last Spanish Muslims, they received the final heritage of Al-Andalus.

Once the Saadians had retaken Agadir (1541), only Mazagan (El-Jadida), Tangier and Ceuta remained in Portuguese hands. Portugal's "Moroccan dream" was extinguished at the Battle of the Three Kings in 1578, when two rival Saadian sultans and Dom Sebastião, the young king of Portugal, all died at Ksar el-Kebir (*see p92*). His uncle, Philip II of Spain, swiftly annexed the Portuguese kingdom.

Saadian prosperity culminated with Ahmed el-Mansour, (1578–1603) whose conquests secured control of Saharan trade, and who set up the *makhzen* (a central administration). Gold from Mali and slaves reached Marrakech. Political and religious links with western Africa, and the presence of African folk culture brought here by slaves, made a mark on Morocco that can still be seen today.

Like their preceding dynasties, the Saadians declined as the result of ambition and disputed succession. In the distant Tafilalt, the ascetic *shorfa*, descendants of Ali, cousin of the Prophet, revolted against the decadence of Saadian rule under Moulay Sherif, and seized control of the region, which they held until 1664.

TIMELINE

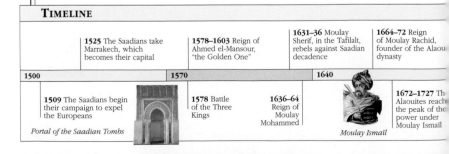

1525 The Saadians take Marrakech, which becomes their capital

1578–1603 Reign of Ahmed el-Mansour, "the Golden One"

1631–36 Moulay Sherif, in the Tafilalt, rebels against Saadian decadence

1664–72 Reign of Moulay Rachid, founder of the Alaou dynasty

1500   **1570**   **1640**

1509 The Saadians begin their campaign to expel the Europeans

Portal of the Saadian Tombs

1578 Battle of the Three Kings

1636–64 Reign of Moulay Mohammed

1672–1727 Th Alaouites reach the peak of the power under Moulay Ismail

Moulay Ismail

ALAOUITE GREATNESS AND EXTERNAL THREATS

The Alaouite dynasty, the sixth and present ruling dynasty, has given the country some rulers of great stature. During its long reign, each ruler concentrated on bringing stability to the country and on countering the threat of imperialist powers. It took ten years for Moulay Rachid (1664–72), founder of the dynasty, to bring the country under his control. The long and glorious reign of his younger brother, Moulay Ismaïl (1672–1727), marked Morocco's final apogee *(see pp54–5)*. He transferred the capital from Fès to Meknès, imposed central authority in the remotest corners of the country, recaptured Mehdya, Tangier and Larache from the Europeans, and maintained relations with the courts of Europe.

After a period of instability, his grandson, Sidi Mohammed ben Abdallah, restored order, expelled the

Trade agreement of 1767. During his reign Sidi Mohammed signed treaties with France, Denmark, Sweden, England, Venice, Spain and the newly created United States

Portuguese from Mazagan and founded Mogador (Essaouira) to facilitate trade with Europe. Under Moulay Yazid and Moulay Sliman, epidemics, uprisings and diplomatic isolation caused the country to withdraw into itself. Moulay Abder Rahman, another great ruler, attempted to modernize the country, but was frustrated by European colonial expansion. He was defeated by the French at Isly in 1844.

Moulay Abder Rahman and his successors, Mohammed III and Hassan I, were forced to concede commercial and consular privileges to Britain, France and Spain. In 1860, Spain took control of Tetouan. Hassan I, a dynamic ruler, attempted to balance the influence of these rivals, but the Conference of Madrid of 1880 sanctioned the intervention of foreign powers in Morocco. On his death, the country was stable and the dynasty's prestige intact, but Morocco was weakened.

French victory at the Battle of Isly, near Oujda, in 1844, depicted by the French painter Horace Vernet

1728–57 Reign of Moulay Abdallah	**1792–1822** Reign of Moulay Sliman, the Pious		**1873–93** Moulay Hassan I attempts to repulse the French	**1894–1908** Reign of Moulay Abdelaziz and regency of Ba Ahmed
'10	1780		1850	
1757–90 Rule of Sidi Mohammed ben Abdallah who establishes his capital in Rabat		**1822–59** Reign of Moulay Abder Rahman	**1859–73** Reign of Moulay Mohammed III	**1907–12** Reign of Moulay Hafidh

Sultan Moulay Hafidh

The Great Age of Moulay Ismaïl

MOULAY ISMAÏL, of partial Saharan parentage and a man of phenomenal vitality, stamped his authority on Morocco during a long and brilliant reign. Ruling for 55 years (1672–1727), he was a contemporary of Louis XIV. He made Meknès his capital and maintained a powerful army, recruited tens of thousands of men for the Black Guard, and modernized the artillery. With these forces, he was able to overcome rebellious tribes and bring temporary peace to the country. He wrenched from European control several fortresses, including Tangier and Larache. He also exchanged ambassadors with the French court.

The capital of Moulay Ismaïl in 1693

Sultan Moulay Ismaïl
He was the greatest, most ruthle ruler of the Alaouite dynasty.

Morocco's Ambassador in Paris (1682)
In conflict with Spain, Moulay Ismaïl sought an alliance with France in order to vanquish the fortresses that Spain held in Morocco. Once in France, the sultan's ambassador, Hadj Tenim, concluded a treaty of Franco-Moroccan friendship in 1682. Morocco then became an important trading partner for European countries.

Moulay Ismaïl's retinue

Black Guard
Moulay Ismaïl greatly expanded the army, which consisted of three contingents: units provided by the tribes, Christian renegades and abid, black slaves and mercenaries, whose exclusive duty was to protect the sultan. This latter regiment led to the formation of the famous Black Guard, which still exists.

Anne Marie de Bourbon

So as to strengthen his links with Europe, Moulay Ismaïl sent a request to Louis XIV for the hand of the princess, the French king's cousin, in marriage. His request was not granted.

Chevalier de Saint-Olon

AUDIENCE GIVEN BY MOULAY ISMAÏL

As depicted in this painting in the Palace of Versailles by M. P. Denis (1663–1742), Louis XIV, the Sun King, sent an ambassador to Meknès in 1689. The ambassador, the Chevalier François Pidou de Saint-Olon, was received with full honours. For 20 years, Louis XIV and Moulay Ismaïl exchanged embassies, but relations between them soured when France declined to engage in conflict with Spain.

THE ARCHITECTURAL HERITAGE OF MOULAY ISMAÏL

Moulay Ismaïl's achievements as a builder are most clearly seen in Meknès. This was formerly a small town overshadowed by the prestigious city of Fès, but the sultan transformed it into Morocco's fourth imperial city. It was enclosed by a double line of defensive walls and was described by some as the Versailles of Morocco. Next to the medina, the sultan built a kasbah, an extensive architectural complex enclosed within its own walls. This was the seat of power and of administration, consisting of several palaces, mosques, garrisons and studs, cisterns and stores for water. It was the ideal imperial city.

Large-scale building projects

undertaken by Moulay Ismaïl, such as the Dar el-Ma, shown here (see p193), *called for an army of craftsmen. These were recruited from other tribes, Christian prisoners and slaves. Contemporary writers record that the cruel sultan supervised the work himself, passing a death sentence on the slowest workers.*

Bab el-Berdaïne,

the Gate of the Pack-Saddle Makers (see p188), *takes its name from the pack-saddle market held nearby. In the 17th century, Meknès was enclosed by triple walls with imposing gates.*

The Sultan's Mausoleum
(see pp194–5), *which was built in the 17th century, was completely restored by Mohammed V in 1959. The clocks in the burial chamber were presented as gifts by Louis XIV.*

Marshal Lyautey, Morocco's first resident-general,
shown here in 1925 with Moulay Youssef

EUROPEAN DOMINATION

When Moulay Abdel Aziz, a weak ruler, ascended the throne in 1894, France already had an imperial presence in Algeria and Tunisia. The French now aimed to secure a free hand in Morocco, parallel with Britain's designs in Egypt and those of Italy in Libya. After controversial fiscal reform, Moulay Abdel Aziz entered into heavy debt with France. Meanwhile, the French military administration in Algeria gradually pushed back the frontier with Morocco, which was to lead to a long-drawn-out conflict. When Kaiser Wilhelm II of Germany arrived in Tangier in March 1905 to claim his share, the "Moroccan question" took on another dimension. The Conference of Algeciras of 1906, in which all the interested powers took part, forcibly opened Morocco to international trade, and assigned France and Spain as administrators.

In 1907, various incidents provided the French forces with the pretext to move into Oujda and Casablanca. In the same year, Abdel

Aziz was deposed by his brother Moulay Hafidh, who attempted to resist but was forced to yield. Numerous uprisings led the French to impose colonial rule, through the Treaty of Fès in 1912. Moulay Hafidh was then replaced by his half-brother, Moulay Youssef.

What was called "pacification" at the time continued until 1934: it took French forces 22 years to bring the whole country under control. In the Rif, a state of war persisted up until 1926. Abd el-Krim Khattabi, a brilliant strategist and organizer, defeated the Spanish at Anoual in 1921, proclaimed a republic in 1922, and long held out against the forces of the Spanish and French colonial powers, led by Francisco Franco and Philippe Pétain respectively. He left the country and died in exile in Cairo in 1963.

Marshal Hubert Lyautey, an exceptional man who was made France's first resident-general in Morocco in 1912, played a decisive role in the imposition of French rule. He installed the capital in Rabat, and worked to promote the country's economic development, but firmly refused to consider assimilation, a process by which colonies were modelled on the mother country. The country's traditional infrastructure was left intact and town planners safeguarded the imperial cities.

On the death of Moulay Youssef in 1927, his third son, Sidi Mohammed ben Yous-

Abd el-Krim Khattabi, heroic leader
of an ephemeral Rifian republic

TIMELINE

1912 Protectorate agreement is signed at the Treaty of Fès

Sultan Moulay Youssef

1921–26 Revolt in the Rif

1930 France imposes the Berber *dahir*

1910	1920	1930

1911 French troops enter Fès

1912–27 Reign of Moulay Youssef, who deposed his half-brother

Marshal Pétain received by Marshal Lyautey in Rabat in 1925

1927 Start of the reign of the sultan Mohammed ben Youssef, the future Mohammed V

sef, who was then 18, succeeded him, taking the name Mohammed V. He was to restore the country's independence.

1930s building, Casablanca, dating from the Protectorate

THE FIGHT FOR ISTIQLAL

Morocco was divided into two zones: a French zone, covering the largest part of the country, and a Spanish zone, in the north and south. Tangier was an international free city.

The French Protectorate was both beneficial and detrimental to Morocco. The country's infrastructure was modernized, its mineral resources were exploited and the most fertile land turned over to agriculture. The population of Casablanca, the economic capital, doubled every ten years, and the city became a major port.

The administration of Lyautey's 13 successors, however, was increasingly direct, so that the role of the local *mukhzen* became redundant. Colonial ideology triumphed in the 1930s. When France imposed a Berber *dahir*, giving Berber areas a separate legal system, the effect was to divide the country.

World War II justified the Moroccan people's desire for freedom. In 1942, the Allies arrived in Morocco and President Roosevelt pledged the sultan his support. Showing a progressively higher profile, Mohammed V drew a following of young nationalists, who set up the Istiqlal (Independence) Party. The Manifesto of Independence called on the sultan to head a movement for independence, a challenge that he formally accepted in a speech in Tangier in 1947. The power struggle with Paris lasted almost a decade. In 1951, the French authorities supported the rebellion of El-Glaoui, the pasha of Marrakech *(see p253)*. The sultan refused to abdicate but the French deposed him in 1953, replacing him with the elderly Ben Arafa. The royal family were forced into exile but the fight for independence gained momentum.

International opinion no longer supported the colonial powers, and the United Nations took over the Moroccan question. After negotiations with France, the deposed sultan made his triumphant return from exile as King Mohammed V, with Hassan, the heir apparent, at his side. The Protectorate ended in 1956, and in 1958 Tangier and the Spanish enclave of Tarfaya were restored to the kingdom. Independence had been won, although national unity was still to be achieved.

Mohammed V and his son, the future king, Hassan II, on their return from exile in 1955

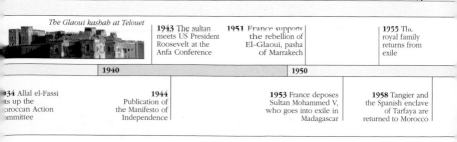

The Glaoui kasbah at Telouet

1943 The sultan meets US President Roosevelt at the Anfa Conference	**1951** France supports the rebellion of El-Glaoui, pasha of Marrakech
1955 The royal family returns from exile	

1940   **1950**

⚫34 Allal el-Fassi ⚫ts up the ⚪roccan Action ⚪mmittee

1944 Publication of the Manifesto of Independence

1953 France deposes Sultan Mohammed V, who goes into exile in Madagascar

1958 Tangier and the Spanish enclave of Tarfaya are returned to Morocco

The future Hassan II, in 1957, with Allal el-Fassi, the founder of Istiqlal, on his right and Medhi Ben Barka, leader of UNFP, on his left

POLITICAL AND SOCIAL CHANGE IN CONTEMPORARY MOROCCO

In the rest of the Arab world monarchies were replaced by authoritarian republican regimes (as in Iraq, Egypt, Yemen and Tunisia). In Morocco, however, Mohammed V's patriotic sentiment united the country behind a monarchy that has long-established roots and that ensures its unity and stability. A pious and outward-looking Muslim, the king encouraged the emancipation of women, the educa-

tion of his people, and agrarian reform. During this period, Morocco, unlike neighbouring countries, embraced political pluralism (albeit in a tightly controlled form) and relative economic liberalism, choices that were decisive for its future. In 1958, having broken away from Istiqlal, the progressive wing of the nationalist movement founded a left-wing party – the Union Nationale des Forces Populaires, the future USFP – with Abder Rahim Bouabid and Mehdi Ben Barka.

The king also had to contend with the impatience of nationalist sentiment, which believed that the country should engage in armed conflict to regain all Saharan territory and that it should give military aid to Algeria, which was still fighting its war for independence.

Mohammed V died suddenly, after an operation, in 1961. His eldest son, Moulay Hassan, who had been closely associated with power for many years, succeeded him as Hassan II. A skilled politician, he was to witness political as well as social change in his country, in the course of a reign lasting 38 years. It was, however, often marked by unrest and mixed success.

THE NATIONAL QUESTION

The question of the reintegration of Moroccan territory is a long-standing theme in contemporary Moroccan politics. At issue is the western Sahara, an area of 266,000 sq km (102,700 sq miles), from which Spain withdrew in 1975. In November that year Hassan II launched a Green March to win back this mineral-rich territory. The Polisario Front, an armed movement supported by Algeria, meanwhile fought for the territory's independence. Open conflict raged until 1988, when both sides accepted a plan drawn up by the United Nations, with consideration for the area's Sahraoui population. Since 1991, a referendum on the issue has been continually postponed because of lack of agreement on voters' lists.

Green March, keeping the national question at the top of Morocco's political agenda

TIMELINE

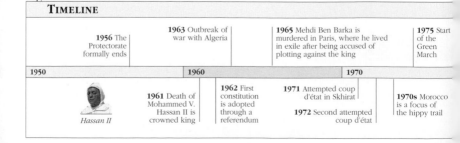

1956 The Protectorate formally ends

1963 Outbreak of war with Algeria

1965 Mehdi Ben Barka is murdered in Paris, where he lived in exile after being accused of plotting against the king

1975 Start of the Green March

1950 — 1960 — 1970

Hassan II

1961 Death of Mohammed V. Hassan II is crowned king

1962 First constitution is adopted through a referendum

1971 Attempted coup d'état in Skhirat

1972 Second attempted coup d'état

1970s Morocco is a focus of the hippy trail

The ceremony marking the Feast of the Throne in Marrakech, during the reign of Hassan II

On the international front, Hassan II firmly steered Morocco in the direction of the Western world, despite some-times stormy relations with Paris, and even spoke of the country joining the European Union. He pursued policies that were distinctive in the Muslim world, leading the Al Qods Committee in Jerusalem and encouraging recon-ciliation between Israel and the Palestinians. By contrast, deep-seated caution marked his relations with neighbouring Algeria, which had gained independence in 1962. Disputes over the border between the two countries led to the outbreak of war in 1963. Algiers also supported the Polisario Front, and the border was closed on several occasions.

On the domestic front, sup-ported by General Oufkir, Dlimi then Driss Basri, Hassan II alter-nated liberalizing policies with repression. The first constitution, drawn up in 1962 and followed by parliamentary elections in 1963, failed to unify the country. A new constitution was drawn up in 1970. Two coups d'état, attempted by a faction close to the king, both failed. Social unrest caused by poverty marked the following years, as public life returned to normal.

When a new constitution was drawn up in 1996, the time had come for a less autocratic style of government.

After parliamentary elections in 1997, Hassan II opened the doors to political change. Abderrahmane Youssoufi, a political opponent who had been imprisoned and exiled, was instructed to form a broad coalition government around the Socialist Union, and wisely brought in thoroughgoing reforms to modernize the country.

The king died suddenly in 1999, and was succeeded by his eldest son, Mohammed VI. Born in 1963, he enjoys great popularity because of his youth. He has addressed human rights issues, has allowed remaining exiles to return, takes a close interest in the northern provinces that were neglected by his father, and has distanced himself from Driss Basri, the all-powerful Minister of the Interior. Fundamental problems – underdevelopment, illiteracy, poverty and social inequality – still remain. After the terrorist bombs of May 2003, the King proclaimed "the end of the era of indulgence", which seems to signal the end of liberty and modernity.

Mohammed VI, still in the early years of his reign, seen as being close to his people

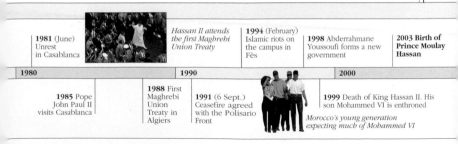

1981 (June) Unrest in Casablanca

Hassan II attends the first Maghrebi Union Treaty

1994 (February) Islamic riots on the campus in Fès

1998 Abderrahmane Youssoufi forms a new government

2003 Birth of Prince Moulay Hassan

1980

1990

2000

1985 Pope John Paul II visits Casablanca

1988 First Maghrebi Union Treaty in Algiers

1991 (6 Sept.) Ceasefire agreed with the Polisario Front

1999 Death of King Hassan II. His son Mohammed VI is enthroned

Morocco's young generation expecting much of Mohammed VI

MOROCCO
REGION
BY REGION

Morocco at a Glance

FROM THE MEDITERRANEAN coast to the High Atlas, beyond which the country stretches out into the boundless expanses of the Sahara Desert, Morocco forms a gigantic semicircle facing onto the Atlantic. Its major towns and cities, the focus of the country's economic and political activity, are located along the Atlantic seaboard from Tangier to Agadir and from Fès to Rabat. Topography, climate and history have together created a multifaceted country which offers everything from beaches, high mountain valleys and fertile agricultural land with almond and peach trees to majestic mountains and an extensive desert dotted with oases and palm groves. In secret medinas, in labyrinthine souks, or at the foot of Almohad and Merinid minarets, traders and craftsmen can be seen continuing ancient artistic traditions.

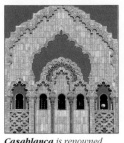

Casablanca *is renowned for its Art Deco architecture. It also boasts the richly decorated Hassan II Mosque (see pp102–3).*

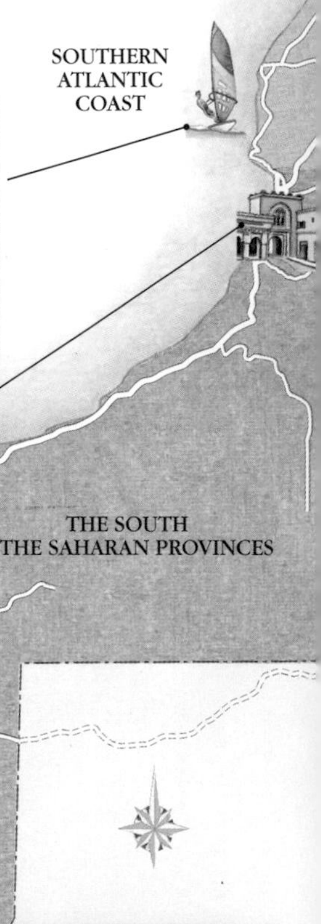

SOUTHERN
ATLANTIC
COAST

Essaouira*, a strikingly white town that appears to rise up out of the water, is also a windsurfer's dream location (see pp120–25).*

THE SOUTH
& THE SAHARAN PROVINCES

Agadir *is the place to go for sun, sand and relaxation. An attractive medina was recently built in the south of the town (see pp286–7).*

The South *is a varied region of deserts, oases, mountains and coastline. The architecture and the colours of the houses in Tafraoute, in the Anti-Atlas, are highly distinctive (see p293).*

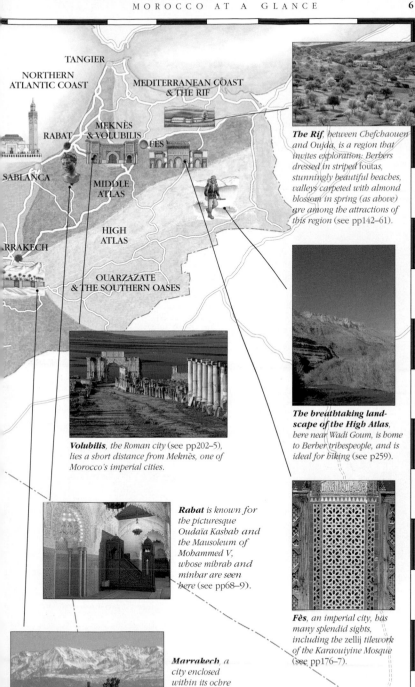

TANGIER

NORTHERN
ATLANTIC COAST

MEDITERRANEAN COAST
& THE RIF

MEKNÈS
& VOLUBILIS

RABAT

FÈS

SABLANCA

MIDDLE
ATLAS

HIGH
ATLAS

RRAKECH

OUARZAZATE
& THE SOUTHERN OASES

The Rif, between Chefchaouen
and Oujda, is a region that
invites exploration: Berbers
dressed in striped foutas,
stunningly beautiful beaches,
valleys carpeted with almond
blossom in spring (as above)
are among the attractions of
this region (see pp142–61).

*The breathtaking land-
scape of the High Atlas*,
here near Wadi Goum, is home
to Berber tribespeople, and is
ideal for biking (see p259).

Volubilis, the Roman city (see pp202–5),
lies a short distance from Meknès, one of
Morocco's imperial cities.

Rabat is known for
the picturesque
Oudaïa Kasbah and
the Mausoleum of
Mohammed V,
whose mihrab and
minbar are seen
here (see pp68–9).

Fès, an imperial city, has
many splendid sights,
including the zellij tilework
of the Karaouiyine Mosque
(see pp176–7).

Marrakech, a
city enclosed
within its ochre
ramparts, stands
in the shadow of
the snowy Atlas
(see pp226–7).

0 km 100

0 miles 100

RABAT

FACING ONTO *the Mediterranean, Rabat is an attractive city of domes and minarets, sweeping terraces, wide avenues and green spaces. It is markedly more pleasant than some other Moroccan cities and is also undergoing fundamental change. Facing Salé, its ancient rival, across Wadi Bou Regreg, Rabat is the political, administrative and financial capital of Morocco, the country's main university town and its second-largest metropolis after Casablanca.*

Archaeological excavations of the Merinid necropolis at Chellah *(see pp80–81)* have shown that this area was occupied by the Romans, and even earlier too. Much later, around 1150, Abd el-Moumen, the first ruler of the Almohad dynasty, chose to establish a permanent camp here and ordered a small imperial residence to be built on the site of a former *ribat* (fortified monastery).

The caliph Yacoub el-Mansour then embarked on the construction of a great and splendid city that was to be known as Ribat el-Fath (Camp of Victory), in celebration of his victory over Alfonso VIII of Castile at the Battle of Alarcos in 1195. On the death of the caliph in 1199, work on this ambitious project ceased: although the city gates and walls had been completed, the Hassan Mosque and its minaret *(see p49)* were unfinished. The Almohads' defeat at the Battle of Las Navas de Tolosa in 1212 weakened their power and led to the city's decline.

In 1610, Philip III of Spain expelled from his kingdom the remaining Moors, who fled to the cities of the Maghreb. Among them were a large colony of emigrants from Andalusia who settled in Rabat.

Rabat became the capital of a minor and relatively autonomous coastal republic. Funds brought by the Andalusian refugees were put to equipping a flotilla of privateers that preyed on European shipping. The "Republic of Bou Regreg", as it was known, was then annexed to the sherif's kingdom in 1666, although piracy was not brought to an end until the mid-19th century.

In 1912 Marshal Lyautey *(see p56)* made Rabat the political and administrative capital of Morocco. Its population now exceeds 1 million.

The medina in Rabat, on the banks of Bou Regreg

◁ The Gate of the Ambassadors at the Dar el-Makhzen (Royal Palace) in Rabat

Exploring Rabat

RABAT HAS four main areas of interest. In the north is the picturesque Oudaïa Kasbah, which is partly enclosed by ramparts dating from the Almohad period. The medina, which contains the city's souks, is bounded to the west by Almohad ramparts and to the south by the 17th-century Andalusian Wall, which runs parallel to Boulevard Hassan II. Avenue Mohammed V is the new town's busy central north-south axis, with residential blocks dating from the Protectorate (1912–56). In the northeast stands the Hassan Tower and Mausoleum of Mohammed V. In the Merinid necropolis at Chellah, to the south, are vestiges of the Roman town of Sala.

The Sliman Mosque and the medina in Rabat

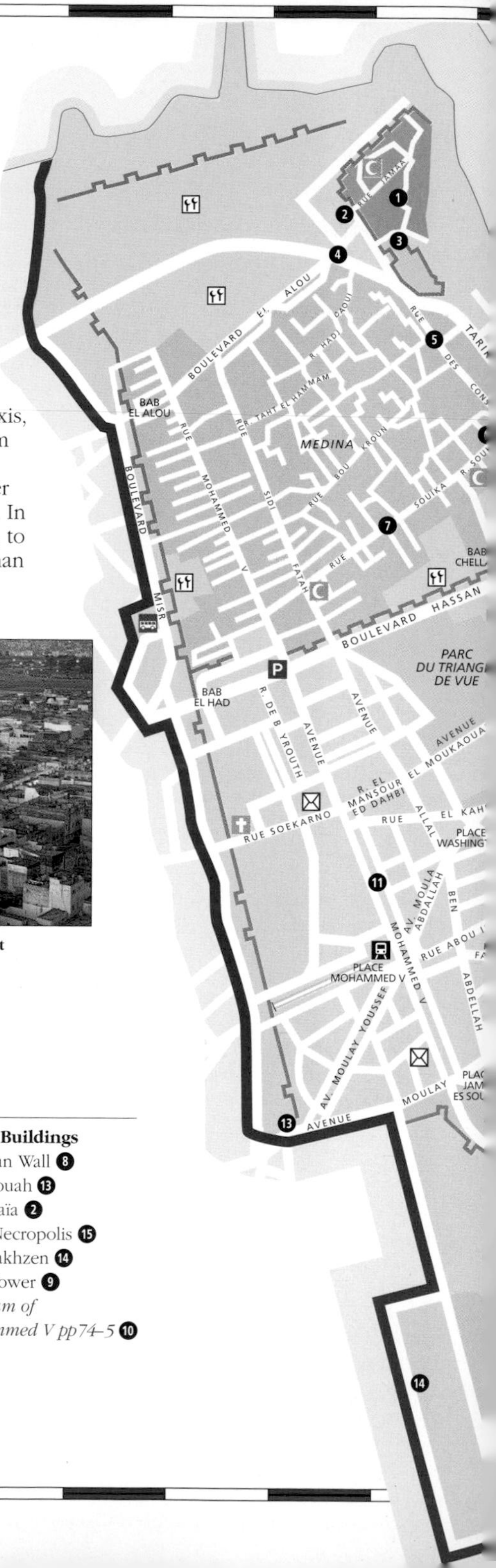

SIGHTS AT A GLANCE

Districts, Streets & Squares

City Walls ❶
Place Souk el-Ghezel and
   Rue Hadj Daoui ❹
Rue des Consuls ❺
Rue Souïka ❼
Rue Souk es-Sebat ❻
Ville Nouvelle ⓫

Museums

*Musée Archéologique
   pp78–9* ⓬
Musée des Oudaïa (Museum
   of Moroccan Crafts) ❸

Historic Buildings

Andalusian Wall ❽
Bab er-Rouah ⓭
Bab Oudaïa ❷
Chellah Necropolis ⓯
Dar el-Makhzen ⓮
Hassan Tower ❾
*Mausoleum of
   Mohammed V pp74–5* ❿

The Andalusian Wall surrounding the medina

SEE ALSO

- *Where to Stay* p302

- *Where to Eat* p322

GETTING AROUND

The main sights of Rabat are easily reachable on foot. The city's many one-way streets, however, make driving difficult. It is best to park on Boulevard Hassan II, since parking spaces are hard to find in the city centre. Although Rabat is served by a bus network, it is often more practical to travel around the city in a *petit taxi*, which is only a little more expensive.

KEY

▨	Street-by-Street map *pp68–9*
▨	Medina
—	City walls
🚆	Railway station
🚌	Bus station
🚢	Port
P	Parking
i	Tourist information
⊠	Post office
✝	Church
✡	Synagogue
C	Mosque
⛾	Muslim cemetery

0 m		400
0 yards		400

Street-by-Street: the Oudaïa Kasbah

Bab Oudaïa

T HE KASBAH takes its name from the Oudaïas, an Arab tribe with a warrior past that was settled here by Moulay Ismaïl (1672–1727) to protect the city from the threat of rebel tribes. Part of the city walls that surround this "fortress", built on the top of a cliff, and Bab Oudaïa, the gate that pierces it, date from the Almohad period (1147–1248). On Rue Jamaa, the main thoroughfare of this picturesque district, stands the El-Atika Mosque, built in the 12th century and the oldest mosque in Rabat.

★ Bab Oudaïa
An archetypal example of Almohad military architecture, this monumental gate was built by Yacoub el-Mansour in the 12th century. ❷

City Walls
The western ramparts were built by Yacoub el-Mansour in 1195, after his victory over Alfonso III. ❶

El-Alou cemetery

★ Musée des Oudaïa
The historic palace of Moulay Ismaïl (see pp54–5), renovated in 1995, now houses a museum with a rich collection of Moroccan folk art and crafts. ❸

★ Andalusian Garden
This pleasant garden, laid out in the Moorish style at the beginning of the 20th century, features a traditional Arabic noria (waterwheel for irrigation).

Café Maure
This is where Rabatis come to relax and pass the time. From here there are views of Salé's medina, of the Bou Regreg and of the Mediterranean. A doorway leads through to the Andalusian Garden.

Narrow Kasbah Street
*Although some elements
date back to the 12th
century, the houses in
the kasbah, lime-washed
in blue or white, were
built in the late 17th to
early 18th centuries, at
the time of the first
Alaouite rulers.*

VISITORS' CHECKLIST

Northern district. *Accessible
via Place du Souk el-Ghezel
and Bab Oudaïa or Place de
l'Ancien-Sémaphore.*
Andalusian Garden ☐
*accessible from the Café Maure.
The narrow streets of the
kasbah are best explored
on foot .*

Fountain

Almohad
walls

Prayer Hall of the El-Atika Mosque
*Founded in about 1150 by Abd el-Moumen, this
place of worship is Rabat's oldest monument.
The mosque was remodelled in the 18th
century, and again under the Alaouites.*

KEY

– – – Suggested route

RUE

ZIRARA

JAMAA

BAZZO

RUE

JAMAA

BAZZO

Carpet
workshop

Pirates' Tower

0 m   50
0 yards   50

**Platform of the Former
Oudaïa Signal Station**
*Built in the 18th century
by Sultan Sidi Mohammed
ben Abdallah, this signal
station defended the Bou
Regreg estuary. The ware-
house to its right contains a
carpet workshop.*

STAR SIGHTS

★ **Andalusian Garden**

★ **Bab Oudaïa**

★ **Musée des Oudaïa**

Walls of the Andalusian Garden, built in the reign of Moulay Rachid

City Walls ❶

In the north of the city. Accessible via Place du Souk el-Ghezel and Place de l'Ancien Sémaphore.

SEPARATED FROM the medina by the Place du Souk el-Ghezel, the Oudaïa Kasbah is defended by thick ramparts. These were built mostly by the Almohads in the 12th century, and were restored and remodelled in the 17th and 18th centuries by the Moriscos *(see p68)* and the Alaouite kings.

Most of the Almohad walls facing onto the sea and running inland survive. The walls surrounding the Andalusian Garden date from the reign of Moulay Rachid (founder of the Alaouite dynasty). The Hornacheros (Andalusian emigrants) who occupied the kasbah and rebuffed attacks from both sea and land rebuilt the curtain wall in several places and constructed the Pirates' Tower, whose inner stairway leads down to the river. They also pierced the walls of the old Almohad towers with embrasures to hold cannons. A complex system of underground passages leading from within the kasbah to the exterior beyond the walls was also dug.

The city walls are built of rough-hewn stone covered with a thick coating of ochre plaster. They are set with imposing towers and bastions, which are more numerous along the stretch of the walls facing the sea and the river. Standing 8 to 10 m (26 to 33 ft) high, and having an average thickness of 2.50 m (8 ft), the walls are surmounted by a rampart walk bordered by a low parapet; part of the rampart walk survives.

This sturdy building and sophisticated military construction defended the pirates' nest and withstood almost all attacks from European forces.

Bab Oudaïa ❷

Oudaïa Kasbah. The gate leads to the kasbah from Place du Souk el-Ghezel.

TOWERING ABOVE the cliffs that line the Bou Regreg, and dominating Rabat's medina is Bab Oudaïa, which is the main entrance into the kasbah. This monumental city gate, built in dressed stone of red ochre, is considered to be one of the finest examples of Almohad architecture. But the particular design and conception of this gateway, built by Yacoub el-Mansour in 1195, make it more of a decorative feature than a piece of military defence work.

Stylized seashell on Bab Oudaïa

Flanked by two towers, it is crowned by a horseshoe arch. The inner and outer façades are decorated with rich ornamentation carved in relief into the stone, starting at the opening of the arch and continuing in several tiers as far up as the base of the parapet. Above the arch, two bands with interlacing lozenges are outlined with floral decoration. Both sides of the gate are crowned by a band of calligraphy. As in all Moorish palaces, the gatehouse of the former

Oudaïa Palace was also a defensive feature and a tribunal. Today, the gatehouse serves as an exhibition hall.

Musée des Oudaïa ❸

Oudaïa Kasbah. Accessible via a gateway in the southwestern walls. **(** *(037) 73 15 37.* **◑** *winter: 8:30am–noon & 2:30–7pm Wed–Mon; summer: 8:30am–noon & 3–6pm Wed–Mon.* **●** *Mar and public holidays.*

IN THE 17th century, Moulay Ismaïl built a small palace within the kasbah. This became the residence of the first Alaouite sultans while they were based in Rabat, as an inscription on the wooden lintels of the central patio indicates: "Unfailing fortune and brilliant victory to our lord Smaïl, leader of the faithful." The palace was completely restored and slightly altered in 1917, during the Protectorate, and, after further phases of restoration, it was renovated in 1995.

The palace as it is today consists of a main building arranged around an arcaded courtyard. The four sides of the courtyard lead off into large rectangular rooms with marble floors and geometrically coffered ceilings. The surrounding buildings include a prayer room for private worship, a hammam (steam bath) and a tower. A beautiful garden laid out in the Andalusian style gives the palace the status of a princely residence.

The Musée des Oudaïa, laid out in a 17th-century palace

Since 1915, the palace has housed the Musée des Oudaïa. On display here are carpets and copperwork, astrolabes (for measuring the altitude of stars) dating from the 14th and 17th centuries, and collections of ceramics and of musical instruments. One room in the museum is laid out as a traditional Moroccan interior, with sofas covered in sumptuous gold-embroidered silk fabrics made in Fès. Another room is devoted to the traditional dress of the region between the Rif and the Sahara.

The museum also contains collections of jewellery, including Berber jewellery, antique pottery, and fine collections of woodcarving and of funerary art.

A small shop in the Souk el-Ghezel district of Rabat

Place Souk el-Ghezel and Rue Hadj Daoui ❹

A CONVENIENT PLACE to start exploring Rabat's medina is the Place Souk el-Ghezel, (Wool Market Square), so named because of the market that once took place here. This was also the place where Christian prisoners were once sold as slaves. Today, it is the fine carpets made in the city that are auctioned here every Thursday morning.

Rue Hadj Daoui, just southwest of Place Souk el-Ghezel, leads into the residential area of the medina, where the streets are quieter and where houses built by the Moriscos are still visible.

The unmistakable mark that the Moriscos made on the architecture of Rabat can be seen in certain styles of building: for example, those involving the use of

semicircular arches and ornamental motifs such as the pilasters consisting of vertically arranged mouldings that decorate the upper parts of doors. The smaller houses are of simple design, most of them built of stone rendered with limewashed plaster. Most of the richer houses tucked away in the quarters of Rabat are built around a central courtyard, like those in other Moroccan medinas, and have a refined elegance.

Walking west along Rue Hadj Daoui leads to Dar el-Mrini, a fine private house built in 1920 and today has been transformed into an exhibition and conference centre.

Rue des Consuls ❺

Eastern part of the medina.

R UNNING THROUGH the medina, Rue des Consuls begins at the Wool Market in the north and leads down towards the Andalusian Wall in the south. Up to the time of the Protectorate, this street was where all foreign consuls in Rabat were obliged to live. Recently covered with rushes

Shops selling leather goods, in the eastern part of the medina

and a glass roof, the street is lined with the shops of craftsmen and traders, making it the most lively quarter in the medina. The two former *fondouks* at No. 109 and No. 137 are now the workshops of leatherworkers and woodworkers.

South of Rue Souk es-Sebat (*see p76*) the street changes name to Rue Ouqqasa, which borders the mellah (Jewish quarter). In Rue Tariq el-Marsa is the Ensemble Artisanal, selling Moroccan crafts, and, a little further on, is a restored 18th-century naval depot.

Rue des Consuls, one of the lively thoroughfares in the medina

Courtyard of the mosque of the Mausoleum of Mohammed V ▷

Mausoleum of Mohammed V ⑩

Copper censer

RAISED IN MEMORY of Mohammed V, the father of Moroccan independence, this majestic building was commissioned by his son, Hassan II. It was designed by the Vietnamese architect Vo Toan and built with the help of 400 Moroccan craftsmen. The group of buildings that make up the mausoleum of Mohammed V include a mosque and a museum devoted to the history of the Alaouite dynasty. The mausoleum itself, in white Italian marble, stands on a platform 3.5 m (11.5 ft) high. Entry is through a wrought-iron door that opens onto a stairway leading to the dome, beneath which lies the sarcophagus of Mohammed V.

★ **Dome with *Muqarnas***
This twelve-sided dome, with painted mahogany muqarnas *(stalactites), crowns the burial chamber.*

★ **Sarcophagus**
Carved from a single block of marble, the sarcophagus rests on a slab of granite, facing a qibla (symbolizing Mecca).

Guard
The traditional attire of the royal guard is white in summer and red in winter (see p75).

Burial vault
containing the body of Mohammed V.

Fountain
Embellished with polychrome zellij tilework and framed by a horseshoe arch of Salé sandstone, this fountain is in the Moorish style.

Stained-Glass Windows
The stained-glass windows in the dome were made in France, in the workshops of the factory at St-Gobain.

VISITORS' CHECKLIST

Boulevard El-Alaouiyine.
🏠 *(037) 68 15 31.* ⏱ *8:30am–6pm daily (also to non-Muslims).*

Brass spheres symbolize a holy or religious building.

Polychrome *zellij* **tilework**

Calligraphy
This marble frieze features a song of holy praise carved in Maghrebi script.

Doorways lead to the balcony from which the sarcophagus can be seen from above.

Esplanade

Doorways
The doorways on the four sides of the mausoleum are fronted by slender columns of Carrara marble.

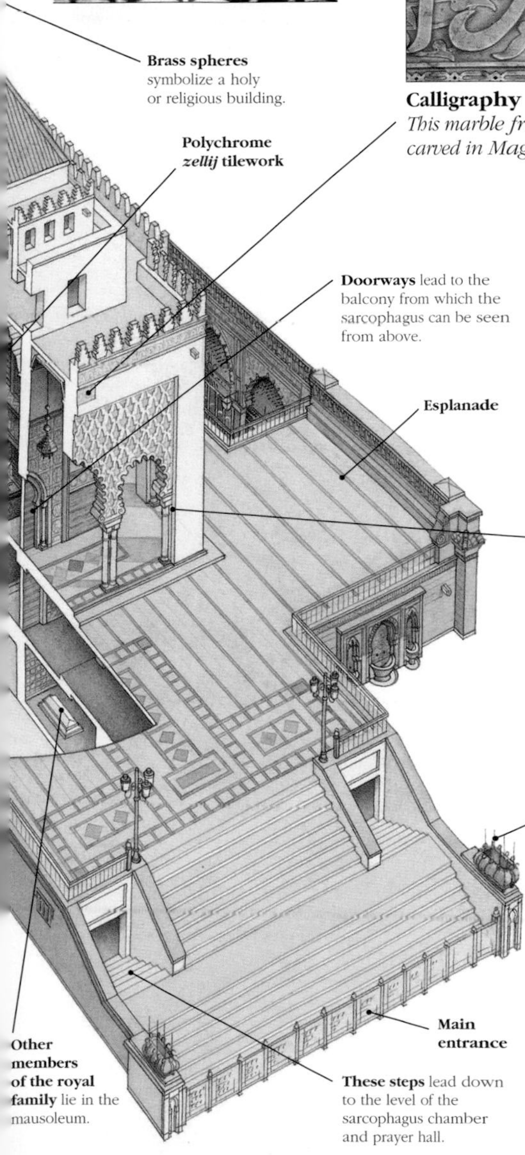

Candelabra
These large candelabra, with slender vertical shafts, are made of pierced and engraved copper.

Other members of the royal family lie in the mausoleum.

Main entrance

These steps lead down to the level of the sarcophagus chamber and prayer hall.

STAR FEATURES

★ **Dome with** *Muqarnas*

★ **Sarcophagus**

Merinid fountain in the Great Mosque district

Rue Souk es-Sebat ⑥

In the medina.

T HIS THOROUGHFARE, which begins at the Great Mosque and ends at Bab el-Bhar (Gate of the Sea) crosses the Rue des Consuls. Covered by a rush trellis, this lively street is filled with the shops of leatherworkers, jewellers and fabric merchants and of traders in all sorts of other goods.

Rue Souïka ⑦

In the medina.
Great Mosque ⬤ to non-Muslims.

R UNNING SOUTHWEST from Rue du Souk es-Sebat, Rue Souïka (Little Souk Street) is the main artery through the medina and also its most lively thoroughfare. Lined with all manner of small shops selling clothes, shoes, food, radios and cassettes, with restaurants and with spice merchants, the street throngs with people several times a day.

At the intersection with Rue de Bab Chellah stands the Great Mosque, built probably

between the 13th and the 16th centuries and remodelled and restored on several occasions during the Alaouite period. The mosque's most prominent feature is the minaret, rising to a height of 33 m (109 ft) and completed in 1939. It is built of ashlars (blocks of hewn stone), decorated with dressed stone, and pierced with openings in the shape of lobed or intersecting arches.

Opposite the mosque is a fountain with a pediment of intersecting arches, built in the 14th century, during the reign of the Merinid sultan Abou Fares Abdelaziz. Further along the street, on the corner of Rue Sidi Fatah, is the Moulay Sliman Mosque, or Jamaa el-Souika. It was built in about 1812 on the orders of Moulay Sliman, on the site of an earlier place of worship.

Andalusian Wall ⑧

Between Bab el-Had and Place Sidi Makhlouf.

I N THE 17TH CENTURY, the Moriscos – Muslim refugees from Andalusia – found the medina undefended and so encircled it with a defensive wall. Named after its builders, the Andalusian Wall stands about 5 m (16 ft) high and runs in a straight line for more than 1,400 m (4,595 ft) from Bab el-Had (Sunday Gate) in the west to the *borj* (small fort) of Sidi Makhlouf in the east. Boulevard Hassan II runs parallel to it. During the Protectorate, a stretch of the walls about 100 m (328 ft) long, and including Bab el-

Tben, was destroyed to allow easier access to a market.

The walls are set with towers placed at intervals of some 35 m (115 ft) and are topped by a rampart walk. This is protected by a parapet that the Andalusians pierced with numerous narrow slits known as loopholes.

To the east of the walls they built the Bastion Sidi Makhlouf, a small, irregular fort which consists of a platform resting on solid foundations, with a tower close by. They also built embrasures over two of the Almohad gates, Bab el-Alou and Bab el-Had.

Moulay Sliman Mosque

Bab el-Had was once the main gateway into the medina. Dating from the Almohad period (1147–1248), it was rebuilt by Moulay Sliman in 1814. On the side facing Boulevard Misr, one of gate's two pentagonal towers stands close to the Almohad walls, which probably date from 1197.

Bab el-Had contains several small chambers which were intended to accommodate the soldiers who were in charge of the guard, the armouries and the billetting of the troops.

Hassan Tower ⑨

Rue de la Tour Hassan.
⬤ to the public.

F OR MORE THAN eight centuries, the Hassan Tower has stood on the hill overlooking Wadi Bou Regreg. Best seen as one approaches Rabat by the bridge from Salé, it is one of the city's most prestigious monuments and a great emblem of Rabat.

It is the unfinished minaret of the Hassan Mosque, built by Yacoub el-Mansour in about 1196. The construction of this gigantic mosque, of dimensions quite out of proportion to the population of Rabat at the time, suggests that the Almohad ruler

Bab el-Had, the "Sunday Gate", built in the 17th century

The Hassan Tower and remains of the Hassan Mosque's prayer hall

intended to make Rabat his new imperial capital. An alternative interpretation is that the Almohads were attempting to rival the magnificent Great Mosque of Córdoba, the former capital of the Islamic kingdom in the West *(see pp48–9)*. Either way, after the death of Yacoub el-Mansour in 1199, the unfinished mosque fell into disrepair. All but the mosque's minaret was destroyed by an earthquake in 1755.

The Hassan Mosque was built to a huge rectangular plan 183 m (600 ft) by 139 m (456 ft); the Great Mosque of Córdoba was just 175 m (574 ft) by 128 m (420 ft). It was the largest religious building in the Muslim West, in size inferior only to the mosque of Samarra in Iraq. A great courtyard lay at the foot of the tower, while the huge columned prayer hall was divided into 21 avenues separated by lines of gigantic columns crowned with capitals. Remains of these imposing stone columns survive and still convey an impression of infinite grandeur.

The minaret, a square-sided tower about 16 m (52 ft) wide and 44 m (144 ft) high, was to have surpassed the height of the Koutoubia Mosque *(see pp236–7)* and the Giralda in Seville *(see pp48–9)*, but it was never completed. According to Almohad custom, it would have reached 80 m (262 ft), including the lantern. Even unfinished it seems huge. Each of its four sides is

decorated with blind lobed arches. On the topmost level of the minaret extended interlacing arches form a *sebkha* motif (lozenge-shaped blind fretwork) as on the Giralda of Seville. The interior is divided into six levels, each of which consists of a domed room. The levels are linked and accessed by a continuous ramp.

It was from the Hassan Tower that Mohammed V conducted the first Friday prayers after independence was declared.

Mausoleum of Mohammed V ⑩

See pp74–5.

Ville Nouvelle ⑪

DURING THE 44 years of the Protectorate, Marshal Lyautey and the architects Prost and Écochard built a new town in the empty part of the extensive area enclosed by the Almohad walls.

Laying out wide boulevards and green spaces, they created a relatively pleasant town. Avenue Mohammed V, the main avenue, runs from the medina to the El-Souna Mosque, or Great Mosque, which was built by Sidi Mohammed in the 18th century. The avenue is lined with residential blocks in the Hispano-Maghrebi style. They were built by the administration of the Protectorate, as were the Bank of Morocco, the post office, the parliament building and the railway station. At No. 93 is the **Musée de la Poste** (Postal Museum), where philatelists can buy stamps to add to their collection.

Rue Abou Inan leads to the **Cathédrale Saint-Pierre**, a pure white building dating from the 1930s.

🏛 **Musée de la Poste**
93 Avenue Mohammed V.
📞 *(037) 70 20 90.* ◯ *daily.*
⛪ **Cathédrale Saint-Pierre**
Place du Golan. ◯ *9am–noon & 2:30–5:30 pm daily.* 📞 *(037) 72 23 01.*

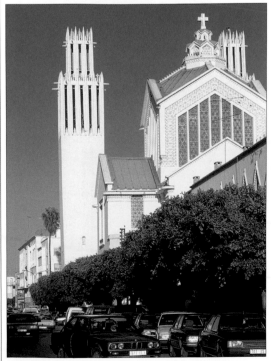

The dazzling white Cathédrale Saint-Pierre, built in the 1930s

Musée Archéologique **⑫**

THE MOST EXTENSIVE collection of archaeological artifacts in the country is housed in the Musée Archéologique. The museum building was constructed in the 1930s, to house the Antiquities Services. The initial prehistoric and pre-Islamic collections, consisting of objects discovered by archaeologists working in Volubilis, Banasa and Thamusida, were put on public display for the first time in 1930–32. The addition of further material from Volubilis in 1957 considerably enlarged the museum's collections, raising it to the status of a national museum. The displays present the collections according to theme. These range from the prehistoric period up to the findings of recent archaeological excavations.

Roman pitcher of the 1st to 2nd centuries, with strainer and spout

The House of the Ephebe, Volubilis *(see pp204–5)*

TEMPORARY EXHIBITIONS

THE SPACE on the ground floor reserved for temporary exhibitions illustrates the results of archaeological investigations in Morocco, using photographs, graphics, models, sculpture and various other objects.

A map of Morocco in the lobby shows the various archaeological sites that have been discovered to date, and the methods used to excavate them are explained. The reconstruction of a mosaic from Volubilis is laid out on the floor of the room opposite. The marble statue in the centre of the room, dating from AD 25–40, is that of **Ptolemy**, king of Mauretania Tingitana and the son and successor of Juba II

Roman bone and ivory carving

and Cleopatra Selene, who was assassinated by the Roman emperor Caligula.

PREHISTORIC CULTURES

ALSO ON the ground floor is a collection of stone artifacts relating to the earliest cultures and civilizations. Exhibits include altars and stelae carved with inscriptions, sarcophagi, tools and implements such as arrows and pebbles, pottery, polished stones, axes and swords, fragments of tombs and mouldings, as well as rock carvings.

Among the cultures highlighted here are the Pebble Culture, known from sites at Arboua, Douar Doum and Casablanca; the

Acheulian culture, known at sites in Sidi Abderrahmane and Daya el-Hamra; the Mousterian culture; and, finally, the Aterian culture of around 4,000 BC. The latter, specific to Morocco, is illustrated by the only human remains to have been discovered at Dar al-Soltane and el-Harhoura.

SALA-CHELLAH AND ISLAMIC ARCHAEOLOGY

THE SITE OF **Sala-Chellah** *(see pp80–81)* is that of a Mauretanian and Roman town which flourished up to the 4th century AD and which in the 13th century became a royal necropolis under the Merinids.

The collection of implements and other objects (including pottery and oil lamps) displayed on the upper floor of the museum traces the history of the site. Particularly striking exhibits include the bronze bust of Juba II (52 BC–AD 23) which was discovered in Volubilis and probably came from Egypt. An Early Christian altar, a Byzantine censer and an ivory figure of the Good Shepherd show the presence of Christianity in Morocco from the 3rd to the 8th centuries.

The section on Islamic archaeology highlights the principal sites that have been

Head of a Berber youth

excavated. The displays of objects that have been unearthed include coins, pottery made in Sijilmassa and other ceramics, notably a 14th-century dish from Belyounech, as well as fragments of carved plaster and sugar-loaf moulds from Chichaoua.

PRE-ISLAMIC CIVILIZATIONS

ARTIFACTS UNCOVERED during excavations at Volubilis, Banasa, Thamusida, Sala and Mogador are arranged by theme, illustrating in an informative fashion the most salient aspects of both pre-Roman Morocco (Mauretanian civilization) and Roman Morocco (Mauretania Tingitana). A range of objects show the extent of trade relations between Morocco and the Mediterranean world, particularly Carthage; and public and private life is illustrated through everyday objects, including the taps that were used in public baths, fragments of terracotta piping, and cooking utensils such as plates, dishes, glasses and knives. A section on the Roman army includes a military diploma from Banasa, certificates of good conduct

Head of Oceanus (1st century BC)

engraved on bronze plaques and military decorations.

The collection of white marble sculpture includes the *Head of a Berber Youth* from Volubilis carved during the reign of Augustus, a *Sphinx* from a votive throne, and a *Sleeping Silenus* from Volubilis. There are also figures of Roman gods such as Venus, Bacchus and Mars, and of Egyptian deities such as Isis and Anubis.

A particularly impressive part of the museum's displays is the collection of antique bronzes which come mainly from Volubilis and which demonstrate the wealth enjoyed by Morocco's Roman towns. A well-preserved bust of *Cato the Younger*, this 1st-century sculpture discovered in the House of Venus was imported into Morocco.

Ephebe Crowned with Ivy is, without a doubt, the star piece in the collection. The naked *ephebe* (young soldier in training) wears a crown of delicate ivy and is depicted in a standing position. The stance suggests that in his left hand he held a torch; this type of representation, known as a "lampadophore", together with the classicism of the statue, are typical of sculpture of the 1st century. The *Dog of Volubilis,* found on the site in 1916 in the

VISITORS' CHECKLIST

23 Rue el-Brihi (behind the Grand Mosque, opposite the Chellah hotel). **⌂** *(037) 70 19 19.* **◷** *9–11:30am & 2:30–5:30pm Wed–Mon (last admission 45 mins before closing).* **●** *Tue, public hols.* **♿**

vicinity of the triumphal arch, dates from the reign of Hadrian (early 2nd century) and was also made outside Morocco. The position of the dog, which is clearly designed to be accompanied by a human figure (undoubtedly Diana), suggests that it was made to decorate a fountain in public baths. The *Lustral Ephebe*, also discovered in Volubilis in 1929, brings to mind the *Lustral Dionysus* of Praxiteles, preserved in a museum in Dresden, in Germany, and known through numerous copies. Finally, the bust of Juba II which dates from 25 BC was probably imported from Egypt.

Roman votive stele from Volubilis, 1st–2nd century AD

GALLERY GUIDE

The museum consists of just four rooms. Visitors can begin their tour of the museum in any one of them.

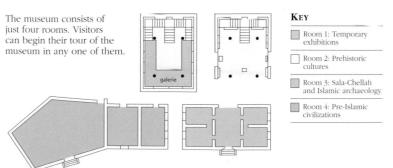

galerie

KEY

▆ Room 1: Temporary exhibitions

☐ Room 2: Prehistoric cultures

▆ Room 3: Sala-Chellah and Islamic archaeology

▆ Room 4: Pre-Islamic civilizations

Bab er-Rouah ⓭

Place an-Nasr. **Gallery** ◻ *daily during exhibitions.*

A STURDY AND imposing Almohad gateway, Bab el-Rouah, the Gate of the Winds, dates from the same period as Bab Oudaïa *(see p68).*

The entrance is decorated with the outline of two horseshoe arches carved into the stone and surrounded by a band of Kufic calligraphy.

The interior of the gate contains four rooms with elegant domes. These rooms are now used for exhibitions.

Bab el-Rouah, a fine Almohad gate with arches set into the stonework

Dar el-Makhzen ⓮

In the northwest of the city. ● *to the public. The exterior of the palace complex is of interest in its own right. The méchouar (assembly place) and the gardens are open to the public.*

A N EXTENSIVE complex enclosed within its own walls, the Dar el-Makhzen (royal palace) is inhabited by about 2,000 people. Built on the site of an 18th-century royal residence, the current palace was completed in 1864, but was constantly enlarged thereafter; today, it even includes a racecourse.

The palace now houses the offices of the Moroccan government, the Supreme Court, the prime minister's offices, the ministry of the Habous (responsible for religious organizations), and the El-Fas Mosque. The *méchouar*, a place of public assembly, is the venue for major gatherings, including the *bayaa,* a ceremony at which senior government ministers swear

Rabat's Dar el-Makhzen (royal palace), where 2,000 people live and work

their allegiance to the king. Traditionally, the king would reside in the former harem though Mohammed VI stays in his own private residence.

Besides private buildings, the palace also includes an extensive garden, immaculately kept and planted with various species of trees and with flowers in formal beds.

Chellah Necropolis ⓯

In the southeast of the city. ◻ *8:30am–6pm daily. Access via Bab Zaer but best reached by taxi.* 📷

A CCESS TO THE Chellah Necropolis is via Bab Zaer. This gate, named after a local tribe, was the only one on the southern side of the ramparts built by Yacoub el-Mansour. The necropolis is nearby.

Detail of the Gate of Ambassadors at the Royal Palace

The entrance to the necropolis itself is marked by an imposing Almohad gate with a horseshoe arch flanked by two towers. Above the arch is a band of Kufic calligraphy with the name of its builder, Abou el-Hassan, and the date 1339. On the left, inside a former guardhouse, there is a café. Through the gate, a stepped walkway leads to a terrace offering spectacular views of the Bou Regreg valley, the Merinid necropolis and the remains of the Roman town of Sala Colonia, which are surrounded by lush vegetation.

It was Abou Yacoub Youssef, the first Merinid caliph, who chose this as the site of a mosque and the burial place of his wife, Oum el-Izz, in 1284. Abou Yacoub Youssef died in Algeciras in 1286, and his body was brought back to the necropolis. His two successors, Abou Yacoub, who died in 1307, and Abou Thabit, who died in 1308, were also laid to rest here. The burial complex was completed by the sultan Abou Saïd (1310–31) and his son Abou el-Hassan (1331–51), and was later embellished by Abou Inan. The walls around the necropolis, which have the ochre tones typical of the earth stone of Rabat, were built by Abou el-Hassan, who probably reconstructed the existing Roman walls. In 1500, Leo Africanus recorded the existence of 30 Merinid tombs.

Situated within the walls of the necropolis are the ruins of the mosque built by Abou

accomplishments include the building of the Bou Inania Medersa in Fès *(see pp172–3)*.

Also within the walls of the necropolis was a *zaouia*, a religious institution that functioned simultaneously as a mosque, a centre of learning and a hostel for pilgrims and students (some of the cells can still be made out). Built by Abou el-Hassan, the *zaouia* is designed and decorated like the medersas in Fès, and it is thought that it may have been even more luxuriously appointed. Abou el-Hassan covered the upper part of the minaret with a decorative design of white, black, green and blue *zellij* tilework, which is still visible today.

The necropolis at Chellah was abandoned at the end of the Merinid dynasty, and in the course of the following centuries was ransacked several times. It was largely destroyed by the earthquake of 1755. Vegetation invaded the stonework and colonies of storks built their nests in the trees and on the minarets, giving the place a super-natural atmosphere, particularly at sunset.

The necropolis has become the subject of much folklore and many legends, as can be seen from the large number of *marabouts* (shrines) of holy men that are scattered about the garden. The sacred eels in the fountain (once the ablutions fountain for the mosque) are also believed to bring good fortune to barren women. These supplicants feed them eggs, symbols of fertility, which are offered for sale by young boys in the square.

ENVIRONS: Archaeological excavations at Chellah have uncovered the remains of the major buildings of **Sala Colonia**. Once a prosperous Roman city, Sala Colonia later declined and by the 10th century had fallen into ruin.

Storks nesting on the minaret of the former *zaouia* at Chellah

Youssef and of the buildings that surrounded it. To the right behind the mihrab is the *koubba* (shrine) of Abou Yacoub Youssef.

Opposite the *koubba*, the Mausoleum of Abou el-Hassan, the Black Sultan and the last Merinid ruler to be buried here, in 1351, lies alongside the walls. His funerary stele is still in place. Also to be seen here is the *koubba* of his wife, who died in 1349. Named Chams el-Doha (which can be translated as "light of the dawn"), she was a Christian who converted to Islam. She was the mother of Abou Inan *(see p51)*, one of the most illustrious Merinid rulers. Her

The interior of the mosque built by Abou Youssef

Still visible today is the *decumanus maximus,* the main thoroughfare that crossed all Roman cities from east to west. It led out from Sala Colonia to the port, built in the 1st century BC and now buried in sand.

From the forum, a road to the right leads towards the Merinid necropolis.

The walls around the Chellah Necropolis, raised by Abou el-Hassan in the 14th century

NORTHERN ATLANTIC COAST

MOROCCO'S NORTHERN ATLANTIC COAST *offers extensive beaches of soft fine sand, lagoons, winter havens for migratory birds, and forests that are highly prized by hunters. But to explore it is also to travel back in time, since the heritage of the Phoenicians and the Romans, the corsairs, the Portuguese and the Spanish, as well as of the colonial epoch is present alongside the new prosperity brought by agriculture, port activity, trade and tourism.*

Although it attracts far fewer tourists than the interior or the imperial cities, the Moroccan coastline from Rabat to Tangier has much to offer visitors. It has not undergone the high level of development that has transformed the coastal area from Rabat to Casablanca and the south. Nevertheless, this region is no less characteristic of the modern, vibrant and outward-looking country that Morocco has become. For 250 km (155 miles), the ocean seems omnipresent, as roads and motorways often skirt the coastline and the beaches. For motorists following the coastal roads, the ocean may suddenly come into sight at an estuary or over a dune. The road follows roughly the course of a Roman road linking Sala Colonia (known today as Chellah, *see pp80–81)* and Banasa, Lixus and Tangier. This is the heart of one of earliest regions of Morocco in which towns and cities were established.

The ocean has shaped the history of the coastal towns: occupied from Phoenician times and into the Roman period, they have attracted pirates, invaders and Andalusian, Spanish and French occupiers, each of whom left their mark. It is also the ocean that gives the region its gentle, moist climate (strawberries, bananas and tomatoes are grown in greenhouses) and that drives industry and port activity from Kenitra to Tangier, where a new port is being built to handle cargo bound for Europe.

Asilah, a small Andalusian-style town *(see p91)*, facing the Atlantic from behind coastal defences

◁ Ruins at the ancient site of Thamusida *(see p87)*, once inhabited by the Romans

Exploring the Northern Atlantic Coast

Travelling along Morocco's Atlantic coast between Salé and Tangier reveals a natural paradise of sea, forests, lagoons, hunting and fishing within sight of beaches that appear to stretch to infinity. The coast is punctuated by ancient sites: Thamusida, nestling in a bend of Wadi Sebou; Banasa, set a little way back from the sea, in the fertile plain of the Rharb; and Lixus, standing on a promontory opposite Larache, on the estuary of the Loukkos. From Salé to Tangier, a succession of small walled towns with interesting monuments bears testament to a rich history: Mehdya, whose kasbah dominates the final meanders of Wadi Sebou; Moulay Bousselham, with its attractive lagoon and beach protected by the tomb of the eponymous saint, which draws numerous pilgrims; Asilah, where walls pierced by mysteriously screened windows enclose narrow, secretive streets; Larache, a charmingly Andalusian town; and Tangier, which looks over the Straits of Gibraltar towards Spain and Europe.

Agriculture in the region of Kenitra

0 km 10

0 miles 10

SIGHTS AT A GLANCE

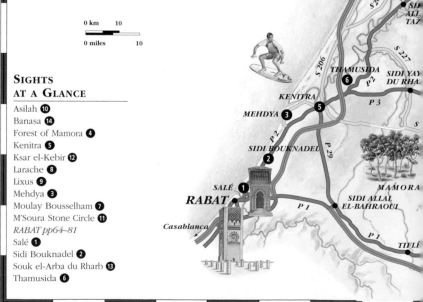

ATLANTIC OCEAN

MOULAY BOUSSELHAM ⑦

Tangier
Tetouan
ASILAH **10**
M'SOURA
STONE CIRCLE
11
P 37
P 2
KUS
9
8
LARACHE
Wadi Loukos
P 2
Chefchaouen
S 603
12
KSAR EL-KEBIR
ARBAOUA
S 216
P 2
16a
S 216
P 23
Ouezzane
SOUK EL-ARBA
13
DU RHARB
UK TELAT
U RHARB
S 221
14
NASA
MECHRA
BEN KSIRI
S 210
S 223
Wadi
Querrha
2014
P 6
SIDI
SLIMANE
Fès
DAR
S 205
SIDI
BEL AMRI
KACEM
P 3
P 4
P 6
ST
4
Meknès
S 205
Meknès
P 1
HEMISSET
Fès

Migratory birds in the lagoon at Moulay Bousselham

SEE ALSO

- *Where to Stay* p303
- *Where to Eat* pp322–3

GETTING AROUND

A motorway (with toll) provides a direct link between Rabat and Larache, and continues towards Asilah, at the junction with the Tétouan road (P37). Even when driving on a motorway, care should be taken: animals or people may try to cross unexpectedly. The P2 goes further inland, reaching the coast at Asilah. From Kenitra, a narrower road, the S2301, is the best way to approach the coast. A bus service running from Rabat and Tangier provides transport to and from most places.

KEY

▬	Motorway
▬	Major road
═	Minor road
═	Track

Colourfully painted doors in the medina at Asilah

The tropical gardens in Sidi Bouknadel

Salé ❶

Road map C2. West of Rabat, on the right bank of Wadi Bou Regreg. 🏠 710,000. ✈ Rabat-Salé , 10 km (6 miles) on the Meknès road. 🚏 Route de Casablanca. 🛈 Rabat; (037) 67 40 13. 🎭 Festival and night-time Candle Procession (on the eve of Mouloud). 🔄 Thu.

FOUNDED IN about the 11th century, Salé was fortified and embellished at the end of the 13th century by the Merinids. They built a medersa, a mosque, a medical school and a magnificent aqueduct, which can still be seen from the road to Kenitra. During the Middle Ages, Salé was a busy port, used by traders from the northern Mediterranean, and in 1609 it provided sanctuary for refugees from Andalusia. Salé shared the lucrative business of privateering with its neighbour and rival Rabat (see pp64–81), with which it came into conflict. When piracy was brought to an end in the 18th century, the town went into decline.

In the 20th century, however, Salé found prosperity once

The walls of Salé, near Bab el-Mrisa

more, as a major centre of the crafts industry.

At the entrance to the town (from the direction of Rabat) stands the 13th-century **Bab el-Mrisa** (Gate of the Sea). This was the entrance to the maritime arsenal built by Yacoub el-Mansour, and a canal linking Wadi Bou Regreg to the harbour passed through it.

Within the town, near Rue Bab el-Khebbaz, the main street through the medina, are the Kissaria and souks, both filled with craftsmen and traders. Nearby are the **Grand Mosque** and the medersa. A doorway framed by a horseshoe arch and covered with a carved wooden porch leads into the medersa. Built during the reign of the Merinid ruler Abou el-Hassan, it is notable for its central tower surrounded by a colonnaded gallery covered in *zellij* tilework and carved plaster and wood. The mihrab has a decorated wooden ceiling.

Chest, Musée Dar Belghazi

The **Seamen's Cemetery**, in the northeast of the town, is dotted with the *marabouts* (shrines) of such holy men as Sidi ben Achir. In the 16th century, he was credited with the power to calm the waves so as allow vessels to

enter the harbour safely. The *marabout* of Sidi Abdallah ben Hassoun (patron of Salé, of boatmen and of travellers) has an unusual dome that abuts the Grand Mosque. Further north along the coast the *marabout* of Sidi Moussa overlooks the sea.

Sidi Bouknadel ❷

Road map C2. 10 km (6 miles) north of Salé on the P2 to Kenitra. 🏠 6,900. 🚍 Rabat. 🔄 Sun.

THE TROPICAL GARDENS (**Jardins Exotiques**) just outside Sidi Bouknadel were laid out in 1951 by the horticulturist Marcel François and are today owned by the State. Some 1,500 species native to the Antilles, South America and Asia grow in the garden.

🌺 **Jardins Exotiques** ⬜ 9am–6:30pm daily. ▦

ENVIRONS: 2 km (1.25 miles) to the north is the **Musée Dar Belghazi**, which contains a wide-ranging collection of fine objects, including jewellery, kaftans, marriage belts, carved wooden doors, minbars, pottery and musical instruments. This privately-run museum was established by a master woodcarver, with bequests from artists and collectors.

🏛 **Musée Dar Belghazi** Km 47, Route de Kenitra. 📞 037 82 21 78. ⬜ 8:30am–6pm daily. ▦

Mehdya ❸

Road map C2. 39 km (24 miles) from Salé on the P2 to Kenitra, at km 29 turning onto the Mehdya-Plage road. 🏠 5,800. 🚍 Kenitra, then by taxi.

THIS SMALL COASTAL resort is much frequented by the inhabitants of Rabat and Kenitra. On the estuary of Wadi Sebou, it stands on the

site of what may have been a
Carthagenian trading post in
the 5th century BC, and then
an Almohad naval base,
which was known at the time
as El Mamora ("the populous
one"). Later, the town was
occupied by the Portuguese,
the Spanish and the Dutch,
and was finally captured by
Moulay Ismaïl *(see p53)* at the
end of the 17th century.

The kasbah which stands
on the plateau, dominating
the estuary, still has its
original walls, which were
built by the Spanish, and its
moated bastions. The monumental gate, built by Moulay
Ismaïl, leads to the governor's
palace, which has a central
courtyard, rooms, outbuildings,
hammam and mosque.

ENVIRONS: the **Sidi Bourhaba
Lagoon**, 27 km (17 miles)
along the Mehdya-Plage road,
is a large bird sanctuary:
thousands of birds, such as
teal and coot, rest here during
their migration between Europe and sub-Saharan Africa.

🦅 **Sidi Bourhaba Lagoon**
[*(037) 74 72 09.* **Exhibition
centre and marked walks**
⏰ *noon–4pm Sat, Sun and public
holidays.*

Forest of Mamora ❹

Road map C2. East of Rabat on the
P2 to Kenitra or the P1 to Meknès.

THE FOREST OF MAMORA,
between Wadi Sebou and
Wadi Bou Regreg, covers an
area 60 km (37 miles) long
and 30 km (19 miles) wide.
Although the forest is now
planted mostly with
eucalyptus, which grows

Pieces of bark stripped from the cork-oak

much faster than other
species, large tracts of it are
still covered with cork-oak,
which is grown for its bark.
At a factory in Sidi Yahia
eucalyptus wood is turned
into a pulp that is used in
paper-making and the
manufacture of artificial silk.

Being intensively exploited
and degraded by the grazing
of cattle, sheep and goats, the
forest is becoming increasingly bare. However, enough
cover remains to allow a
refreshingly cool walk in
summer, when wood pigeons,
kites, rollers and spotted
flycatchers can be seen.

Kenitra ❺

Road map C2. 🏛 *300,000.*
🚉 🚌 *Rabat.* 🛒 *Mon & Sat.*

ESTABLISHED IN 1913 in the
early days of the French
Protectorate, from 1933 to
1955 this town was known as
Port-Lyautey. Nowadays,
Kenitra consists of distinct
districts: residential areas with
villas, a European-style town
centre and poorer suburbs.

In the harbour, on the right
bank of Wadi Sebou, regional
produce from the Rharb (such
as citrus fruit, cork, cotton,
cereals and pulp
for papermaking)
are unloaded for
use in local indus-
tries. Once a
marshy area where
malaria was rife
(but still used for
extensive stock-
farming), the
alluvial plain of
the Rharb has
been transformed
by irrigation. It is

now one of Morocco's major
agricultural areas, specializing
in rice, sugar beet, cotton and
citrus fruits.

The Roman baths at Thamusida,
on the banks of Wadi Sebou

Thamusida ❻

Road map D2. 55 km (34 miles) northeast of Rabat, 17 km (10.5 miles) northeast of Kenitra. Motorway exit: Kenitra N.

ON THE P2, at the milestone
indicating "Kenitra 14 km,
Sidi Allal Tazi 28 km", a track
heading westwards leads to
this ancient site on Wadi
Sebou. It was inhabited by the
Romans from the 2nd century
BC to the 3rd century AD.

Part of the walls can still be
seen, along with the outline
of the Roman army camp
(with streets intersecting at
right angles) and the site's
most prominent feature, the
praetorium (headquarters),
with columns and pilasters.
To the northeast the remains
of baths and a temple with
three chambers, or *cellae,* can
be made out. North of Wadi
Sebou are vestiges of the
harbour docks.

Fishing harbour at Mehdya, on Wadi Sebou

Cork-oaks in the Forest of Mamora ▷

Moulay Bousselham ❼

Road map D2. 48 km (30 miles) south of Larache. *Motorway then 10 km (6 miles) on the S216.* 🚶 *900.* 🚤 **Boat trips** *available from Café Milano.* 🎪 *Moussem (early summer).*

THE SMALL TOWN of Moulay Bousselham is a coastal resort that is very popular with Moroccans. The mosque and the tomb of Moulay Bousselham tower above the ocean and the Merja Zerga lagoon. As the burial place of Moulay Bousselham, the 10th-century holy man, it is also a major place of pilgrimage, attracting many followers in late June and early July.

The life of the holy man is wreathed in legends associated with the ocean and its perils. The Moulay Bousselham sandbar is, indeed, highly dangerous: the waves come crashing in over the reefs and onto the beach. The waters of the lagoon are calmer; boat trips are organized to see the thousands of birds – herons, pink flamingoes, gannets and sheldrake – that come to the lagoon on their migrations in December and January. Boat trips around the lagoon depart from the small fishing harbour.

The town of Moulay Bousselham and the Merja Zerga lagoon

Larache ❽

Road map D1. 🚶 *95,000.* 🚌 *from Tangier, Rabat.* 🛍 *Sun.*

SET A LITTLE WAY back from major roads, Larache is both an Andalusian and an Arab town. The modern part bears obvious signs of the Spanish Protectorate.

Established in the 7th century by Arab conquerors, by the 11th century Larache was an important centre of

Andalusian-style fountain on Place de la Libération, Larache

trade on the left bank of Wadi Loukkos. In the 16th century it was used as a base by corsairs from Algiers and Turkey, and was subject to reprisals by Portuguese forces from Asilah. The town passed to Spain in 1610, and was then taken by Moulay Ismaïl at the end of the 17th century. During the Spanish Protectorate (1911–56) Larache was held by Spain.

The medina is reached from Place de la Libération, a very Spanish plaza, and through Bab el-Khemis, a brick-built gate roofed with glazed tiles. In the fabrics souk – the *kissaria (socco de la alcaicería)* – a market offers a wide range of goods. Narrow streets lined with houses with floral decoration lead down towards the harbour. Bab el-Kasba separates the southern edge of the fabrics souk from Rue Moulay el-Mehdi, a street covered with overhead arches that leads to an octagonal minaret and a terrace overlooking the meandering Wadi Loukkos, salt-marshes and the Lixus promontory.

The **Musée Archéologique**, arranged in a bastion of the old walls, contains objects discovered during excavations at Lixus.

Not far from Lixus is the Château de la Cigogne (Stork's Castle), a fortress that was built in 1578 by the Saadian rulers and then remodelled by the Spanish in the 17th century. It is closed to the public.

It is pleasant to stroll along the seafront – the "balcony of the Atlantic". Nearby is the

Moorish market. Finally, in the **Catholic Cemetery**, the tomb of the French writer Jean Genet (1910–86) can be found, lying facing the ocean.

🏛 **Musée Archéologique**
📞 *(039) 91 20 91.* 🕐 *11am–1:30pm & 3–6pm Wed–Mon.* ● *Mar.* 🈲

Lixus ❾

Road map D1. 5 km (3 miles) northeast of Larache on the P2. 🚤 *from Larache.*

THIS ANCIENT SITE, which commands a view of the ocean, of Wadi Loukkos and of Larache, is to become one of UNESCO's World Heritage Sites. According to legend, this is where one of the Labours of Hercules – picking the golden apples in the Garden of the Hesperides – took place.

In the 7th century BC the Phoenicians established a trading post here, serving as a stage on the Gold Route. After it had been taken by the Romans between 40 and 45 AD, Lixus became a colony

The Roman ruins of Lixus, set on a magnificent promontory

and a centre of the manu-
facture of *garum*, sauce made
with scraps of fish marinaded
in brine from salting vats. The
Romans abandoned Lixus at
the end of the 3rd century AD.

The vats in which meat and
fish were salted and *garum*
made – Morocco's major
industry in Roman times –
can be seen around the edges
of the site. In the amphitheatre, with its circular arena,
public games took place.

The **Acropolis** above the
town has its own walls; only
on the western side, where
there is a sheer drop, do they
coincide with the town walls.
An apsidal building, preceded
by an atrium with a cistern,
has been excavated. The
Great Temple (1st century
BC–1st century AD), to the
south, features an arcaded
area (courtyard). The *cella,*
where the god dwelt, on the
axis of the peristyle, backs
onto an apsidal wall; opposite
is a large semicircular apse
with a mosaic floor.

Asilah

Road map D1. 👥 *25,000.*
🚉 *2 km (1.5 miles) north of
town.* 🚌 *from Tangier or Rabat.*
🎭 *Cultural Festival (Aug).* 🛒 *Thu.*

E STABLISHED BY the
Phoenicians, Asilah was
an important town in Mauretania's pre-Roman period
(when coins where minted
here), and also under the
Romans. It was captured by
the Portuguese in 1471 and
became a centre of trade with
connections to the Medi-
terranean countries. The town
came under Moroccan control
in 1691, during the reign of
Moulay Ismaïl.

At the end of the 19th
century, Raissouli, a pretender
to power and a brigand,
extortioner and kidnapper,
made Asilah his base. In
1906, taking advantage of the
intrigues that surrounded the
sovereign, Abdul Aziz, he
assumed the mantle of pasha
then that of governor of the
Jebala. He built himself a
palace facing the sea, from
which he was expelled by the
Spanish in 1924.

Colourful display of fruit on a stall in the market at Asilah

This small Andalusian-style
town is enclosed within
ramparts. The narrow streets
are paved or limed, and lined
with houses fronted by
balconies with restrained
mashrabiyya, and with blue-
or green-painted woodwork.

The Criquia jetty, northwest
of the town, overlooks a tiny
cemetery with tombstones
covered with glazed tiles. At the
foot of the square tower on
Place Ibn Khaldoun stands
Bab el-Bahr (Gate of the Sea).
On the opposite side of the
square, Bab Homar (Gate of
the Land), with the Portuguese royal coat of arms,
leads out from the ramparts
and into the new town.

In summer, the **Centre
Hassan II des Rencontres
Internationales**, in Rue de la
Kasba, within the walls, hosts
cultural events and
exhibitions. Asilah is also
frequented by painters, who
are fond of marking the walls
with signs of their passing.

M'Soura Stone Circle

Road map D1. El-Utad to Chouahed.
27 km (17 miles) southeast of Asilah
on the P2, then P37 towards Tetouan.

T HIS NEOLITHIC SITE is
reached via a 7-km
(4-mile) track running from
Sidi el-Yamani towards Souk
et-Tnine. Perhaps the burial

place of an important local
ruler, it consists of 200 mono-
lithic standing stones ranging
in height from 50 cm (20
inches) to 5 m (16 ft) and
surrounding a burial area
about 55 m (180 ft) in circum-
ference. Unique in the
Maghreb and the Sahara, by
its sheer size this monument
is reminiscent of those seen in
Spain. The type of pottery
decorated with impressions of
cardium shells and bronze
weapons, which excavations
have brought to light, are also
identical to Spanish examples.

One of the 200 standing stones at
the M'Soura Neolithic stone circle

Sugarcane plantation in the fertile region around Ksar el-Kebir

Ksar el-Kebir ⓬

Road map D1. 👥 *107,000.*
🚉 *Moulay el-Mehdi (approx.*
3 km/2 miles) 🚌 *from Tangier.* 🔵 *Sun.*

THE TOWN takes its name
from a great fortress which,
during the Almoravid and
Almohad periods, controlled
the road leading to the ports
along the Straits of Gibraltar.

It was at Wadi el-Makhazin
nearby that the Battle of the
Three Kings took place in
1578. The conflict has been
described as the "last crusade
undertaken by the Christians
of the Mediterranean". It was
instigated by the Saadian
sultan El-Mutawakkil, who,
having been driven from
Morocco, was zealous for a
crusade. In alliance with
Sebastião I, king of Portugal,
he made a bid to win back
his kingdom. Sebastião,
El-Mutawakkil and their
opponent, the Saadian sultan
Abd el-Malik (who was
victorious over the invaders),
all died in the battle. Moulay
Ahmed, brother of Abd
el-Malik, succeeded him,
becoming known not only
as Ahmed el-Mansour ("the
Victorious") but also as
Ahmed el-Dhebi ("the
Golden"), because of the
ransom that he exacted.

Ksar el-Kebir is, today, a
sizeable country town. A
particularly large souk is held
here on Sundays: goods on
offer include the produce of
local market gardens, as well
as that of the area's olive
plantations and citrus groves.

Souk el-Arba du Rharb ⓭

Road map D2. 👥 *38,000.*
🚉 🚌 *Rabat, Tangier.* 🔵 *Wed.*

A MAJOR AGRICULTURAL centre
on the northwest border
of the Rharb, Souk el-Arba du
Rharb is especially busy on
Wednesdays, when the souk
is held. The town's position
on the intersection of roads
leading to Tangier, Rabat,
Meknès and the coastal town
of Moulay Bousselham has
made it a key staging post.

Banasa ⓮

Road map D2. 103 km (64 miles)
northeast of Rabat on the P2 or
Rabat-Tangier freeway (Kenitra North
exit).

THIS ANCIENT TOWN, an in-
land port on Wadi Sebou
and the most developed in
Mauretania Tingitana, was a
centre of ceramic production
from the 3rd century and
during the 1st century BC.
A Roman colony from 33 to
25 BC, Banasa was a
prosperous and bustling
commercial town until the
end of the 3rd century AD.

The entrance to the town,
through a vaulted gateway,
leads to the basilica and the
paved and arcaded forum.
South of the forum rises the
capitol, where several altars
stand before the temple's five
cellae (chambers). In the
public baths to the west, the
various rooms for the Roman
ritual of bathing – robing
rooms, a *caldarium* and *tepi-
darium* (hot and warm rooms)
with underfloor heating, and
frigidarium (cold room) can
be distinguished. Wall paintings and a brick floor paved
in a herringbone pattern can
be made out in another bath-
house at a lower level.

A famous document
engraved on bronze was
discovered at Banasa. Known
as the *Banasa Table*, it was
an edict by which Caracalla
granted the province relief
from taxes in return for lions,
elephants and other animals
that the emperor desired for
public spectacles in Rome.

From the P2 or freeway,
Banasa is reached by taking
the S210A, then, 3 km (2 miles)
before Souk Tleta du Rharb,
by turning off onto the S210.
As it approaches the site, the
road is reduced to a track.

**Stele with an inscription in Latin,
standing in the ruins of Banasa**

Roman Towns in Morocco

URING THE reigns of Juba II and Ptolemy, kings of Mauretania who ruled under the aegis of Rome, towns were established in Morocco. Under Roman control, they developed either into *coloniae* (colonies such as Lixus and Banasa) or *municipiae* (free towns such as Sala and Volubilis).

The inhabitants, who grew prosperous through the cultivation of the land, endowed their towns with such civic features as forums, basilicas, capitols and triumphal arches. Adapting

Head of Hercules

to the Roman way of life, they built houses with columned courtyards and mosaic floors in the Roman style, and imported bronze sculptures from Egypt and Italy and pottery from Etruria. Public and private baths fulfilled the desire for personal cleanliness and also acted as places in which to socialize. The arcades along the *decumanus maximus* (main thoroughfare) were filled with shops, while cottage industries were established around the edges of the town.

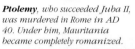

Juba II *(52 BC–AD 23), who married the daughter of Cleopatra and Mark Antony, turned Mauretania into a highly prosperous country.*

Ptolemy, *who succeeded Juba II, was murdered in Rome in AD 40. Under him, Mauritania became completely romanized.*

ROMAN RULE

Juba II was made king of Mauretania by Augustus. After Ptolemy's death, the province was administered by Rome under Claudius. Triumphal arches were built during the reigns of Commodius and Caracalla. In the late 3rd century, under Diocletian, the country was administered with the province of Spain.

Mauretania's cities *were centres of trade and administration, as well as garrison towns. As in Rome, the focal point was the forum (a market place and public area) and the basilica, simultaneously a monetary exchange, law court and meeting place. The capitol was the city's religious centre.*

The basilica and the columns of the capitol at Volubilis

ART

As Rome imposed political unity, so Roman artistic influence spread throughout the Maghreb.

Head of the young Bacchus, *with soft, rounded features and an effeminate appearance, in the artistic style that prevailed at the time in Rome.*

Roman funerary art *can be seen in Morocco. Many stelae (free-standing stone columns) take the shape of a pointed rectangle carved with a figure dressed in a full-length tunic.*

Mosaic depicting Aeolus, *Roman god of wind, whose breath restores nature to life. It comes from the floor of the house in Volubilis.*

CASABLANCA

TRADDLING EAST AND WEST, *Casablanca, the commercial and financial capital of Morocco, is a baffling metropolis where tradition and modernity co-exist. A city where skyscrapers stand in stark contrast to the small shops of the medina, with its narrow, winding streets, this is where the prosperous rub shoulders with paupers.*

In the 7th century, Casablanca was no more than a small Berber settlement clinging to the slopes of the Anfa hills. However, for strategic and commercial reasons, it was already attracting the attention of foreign powers. In 1468, the town was sacked by the Portuguese, who wrought wholesale destruction on the city's privateer ships. Then, in the 18th century, with the sultanate of Sidi Mohammed ben Abdallah, Dar el-Beïda (meaning "White House" – "Casa Blanca" in Spanish) acquired a new significance. This was thanks to its harbour, which played a pivotal role in the sugar, tea, wool and corn markets of the Western world. But it was in the 20th century, under the French Protectorate *(see pp56– 7)*, that Casablanca underwent the most profound change. Against expert advice, Marshal Lyautey, the first resident-governor, proceeded with plans to make Casablanca the country's economic hub. To realize this vision, he hired the services of town planners and modernized the port. For almost 40 years, the most innovative architects worked on this huge building project. Casablanca continued to expand even after independence. Futuristic high-rise buildings and a colossal mosque sending its laser beams towards Mecca once again expressed the city's forward-looking spirit. With almost 3.5 million inhabitants, Casablanca is, today, one of the four largest metropolises on the African continent, and its port is the busiest in Morocco.

Moroccans relaxing on the terrace of a café in the Parc de la Ligue Arabe

◁ Casablanca's Mosque of Hassan II, seen from the sea

Exploring Casablanca

THE CENTRE of the new town (Ville Nouvelle) revolves around two focal points: the Place des Nations Unies and the Place Mohammed V, squares that are lined with fine 1930s buildings. To the north, the old medina is still enclosed within ramparts, while to the southeast extends the Parc de la Ligue Arabe, Casablanca's green lung. Further out, towards the west, is the residential district of Anfa and the coastal resort of Aïn Diab. The Boulevard de la Corniche leads to the monumental Mosque of Hassan II. The Quartier Habous, a modern medina built in the 1920s, also features some interesting architecture.

SIGHTS AT A GLANCE

Avenues and Boulevards
Avenue des Forces
    Armées Royales **2**
Boulevard Mohammed V **3**

Squares
Place Mohammed V **4**
Place des Nations Unies **1**

Districts
Anfa **12**
Corniche d'Aïn Diab **13**
Old Medina **6**
Port **7**
Quartier Habous
    (New Medina) **9**

Park
Parc de la Ligue Arabe **5**

Building
Casablanca Twin Center **10**

Mosque
Mosque of Hassan II
    pp102–3 **8**

Museum
Musée du Judaïsme
    Marocain **11**

Environs
Mohammedia **14**

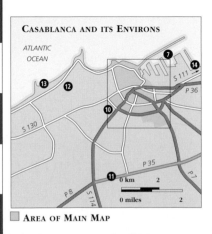

CASABLANCA AND ITS ENVIRONS

ATLANTIC
OCEAN

7
14
S 111
P 36
13   **12**
10
S 130
P 35
P 7
11   0 km   2
P 8   S 114   0 miles   2

☐ AREA OF MAIN MAP

Detail of a 1930s façade in Casablanca

GETTING AROUND

Allow at least one day to explore
Casablanca. The old medina and the new
town, with their fine architectural heritage,
are best seen on foot. By contrast, the
Quartier Habous and the Mosque of
Hassan II can be reached only by
motorized transport. Parking is not a
problem as there are many car parks.
It is also possible to travel around
Casablanca by bus. Bus routes
serve both the city centre
and outlying
districts.

**Stained-glass window in the
Church of Notre-Dame-de-Lourdes**

KEY

- Medina
- Ramparts
- Railway station
- Bus station
- Parking
- Tourist information
- Post office
- Church
- Mosque
- Jewish cemetery
- Motorway
- Major road
- Minor road

SEE ALSO

- **Where to Stay** pp303–4
- **Where to Eat** pp323–4

The Moretti Milone apartment
block, one of the highest in 1934

Place des Nations Unies ❶

South of the old medina.

AT THE BEGINNING of the
20th century, this was
still no more than a market
square, a place which, by
evening, would become the
haunt of storytellers and
snake charmers.
Today, it is the
heart of the new
town, a hub where
major thoroughfares
converge.
   When the square
was laid out in
1920, it was known
as Place de France,
but was later
renamed. Beneath the arcades
of 1930s apartment blocks are
rows of brasserie terraces and
souvenir shops. In the
northeast corner of the
square, the **clocktower**,
which dates from 1910, was
demolished in 1940 and then
rebuilt to an identical design.
At the time that it was built,
the clock symbolized colonial
rule, indicating to the
population that it should
now keep in time with an
industrial society.
   At the **Hyatt Regency
Hotel** memories of
Humphrey Bogart and Ingrid
Bergman, stars of the famous
film *Casablanca*, made in
1943 by Michael Curtiz, hang
in the air. In the southeast
corner of the square is the
Excelsior Hotel (1914–16),
with Moorish friezes and

Window of the
Excelsior hotel

balconies, which was the first
of Morocco's Art Deco hotels
and is one of the square's
finest buildings. In 1934, the
11-storey **Moretti Milone**
apartment block, at the corner
of Boulevard Houphouët
Boigny, was the first high-
rise building in central
Casablanca. **Boulevard
Houphouët Boigny**, lined
with shops and restaurants,
runs from the square to the
port. At the end, on the right,
the *marabout* of Sidi Belyout,
patron saint and protector of
Casablanca, stands in stark
contrast to the neighbouring
residential buildings.

Avenue des Forces Armées Royales ❷

South of the old medina, running
between Place Oued el-Makhazine
and Place Zellaga.

LINED WITH HIGH-RISE buildings, major hotels such
as the **Sheraton** and **Royal
Mansour**, with airline offices
and travel
agents and the
towering, futuristic
glass building of
**Omnium Nord
Africain** (ONA), this
avenue marks the
boundary of the
commercial district.
Further develop-
ment is planned for
its continuation towards the
Mosque of Hassan II.

Boulevard Mohammed V ❸

Running from Place des Nations Unies
to Boulevard Hassan Seghir.

RUNNING THROUGH the city
like a spine, this boule-
vard links Place des Nations
Unies with the railway station
in the east of the city. When
it was built in 1915, it was
intended to be the major

No. 208 Boulevard Mohammed V,
faced with friezes and balconies

artery through the commercial
heart of Casablanca. On both
sides, covered arcades house
shops and restaurants.
   A raised strip sections off
traffic and widens into a
square level with the **Central
Market**. The high-rise
buildings here are notable for
their façades, which feature
loggias, columns, *zellij* tile-

The Glaoui residential block, built in 1922 by M. Boyer

The Palais de Justice, built in the Moorish style in 1922

work and geometric carvings. Peculiar to the buildings of this period is the mixture of styles – Art Deco, on the one hand, seen in white façades of simple design, and the typically Moroccan, more decorative style on the other. Among the finest of these buildings are three residential blocks: the **Glaoui** (designed by M. Boyer, 1922), on the corner of Rue El-Amraoui Brahim; the **Bessonneau** (H. Bride, 1917), opposite the market; and the **Asayag** (M. Boyer, 1932), at the corner of Boulevard Hassan Seghir. The latter, very innovatory at the time it was built, is five storeys high and has three towers set around a central hub. From the fourth storey upwards, terraces extend the studio apartments. Buildings at numbers 47, 67 and 73 are also fine examples, with overhanging loggias and rounded balconies.

Another particular feature of Boulevard Mohammed V is its covered arcades, which are similar to the shopping arcades built during the same period (the 1920s) along the Champs-Élysées in Paris. Among the most interesting of these arcades is the **Passage du Glaoui**, which links Boulevard Mohammed V to Rue Allal ben-Abdallah. Lit by prismatic lamps, the arcade is punctuated by glass rotundas. **Passage Sumica**, opposite Passage du Glaoui, is closer to the Art Deco style. This runs through to **Rue du Prince Moulay Abdallah**, which also contains some

notable 1930s apartment blocks. This pedestrianized street is very popular with shoppers.

In Rue Mohammed el-Quori, off Boulevard Mohammed V, stands the **Rialto**. This former cinema is renowned for its fine ornamentation, stained-glass windows and Art Deco lighting.

 **Central Market**
Boulevard Mohammed V *(almost opposite the tourist information centre).* ◻ 7am–2pm daily.

Place Mohammed V ❹

North of the Parc de la Ligue Arabe.

Exemplifying the architecture of the Protectorate, this square, the administrative heart of Casablanca, combines the monumentality of French architecture with Moorish sobriety. This is the location of the Préfecture, the law courts, the central post office, banks and cultural organizations.

The **Préfecture** (by M. Boyer, 1937), over which towers a Tuscan-style campanile 50 m (164 ft) high, stands on the southeastern side of the square. Its buildings are set around three courtyards, each with a tropical garden. The central stairway is framed by two huge paintings by Jacques Majorelle *(see p243)* depicting the festivities of a *moussem*

Zellij decoration on the façade of the Post Office

and the performance of the *ahwach*, a Berber dance.

Behind stands the **Palais de Justice** (law courts, designed by J. Marrast and completed in 1922). The strong verticality of the Moorish doorway, with its awning of green tiles, contrasts with the horizontal lines of the arcaded gallery, which are emphasized by a carved frieze running the length of the building.

Two buildings set slightly back abut the façade of the law courts on either side. On the right is the **Consulat de France** (French Consulate, by A. Laprade, 1916), whose gardens contain an equestrian statue of Marshal Lyautey, by Cogné (1938), which stood in the centre of the square until Moroccan independence. On the left, in the northeastern corner, is the **Cercle Militaire** (by M. Boyer). To the north is the **Post Office** (A. Laforgue, 1920), fronted by an open arcade decorated with *zellij* tile-work and semi-circular arches, which leads through to an Art Deco central hall within.

Opposite, along Rue de Paris, a small area of greenery where people like to stroll gives a more picturesque feel to the square, in the centre of which is a monumental **fountain** dating from 1976. At certain times of day, the fountain plays music and gives light displays.

A long, straight walkway in the Parc de la Ligue Arabe

Parc de la Ligue Arabe ❺

South of Place Mohammed V
(between Boulevard Rachidi and
Boulevard Mohammed Zerktouni).

LAID OUT BY the architect
A. Laprade in 1919, this
huge garden incorporates café
terraces and is a popular
place for a stroll. Avenues
lined with impressively tall
palm trees, ficus, arcades and
pergolas frame some stunning
formal flowerbeds. The streets
surrounding the park,
including Rue d'Alger, Rue du
Parc and Boulevard Moulay-
Youssef, contain Art Nouveau
and Art Deco houses.

Northwest of the park
stands the **Église du Sacré-
Cœur**, built in
1930–52 by
Paul Toürnon.
A white
concrete
twin-towered
building with
an Art Deco
flavour to
its façade, it
is now de-
consecrated
and used for
cultural events.

To the southeast stands the
**Église Notre-Dame-de-
Lourdes** (1956). Its stained-
glass windows depict scenes
from the life of the Virgin
against motifs taken from
Moroccan carpets. They are the
work of G. Loire, a master-
craftsman from Chartres.

To the southwest is the **Villa
des Arts** displaying contemporary Moroccan paintings

🚪 **Église du Sacré-Cœur**
Rond-point de l'Europe. ☐ only for
concerts and other events.
🏛 **Villa des Arts**
30 Bd Brahim Roudani. ☎ (029) 50
87 94. ☐ 11am–7pm Tue–Sat. 📷

Old Medina ❻

Between Boulevard des Almohades
and Place des Nations Unies.

AT THE BEGINNING of the 20th
century, Casablanca consisted only of the old medina,
which itself comprised no
more than a few thousand
inhabitants. The walls around
the old town
were origin-
ally pierced
by four gates,
two of which
survive today.
**Bab Marra-
kech** and **Bab
el-Jedid**, on
the western
side, face onto
Boulevard Tahar
el-Alaoui. A
daily **market**, with jewellers,
barbers, public letter-writers
and so on, stretches out along
the length of the walls.

Opposite the fishing harbour
is the *sqala*, a fortified bastion
built in the 18th century,
during the reign of Sidi
Mohammed ben Abdallah.
Behind the bastion, the

A cannon in the *sqala*, facing
the port and onto the ocean

marabout (shrine) with a
double crown of merlons
contains the **Tomb of Sidi
Allal el-Kairouani**, who
became Casablanca's first
patron saint in 1350. **Bab
el-Marsa** (Gate of the Sea),
which opens onto Boulevard
des Almohades, also dates
from the 18th century. It was
at this spot that the French
disembarked in July 1907.

Port ❼

East of the old medina.

CASABLANCA IS Morocco's
principal port. Covering
an area of 1.8 sq km (0.70 sq
miles), the port was built
during the Protectorate and is
entirely artificial. A groyne

A fish auction on the quay, where
fishing boats land their catch

protects it from the pounding
of the ocean that destroyed
several earlier constructions.
With its long piers, one of
which stretches for over 3 km
(2 miles), the port is equipped
with ultra-modern commercial,
fishing and leisure facilities.
Grain, metals, citrus fruit and
vegetables make up most of
the cargoes here.

Access to the port complex
is via the fishing harbour.
The **Centre 2000**, near the
Casa-Port railway station,
houses luxury shops and
restaurants. On the seafront
in the port itself, as well as
along the avenue leading
down to it, some excellent
fish restaurants are to be
found (see p324).

Architecture of the 1920s and 1930s

IN 1907, when innovative architects set to work to create buildings in a range of contemporary styles, Casablanca began to look like a huge building site. In the early 1920s, numerous teams of architects were working in the city. Whatever the style, avant-garde tendencies were often counterbalanced by the traditional Moroccan style.

Thus, as the architects drew on the repertoire of Neo-Classicism, Art Nouveau and Art Deco, which were fashionable at the time, they also

Architectural detail, 1930

took inspiration from the Moorish style that Europeans found so fascinating. Towards the end of the 1920s and into the early 1930s, a new taste for simplicity became apparent. Emphasizing shape and outline at the expense of decoration, this gave prominence to the interplay of convex and concave shapes, and to balconies and bow windows. Another significant factor was the expectations of the colonial population and of European speculators: lifts, bathrooms, kitchens and parking areas appeared.

FAÇADES

The façades of residential blocks were encrusted with putti, fruit, flowers and pilasters and featured roofs covered in green tiles, stucco and *zellij* tilework. Colonial houses, in the suburbs, were built in a style that was a cross between a grand Parisian town house and a Moroccan-style seaside residence.

The dome is an example of the Western use of a Moorish architectural element.

Balconies are an adaptation to the sunny climate and bright light.

Mosaic decoration

Wrought-iron balconies, like this one from the Darius Boyer House, are typical of the Art Nouveau ironwork that often graced French windows and balconies.

Mosaic decoration on the law courts consists of multi-coloured zellij tilework in geometric shapes overlying a frieze of stucco carved with inscriptions.

1930s architecture *features traditional Moorish elements, including semicircular arches and decoration in the form of carved stucco.*

This building has an elegantly classical appearance, with decoration consisting of columns, belvederes and a dome with Art Nouveau motifs.

Casablanca's main post office *has a loggia of semicircular arches and zellij tilework.*

Mosque of Hassan II ❽

Mosque door, interior view

WITH A PRAYER HALL that can accommodate 25,000, the Mosque of Hassan II is the second-largest religious building in the world after the mosque in Mecca. The complex covers 9 hectares (968,774 sq ft), two-thirds of it being built over the sea. The minaret, the lighthouse of Islam, is 200 m (656 ft) high, and two laser beams reaching over a distance of 30 km (18.5 miles) shine in the direction of Mecca. The building was designed by Michel Pinseau, 35,000 craftsmen worked on it, and it opened in 1993. With carved stucco, *zellij* tilework, a painted cedar ceiling and marble, onyx and travertine cladding, it is a monument to Moroccan architectural virtuosity.

★ The Minaret
Its size – 25m (82 ft) wide and 200 m (656 ft) high – and its decoration make this an exceptional building.

Fountains
These are decorated with zellij tilework and framed with marble arches and columns.

Marble
Covering the columns of the prayer hall and seen on doorways, fountains and stairs, marble is ubiquitous, sometimes used in combination with granite and onyx.

Minbar
The minbar, or pulpit, located at the western end of the prayer hall, is particularly ornate. It is decorated with verses from the Koran.

STAR FEATURES

★ Minaret

★ Prayer Hall

Women's Gallery
Above two mezzanines and hidden from view, this gallery extends over 5,300 sq m (57,000 sq ft) and can hold up to 5,000 women.

VISITORS' CHECKLIST

Accessible from the port, southwards along the seafront.
📞 (022) 22 25 63. 🕐 9am, 10am, 11am & 2pm Sat–Thur.
⬤ Fri, to non-Muslims. 🚻

Dome
The cedar-panelled interior of the dome over the prayer hall glistens with carved and painted decoration.

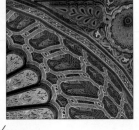

Royal Door
This is decorated with traditional motifs engraved on brass and titanium.

Columns

Doors
Seen from the exterior, these are double doors in the shape of pointed arches framed by columns. Many are clad in incised bronze.

Mashrabiyya screenwork at the windows protects those within from prying eyes.

Hammam

★ Prayer Hall
Able to hold 25,000 faithful, the prayer hall measures 200 m (656 ft) by 100 m (328 ft). The central part of the roof can be opened to the sky.

Stairway to the Women's Gallery
The stairway features decorative woodcarving, multiple arches and marble, granite and onyx columns, arranged in a harmonious ensemble.

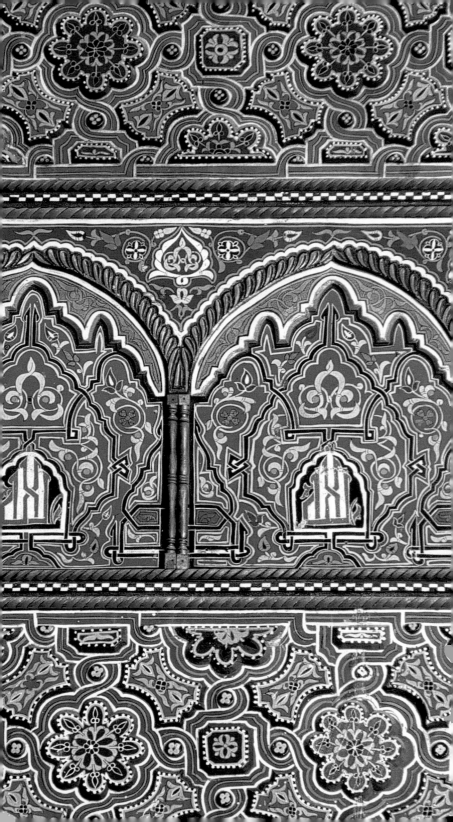

The copper and brass souk in the Quartier Habous

Quartier Habous (New Medina) ❾

In the southeast of the city centre, near Boulevard Victor Hugo.

IN THE 1930s, in order to address the problem of an expanding urban population and to prevent Casablanca's underprivileged citizens from being forced to settle in insalubrious quarters, French town planners laid out a new medina (Nouvelle Medina). Land to the south of the existing city centre earmarked for this development was given over to the Habous, the administration of religious foundations, hence the new town's name.

This new town – which did not, however, forestall the later development of shanty towns – was built in the traditional Arab style at the same time as obeying modern town planning and public health regulations. It contains public areas, such as a market, shops, mosques, a *kissaria* and baths, as well as private dwellings (arranged around a courtyard separated from the street by a solid wall).

The new medina is another facet of colonial town planning during the Protectorate, and its flower-filled, arcaded streets offer the opportunity for a stroll in a scenic quarter of the city. While the most modest houses are located around the market, the finest are set around the mosque.

Northeast of the medina are the copper and brass Souk and **Chez Bennis**, Casa-

blanca's most famous patisserie, which sells pastries known as *cornes de gazelle* (gazelles' horns), fritters and *pastilla*. There are also shops specializing in curios and collectors' items, and they can be good places to find Art Deco objects. A wide range of Moroccan rugs and carpets is also on sale at the weekly auction in the carpet souk.

Northwest of the Quartier Habous is the **Mahakma du Pacha**, a formal tribunal and today one of the city's eight *préfectures* (administrative headquarters). The building (by A. Cadet, 1952), which centres around a tall tower and two courtyards, is a fine example of the adaptation of traditional Arab architecture to modern needs. The traditional Arabic decoration of its 64 rooms is the work of Moroccan craftsmen: it consists of carved stucco and *zellij* tilework on the walls, carved cedarwood panels on the ceiling and wrought iron on the doors.

The **Royal Palace**, on the fringes of the Quartier des Habous and set in extensive Mediterranean gardens, was built in the 1920s by the Pertuzio brothers, whose aim was to create a luxuriously appointed yet modern dwelling.

🏛 **Mahakma du Pacha**
Boulevard Victor Hugo.
♜ **Royal Palace**
Between Boulevard Victor Hugo and Rue Ahmed el-Figuigui.
⬤ to the public.

Carpets displayed for sale in the Quartier Habous

The Twin Center, shaped like the hull of a ship, and its two towers

Casablanca Twin Center ❿

At the intersection of Boulevard Zerktouni and Boulevard El-Massira.

DOMINATED BY its two towers, which rise to a height of 100 m (328 ft), this extensive complex is proof and symbol of the city's economic importance. Built by Ricardo Bofill and Elie Mouyal, it comprises offices, shopping malls and a conference centre. By its outward appearance no less than in its infrastructure, the building signals the economic role that Casablanca plays on both the national and international stage.

Musée du Judaïsme Marocain ⓫

81 Rue Chasseur Jules Gros, Quartier de l'Oasis. ☎ (022) 99 49 40.

THE RECENTLY modernized Museum of Moroccan Judaism contains displays of scarves, kaftans, prayer shawls and other religious objects, and the reconstruction of a synagogue.

From Roman times up to independence in 1956, Morocco had a sizeable Jewish community. Today numbering some 5,000, Morocco's Jews occupy prominent positions in the spheres of politics, economics and culture.

◁ Painted plasterwork in the prayer hall of the Mosque of Hassan II

The Anfa quarter occupies a hill overlooking the city

Anfa ⑫

Northwest of the city.

OCCUPYING A HILL that overlooks Casablanca from the northwest, Anfa is a residential quarter with wide flower-lined avenues where luxurious homes with terraces, swimming pools and lush gardens bring to mind Beverly Hills. Since the 1930s, villas in a great variety of styles have been built here, and they constitute a catalogue of successive architectural styles and fashions.

It was at the Hôtel d'Anfa, now demolished, that the historic meeting between US president Franklin D. Roosevelt and British prime minister Winston Churchill took place in January 1943, during World War II, at which the date of the Allied landings in Normandy was decided. Although they got wind of the meeting, the Germans were misled by the literal translation of "Casablanca".

Under the impression that the location was to be the White House in Washington, they failed to prevent it from going ahead.

During the meeting, President Roosevelt also formally pledged his support to Sultan Mohammed V in his aim to obtain independence from France, thus opening new avenues for Morocco in the postwar period.

Corniche d'Aïn Diab ⑬

West of the Mosque of Hassan II.

THE CORNICHE D'AÏN Diab has been an upmarket part of Casablanca since the 1920s. Running from the **El-Hank Lighthouse** (built in 1916) in the east, to the *marabout* of Sidi Abderrahman in the west, this coastal avenue is lined with a succession of institutes of thalassotherapy, tidal

swimming pools, hotels, restaurants and fashionable nightclubs.

The earliest establishments to be built here – with the needs of a wealthy clientèle in mind – opened in the 1930s, one of them being **Le Lido** restaurant. A little further on is **La Réserve**, a restaurant with panoramic views. It was built in 1934, right over the sea, and rests on piles driven into the sand.

At the foot of the hill of Anfa, near the **Palais Ibn Séoud**, the foundation of the same name houses a mosque and one of the most comprehensive libraries on the African continent. At the western end of the Corniche, 3 km (2 miles) further on, the **Marabout of Sidi Abder-rahman**, perched on a rock, is accessible only at low tide. It attracts Muslim pilgrims suffering from nervous disorders and those who have had evil spells cast on them.

Mohammedia ⑭

28 km (17 miles) northeast of Casablanca. 🚉 🚌

AT THE BEGINNING of the 20th century, Mohammedia was nothing more than a kasbah. This changed in the 1930s, when its port began to receive oil tankers.

Today, petroleum accounts for 16 per cent of all Moroccan port traffic. Although the flaming chimneys of the refineries blight the landscape, this town of 150,000 habitants, now part of greater Casablanca, is still residential. It has large, modern hotels, geared to the needs of business people, a golf course, a casino and a yacht club, which have helped to turn Mohammedia also into an upmarket coastal resort for wealthy Moroccans.

El-Hank lighthouse

A visit to the kasbah and the fish market can be followed by a stroll along the seafront. From the port, the clifftop walk offers fine views of the sea and Mohammedia.

SOUTHERN ATLANTIC COAST

IKE THE WHOLE *of Morocco's Atlantic coastline, the area south of Casablanca is of variable interest to visitors. It is, however, worth the detour, as much for the architecture of the fortified towns built by the Portuguese, such as Asilah and Essaouira, as for the breathtaking coastal scenery. In addition, there is also the coastal resort of Oualidia, which has a very safe beach.*

Morocco's southern Atlantic coastal area contains many smaller towns and resorts, which are especially attractive to those who wish to escape the frenetic activity of the imperial cities.

This region, more than almost any other part of Morocco, has always had contact with the outside world. The Phoenicians, then the Romans, established trading posts here. The Portuguese and the Spanish built military strongholds and centres of trade along the coast, whose topography also made it a haven for pirates. Fortified towns like El-Jadida, Safi and, most especially, Essaouira bear witness to the Spanish and Portuguese contribution to Morocco's history. Under the French Protectorate, the region became the country's economic and administrative centre. Today, this stretch of coastline is industrial and visibly oriented toward the modern world: most of the country's phosphate is produced here, the industry attracting a large workforce from the interior.

The entire coastline, punctuated by scenic viewpoints over the ocean, is ideal for bird-watching and palaeontology. Gourmets will also enjoy Oualidia's famous oysters.

The road, excellent from Casablanca to Essaouira, passes stunningly beautiful deserted beaches that are ideal for surfing. It winds on to Agadir, the great sardine-processing port and Morocco's most popular coastal destination. The wild landscape is dominated by the curious argan tree, with goats climbing in its branches *(see p127)*. It produces the highly prized argan oil.

Fishing boats in the harbour at Imessouane, south of Cap Tafelney

◁ The caretaker of the kasbah at Boulaouane *(see p112)*

Exploring the Southern Atlantic Coast

THIS PART OF MOROCCO'S Atlantic coastline is punctuated by
the fortified towns of Azemmour, El-Jadida, Safi and
Essaouira, which were established by the Portuguese in the
15th and 16th centuries. The road running inland from
Settat to Boulaouane crosses a stunningly beautiful plateau,
carved out of the landscape by Wadi Oum er-Rbia (Mother
of Spring), where all the colours of the splendid Doukkala
region can be seen. Further south, the road leading to
Agadir offers interesting tours up into the lower foothills of
the High Atlas. In the 1970s, the most accessible part of the
foothills was given the name Paradise Valley. The well-
marked road that winds between luxuriant cascades
provides points of departure for hikes in the mountains,
and it eventually leads to Imouzzer des Ida Outanane,
a quiet summer resort.

GETTING AROUND

The quickest route from Casablanca
to Agadir is the P8. This major road
follows the coastline as far as El-Jadida,
which is 99 km (62 miles) from
Casablanca. It then goes inland as far
as Essaouira, 360 km (224 miles) from
Casablanca, and runs near or actually
on the coast for the 165 km (103 miles)
between Essaouira and Agadir. The
S121, a minor road that is more scenic
because it follows the coast, runs
between El-Jadida and Essaouira,
passing through Oualidia and Safi,
241 km (150 miles) from Casablanca.
The P7 and S114 run inland from
Casablanca towards Settat (and
Marrakech). From Settat, the S105
leads to Kasbah Boulaouane, from
where it is easy to rejoin the coast road.

Azemmour, on Wadi Oum er-Rbia

SEE ALSO

• *Where to Stay* pp304–6

• *Where to Eat* pp324–6

CASABLANCA

S 130

P 8

S 114

P 7

P 7

Khouriba

SETTAT

P 7

S 104

AZEMMOUR

ADIDA

LAY
ALLAH

S 105

P 8

SIDI
SMAÏL

S 124

**KASBA DE
BOULAOUANE**

23

1340

P 9

S 125

USSOUFLA   S 125   S 503

BEN GUERIR

P 12

P 7

P 9

6453

MARRAKECH   Beni Mellal

P 10

Asni   Ouarzazate

SIGHTS AT A GLANCE

AGADIR pp286–7
Azemmour **3**
CASABLANCA pp94–107
Chiadma Region **9**
El-Jadida **4**
Essaouira pp120–25 **10**
Kasbah Boulaouane **2**
Kasbah Hamidouch **8**
MARRAKECH pp222–43
Moulay Abdallah **5**
Oualidia **6**
Safi **7**
Settat **1**
Tamanar **11**
Tamri **12**

Tour
Imouzzer des Ida
  Outanane **13**

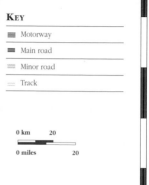

The *sqala* (bastion) in the harbour at Essaouira

KEY

▬	Motorway
▬	Main road
▬	Minor road
▬	Track

0 km   20

0 miles   20

The Portuguese Cistern at El-Jadida

A village near Settat, on the fertile coastal plain of Chaouia

Settat ●

Road map C3. 🏔 *100,000.* 🚌 🚉
🏨 *Avenue Hassan II, El-Haram
building; (023) 40 58 07.* 📷
*Moussem of the Chaouia (first week
in July or in Sept), Chaouia Folk Art
Festival (final week in Nov).* 🏪 *daily;
livestock market Sat.*

A CROSSROADS BETWEEN north and south, Settat is the capital of a province with some 850,000 inhabitants. It is the economic hub of the Chaouia, a coastal plain that is known as Morocco's grainstore. While the north of the region is renowned for its fertile agricultural land, the southern part is given over to livestock (*chaoui* means "breeder of sheep").

When Moulay Ismaïl built the Kasbah Ismaïla, at the end of the 17th century, the security and stability of the region – which was traversed by major caravan routes – was strengthened. The sultan would stay in the kasbah on his travels between Fès and Marrakech. Vestiges of the building can still be seen in the modern town.

Settat, as it is today, offers little of interest to tourists. However, under the aegis of Driss Basri, a native of the region and Minister of the Interior for almost 20 years, it stood as a model of urban development in the 1990s. The merits of this distinction can be seen from Place Hassan II, in the town centre, in the arrangement of open spaces and of pedestrian and shopping areas, and in build-ings combining Art Deco and Moorish styles.

ENVIRONS: the tiny village of **Boulaouane** can be reached by road from Settat. The journey there gives a foretaste of the semi-arid southern land-scapes. The roads are lined with Barbary fig trees, and donkeys can be seen carrying barrels of the local rosé wine.

Kasbah Boulaouane ●

Road map C3.

L OCATED IN A meander of Wadi Oum er-Rbia, this kasbah stands on a promon-tory in the heart of a forested area covering 3,000 hectares (7,400 acres). It was apparent-ly built by the Almohads, who made it an imperial stopping place on the road running along the coast and inland to Fès. At the beginning of the 16th century, it was the scene of a battle that halted the advance of the Portuguese towards the interior. Moulay Ismaïl revitalized the village by choosing to build a kasbah here in 1710 – in an attempt to pacify and control the region.

The stone-built fortress is encircled by a crenellated wall set with bastions and pierced by an angled gate with three pointed arches. Above the gate is an inscription with the name of Moulay Ismaïl and the date of the kasbah's foundation.

This gate, which accom-modated sentries, is the only point of entry into the fortress. It leads through to the sultan's palace, which is built around a central courtyard with mosaic decoration. Beside the palace, a square tower about 10 m (33 ft) high, and now disfigured by cracks, afforded a vantage point over the surrounding territory. Disused vaulted armouries were used for storing food supplies. The mosque, with five aisles, is in a very bad state of preservation. Next to it is the tomb of a saint named Sidi Mancar, whom the region's inhabitants still revere today, since he is believed to have the power to cure paralysis and sterility.

Ceaselessly battered by the elements, the kasbah has suffered deterioration over the centuries. It was declared a historic monument in 1922. A restoration programme has been under way since 1995,

Kasbah Boulaouane, built in the 18th century

BOULAOUANE WINE

Extensive vineyards near Boulaouane

Connoisseurs consider that the wine known as Gris de Boulaouane, a rosé with an orange tint, is one of the best Moroccan wines. Although the Romans successfully exploited the soil and climate of Mauretania Tingitana to grow vines, the establishment of Islam in the Maghreb did not further the upkeep of the vineyards. Under the French Protectorate, the vineyards were revived, and in 1956 wine production passed into state control. The state-owned company that marketed Gris de Boulaouane collapsed, however, and the quality of the wine deteriorated. The French company Castel retook control of Moroccan wine production in the 1990s: the old vines were dug up and new stock planted, this time Cabernet-Sauvignon, Merlot, Cinsault, Syrah and Grenache gris. Today, Moroccan vineyards cover 350 hectares (865 acres) in the district of Boulaouane, the Doukkala region, the foothills of the Atlas and along the Atlantic coast. The vines are planted in sand, the heat of which prevents the development of phylloxera. The grapes are hand-harvested at the end of August and the wine, bottled in France, is exported mostly to Europe.

A bottle of Gris de Boulaouane

but progress has been hampered by a lack of funds.

The region is also famous for its tradition of falconry, a sport still practised today by falconers from several important local families.

Azemmour ③

Road map B2. 𝌆 *32,800.* 🚌
🛈 *Avenue Mohammed V.*
🎪 *Moussem (Aug).* 🛍 *Tue.*

AN ANCIENT Almohad town located on the left bank of the Wadi Oum er-Rbia estuary, Azemmour is also known by the name of Moulay Bouchaïb – the town's patron saint, who, in the 12th century, was also patron saint of the trade that then flourished between the town and Málaga, in Spain.

In 1513, the Portuguese took control of the town. The fort that they built became the kasbah that can be seen today.

A door in the medina, Azemmour

They abandoned the town when Agadir fell in 1541.

Despite its year-round gentle climate and coastal location, Azemmour has few hotels and not many tourists come here. The narrow white streets of the medina are peppered with architectural features recalling the former Portuguese presence – the style of the doors being particularly prominent in this respect. The town also has a tradition of Portuguese-style embroidery, which famously features dragons and lions depicted face to face, an exclusively Moroccan motif. The mellah (Jewish quarter), once within walls, is now derelict. The synagogue, however, has a notable pediment with an inscription in Hebrew.

ENVIRONS: 8 km (5 miles) north on the coast road, the **Sidi Boubeker lighthouse** offers a view of the town's Portuguese defences. **Haouzia** beach, starting 2 km (1.5 miles) southeast of Azemmour, stretches for 15 km (9 miles) from the Oum er-Rbia estuary to El-Jadida. Along the way it passes a forest of eucalyptus, pine and mimosa with flowering cacti.

Embroidery with dragon motifs, of Portuguese inspiration and typical of Azemmour

El-Jadida ❹

THE PORTUGUESE settled here in 1502 and built a fort that they named Mazagan. In time, the town became a major centre of trade, and ships from Europe and the East anchored here to take on provisions. In 1769, the sultan Sidi Mohammed expelled the Portuguese, who dynamited it as they fled. It was resettled by local Arab tribes and a large Jewish community from Azemmour at the beginning of the 19th century. The town was then known as El-Jadida (The New One), but temporarily reassumed its original name – Mazagan – under the French Protectorate.

Bastion de l'Ange, commanding a fine view of El-Jadida's harbour

♠ Ramparts

Entry into the old town is through a gateway that leads to Place Mohammed ben-Abdallah. The walls were originally fortified with five bastions but only four of these were rebuilt after the Portuguese had destroyed the town as they escaped Sidi Mohammed in 1769. The rampart walk leads to the Bastion de l'Ange, which commands a panoramic view over the old town. The Bastion de St Sébastien was once the seat of the Inquisition's tribunal and the prison.

♠ Medina

The main street leads to the sea gate (Porta do Mar), from where there is access to the rampart walk. This gate, now blocked in, once linked the town to the seashore. Halfway along the main street is the entrance to the Citerne Portugaise, originally an underground arsenal, which is one of El-Jadida's most interesting sights and should not be missed.

The mellah has a deserted air: most of the Jewish community emigrated to Israel in the early 1950s.

The old town of El-Jadida, built by the Portuguese

CITERNE PORTUGAISE (PORTUGUESE CISTERN)

The Portuguese built this underground "cistern" in 1514. First an arsenal, then an armoury, it came to be used as a cistern only in 1541. The reflection of the columns and the vaulting on the water is an unreal and mysterious sight.

A well, 3.5 m (11.5 ft) across, was sunk through the central span, allowing daylight to enter.

The vaults rest on five lines of columns.

The cistern takes the form of a square 34 m by 33 m (111 ft by 108 ft).

The 25 pillars are reflected in the stagnant water.

OUALIDIA OYSTERS

Lovers of seafood hold Oualidia oysters in especially high esteem. The species of edible oyster that is raised in the local oyster farms is related to those from the Marennes-Oléron region of France, which were imported in the 1950s. Oyster Farm No. 7, which was set up in 1992 in the lagoon here, is one of the most modern in Morocco. The oysters and other shellfish that are farmed here are raised according to stringent European health and hygiene regulations.

Oualidia oysters

🐟 Citerne Portugaise

🕐 9am–1pm & 3–6pm daily. 🏷

This former armoury, in the Manueline Gothic style, was converted into a cistern after the citadel was enlarged in 1541. It was then constantly fed by fresh water so as to guarantee the town's water supply in the event of a prolonged siege. Rediscovered by chance in 1916 when a shopkeeper was knocking down a wall to enlarge his shop, it has fascinated many artists as well as visitors. Orson Welles used it as a location for certain scenes of his film *Othello*, released in 1952.

ENVIRONS: El-Jadida is a short bus ride away from the very popular **Sidi Bouzid** beach, which is about 5 km (3 miles) further south.

Moulay Abdallah ❺

Road map B3. 11 km (7 miles) south of El-Jadida and 82 km (51 miles) north of Oualidia. 🎏 *Moussem (Aug).*

THE ORIGINS OF this fishing village lie in a 12th-century Almohad settlement which was then known as Tit. The old site's impressive ruins can still be seen today, together with a minaret dating from the same period as that of the Koutoubia Mosque in Marrakech *(see pp236–7).* The settlement was, at that time, a *ribat*, or fortified monastery, built around the cult of the saint Moulay Abdallah, whose purpose was to guard the coast. It became a busy port, but was destroyed in the early 16th century to prevent the Portuguese, who were at

Azemmour, from taking it. The fishing industry revived the village, which then assumed the name of the saint in whose honour it was established. The *moussem* held here in early August is renowned for its fantasias *(see p35).*

ENVIRONS: from the coast road leading south from Moulay Abdallah you can see the gigantic installations of the mineral **Port de Jorf Lasfar**, the largest port in Africa. Built in the 1980s, it has a chemical complex and petrol refinery.

Oualidia ❻

Road map B3. 🏯 3,000. 🚌 ⛵ Sat.

THIS SMALL COASTAL resort takes its name from the sultan El-Oualid, who built a kasbah here in 1634. The rather unattractive town centre leads through to a stunningly beautiful beach on the edge of a lagoon. Swimming is safe here but on either side, the sea is rough and foaming. This is one of the beaches on the Atlantic coast that is good for surfing, particularly for beginners. Among the summer villas here is the residence built for Mohammed V.

The town is an important centre of the oyster industry. A visit to the oyster farms *(parcs à huîtres),* particularly **Oyster Farm N° 7** – taking in the purification and calibration tanks and including the opportunity to sample some oysters – is a pleasant way to spend a morning or afternoon.

Oyster Farm No. 7
On the El-Jadida road.
📞 (023) 36 63 24.

ENVIRONS: the coast road running southwards along the clifftop leads to **Cap Beddouza**, and on to Safi.

Heaps of phosphate in the mineral port of Jorf Lasfar

Safi 7

Road map B3. 👤 *260,000.* 🚌 🚉
ℹ️ *tourist office, Rue Imam-Malek & main market, Ave de la Liberté; (044) 46 38 95.* 🎭 *Moussem of the Seven Saints (mid-Aug), Moussem of Lalla Fatna (mid-Nov.)* 🗓 *Mon.*

AN IMPORTANT Moroccan port since the 16th century, the town of Safi is today an industrial centre and a major sardine-processing port. It owes its importance to the growth of the fishing industry and to the processing and export of phosphates, as well as to its pottery. A rapidly expanding town, Safi has an interesting medina as well as traces of its Portuguese history.

🏛 Medina
The area covered by the medina takes the form of a triangle whose widest side faces onto the coast. Rue du Souk, lined with shops and workshops, leads to Bab Chaaba (Gate of the Valley). Near the Grand Mosque, south of the medina, is the **Portuguese Chapel**, originally the choir of Safi's cathedral, built by the Portuguese in 1519.

⚓ Dar el-Bahr
⏱ *8:30am–noon & 2:30–5:30 pm Wed–Mon.*
This small fortress, also known as the Château de la Mer, overlooks the sea. It was built by the Portuguese at the beginning of the 16th century, and served as a residence for the governor, then for the sultans in the 17th century. On the esplanade are cannons cast in Spain, Portugal and Holland.

Kasbah Hamidouch, built by Moulay Ismaïl

🏛 Musée National de la Céramique
Kechla. 📞 *(044) 46 49 87.*
⏱ *Wed–Mon, 8:30am–noon & 2–6pm.*
Built by the Portuguese in the 16th century, the citadel, known as the Kechla, encloses a mosque and garden dating from the 18th and 19th centuries. Since 1990 the Kechla has housed the Musée National de la Céramique, which contains displays of traditional and modern ceramics, including blue-on-white wares made in Safi, pottery from Fès and Meknès, and pieces by Boujmaa Lamali (1890–1971).

Safi candlestick, 20th century

🏛 Colline des Potiers
In the Bab Chaaba district, craftsmen can be seen making the ceramic wares that have made Safi famous. Finished pieces are displayed and offered for sale in commercial showrooms and visitors can follow the various stages of pottery production at the training school.

Kasbah Hamidouch 8

Road map B3. 29 km (18 miles) south of Safi on the coast road.

THIS KASBAH forms part of a system of fortified outposts that Moulay Ismaïl *(see pp54–5)* established along the main routes of communication so as to control the region and accommodate travellers.
The kasbah is encircled by an outer wall, within which stand a mosque and various buildings, now in ruins. An inner wall, set with square towers and reinforced by a dry moat, surrounds a courtyard that is lined with shops, various houses and a chapel.

Chiadma Region 9

Road map B3–4.

THE TERRITORY of the Chiadma, in the provinces of Safi and Essaouira, is inhabited by Regraga Berbers. They are descended from seven saint apostles of Islam, who, during a journey to Mecca, were directed by the Prophet Mohammed to convert the Maghreb to Islam. In spring, a commemorative pilgrimage is made, ending at the small village of **Ha Dra**.
A souk, one of the most authentic markets in the area, takes place in Ha Dra on Sunday mornings. Grain, spices, animals and a wide range of goods, mostly food, are offered for sale.

A potter at work in Safi, where a particularly high-quality clay is used

◁ **Fishing boats on the shore below Essaouira's ramparts**

Sea Fishing in Morocco

THE MOROCCAN COASTLINE, which is over 3,500 km (2,175 miles) long, faces both the Atlantic Ocean and the Mediterranean Sea, and gives the country access to some of the richest fishing grounds in the world – with some 240 species of fish. Morocco brings in the largest catches of fish in the whole of Africa. Its pre-eminence is due especially to sardines, of which Morocco is the largest processor and exporter in the world. Coastal fishing has created a major canning industry, too. The Moroccan sea fishing industry employs some 200,000 people and exports bring in US $600 million per year. Modern fishing methods, however, have not completely replaced traditional ways.

Small trawlers, many of them made of wood, as well as motorized dinghies, ply the coastal waters as far out to sea as the edge of the Continental Shelf. Their catches consist of many different species of fish.

Sardine fishing in Essaouira uses swivel nets. In spite of their expert knowledge of the sea bed, the fishermen often have to repair damaged nets when they return to harbour every day.

Cheap eateries in Essaouira's harbour invite customers to select a plateful of fish and eat it on the spot. Many such establishments are to be found in the port, at the exit from the sqala.

The fish market at Agadir, one of the largest sardine ports in the world, was modernized only a few years ago. Every day, an auction of almost 250 different kinds of fish takes place here.

Crates of fish are packed ready for sale. Sardines are the most important catch, but other fish, including hake and grey mullet, are also on offer.

Consernor, the canning company, is one of Safi's major industries. It revitalized the local economy in the 1920s.

Essaouira ⑩

Burnous

WITH THE BRILLIANT WHITENESS of its lime-washed walls and the sight of women enveloped in voluminous *haiks*, Essaouira, formerly Mogador, is a quint-essentially Moroccan town and one of the most enchanting places in the country. By virtue of its location on this stretch of the Atlantic coast, where trade winds prevail almost all year round, the town enjoys a particularly pleasant climate. It is a prime location for windsurfing, but has managed to escape mass tourism. A mecca for hippies during the 1970s, it is still an artists' town and is very fashionable with independent travellers.

Women in Essaouira wearing the characteristic white *haik*

Exploring Essaouira

In the 7th century BC, the Phoenicians founded a base on the site where Essaouira now stands, and in the 1st century BC Juba II made it a centre of the manufacture of purple dye. The Portuguese established a trading and military bridgehead here in the 15th century, and named it Mogador. The town itself, however, was not built until around 1760, by the Alouite sultan Sidi Mohammed ben Ab-dallah (Mohammed II), who had decided to set up a naval base here. The town, the harbour and the fortifications, in the style of European fortresses, were designed and built by Théodore Cornut, a renowned French architect who had worked for Louis XV.

♣ Ramparts

On the side facing the sea, the outer walls, which have bevelled crenellations, were designed to give protection from naval attack and are thus typical of European fortifications. By contrast, the inner walls, which have square crenellations and are similar to the fortifications around Marrakech, are Islamic in style. These are built in stone and roughcast with a facing of earth. The walls are pierced by gates – Bab Sebaa on the southern side, Bab Marrakech on the eastern side and Bab Doukkala on the northeastern side – that lead into the medina.

♣ Sqalas

Two *sqalas* (sea bastions) were built to protect the town: the Sqala de la Ville, in the northwest, and the Sqala du Port, in the south.

The Sqala de la Ville consists of a crenellated platform

The Porte de la Marine, built by Sidi Mohammed ben Abdallah

featuring a row of Spanish cannons and defended at its northern end by the North Bastion. This was built by Théodore Cornut on the site of the Castello Real, a citadel constructed by the Portuguese in about 1505. The esplanade (where scenes from Orson Welles' film *Othello* were shot in 1949) commands a view of the ocean and the Îles Purpuraires. A covered passage leads from the bastion to the former munitions stores, which now house marquetry workshops.

Port

Sqala du Port. ⬜ *daily.* 🖼

The Porte de la Marine, leading to the docks, is crowned by a classical triangular pediment and dominated by two imposing towers flanked by four turrets. The rectangular Sqala du Port is surmounted by battlements.

From the 18th century, 40 per cent of Atlantic sea traffic passed through Essaouira. It became known as the Port of Timbuctu, being the destination of caravans from sub-Saharan Africa bringing goods for export to Europe. Once one of Morocco's largest

Sqala de la Ville, a favourite place for strolls at sunset

View of the Sqala du Port, at the southern entrance to the town

sardine ports, Essaouira now provides a living for no more than 500 to 600 families. But it still has its traditional ship-yard, where vessels are made out of wood. Visitors can also watch the fish auction and sample freshly grilled sardines.

🚪 Medina

For an old Moroccan town, the layout of Essaouira is unusual in that it was planned before the town was actually developed. It was laid out by the French architect Cornut, who, between 1760 and 1764, built the Sqala de la Ville and the Sqala du Port, endowing them with fortifications and batteries of cannons, as well as outer and inner walls.

As elsewhere in Morocco, the medina in Essaouira is a labyrinth of narrow streets; the town itself, by contrast, has straight, wide streets laid out at right angles to one another and cut by gateways. The huge market, the Souk Jdid, is divided into four by the intersection of two thoroughfares: there is a daily souk for fish, spice and grains, and a souk for second-hand and collectable items, known as *joutia*.

The daily spice souk, laid out next to the fish souk

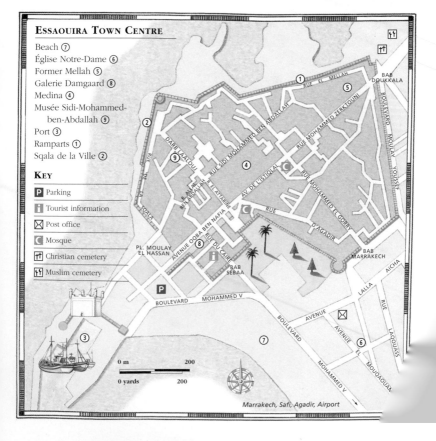

ESSAOUIRA TOWN CENTRE

Beach ⑦
Église Notre-Dame ⑥
Former Mellah ⑤
Galerie Damgaard ⑧
Medina ④
Musée Sidi-Mohammed-
   ben-Abdallah ⑨
Port ③
Ramparts ①
Sqala de la Ville ②

KEY

🅿 Parking
ℹ Tourist information
✉ Post office
🅲 Mosque
✝ Christian cemetery
🕍 Muslim cemetery

RUE EL MELLAH
BAB DOUKKALA
BOULEVARD MOULAY YOUSSEF
RUE MOHAMMED ZERKTOUNI
RUE SIDI MOHAMMED BEN ABDALLAH
DARB LAALOUJ
RUE ATTARINE EL XTARINE
ABDALLAH BEN
AV. DE L'ISTIQLAL
RUE MOHAMMED EL QORRY
RUE D'AGADIR
RUE
BAB MARRAKECH
AICHA
LALLA
AVENUE OQBA BEN NAFIA
RUE DU CAIRE
PL. MOULAY EL HASSAN
BAB SEBAA
RUE LAQOUASS
AVENUE EL MOUQAOUAM
BOULEVARD MOHAMMED V
BOULEVARD AVENUE
AVENUE MOHAMMED V

0 m   200
0 yards   200

Marrakech, Safi, Agadir, Airport

Working with Thuya

THUYA, A HIGHLY PRIZED WOOD with a delicious perfume, grows abundantly in the region of Agadir and Essaouira, and has been the source of that latter's prosperity. Thuya is a very dense hardwood, and almost every part of the tree apart from the branches can be used: the trunk, with its relatively light-coloured wood; the stump, used for making small objects; and the gnarl, a rare excrescence streaked with brown and pink. The gnarl is polished, inlaid with decorative motifs in citron wood, mother-of-pearl or ebony and sometimes with threads of silver or copper, or slivers of camel bone. It is used to make such items as coffee tables, caskets, small statues, boxes in all shapes and sizes, trays and jewellery. The country's best marquetry craftsmen can be seen working at this traditional craft in the former munitions stores beneath Essaouira's ramparts.

MARQUETRY
Essaouira's cabinet-makers were already renowned in antiquity, and the town has remained the capital of marquetry ever since. Tradition dictates that the artistically skilled part of the work (from the construction of a piece to its decoration) be done by men. Women and children are given the task of polishing the finished items.

The high sheen
of this bread box is produced by polishing the surface with methylated spirit and gum arabic. Linseed oil feeds the wood and prevents it from developing cracks.

The decoration
of this dish is based on a geometric scheme. The border pattern consists of an inlay of alternating pieces of ebony and citron wood.

THE THUYA GNARL
This excrescence, which grows on certain trees, particularly the thuya, is very sought after by cabinet-makers for its veined and speckled appearance.

Craftsmen apply all their ingenuity and imagination to produce novel shapes.

The thuya gnarl is separated from the trunk.

The old part of the Jewish cemetery at Essaouira

⊞ Former Mellah

From Bab Doukkala, accessible via Rue Mohammed Zerktouni.
◆ *Controlled access.*

Having risen to prominence and prosperity in the 18th and 19th centuries, the Jewish community in Essaouira came to hold an important economic position in the town, and Jewish jewellers acquired wide renown.

The town's former Jewish quarter is no longer inhabited by Jews, but on Rue Darb Laalouj the former houses of Jewish businessmen can still be seen; they are now converted into shops. In contrast to Muslim houses, they are fronted by balconies opening onto the street and some have lintels with inscriptions in Hebrew.

Rue Mohammed Zerktouni, the main street in the quarter, has a very lively market. Leaving by Bab Doukkala, you will pass the austere Jewish cemetery, which is worth a visit. (The keys are available on request from the caretaker.)

🔒 Église Notre-Dame

Avenue El-Moukaouama, south of the post office. ⏰ *8:30am Mon–Sat, 10am Sun.* ☎ *(048) 47 58 95.*
This Catholic church stands outside the walls of the medina, on the road leading to the beach. It is one of the few churches in the country where the bells are rung on Sundays to summon the faithful to mass at 10am.

Most of the church furnishings are made of thuya wood. On an alternating basis, the services here are said in one of four languages: French, English, Dutch or German.

🏖 Beach

Essaouira's beach, to the south of the town centre, is known as one of the finest in Morocco. All through the summer, the trade winds keep this part of the coast surprisingly cool. At times, however, the gusty winds are so strong that they drive people to seek shelter in the medina.

At the estuary of Wadi Qsob, on the far side of the beach, vestiges of the system of defences built on a rocky promontory by the sultan Sidi Mohammed are visible. Although they have crumbled, thick walls can still be made out.

By following the *wadi* upstream, after a tumbled-down bridge, you reach the village of Diabet. It is also accessible via the road to Agadir, turning off to the right after 7 km (4 miles). An interesting sight here are the

Surfer

ruins of **Dar Soltane Mahdounia**, a palace built by Sidi Mohammed ben Abdallah in the 18th century and now almost completely engulfed in sand. It inspired Jimi Hendrix (who lived in Diabet for several years) to write the song *Castles in the Sand*.

Windsurfers will particularly enjoy the many beaches each side of Essaouira. Thanks to the enterprise of dynamic local associations, Morocco is about to become one of the top destinations for surfers and windsurfers. (The Océan Vagabond café is a good place to hire surfing equipment.) The windiest time of year in the Essaouira area, and therefore the best time for surfing and windsurfing here, is from April to September.

However, while the air, at 20 to 30 °C (68 to 86 °F), is always pleasantly warm, the water is always a very cool 16–18 °C (61–64 °F).

South of Essaouira, at **Cap Sim** (beyond Diabet) and at **Sidi Kaouki**, and to the north, at **Moulay Bouzerktoun**, the waves are very strong, and safe only for experienced surfers. Also to the south, at **Tafelney** (beyond the village of Smimou), there is a magnificent bay where the water is warmer. In spite of the constant gusty wind, it is easier to get into the water on the beach at Essaouira, as the waves are much gentler.

Essaouira beach, swept by strong gusts of ...

🏛 Galerie Damgaard

Avenue Oqba Ibn Nafia.
📞 (044) 78 44 46. FAX (044) 47 58 57. ⬤ 9am–1pm & 3–7pm daily.

For about a quarter of a century, a generation of painters and sculptors has made Essaouira an important centre of artistic activity. Many talented artists have been brought to public attention by the Dane Frederic Damgaard.

Formerly an antique dealer in Nice, since 1988 he has devoted his energies to the art produced in Essaouira, opening his own art gallery in the heart of the medina. On display here is the work of artists from the humblest walks of life. Among the best known are Mohammed Tabal, a Gnaoua painter who has become known as "the trance painter", Zouzou, Ali Maïmoune, Rachid Amarlouch and Fatima Ettalbi. Others are stiill to be discovered, like the expressionist Ali, whose style is midway between naive and Brutalist. All of them draw their inspiration from Essaouira's cultural variety, and reflect the traditions of different schools. In recent years, many exhibitions and other projects, in Morocco and throughout the world, have been devoted to the painters of Essaouira.

Art gallery of Frederic Damgaard, the great discoverer of artistic talent

Rbab, in the Musée Sidi-Mohammed

🏛 Musée Sidi-Mohammed-ben-Abdallah

Rue Darb Laalouj. 📞 (048) 47 53 00. ⬤ call for details. 🖼

This small ethnographic museum is laid out in a 19th-century house that was a former pasha's residence and the town hall during the Protectorate. It contains fine displays of ancient crafts and of weapons and jewellery. There are also instruments and accessories used by religious brotherhoods, Moorish musical instruments and some stunning examples of Berber and Jewish costumes in silk, velvet and flannel. Carpets illustrating the traditional weaving of local tribes are also exhibited.

ENVIRONS: on the **Îles Purpuraires**, visible across the bay from Essaouira, is a bird sanctuary where gulls and the rare Eleonora's falcon, a threatened species, and other birds can be seen. Phoenician, Attic and Ionian amphorae discovered on the Île de Mogador, the main island, and now in the Musée Archéologique in Rabat *(see pp78–9)*, prove that trade was taking place here from the 7th century BC. In the 1st century BC, Juba II *(see p45)*, founder of Volubilis, set up a centre for the production of purple dye, from which the islands take their name. Purple dye, highly prized by the Romans, was obtained from the murex, a mollusc. The ruins of a prison, built in the 19th century by the sultan Moulay el-Hassan, are also visible.

Some 12 km (7.5 miles) south of Essaouira, the splendid beach at **Sidi Kaouki** is very popular with windsurfers. A mausoleum, which appears to rise up out of the water, contains the tomb of a *marabout* (holy man) who, according to legend, had the power to cure barren women. An annual pilgrimage, with many devotees, takes place here in mid-August.

🔅 Îles Purpuraires

Controlled access (information available from the tourist office).

he far end of a spectacularly extensive beach south of Essaouira

The Painters of Essaouira

Essaouira, a town imbued with art and culture, is home to a group of painters known as "free artists", each of whom has his or her own unique style. Their talents have won recognition abroad and their work has been shown in many European art galleries. Using bright colours, their naive or "tribal" art is inspired by the myths,

Detail of a work by Tabal

Arab-Berber history and African origins of Moroccan popular culture. These self-taught painters are also woodcarvers, sailors and builders, and they have in common an unconditional love of their town. Arabesques, geometric designs, dots, stippling and a swarm of objects, animals and human figures populate their poetic world.

MOHAMMED TABAL

A leading figure in Essaouira's artistic circles, Mohammed Tabal draws inspiration from his Gnaoui ancestry – from the ritual of spiritual possession and from the trances that form part of the rites of this popular brotherhood of African origin *(see p27)*. His paintings are splashed with bright, contrasting colours and feature a multitude of tiny details, such as naive motifs rich in symbolism.

Mohammed Tabal's paintings *are imbued with mysticism.*

Abdallah Elatrach *is inspired by scenes of daily life in the souks and by the traditions of various brotherhoods whose rituals involve trance.*

Ali Maïmoune *paints tree-filled worlds that are populated by terrifying monsters, animals and fantastic warriors.*

Imouzzer des Ida Outanane ⑬

THIS TOUR FOLLOWS a very scenic river valley with many natural swimming pools surrounded by palm trees. From Agadir, a winding road leads to the village of Imouzzer, set on a hilltop in the foot-hills of the High Atlas. It is the heart of the territory of the Ida Outanane, a confederation of Berbers whose traditional speciality is gathering honey. Despite the exodus from the country into the towns, many women – dressed in brightly coloured robes – can still be seen at work on the hillsides.

Win t'mdoum Caves ①
Located 35 km (22 miles) from Imouzzer, these caves are the most extensive in North Africa. Work is under way to make them accessible to the public.

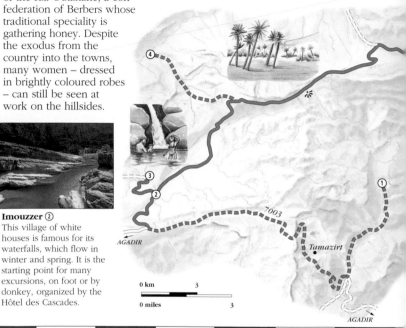

Imouzzer ②
This village of white houses is famous for its waterfalls, which flow in winter and spring. It is the starting point for many excursions, on foot or by donkey, organized by the Hôtel des Cascades.

0 km   3

0 miles   3

Tamanar ⑪

Road map B4. 🏛 *Thu in Tamanar, Fri in Arba des Ida Outrhouma, 10 km (6 km) south of Tamanar.*

THE SMALL TOWN of Tamanar, which extends along its one main street, is a regional administrative centre and, effectively, the capital of the argan industry. It is at the heart of Haha territory, home to a sedentary yet dynamic Berber population which was self-governing in the 15th century.

On the way out of the village, near Café Argane, is a store selling locally produced argan oil. The highly organized women who run it show the fruits of their labour in a friendly atmosphere and sell their products in a cooperative.

Landscape near Tamanar

ENVIRONS : Between Smimou (where there is a picturesque souk on Sundays) and Tamanar, a small sign saying "Tafadna" indicates the route to **Tafelney**. Two-thirds along this road, the landscape takes

on a majestic beauty. The road comes to a sudden stop at a magnificent bay, where fishermen can often be seen mending their nets on the beach.

To the left, a huddle of identical shanty houses are home to thousands of birds. To those with a taste for remote spots, the strange beauty of this place will have a strong appeal.

Tamri ⑫

Road map B4. ✖

THIS VILLAGE is located on the estuary of a river that in winter is fed partly by the waterfall at Imouzzer *(see above)*. There is an extensive

Tamaroute ③

The waterfalls in this attractive village are known as "The Bridal Veil". They are the southernmost waterfalls above the Sahara. Flowing from several levels, the waters are abundant when the snow begins to melt in spring.

Assif el-Had ④

The natural bridge at Assif el-Had was created by water flowing down from the mountains.

Imi Irhzer ⑤

In February, the red-ochre houses of the villages almost disappear in a sea of almond blossom. A sheepfold has been converted into a gîte.

ARGANA,
MARRAKECH

Biramane ●

● Tasguint

AGADIR ↓

Bigoudine ⑥

The road to Bigoudine offers a succession of panoramic views. This is where the argan forests begin. When it is completed, a new road crossing the P40 and passing through Bigoudine will provide a link to Imouzzer.

KEY

▬ Itinerary (road)

▪▪ Itinerary (track)

= Other roads

== Other tracks

🌿 View point

TIPS FOR TRAVELLERS

Departure : Imouzzer des Ida Outanane, at Hôtel des Cascades. *How to get there:* from Agadir, northwards on the P8, turning off after 12 km (7.5 miles) onto the 7002. From the north, turn left onto the road 20 km (12 miles) after Cap Rhir. From Agadir, a bus departs from next door to the bus station at about 12:30pm daily (allow three and a half hours), returning from Imouzzer at 8am the next day. *Stopping-off points:* at Tifrit, 18 km (11 miles) from Imouzzer, Hôtel Tifrit and Chez Zénid café. At Imouzzer, Hôtel des Cascades.

banana plantation. On the left, as you approach Tamri from the north, an inland road leads to a major bird-watching area, where Audouin's gulls, Barbary falcons, Lamier's falcons, sparrows and various other species can be seen.

ENVIRONS: about 19 km (12 miles) north of Agadir is **Taghazoute**, a fishing village that is popular with surfers. It was also colonized by the hippie movement, and, on the way out of Taghazoute, you can see curious signs saying "Banana Village" and "Paradise Valley" – names that were originally given by those who followed in the footsteps of Jimi Hendrix in the 1970s.

THE ARGAN TREE

Bottle of argan oil

The argan (*Argania sideroxylon*) is North Africa's weirdest tree. It is interesting not only in its own right, but is also important ecologically and economically. This tenacious, twisted tree, which never grows higher than 6 m (19.5 ft), has a multitude of uses. Being a very hard wood, it is ideal for making charcoal. It is also used to feed animals (camels and goats find the leaves and fruit delectable), and to make argan oil, which is extracted from the kernal. The vitamin-rich oil has a wide range of applications, according to the degree to which it is refined. It is used in cosmetics for what are thought to be its hydrating and anti-ageing properties, and in medicine to combat arteriosclerosis, chicken pox and rheumatism. Argan oil also has culinary uses – a few drops are enough to bring out the flavour of salads and *tajines* – and is used as fuel for lamps.

Goat perched in an argan tree, feeding on its fruit

TANGIER

O NCE AN INTERNATIONAL CITY, *Tangier has a special character that sets it apart from other Moroccan cities. It has drawn artists and writers, from Henri Matisse to Paul Bowles and writers of the Beat generation. Tangier's port, dominated by the medina, is the main link between Africa and Europe. With a new road linking Tangier to Rabat and the construction of a new port, the city continues to expand.*

The history of Tangier has been shaped by the sea and by its stragetic location on the Straits of Gibraltar. The Phoenicians established a port here in the 8th century, and it was later settled by the Carthaginians. In 146 BC, Tangier, known as Tingis, became a Roman town and the capital of Mauretania, to which it gave the name Tingitana. In 711, Arab and Berber forces gathered here to conquer Spain. By the 14th century, the town was trading with Marseilles, Genoa, Venice and Barcelona. Tangier was captured by the Portuguese in 1471, by the Spanish (1578–1640) and then the English, who were expelled from the city by Moulay Ismaïl in 1684. In the 19th century, Morocco was the object of dispute between European nations. When, in 1905, Kaiser Wilhelm II denounced the *entente cordiale* between France and Britain, the stage was set for Tangier's transformation into an international city. This was sealed by the Treaty of Algeciras (1906), after which the diplomatic corps in Tangier took over Morocco's political, financial and fiscal affairs. When colonial rule was established in 1912, Spain took control of the northern part of the country. Tangier, however, remained under international administration. This was the city's heyday. Its image as a romantic and sensuously exotic place was made in literature and on the big screen.

After independence in 1956, Tangier was returned to Morocco, but suffered political ostracism. However, the city became industrialized, and new districts sprang up. Mohammed VI now includes it in his royal visits, and this has given a boost to the city.

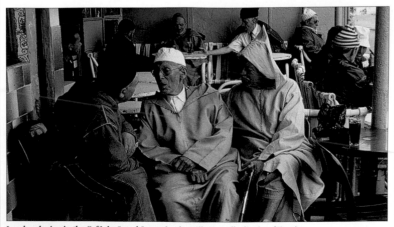

Locals relaxing in the Café du Grand Socco in the Ville Nouvelle district of Tangier

◁ The elegant whitewashed façade of Tangier's Ancien Palais du Mendoub, built in 1929

Exploring Tangier

THE BEST OVERVIEW OF THE CITY is from the vantage point of the Colline du Charf or Colline de Bella-Vista, to the southeast. While the historic heart of Tangier is the medina, the soul of the city is the kasbah, which has a palace-museum, narrow streets, gateways and a seafront promenade. In the evening, when it is wise not to linger in the medina, visitors who explore Ville Nouvelle (New Town), along Avenue Pasteur and Avenue Mohammed V will come across the Spanish custom of the *paseo* (evening promenade). Alternatively, the cafés on Place de France and Place de Faro offer relaxing views of the port and the Straits of Gibraltar, and, in clear conditions, a sight of the lights along the coast of Spain.

SIGHTS AT A GLANCE

Avenues, Streets and Squares
Avenue Pasteur **14**
Place de France & Place de Faro **13**
Rue de la Liberté **12**
Rue Es-Siaghine **6**

Quarters and Promenades
Bay of Tangier **19**
Colline du Charf **18**
Grand Socco
   (Place du 9 Avril 1947) **8**
Kasbah **1**
Petit Socco **4**
Quartier du Marshan **17**
Ramparts **3**

Mosque and Church
Anglican Church of
   St Andrew **9**
Grand Mosque **5**

Historic Buildings
Ancien Palais
   du Mendoub **15**
Café Hafa **16**
Fondouk Chejra **11**

Museums
American Legation **7**
Musée d'Art
   Contemporain **10**
Musée des Arts Morocains
   et des Antiquités **2**

0 m   200

0 yards   200

GETTING AROUND

Parking is available in Ville Nouvelle, on Place du 9 Avril 1947 (Grand Socco) or on the Plateau du Marshan. The medina and kasbah must be explored on foot. The only practical use for cars and taxis is for reaching the Colline du Charf and Colline de Bella-Vista, the Plateau du Marshan and La Montagne, or for a trip along the bay, from the port to the edge of the wooded hills before Cap Malabata.

ENVIRONS OF TANGIER

0   1 km

0 yards   1000

AREA OF MAIN MAP

KEY

▢	Medina
▢	Former sultan's palace
—	Ramparts
🚌	Bus station
P	Parking
i	Tourist information
✝	Church
✡	Synagogue
C	Mosque
⊞	Christian cemetery
✦	Jewish cemetery
⚰	Muslim cemetery
▬	Major road
═	Minor road

Port

Bab el-Assa, leading through to Place de la Kasba

The fountain at Bab el-Assa, a gateway in the Kasbah, with mosaic decoration and ornamental stuccowork and woodcarving

Kasbah ❶

From the Marshan, accessible via Bab el-Kasbah; from the medina, via Rue Ben Raissouli and Bab el-Assa; from the Grand Socco, via Rue d'Italie and Rue de la Kasba.

THE KASBAH was built on the site of the Roman settlement. Its present appearance dates from the Portuguese period and that of Moulay Ismaïl *(see pp54–5)*. With its quiet streets and friendly inhabitants, it has a special character, and its walls and gates command stunning views over the strait, the bay and the city.

Place de la Kasba was once the *méchouar* where the sultan or his pashas held public audiences. It is also the location of the Dar El-Makhzen, the former palace that is now a museum *(see below)* and of the **Kasbah Mosque**, whose octagonal minaret is clad in coloured tiles. Its present form dates

from the 19th century; the *mendoub* led Friday prayers here. Also on the square is the Dar ech-Chera, the former tribunal, fronted by an arcade of three white marble columns. The large fig tree growing against the wall of an elegant house is supposed to be the place where Samuel Pepys wrote about Tangier in his diary in the 17th century.

Bab el-Assa (Gate of Bastinado) leads from the square to the medina. It was set at an angle so as to make it more difficult to attack. The gate gets its name from the bastinado (caning the soles of the feet) that was once the punishment of criminals. In the lobby, between the two porches, stands a fountain decorated with mosaics, stuccowork and woodcarving. Gnaouas *(see p27)*, distantly related to those of Marrakech and Essaouira, regularly perform music and dance here. In the evening, audiences can talk with them about their

musical traditions and their repertoire. From the lobby, a narrow passage allows sight of a small *derb* (alleyway) lined with very fine houses, while beyond the gate is a view over the city. Nearby is the small **Musée de Carmen-Macein**, a private museum where sculpture, paintings and lithographs by artists including Picasso, Max Ernst and Georges Braque are shown.

🏛 **Musée de Carmen-Macein**
Bab el-Assa. 📞 *(039) 94 80 50.*
⏰ *Jul only: 8:30am–noon & 2–6pm.*

Central courtyard, Musée des Arts Marocains et des Antiquités

Musée des Arts Marocains et des Antiquités ❷

Place de la Kasba. 📞 *(039) 94 80 50.*
⏰ *9am–noon & 3–6pm Wed–Mon.*
♿

THE MUSEUM of Moroccan Crafts and Antiquities is laid out in the Dar el-Makhzen, a former sultans' palace built in the 17th century, during the reign of Moulay Ismaïl, and remodelled and enlarged several times in the 17th and 19th centuries. Bit el-Mal, the treasury – a separate room with a magnificent painted cedar ceiling – contains large 18th-century coffers with a complex system of locks.

A gallery leads to the palace itself. It is built around a central courtyard paved with *zellij* tilework and

The octagonal minaret on the Kasbah Mosque

surrounded by a gallery supported by white marble columns with Corinthian capitals. The eight rooms opening onto the courtyard contain displays of every aspect of Moroccan crafts, from carpets, ceramics and musical instruments to embroidery, brocades and jewellery, armour and leatherwork.

The Petit Socco, or Souk Dakhli, a pale reflection of its lively past

A small archaeological museum is housed in the former palace kitchens. *The Voyage of Venus*, a Roman mosaic from Volubilis *(see pp202–5)*, is displayed in the museum's courtyard. Reproductions of several famous bronzes from the Musée Archéologique in Rabat *(see pp78–9)* are also on display. One room is devoted to Morocco's major archaeological sites. On the upper floor, the prehistory and history of Tangier and its environs, from the Neolithic period to its occupation by foreign powers, are presented through displays of grave goods, pottery and coins.

Adjacent to the palace is the Andalusian Garden, with fragrant herbs and shrubs.

Ramparts ❸

Place de la Kasba. *Accessible via Bab el-Bahar.*

ON THE SIDE of the square facing the sea, opposite Bab el-Assa, stands Bab el-Bahar (Gate of the Sea), which was built in the walls in 1920. From the terrace there is a breathtaking view of the port, the straits and, in clear conditions, the Spanish coast.

The walkway, which starts on the left, follows the outside of the ramparts and leads to the impressive **Borj en Naam**, a fort. Continuing along the seafront and through residential districts, the route leads to Hafa.

🏛 **Borj en Naam.**
⬤ *to the public.*

Petit Socco ❹

Accessible via Rue Es-Siaghine or Rue Jma el-Kbir.

KNOWN TODAY as the Souk Dakhli, the Petit Socco probably corresponds to the area on which the forum of Roman Tingis once stood. It was a country souk, where people would come to buy food, and with the arrival of the Europeans at the end of the 19th century it became the pulsing heart of the medina. This was where business was done; diplomats, businessmen and bankers, whose offices were located around the square or in the close vicinity, could be seen in the cafés, hotels, casinos and cabarets of the Petit Socco. The Fuentes, a café-restaurant and hotel, now gives but a faint impression of these halcyon days. From the 1950s, the hub of city life shifted to Ville Nouvelle, leaving the Petit Socco to a few writers, and to idlers, smokers of kif and shady traffickers.

Doorway of the Grand Mosque

Grand Mosque ❺

Rue Jma el-Kbir. ⬤ *to non-Muslims.*

THE GRAND MOSQUE, built on the site of a Portuguese cathedral, probably also overlies a former Roman temple dedicated to Hercules. Dating from the reign of Moulay Ismaïl, it was enlarged in 1815 by Moulay Sliman. Mohammed V led Friday prayers here on 11 April 1947, during a visit to Tangier, when he also made a historic speech in the Mendoubia Gardens *(see p138)*. Opposite the mosque, the state primary school (established by nationalists during the French Protectorate) is a former Merinid medersa that was remodelled in the 18th century.

Nearby, the Borj el-Hadjoui commands a view of the port and a pair of Armstrong cannons, each weighing 20 tonnes. They were purchased from the British in Gibraltar, but were never used.

From the *borj*, Rue Darel Baroud leads to the **Hôtel Continental**, located opposite the port and one of Tangier's oldest hotels. The building's architectural style, its Andalusian-style lounges and its open terraces give this establishment great appeal. Its patrons have included writers and painters – among them Edgar Degas – and film producers.

🏨 **Hôtel Continental**
36 Rue Dar el-Baroud.
📞 (039) 93 10 24. ⬤ *daily.*

The Hôtel Continental, one of the oldest hotels in Tangier

A jeweller's shop near Rue Es-Siaghine

Rue Es-Siaghine **⑥**

Running from the Petit Socco to the Grand Socco.

Tᴴɪꜱ ꜱᴛʀᴇᴇᴛ ᴡᴀꜱ once the *decumanus maximus*, the main axis and busiest thoroughfare of the Roman town. It led from the harbour out through the southern gate, marked today by Bab Fahs. Lined with cafés and bazaars, the street is as lively now as it must have been in antiquity.

The small administrative building at No. 47, with a courtyard planted with orange trees, was from 1860 to 1923 the residence of the *naib*, the Moroccan high official who served as intermediary between the sultan and foreign ambassadors. The Spanish **Church of the Immaculate Conception** (La Purísima), at

No. 51, was built by the Spanish government, work beginning in 1880. It was used by the whole city's Christian community, as well as by foreign diplomats. It is now used for social activities.

Further up the street, on the left, is Rue Touahine, which is lined with jewellers' shops and which leads to the **Fondation Lorin**, an arts centre in a disused synagogue. On display here are newspapers, photographs, posters and plans relating to the political, sporting, musical and social history of Tangier since the 1930s. Temporary exhibitions of paintings also take place here.

🏛 Fondation Lorin
44 Rue Touahine. **ℹ** *(039) 33 46 96.*
⏲ *11am–1pm & 3:30–7:30pm Sun–Fri.* ⬤ *Sat.*

American Legation **⑦**

8 Rue d'Amérique. **📞** *(039) 95 53 17.* ⏲ *10am–1pm & 3–5pm Mon–Thu.*

Tʜᴇ ᴀᴍᴇʀɪᴄᴀɴ ʟᴇɢᴀᴛɪᴏɴ consists of a suite of rooms that originally formed part of the residence that Moulay Sliman presented to the United States in 1821, and which served as the United States Consulate for the next 140 years. Another suite, on several floors looking out onto a garden, was presented by a Jewish family: the doors, windows and ceilings were decorated by craftsmen from Fès.

The rooms contain engravings of Gibraltar and Tangier, old maps, and paintings (by Brayer, Mohammed ben Ali Rbati, James McBey, Claudio Bravo and others), which were given to the legation by Margarite McBey, wife of James McBey and a resident of Tangier. Through photographs, early editions and recordings, a room devoted to Paul Bowles gives an overview of the writer's life and work during the years that he lived in Tangier. A reference library is also available for the use of scholars and specialists on North Africa.

The elegant interior courtyard of the American Legation

Artists and Writers in Tangier

AT THE BEGINNING of the 20th century, many writers from Europe and the United States came to Tangier, most of them settling here more or less permanently. Drawn not only by the climate, they also came in search of stimulation and spiritual wellbeing, and in particular sought the atmosphere, freedom and sense of adventure that the city seemed to project. Tangier's exotic reputation as a den of traffickers and spies, and of drugs, sex and dissipation was also a powerful draw.

PAINTERS

The light, architecture and inhabitants of Tangier have inspired many European and American painters. Discovered by Eugène Delacroix at the end of the 19th century, the city later became the subject of paintings by Georges Clairin, Jacques Majorelle, James Wilson Morrice, Kees Van Dongen, Claudio Bravo and the Expressionist painter Henri Matisse.

© Succession H. Matisse 2001

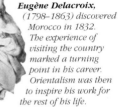

Eugène Delacroix, (1798–1863) discovered Morocco in 1832. The experience of visiting the country marked a turning point in his career. Orientalism was then to inspire his work for the rest of his life.

Henri Matisse *(1869–1954) was one of the greatest Fauvist painters. His* Odalisque à la Culotte Grise *is typical of his work.*

WRITERS

In the wake of Paul Bowles came writers and musicians of the Beat, Rock and Hippie generations. Tennessee Williams arrived in 1949, followed by Truman Capote, who came to Tangier "to escape from himself". William Burroughs lived here for longer than all other foreign writers, finding Tangier a city where "throbbed the heartbeat of the world".

Paul Bowles, *who came to Tangier for the first time in 1931 on the advice of Gertrude Stein, settled there permanently in 1947. He died in 1999.*

Mohammed Choukri, *born in the Rif in 1935, was a friend of Jean Genet and Tennessee Williams. Discovered by Paul Bowles, he came to fame in the 1980s with* For Bread Alone.

Paul Morand, *a diplomat and writer, and also a great traveller, wrote* Hécate et ses chiens *in Tangier in 1955. A unique atmosphere pervades this short novel on the subject of couples: "In Africa, the first thing you learn is to live life as it comes."*

Grand Socco (Place du 9 Avril 1947) **8**

THE LINK BETWEEN the medina and Ville Nouvelle, Place du Grand Socco was renamed Place du 9 Avril 1947 in memory of the speech that Mohammed V made in support of independence. The square comes to life in the evenings, when vendors spread out their wares – extensive displays of a huge variety of second-hand goods – on the ground. A colourful market, where peasant women in striped *foutas* and wide-brimmed straw hats come to sell fruit and fowl, takes place above the square, near the Anglican Church of St Andrew, at the far end of Rue d'Angleterre.

The minaret of the **Mosque of Sidi Bou Abib** (1917), decorated with polychrome tiles, overlooks the square from the southwest. Near Bab Fahs, a double gateway leading into the medina, are the grounds of the Mendoubia. This was the residence of the *mendoub* when Tangier was under international administration (1923–56).

Anglican Church of St Andrew **9**

Rue d'Angleterre. ⬜ 9:30am–12:30pm & 2:30–6pm. Keys obtainable from the caretaker. ✝ 11am Sun.

BUILT ON LAND that Moulay Hassan donated to fulfil the needs of an increasingly

Church of St Andrew, with a bell-tower in the shape of a minaret

large British population in Tangier, the church of St Andrew was completed in 1894. The interior is a curious mixture of styles, in which the Moorish style predominates.

The lobed arch at the entrance to the choir, and the ceiling above the altar, which is decorated with a quotation from the Gospel in Arabic, are of particular interest. The belltower, in the shape of a minaret, overlooks the cemetery. Among those buried here are Walter Harris, a journalist and correspondent for *The Times,* and Sir Harry McLean, a military adviser to the sultans.

A plaque at the west end of the church commemorates Emily Kean: she came to Tangier in the 19th century, married the Cherif of Ouezzane and devoted her life to the welfare of the people of northern Morocco.

Musée d'Art Contemporain **10**

Rue d'Angleterre. ⓘ (039) 94 80 50. ⬜ 9am–12:30pm & 3–6pm Wed–Mon. 🖼

PAINTINGS BY Chrabia Tallal, Fatima Hassan, Mohammed Kacimi, Abdelkebir Rabia, Fouad Belamine and others are shown in this art gallery, the former British Consulate. They form a comprehensive cross-section of contemporary Moroccan painting.

Fondouk Chejra **11**

Rue de la Liberté. Accessible via the steps below the level of the Hôtel el-Menzah. ⓘ (039) 94 80 50.

THE BUZZING ATMOSPHERE in Fondouk Chejra, known as the Poor People's Souk or Weavers' Souk, is that of an Oriental bazaar. Above the shops on the ground floor, the rooms that were once used by travellers and passing tradesmen have been converted into weavers' workshops, where the white and red fabric that is typical of the Rif is produced. The original layout of the former *fondouk*, or caravanserai, is difficult to make out, the central courtyard having been much altered.

Rue de la Liberté **12**

THIS STREET RUNS from Place du 9 Avril 1947 (or Grand Socco) to Ville Nouvelle. It was formerly known as Rue de Fès, then as Rue du Statut, its current name dating from the beginning of Moroccan independence. The French Consulate, which is set in the centre of a pleasant and attractive park, dates from 1929; the classical arcade of the façade is offset by decoration in the Moorish style.

In the **Galerie Delacroix**, next door, temporary exhibitions are organized by the Institut Français. The Hôtel el-Minzah, dating from 1930, is one of the most illustrious hotels in Morocco, with an

The Grand Socco, also known as Place du 9 Avril 1947

◁ **Residential quarter of Tangier, with the minaret of the Kasbah Mosque rising in the background**

Andalusian-style courtyard and gardens, comfortable lounges and bars. Winston Churchill, Paul and Jane Bowles, Jean Genet and Hollywood stars from Rita Hayworth and Errol Flynn to Anthony Quinn regularly stayed in this magical place.

🏛 **Galerie Delacroix**
86 Rue de la Liberté. ☎ (039) 93 21 34.
◻ 11am–1pm, 4–8pm Tue–Sun.

Place de France & Place de Faro ❸

Place de France is a major meeting place for the inhabitants of Tangier. The **Café de Paris**, which opened in 1920, was the first establishment to open outside the medina. Among its regular customers were Paul Bowles, Tennessee Williams and Jean Genet, as well as foreign

The Café de Paris, once one of the most fashionable cafés in Tangier

diplomats. The café has remained a hub of city life.
Very near Place de France, on Avenue Pasteur, is Place de Faro (named after the Portuguese town twinned with Tangier in 1984), complete with cannons. It is one of the few places to have escaped the attentions of the developers. It offers a view of the medina and of ferry traffic in the harbour and the strait.

Avenue Pasteur ❹

Together with Avenue Mohammed V, which extends eastwards from it, Avenue Pasteur is Ville Nouvelle's main artery and its economic centre. In the evening, the avenue is given

The dilapidated Art Deco façade of the Gran Teatro Cervantes

over to the Spanish custom of the *paseo*. The Moroccan tourist office, at No. 29, occupies the first building to be constructed on the avenue, while the villa at No. 27 houses the **Great Synagogue**. The **Librairie des Colonnes**, the bookshop at No. 54, has lost some of its former prestige and importance. All the writers in Tangier, whether visitors or residents, regularly patronized this bookshop, which stocks most available books on Tangier. Lectures and signing sessions are still held here.
The **Gran Teatro Cervantes** (accessible from Avenue Pasteur, which is reached along Rue du Prince Moulay Abdallah and via steps continuing from it) opened in 1913. One of North Africa's major theatres, it was here that the greatest singers and dancers of the age performed. The building, with an Art Deco façade, is in a bad state of repair. Restoration has been delayed by disputes between the city and the Spanish state, which had undertaken to finance its upkeep.

✡ **Great Synagogue**
27 Avenue Pasteur. ℹ (039) 94 80 50.

📖 **Librairie des Colonnes**
54 Avenue Pasteur. ☎ (039) 93 69 55.

Ancien Palais du Mendoub ❺

Avenue Mohammed Tazi *(in the northwest of Ville Nouvelle).*
● *to the public.*

The *Mendoub* was the sultan's representative during the international administration of Tangier. While his main residence was the Mendoubia, near the Grand Socco, this palace, built in 1929, was used mostly for receptions. It was acquired in 1970 by Malcolm Forbes (1919–90), the American multimillionaire who founded *Fortune* magazine. It became a luxury residence where

The elegant Ancien Palais du Mendoub

Forbes threw lavish parties and where such international stars as Elizabeth Taylor were guests. The house also contained a display of Forbes' 120,000 piece collection of toy soldiers. The Palace is now state-owned and will be used as a residence for important visitors from abroad.

Café Hafa ⑯

Rue Mohammed Tazi *(in a narrow street opposite the football stadium, leading towards the sea).*

THE CAFÉ OPENED in 1921, and neither the furniture nor the décor seem to have changed since then. Assorted tables and rush matting are laid out on terraces rising in tiers from the edge of the cliff, offering a breathtaking view of the strait. Writers and singers, from Paul Bowles to William Burroughs and from the Beatles to the Rolling Stones, have come here, seeking out Tangier's young generation or the company of local fishermen. People come here to smoke and drink mint tea, which is probably brewed exactly as it was in 1921.

Quartier du Marshan ⑰

Rue Mohammed Tazi, Rue Assad Ibn Farrat, Avenue Hassan II *(western part of the kasbah).*

LOCATED WEST of the kasbah, the Quartier du Marshan was developed from the late 19th to the early 20th century. Being removed from the bustle of the medina and of Ville Nouvelle, it was an attractive residential location, and high officals and the *shorfa* of Ouezzane built their palaces and grand villas here in the late 19th century. The Italian Consulate (Rue Assad Ibn Farrat), rebuilt in 1916 and with walls covered in *zellij* tilework, housed Garibaldi in 1849–50. The former palace of the sultan Moulay Hafid, in Moorish style, became the Palais des Institutions Italiennes in 1926. On the edge of the strait, the

An elegant villa in the Quartier du Marshan

Beaches around Tangier

THE BAY OF TANGIER, a grand crescent that is some-times likened to the Baie des Anges in Nice or to Copacabana in Rio de Janeiro, stretches for almost 4 km (2.5 miles) from the edge of the port round to the residential districts and resort areas and to the first spurs of land that mark its eastern extremity. The proximity of the city and the rivers that flow into it unfortunately make this the most polluted beach in Morocco. For swimming and sunbathing, it is better to make for the beaches between Cap Spartel and the Grottes d'Hercule and beyond, or for the coves of Cap Malabata, or, further east, the beaches at Sidi Khankroucht and Ksar es-Seghir.

③ **The Bay of Tangier** *forms a splendid and extensive sweep, but is unfortunately very polluted.*

② **Between Tangier** *and Cap Spartel, small coves are reachable on foot from the Perdicaris Belvedere. The walk down passes through mimosa and woods of umbrella pine.*

① **Between Cap Spartel** *and the Grottes d'Hercule are many attractive little bays separated by rocky outcrops.*

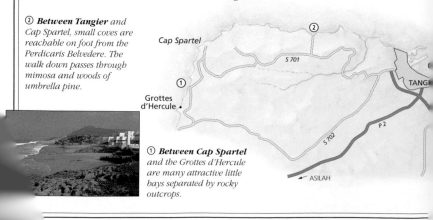

Marshan ends at the limits of Hafa, a poorer residential district with a great deal of local colour, up on the sea cliff.

Colline du Charf ⑱

In the southeast of the city.

A HILL RISING TO a height of about 100 m (328 ft), the Colline du Charf commands the most impressive and most complete view of Tangier.

The panorama stretches from Cap Malabata in the east to La Montagne, which rises over the old town to the west. From here the beach appears as a strip lining the bay, and the white, densely packed medina seems to cling to the hillside as it slopes down towards the port, while the high-rise blocks of Ville Nouvelle stand along its wide avenues. Poorer residential districts stretch

out southwards: in among them, at the foot of the hill, can be seen Plaza Toro, whose bullrings are now used for public functions. Further north is the Syrian Mosque, with a style of minaret rarely seen in the Maghreb.

The mosque-like building on the hill was a café during Tangier's international period. A favourite form of relaxation for the inhabitants of Tangier is to stroll on the hill or sit and gaze out over the strait.

Bay of Tangier ⑲

BETWEEN THE PORT and Cap Malabata, the bay forms a beach-lined semicircle. Avenue d'Espagne, which runs along the bay, is lined with hotels, from small guesthouses to large modern establishments. Dotted with the blues, reds and whites of

Tangier's fishing harbour, at the foot of the medina

the boats and the ochre, green and orange of the nets, the small fishing harbour is a colourful sight, and the freshly caught fish that is offered makes a delicious meal.

It was on Avenue d'Espagne that Bernardo Bertolucci shot scenes for his 1990 film *The Sheltering Sky*. Many literary works, by William Burroughs and others, took shape in the small guesthouses here. The French philosopher Michel Foucault would stay at the Hôtel Cecil, while Samuel Beckett preferred the Solazur.

④ **The beach at Mrissa**, beneath Cap Malabata, has fine, soft sand and is well sheltered by stands of pine.

⑤ **Plage des Amiraux** has developed in front of the elegant houses of a small, newly created village.

⑥ **The double beach at Sidi Khankroucht**, at Km 18, beneath shaded hills, is clean and pleasant. Chez Hassan is a small, friendly restaurant here.

⑦ **Wadi Aliane** is an attractive sandy beach with a small resort complex that is still in the process of being built.

Ksar es-Seghir ⑧
CEUTA

Malabata

TÉTOUAN

KEY

— Major road

= Minor road

0 km   2

0 miles   2

⑧ **At Ksar es-Seghir**, 33 km (20 miles) along a road with beautiful scenery, a splendid beach stretches out in front of woods and groves from which emerge the ruins of Almohad, Merinid and Portuguese buildings.

MEDITERRANEAN COAST & THE RIF

THE GREAT MOUNTAINOUS CRESCENT *of the Rif forms a natural barrier across northern Morocco. Its proud Berber-speaking inhabitants haughtily guard their traditions and independence, and historically the Rif has always resisted conquest. The Rif, today, is friendly and welcoming, with sandy Mediterranean coves and beaches, many of them with a backdrop of majestic cliffs.*

Inaccessible and intricately partitioned, the Rif reaches a height of 2,452 m (8,047 ft) at Jbel Tidirhin, in the central part of the mountain range, then tails away eastwards towards the Moulouya estuary and the Algerian border. The northwestern Rif is a region of low mountains and hills dotted with villages, while the central part consists of lofty summits and enclosed valleys. To the east, what is regarded as the real Rif gently slopes away.

All Riffians fiercely defend their cultural identity. The Spanish, to whom the region fell when Morocco was divided under the French Protectorate, came face to face with this intransigence during the uprisings of 1921–6 and were soundly defeated at Anoual

in 1921 *(see p56)*. The history of the Rif and its coastline is closely linked to that of Spain. For Morocco, the Mediterranean became a bridgehead for the conquest of Spain. From the 15th century, the Portuguese occupation, followed by that of the Spanish, cut Morocco off from the Mediterranean and accelerated its decline. Spain still maintains a foothold in Ceuta and Melilla, and on a few rocky islets. Morocco has worked for closer cooperation with Spain and Europe to tackle problems of illegal trafficking and emigration here. By 2007, the new port of Tanger Méditerranée, as well as a new airport, will dramatically change the area between Tangier and Ceuta.

The fishing harbour at Al-Hoceima

◁ A brightly painted wooden door in Chefchaouen

Exploring the Mediterranean Coast & the Rif

STRETCHING FROM the land of the Jebala in the west to Morocco's eastern frontier, the Rif presents a great variety of landscapes. Here are high, steep valleys where almond trees blossom and oleanders flower, mountain roads that command wild and magnificent vistas, forests of cedar, fir and oak, and villages and isolated houses with pitched tin roofs. Between Ceuta and Cabo Negro, the coast is punctuated by sweeping beaches of golden sand and, from Wadi Laou to Al-Hoceima and Saïdia, by more secluded bays beneath rocky cliffs. The medinas of Tetouan and Chefchaouen are among the most picturesque in Morocco.

SPAIN

GIBRALTAR

CAP MALABATA
CAP SPARTEL
KSAR ES-SEGHIR
CEUTA
GROTTES D'HERCULE
Asilab, Larache
Larache
SOUK EL-ARBA DES BENI HASSAN
Ksar el-Kebir
Souk el-Arba du Rharb
OUEZZANE
Moulay Idriss
FÈS EL-BALI
Fès

TETOUAN
MEDITERRANEAN SEA
BOU AHMED
EL-JEBHA
TORRES DE ALCALÁ
AL-HOCEI
CHEFCHAOUEN
BAB BERRET
KETAMA
TARGUIST
RIF
TAHAR SO
Wadi Ouerrba
AÏN AÏCHA
Fès

KEY

Main road
Minor road
Track

Narrow street in Chefchaouen

SIGHTS AT A GLANCE

LOCATOR MAP

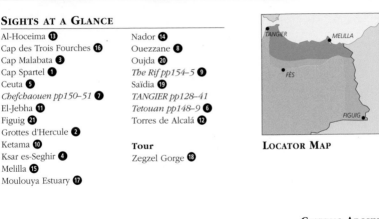

GETTING AROUND

Air links to the region depart from Tangier, Al-Hoceima and Oujda. Once there, it is better to hire a car rather than use *grands taxis*. Having your own means of transport gives you the freedom to stop off at secluded beaches and seek out the high valleys. In this mountainous environment, the roads are sometimes in a bad state of repair: roadworks go on permanently, particularly along arterial routes.

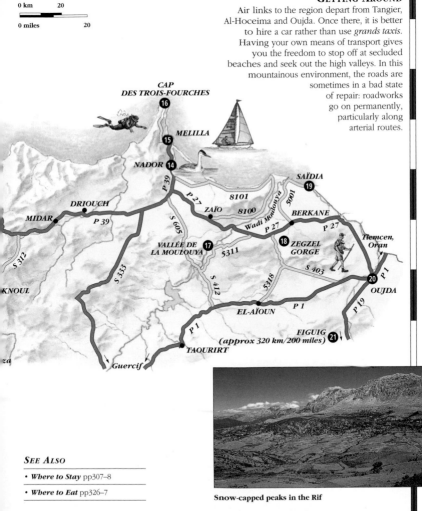

Snow-capped peaks in the Rif

SEE ALSO

Cap Spartel ①

Road map D1. 14 km (9 miles) west of Tangier.

From Tangier, the road leading to Cap Spartel runs through La Montagne, the city's western suburb, which is bathed in the perfume of eucalyptus and mimosa. Long walls surround the residences of Moroccan, Kuwaiti and Saudi kings and princes and the luxury villas dating from the golden age of Tangier's international period. Beyond stretch forests of holm-oak, cork oak, umbrella pine, mastic-tree, broom and heather, which all flourish here, watered by the highest rainfall in Morocco.

At the cape, the most northwesterly point of Africa, is the promontory known in antiquity as Cape Ampelusium or Cape of the Vines, and a lighthouse dating from 1865.

The lighthouse at Cap Spartel, where sea and ocean meet

From beneath the lighthouse, there is a breathtaking view of the ocean where the Mediterranean and Atlantic meet, and on clear days you can see the strait and coast of Spain from Cape Trafalgar to the Rock of Gibraltar.

Grottes d'Hercule ②

Road map D1. 5 km (3 miles) southwest of Cap Spartel.

At the place known as Achakar, the sea has carved impressive caves out of the cliff. The people who, from prehistoric times, came

The unfinished medieval "castle" at Cap Malabata

to these caves knapped stones here and quarried millstones for use in oil presses. The opening to the caves, facing onto the sea, is a cleft shaped like a reversed map of Africa.

According to legend, Hercules slept here before performing one of his 12 labours – picking the golden apples in the Garden of the Hesperides. The location of the legendary garden belonging to these nymphs of darkness and guarded by the dragon with 100 heads is said to be further south, near Lixus.

The best time to visit the caves is in the late afternoon, after which the light of the setting sun can be enjoyed from the cafés nearby. Further south, beneath the level of the caves, are the **Ruins of Cotta** (1st century BC to 3rd century AD). With vats for salting fish, making *garum* and producing purple dye, this was one of the largest industrial centres of the Punic-Mauretanian period.

The Grottes d'Hercule, like a reversed map of Africa

Cap Malabata ③

Road map D1. 12 km (7.5 miles) east of Tangier. *Road S704, from Ksar es-Seghir and Ceuta, along the coast.*

The route out of Tangier skirts an area of large tourist hotels and continues eastward round the curve of the bay. Soon after a tiny estuary, at the edge of the road, are the remains of a 16th-century fortress, from which Moroccan soldiers could watch and attack the Portuguese, Spanish and English occupiers of Tangier. Nearby, white crenel-lated walls surround the lush and extensive grounds of the **Villa Harris**. The residence of Walter Harris (1866–1953), a journalist and diplomatic correspondent for *The Times* in Tangier from 1892, now houses a Club Méditerranée resort.

The road ascending the hills passes through magnificent pine forests and by many small coves where there are cafés which, like Café Ryad, have an old-world charm. Just before the cape, a strange building appears. Conceived in the medieval style, it was the work of a whimsical Italian, who left it unfinished in the 1930s.

The view from Cap Malabata is stunning, especially in the morning, looking westwards over the city and suburbs of Tangier and across to the Straits of Gibraltar, and eastwards to Jbel Moussa, which rises over Ceuta.

Ksar es-Seghir ❹

Road map D1. 33 km (20 miles) east of Tangier. 🚶 8,800. 🚌 Sat.

A TOWN WITH A small fishing harbour and a fine beach, Ksar es-Seghir faces the Spanish town of Tarifa across the Straits of Gibraltar. The souk that takes place here on Saturdays is filled with women of the Rif, conspicuous in their white, red-striped *foutas*.

Since the 17th century, forts have stood on this well-sheltered spot on an estuary, and it was from here that Moroccan troops set sail for Spain. The Almohads made it an important centre of ship-building and skilled crafts. The remains of buildings in a small forest are those of a town built by the Merinids in the 14th century. The circular walls that surround it are unusual, but were obviously preferred to the customary square plan by the town's Muslim builders; the gateway facing the sea is the best-preserved. The Portuguese, who held the town from 1458 to 1549, strengthened it with new fortifications that reached to the sea.

Ksar es-Seghir, an attractive coastal town

Ceuta ❺

Road map D1. 63 km (39 miles) east of Tangier. 🚶 75,000. ℹ️ *Quai Cañonero Dato; (056) 51 13 79. Also Calle Alcade José Victori Gonalons; (056) 51 40 92.*

S TANDING ON A narrow isthmus between Monte Hacho and the mainland, Ceuta occupies a favourable location opposite Gibraltar. The Rock of Gibraltar and Monte Hacho are the two legendary Pillars of Hercules.

From the 12th century, the town was visited by traders

Ceuta, like an amphitheatre on the isthmus linking it to the mainland

from Genoa, Pisa, Marseilles and Catalonia. In 1415, it became a Portuguese enclave, then passed to Spain in 1578. Today, Ceuta is an important garrison town. Its livelihood depends mainly on the tax-free trade that its status as a free port allows. It is a self-governing town within the Spanish state. However, Morocco has claimed it back, and the town faces an uncertain future.

The 12-km (7.5-mile) circuit of Monte Hacho (part of it accessible by road) affords views over the town, the mountains and coast of the Rif and Gibraltar, especially from the lighthouse at Punto Almina. The Castillo del Desnarigado, a fortress that is now a military museum, encloses the Ermita de San Antonio. This chapel draws a large pilgrimage on 13 June each year.

The **Plaza de Africa** is, in architectural terms, the centre of the town, where the main public buildings are concentrated. The cathedral, whose present appearance dates from the 18th century, stands on the site of a Grand Mosque. Religious paintings and objects are displayed in its museum.

Nuestra Señora de Africa (the Church of Our Lady of Africa) was built in the early 18th century, also on the site of a mosque, in an arresting Baroque style. On the high altar stands a statue of the Virgin, patroness of Ceuta, who is believed to have saved the town from an epidemic of plague in the 16th century. The cathedral treasury contains some fine paintings, banners and 17th-century illuminated books.

The **Ayuntamiento** (town hall), built in 1929, is of interest to visitors for the paintings that it contains by Mariano Bertuchi, an artist active during the colonial period.

The **Museo Municipal** (Archaeological Museum) is laid out above underground passages dug in the 16th and 17th centuries to supply the town with water. The displays include Neolithic, Carthaginian and Roman pottery, including amphorae, as well as coins and armour.

Through maps, photographs and visual displays, the **Museo de la Legión** documents the activities of the Spanish Foreign Legion and its efforts in 1921–6 to subdue the Rif uprising and the rebel leader Abdel Krim. The legion, formed in 1920, suffered serious losses during this war.

🏛 **Museo Municipal**
On the corner of Paseo de Revellín and Calle Ingenieros. 📞 (056) 51 40 92. 🕐 9am–2pm, Mon–Fri. 🈺
🏛 **Museo de la Legión**
Paseo de Colón. ⬤ Sun. 🈺

Tetouan ❻

IN THE WORDS of Arab poets, Tetouan is a white dove, "the sister of Fès", "the little Jerusalem" or "the daughter of Granada ". The town, built partly on the slopes of Jbel Dersa, was inhabited by Jewish refugees from Granada in the 15th century, then by Moors from Andalusia in the 17th century. The town's Andalusian heritage can be seen in its medina, and also in its culinary traditions, as well as in its music and in the craft of embroidery. From the 15th to the 18th centuries, Tetouan was a lively centre of privateering, then of thriving trade with Europe, becoming a sort of city-state comparable to Florence or to Venice at the time of the doges. In the 18th century, the town was the diplomatic capital of Morocco. The Spanish, who held it from 1860 to 1862, made it their capital during the Protectorate, building a new town on the west side of the old Andalusian medina.

The church on Place Moulay el-Mehdi, built in 1926

Place Hassan II, a link between Ville Nouvelle and the medina

⛪ Ville Nouvelle
Place Moulay el-Mehdi and Boulevard Mohammed V.
It is on Place Moulay el-Mehdi – which is sometimes still referred to by the town's inhabitants as Place Primo (after the Spanish politician José Primo de Rivera) – that the Spanish colonial architecture of Ville Nouvelle (New Town) is at its most eloquent. With a main post office, bank and church (1926), the square looks like any other central town square in Spain. Elegant homes with doors, windows and balconies with Moorish-style ornamentation can be seen on Boulevard Mohammed V, the town's principal thoroughfare.

Place Hassan II links Ville Nouvelle and the medina. Modern tiling has replaced the old mosaic decoration of the royal palace that stands on the side of the square nearest the medina. Both the boulevard and the square come to life in the evenings with the *paseo* (promenade), a Spanish custom that is more deeply ingrained in Tetouan than elsewhere.

🏛 Musée Archéologique
Boulevard El-Jazaïr, near Place El-Jala. ℂ (039) 96 73 03. ◯ Mon–Fri pm only.
The rooms of the Archaeological Museum contain objects dating from the Roman period that were discovered at Volubilis, Lixus and Thamuda, a Roman site on the outskirts of present-day Tetouan (on the road to Chefchaouen). Mosaics, including a depiction of the Three Graces of classical mythology, as well as pottery, coins, bronzes and other pieces, are displayed. The most interesting exhibits – such as ancient inscriptions, mosaic floors and Muslim funerary stelae with the Star of David – are laid out in the garden.

⛪ Medina
Entry through Place Hassan II, then via Rue Ahmed Torres to the southeast.
Tetouan's medina, now a World Heritage Site, is the most strongly Andalusian of all Moroccan medinas. Emigrants from Spain who arrived in the 15th and 17th centuries implanted their architectural traditions here, including a taste for wrought-iron decoration and a liking for doors with elaborate metal fittings.

The aroma of spices, freshly sawn wood and *kesra* (bread) fills the medina's narrow streets, squares and souks, which bustle with carpenters, slipper-makers, drapers, tanners and sellers of second-hand goods. Rue El-Mokadem (between Place Souk el-Fouqui and Place Gharsa el-Kebira) is the street most densely packed with shops, but also one of the most

Kesra (bread) on sale in the El-Fouqui Souk

The medina, on the slopes of Jbel Dersa

VISITORS' CHECKLIST

Road Map D1.  310,000.
5 km (3 miles). Tnine-Sidi-
Lyamani. 30 Bld Moham-
med V; (039) 96 19 15. Wed,
Fri, Sun by Place Moulay-el-Medhi.

school teaches leatherwork,
pottery, mosaic-making,
carpet-weaving and deco-
rative plasterwork. The
students' work is displayed
in a domed exhibition hall.

noteworthy for its impressive
white buildings and its paving.
Sellers of Riffian fabrics and
pottery fill the small shady
square where the El-Houts
Souk takes place. It leads to
the former mellah, Tetouan's
Jewish quarter, where the
balconied houses have large
windows, wrought-iron gates
and arcaded façades.

🏛 Musée d'Art Marocain

Avenue Hassan Iᵉʳ and Rue Sqala,
near Bab Oqla. 📞 (039) 97 05 05.
🕐 9am–noon & 2–6pm Wed–Mon.
Occupying a bastion built in
1828, the museum is laid out

in an Andalusian palace with
a garden, a fountain clad in
zellij tilework, and red-tiled
awnings, typical of buildings
in Tetouan. The furniture, the
craftsman-made pieces, the
costumes and musical instruments illustrate the town's
traditions. Tetouani rooms, with
marriage scenes (such as putting together the trousseau and
presenting the bride), have also
been convincingly re-created.

The Craft School, near the
museum, opposite Bab Oqla,
occupies a residence built in
1928 in Moorish style. Specializing in local traditions, the

Detail of a façade on
Boulevard Mohammed V

TETOUAN'S JEWS

A large Jewish community, expelled from Spain
at the end of the Christian Reconquest, settled in
Tetouan, thrived here and reached its height in
the 16th century. Like the many Muslims who
had also arrived from Spain, these Jews
cherished the memory of Andalusia as a lost
paradise. On feast days, they would listen to
Andalusian music and don Andalusian costume
and jewellery.

Exploiting their contacts in Gibraltar, Antwerp,
Amsterdam and London, Tetouan's Jews played a
central role in the economic life of the town and
through them it became an important trade link
with the West. At the beginning of the 19th
century, subjected to violence and heavily taxed,
the Jews repaired to a quarter of their own, the
judería. Marginalized in professional and social
life, many Jews left to settle in Melilla, Gibraltar
or Iran, and also in Latin America. Despite an
improvement in their situation under Spanish
rule, the Jewish community – which still counted
some 3,000 people in 1960 – continued to shrink
progressively after independence, many leaving
for Israel. By the early 1990s, there were no
more than 200 Jews remaining in Tetouan.

Jewish Feast Day in Tetouan, painting by
Alfred Dehodencq (1822–82)

Chefchaouen ⓿

THE WHITE TOWN of Chefchaouen nestles in the
hollow of the two mountains – ech-Chaoua (The
Horns) – from which it takes its name. Steep narrow
streets with white and indigo limewashed buildings,
small squares, ornate fountains and houses with
elaborately decorated doorways and red tile roofs
make this a delightful town. It was founded in 1471 by
Idrissid *shorfa*, descendants of the Prophet Mohammed,
as a stronghold in the fight against the Portuguese.
Chefchaouen, esteemed as a holy town, has eight
mosques and several *zaouias* and *marabouts*.

Courtyard of the kasbah, around
which the museum is laid out

A café on Place Uta el-Hammam, in the heart of the town

⊞ Place Uta el-Hammam

The square is the heart of the
old town and the focal point
on which all the streets of the
medina converge. It is lined
with trees, and paved with
stones and pebbles, and in
the centre stands a four-sided
fountain decorated with arches
and crowned by a pavilion of
green tiles. With shops and
cafés, this is an ideal place for
a relaxed stroll.

⬛ Grand Mosque

Place Uta el-Hammam.
🚫 to non-Muslims.
The Grand Mosque was
founded probably in the 16th
century and has been re-
modelled several times since.

The later minaret, which dates
from the 17th century, is
distinctive in being octagonal.
It is decorated with three tiers
of plain and lobed arches on
a painted ochre background.
The uppermost tier is
decorated with *zellij* tilework.

⊞ Fondouk

Corner of Place Uta el-Hammam and
Rue Al-Andalus.
The *fondouk* still serves the
purpose for which it was
originally built. About 50
rooms, arranged around the
courtyard, still accommodate
travellers and passing traders.

It is a building of strikingly
simple design, with a gallery
of semicircular arches lining
the pebble-paved
courtyard. The only
contrast to this
simplicity is
provided by the
main entrance; the
doorway is
surmounted by an
awning and framed
by a broken
horseshoe arch
surrounded by
interlacing arches.

⊞ Kasbah and Museum

West corner of Place Uta el-Hammam.
◯ Wed–Mon. ● Tue & Fri pm. ▨
The kasbah, with crenellated
walls of red beaten earth and
ten bastions, is the essential
heart of the town. The
fortress was begun in the 15th
century by Moulay Ali ben
Rachid, and was completed
by Moulay Ismaïl in the 17th
century, as was the residence
within. The kasbah's plan and
architectural style show Andalusian influence. A pleasant
garden with fountains is laid
out within, from where there
is a good view of the walls
and the rampart walk. The
Musée Ethnographique
(Ethnographic Museum)
occupies the residence built
in the garden. This is a
traditional Moroccan house
with a courtyard and gallery
on the first floor. The
museum contains displays of
pottery, armour, embroidery,
costume, musical instruments,
palanquins and painted
wooden chests.

⊞ Medina

A small street running
between the kasbah and
the Grand Mosque leads
to the Souïka district. This
is the oldest district of
Chefchaouen, and the town's
finest houses, with carved
and decorated doors, are
found here. The name *souïka*,
meaning "little market",
comes from the district's
kissaria, where there are
many small shops along its
narrow streets.

The medina contains more
than 100 weavers' workshops.

The *fondouk*, with rooms round the courtyard

Narrow street with houses painted white and blue

Indeed, Chefchaouen is famous for the woollen *jellabas* that are woven here, as well as for the red and white striped fabrics worn by the women of the Jebala, a tribe of the western Rif. One such weaver's workshop is located in Rue Ben Dibane, identifiable by an exterior stairway.

One of the most distinctive fountains in Chefchaouen is Aïn Souika, set in a recess in the district's main street. Covered by a porch, it has a semicircular basin and interlaced lobed arches.

⊞ Quartier Al-Andalus

This district is reached from the northwestern corner of Place Uta el-Hammam, leaving the *fondouk* on the left. The Quartier Al-Andalus received the second wave of immigrants – Muslims and Jews expelled from Spain – who arrived in 1492, after the fall of Granada.

Here, the houses, painted white, green or blue, have decorated doors and wrought-iron railings at some of their windows. They follow the steep gradient of the terrain, which makes for many exterior stairways and entrances at various levels.

⚑ Ras el-Ma and the Mills

The steep streets of Al-Andalus leading up towards the mountain pass through Bab el-Ansar, the town's

VISITORS' CHECKLIST

Road map D1. 🏠 *45,000.*
📧 🖼 *Moussem of Sidi Allal el-Hadj (9 Aug).* 🏛 *Mon & Thu.*

northwest gateway, which has been restored and renovated.

Beyond is the spring of Ras el-Ma, which is now enclosed by a building. The presence of this underground spring was the reason why the town was established. It accounts for the town's lush gardens, and the water also powers the mills. Steps leading towards the metalled road run alongside the wash-houses, then the mills, whose origins go back to the arrival of the Andalusian refugees.

The route then leads to the bridge across Wadi Laou, which is built in the form of a semicircular arch with bevelled buttresses. With its cascades, wash-houses and cafés, this is one of the most pleasant quarters of Chefchaouen

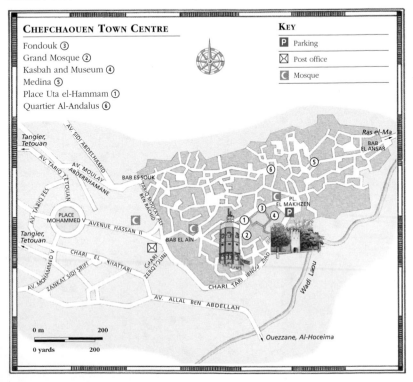

CHEFCHAOUEN TOWN CENTRE

Fondouk ③
Grand Mosque ②
Kasbah and Museum ④
Medina ⑤
Place Uta el-Hammam ①
Quartier Al-Andalus ⑥

KEY

🅿	Parking
⊠	Post office
©	Mosque

Tangier, Tetouan

AV. SIDI ABDELHAMID
AV. MOULAY ABDERRHAMANE
AV. TARIQ TETOUAN
AV. TARIQ FES
BAB ES-SOUK
TARIQ MOULAY ALI BEN RACHID
PLACE MOHAMMED V
AVENUE HASSAN II
Tangier, Tetouan
AV. MOHAMMED V
CHARI EL KHATTABI
ZANKAT SIDI SRIFI
BAB EL AÏN
CHARI ZERQUNI
CHARI TARI IBN ZIAD
CHARI TARI IBN ZIAD
AV. ALLAL BEN ABDELLAH

Ras el-Ma
BAB EL ANSAR
PL. EL MAKHZEN

Wadi Laou

Ouezzane, Al-Hoceima

0 m   200
0 yards   200

A mantle of olive trees covering the hills near Ouezzane

Ouezzane ❽

Road map D2. 60 km (37 miles) south of Chefchaouen. 🚌 🏙 *70,000.* 🛒 *Thu.*

A LARGE MARKET town, Ouezzane spreads out over the slopes of Jbel Bou Hillal, in a landscape of extensive olive groves and plantations of fig trees fed by abundant springs. It is important for its textiles (*jellabas* and carpets) and olive oil.

In the 15th century, the town, which was populated by Andalusians, also counted many Jews among its inhabitants. It began to prosper in the 18th and 19th centuries under the influence of the Idrissid *shorfa*. In 1727, a descendant of Idriss II established the religious brotherhood of the Taïbia, whose influence spread throughout Morocco, Algeria and Tunisia.

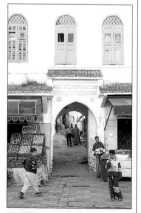

The medina at Ouezzane

In the 19th century, the *shorfa* played a prominent religious and political role in Morocco. The sherif of Ouezzane's policy of openness also assisted trade relations with France. The Zaouia (or Green Mosque) and, with its *zellij*-covered minaret, the Mosque of Moulay Abdallah Cherif, founder of the Taïbia brotherhood, attract many pilgrims.

Jews also come to **Asjen**, 8 km (5 miles) west of the town, to venerate the tomb of Rabbi Abraham ben Diouanne, who died in about 1780. The pilgrimage that takes place 33 days after Easter is an occasion when Morocco's Jewish community acknowledges its allegiance to the king.

The Rif ❾

See pp154–5.

Ketama ❿

Road map D-E1.107 km (66 miles) east of Chefchaouen on the P39, the "Route des Crêtes" (Mountain Crests Road). 🛒 *Wed.*

L OCATED IN THE HEART of a forest, Ketama used to be a popular summer and winter resort but the presence and perseverance of illegal kif and hashish salesmen will make most visitors move on.

Leaving the town, the road eastward reveals the slopes of Jbel Tidirhin (or Tidiquin), at 2,448 m (8,034 ft) the highest peak in the Rif. In the valleys,

the houses have pitched roofs, with a covering of planks and corrugated metal, the modern substitute for thatch. In some villages, such as Taghzoute, the craft of leather embroidery is very much alive.

El-Jebha ⓫

Road map D1. 137 km (85 miles) east of Tetouan along the coast road S608, 73 km (45 miles) from Ketama on the P39 then the 8500. 🛒 *Tue.*

T HE SMALL fishing town of El-Jebha nestles at the end of Fishermen's Point. Its one-storey, cube-like houses, covered in white roughcast, give it a typically Mediterranean air. On the right of the harbour, where *lamparo* boats are moored, is Crayfish Cove, which is ideal for underwater fishing. On the left, a soft sandy beach stretches away towards the west.

Torres de Alcalá ⓬

Road map E1. 144 km (89 miles) from Chefchaouen and 72 km (45 miles) from Ketama on the P39 then the 8501.

L OCATED ON THE estuary of Wadi Bou Frah, the fishing village of Torres de Alcalá lies at the foot of a peak crowned by the ruins of a Spanish fortress. About 5 km (3 miles) further east is **Peñon de Velez de la Gomera**, a tiny island attached to the mainland by a narrow spit of sand. Held by the Spanish from

1508 to 1522, it later became a hide-out for pirates and privateers. A convict station under the Protectorate, it is still under Spanish sovereignty. Some 4 km (2.5 miles) west of Velez is **Kalah Iris**, a cove that is an oasis of calm outside the summer season.

Al-Hoceima ⑬

Road map F1. 🏚 *65,000.*
✈ *17 km (10 miles).* 🚌 ℹ *Avenue Marrakech; (039) 98 54 76.*
🎭 *Festival late Jul–early Aug.* 🛒 *Tue.*

Peñon de Velez de la Gomera, still under Spanish sovereignty

T HIS ANCIENT fishing and trading port, seat of the emirate of Nokour during the Middle Ages, was long the object of dispute between European traders. The modern town was founded by General Sanjurjo in 1926, at the place where the Spanish garrison landed, and was known initially as Villa Sanjurjo.

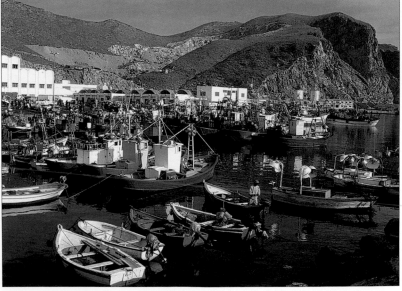

Peñon de Alhucemas, a small island held by Spain

The town's location is one of the most beautiful along Morocco's Mediterranean coast. Whitewashed houses line the bay – an almost perfect semicircle between two hilly promontories. The coastline to the east, opposite the **Peñon de Alhucemas**, a small island held by Spain, commands the most impressive view of the bay.

A few dozen trawlers are usually moored in the harbour; in the evenings their *lamparos* are lit up ready for a night's fishing. **Plage Quemado** stretches out in front of the town. This beach is better than others near Al-Hoceima, such as that at **Asfiha**, in the direction of Ajdir, opposite the small island known locally as Nokour's Rock.

The souk at **Im Zouren**, 17 km (10 miles) east on the road to Nador, is unusual: for the first few hours in the day, only women may go there. Both **Im Zouren** and **Beni Bou Ayach**, large market towns on the road out of Al-Hoceima, have a slightly unreal appearance, created by residential blocks painted in ochres, blues, greens and pinks. The towns come to life for only a few weeks of the year, when emigrant workers based in Germany and Holland return.

Trawlers and fishing boats moored in the harbour at Al-Hoceima, with warehouses in the background

The Rif **⑨**

THIS REGION is well-known for its atmospheric and beautiful medinas but, covering an area of some 30,000 sq km (11,580 sq miles), it offers much else besides. Among its natural wonders are high mountains, capes, gorges and rock formations. The country souks held weekly in Riffian towns and villages provide the opportunity to come into contact with local people as they go about their daily business. In July, the *moussem* of Jbel Alam, one of Morocco's best-known pilgrimages, takes place: the object is the tomb of Moulay Abdesselam ben Mchich, a highly venerated Sufi mystic who died in 1228. In the environs of Chefchaouen, ramblers and those with four-wheel-drive vehicles can visit one of the rare collective granaries of the western Rif at Akrar d'El-Kelaa, and the nature reserve at Talassemtane, where the fir forests are protected.

Souk at Wadi Laou
The Saturday souk, where women in foutas *sell their hand-made pottery goods, is the largest and most colourful in the Rif.*

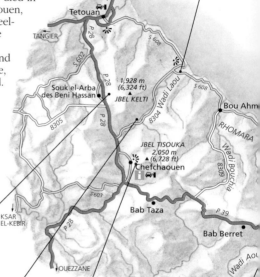

The Jebala District
In a landscape of hills and middle-altitude mountains, the villages of the Jebala tribe have taken root where springs cascade from the hillside, surrounded by olive groves and smaller cereal plantations.

The terrace of the Hôtel Asma, in Chefchaouen, has a view of the enclosed medina, with the tower of the kasbah rising over it.

Gorge of Wadi Laou
Running between sheer high cliffs and below precariously perched villages, the gorge offers stunningly beautiful sights.

Mountain Crests Road
This road commands breathtaking views of the mountains, villages and isolated houses of the Rif, as well as of the cultivated terraces, olive groves and forests of holm-oak that typify the region.

Riffian Coastline
East of the small village of Torres de Alcalá there are some attractive and unspoilt caves and bays, including Kalah Iris, a haven of calm and solitude.

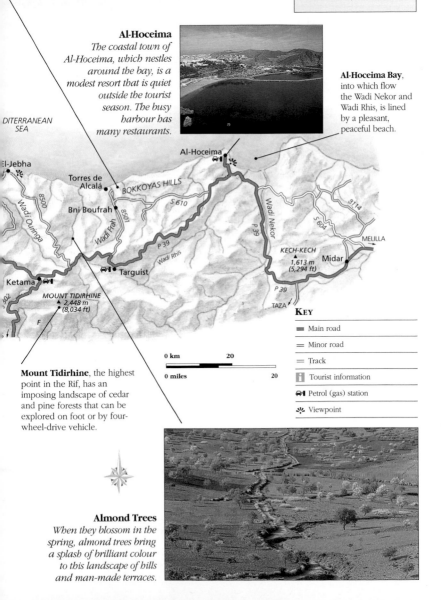

Al-Hoceima
The coastal town of Al-Hoceima, which nestles around the bay, is a modest resort that is quiet outside the tourist season. The busy harbour has many restaurants.

Al-Hoceima Bay, into which flow the Wadi Nekor and Wadi Rhis, is lined by a pleasant, peaceful beach.

KEY

▬	Main road
═	Minor road
═	Track
ℹ	Tourist information
⛽	Petrol (gas) station
☀	Viewpoint

Mount Tidirhine, the highest point in the Rif, has an imposing landscape of cedar and pine forests that can be explored on foot or by four-wheel-drive vehicle.

Almond Trees
When they blossom in the spring, almond trees bring a splash of brilliant colour to this landscape of hills and man-made terraces.

Nador ⑭

Road map E1. 154 km (96 miles) east of El-Hoceima and 13 km (8 miles) south of Melilla. ⚇ *200,000.* ▦ ⬙ ⬙ *Sun & Mon.*

WITH WIDE AVENUES, shops, a multitude of cafés, restaurants and hotels, banks and residential blocks, Nador, somewhat unexpectedly, has all the trappings of a major town. It is, indeed, enjoying great prosperity.

Nador's dramatic economic growth has been fuelled both by its traditional industries, such as metallurgy (its metal-processing complex is supplied with iron ore from the Rif and anthracite from Jerada) and by new ones, namely textiles, chemicals and electrics. The waves of emigration that have affected the whole of the eastern Rif have also contributed significantly to Nador's development. While immigrants here are key investors and consumers, funds sent home by workers from abroad have swelled the town's economy.

Nador's location, 13 km (8 miles) from the Spanish enclave of Melilla, also accounts for the town's prosperity, through illegal trafficking. Through well-oiled channels, goods cross the border at many points, including **Beni Enzar**, the border post nearest Melilla. Here, small consignments are transported across the border several times a day, packed in

The mountainous Mediterranean coastline near Melilla

small trucks or loaded onto the backs of women and children. The goods are then disposed of in broad daylight in two huge markets in Nador.

Beni Enzar, on the edge of Nador, is the foremost fishing port on the Mediterranean coast, and it also has modern naval dockyards.

Melilla ⑮

Sovereign Spanish town.
Road map E1. 167 km (104 miles) east of El-Hoceima and 153 km (95 miles) northwest of Oujda. ⚇ *70,000.* ▦ ❙ *Tourist and information office near Plaza de Toros; (952) 67 54 44.* ⬙ *Easter Week; Festival of Spain (early Jul); Our Lady of Victory (early Sep).*

ALTHOUGH ABOUT 40 per cent of the population of the Spanish town of Melilla is Moroccan, the way of life here is still very Andalusian.

It was once a Carthaginian, then a Roman, trading post. Located on the road from Fès and being the destination of caravans from Sijilmassa and the Sahara, Melilla became a busy port during the Middle Ages. The town has been in Spanish hands since 1497.

Under the Protectorate, Melilla underwent rapid development thanks to its status as a free zone. However, Moroccan independence and the closure of the border with Algeria cut it off from the hinterland. The town is now experiencing a difficult period. Consumer demand in this Spanish town means that tax-free goods find a ready

market. This has contributed to a thriving illegal trade, which in turn creates the appearance of prosperity.

Set on a rocky peninsula and enclosed within 16th- and 17th-century walls, the fortress-like Medina Sidonia district constitutes the upper town. The Puerta de la Marina leads through to a tracery of alleys, vaulted passages, steps and several small squares, some with a chapel or church. The Puerta de Santiago leads through to Plaza de Armas, west of the old town.

The church of **La Purísima Concepción**, in the north-

General view of Melilla

west of the old town, contains some fine Baroque altarpieces; on the high altar stands an 18th-century statue of Our Lady of Victory, patron saint of Melilla. Passing behind the church and following the ramparts, you will come to the **Musée Municipal** (Town Museum). Here, Melilla's Phoenician, Carthaginian and Roman periods are represented by ceramics, coins and brace-lets that were discovered in the vicinity of the town.

Mediterranean cactus

◁ **Blossoming almond trees in the Nekkor valley**

KIF

Kif plantation in the Rif

Until relatively recent times, the cultivation of kif (cannabis) was the preserve of a few tribes around Ketama. Kif plantations have multiplied and are now found in several provinces between Chefchaouen and Al-Hoceima. Once grown only in the high valleys of the central Rif, the plant is today also cultivated on the slopes of low-lying valleys. Growing *Cannabis sativa*, "the curative herb", as well as Indian hemp, is highly lucrative and underpins the entire economy of the Rif. Although growing and smoking it (which are traditional in the region) are tolerated on a localized basis, its commercial exploitation is illegal. This has given rise to a major smuggling trade, which the Moroccan authorities are fighting with financial assistance from the European Union. The proposed solution is to introduce alternative crops and to open up the Rif by building a coastal road from Tangier to Saïdia, passing through Ceuta and Al-Hoceima.

Various stone implements from the western Sahara are also exhibited.

The circular Plaza de España links the old town with the new, which was begun at the end of the 19th century. Avenida del Rey Juan Carlos is the new town's busiest street.

🏛 **Musée Municipal**
🕐 *Tue–Sun.* 🈺

Cap des Trois Fourches ⓰

Road map E1. 30 km (18 miles) from Melilla by road then track.

THE ROAD FROM Beni Enzar to the Cap des Trois Fourches offers some stunning views of Melilla and the Mediterranean Sea. The part of the cape beyond the Charrana lighthouse is one of

the most beautiful promontories in Morocco.

The cape is lined with bays and beaches nestling against the rocky coast. However, the coast road is narrow and difficult to drive, so care should be taken.

Moulouya Estuary ⓱

Road map E1. From Nador to Ras Kebdana, then on to Saïdia, road 8101, then roads 8100 and S401.

THE WHOLE AREA between the Bou Areg lagoon and the estuary of Wadi Moulouya is a rich and fascinating nature reserve. A great variety of birds – dunlin, plover, oystercatcher, little egret, redshank, black-tailed godwit and flamingoes, terns, and different species of gulls –

Peasant woman, Moulouya valley

come to spend the winter in this marshy area. The dunes are home to woodcock, plovers, herons and storks.

The vegetation in this area is equally diverse: spurge and sea holly grow on the dunes, while glasswort, reeds and rushes cover the marshes, which are the habitat of dragonflies, grasshoppers and sand spiders.

The Cap des Trois Fourches, offering some breathtaking views and stunning coastal landscapes

Zegzel Gorge ⑱

ONE OF THE MOST scenic routes in Morocco is road 5306 from Berkane to Taforalt. It follows the course of Wadi Zegzel as the river winds through deep gorges and along valleys and hillsides. Many of the caves that have been hollowed out of the cliffs by the action of water, such as the Grotte du Chameau and Grotte de Tghasrout, contain impressive stalactites and stalagmites. A return by road 5308 offers the opportunity to enjoy breathtaking views of the mountains and the Angad plain, and of almond groves, villages and isolated *marabouts*. Road 5319, then road P27, lead back to Oujda, or Berkane via Ahfir, a town established by the French in 1910.

Grotte du Chameau ②
Dug into the mountainside by a hot underground stream, Grotte du Chameau (Camel Cave) contains several great halls with stalactites and stalagmites.

Wadi Zegzel Gorge ①
With the reddish cliffs of the mountainside towering above, the river valley traverses a lush green landscape, sometimes widening in places where it cuts through terraces planted with olive and fruit trees.

Beni-Snassen Mountains ③
In several places, the road offers spectacular views of the mountains, which bear the marks of erosion. Here also are hamlets with pisé houses and terraces with vines and olive trees.

Saïdia ⑲

Road map F1. 50 km (31 miles) northwest of Oujda. 🏘 2,800. 🚌 🎭 *Folk Arts Festival (Aug).* 🛍 *Sun.*

AT THE NORTHERN extremity of the fertile Triffa plain, an agricultural and wine-growing area, is the little town of Saïdia, located on the Wadi Kiss estuary. For the last 20 km (12 miles) before it reaches the sea, this river constitutes the border between Morocco and Algeria.

Saïdia is a coastal resort with a fine beach edged with mimosa and eucalyptus, the reason behind the town's name "Blue Pearl". In summer the beach is crowded with Moroccan tourists. A folk arts festival is held at the Palais du Festival on Boulevard Mohammed V in August.

Saïdia may soon be home to a new resort which will overlook a new marina and will accommodate over 1000 guests.

Oujda ⑳

Road map F2. 🏘 800,000. ✈ 15 km (9 miles) 🚌 🚋 🚉 ℹ *Place du 16 Août 1953; (056) 68 43 29 or (055) 68 15 31, and railway station.* 🎭 *Moussem of Sidi Yahia (Sep).* 🛍 *Wed & Sun.*

THE HISTORY of Oujda has been shaped by its geographical location on a crossroads. In the Ville Nouvelle, the main shops and the banks, and several large brasseries with spacious terraces, are concentrated on Avenue Mohammed V and around Place du 16 Août 1953.

The medina, still partly enclosed by ramparts, is easy to explore, being small enough to wander about in without becoming disoriented. Rue el-Mazouzi, a major axis, crosses the medina from west to east, ending at Bab Sidi Abdel Ouahab. Various souks are located on this main street. The *kissaria*, which is lined with arcades, has shops selling various types of textiles, kaftans and velvets as well as looms and skeins of wool. The small squares where the

View of Jbel Fourhal ④
The highest point of the Beni Snassen mountains, Jbel Fourhal (1,532 m/5,025 ft) is partly covered with forests of holm-oak and scarred by areas of limestone scree.

KEY

- Suggested route
= Other roads
⚐ Viewpoint

0 km   3

0 miles   3

TIPS FOR DRIVERS

Departure point: Berkane, 60 km (37 miles) from Oujda on the P27.
Length: 134 km (83 miles).
Follow the 5306 for 20 km (12 miles) along the Zegzel Gorge. Road 5308, the Route de Corniche, skirts the Beni Snassen Mountains but is in a bad state of repair. Road 5319 leads back to the P27, for the return trip to Oujda.
Stopping-off points: Although it is possible to find a meal in Ahfir, it is best to take a picnic. Berkane (Hotel Laetizia) offers basic accommodation. For this trip it is more convenient to stay at Oujda (Hotel Moussafir, Place de la Gare. 📞 *056 68 82 02).*

SAÏDIA
Ahfir
Col de Guerbouss
539 m
(1,769 ft)
MOUNTAINS
Almou
OUJDA

Oulad Jabeur Fouaga ⑤
In this small village the houses that cluster around the mosque have roofs of earth and thatch, which is typical of the region. Some have a central courtyard.

Almond Trees ⑥
Almond trees, grown on terraces, are widely cultivated in the region. Their blossom adds a splash of colour to this often harsh, high limestone environment.

Beni-Snassen Mountain Road ⑦
This mountain road winds up the hillsides and threads its way above dramatic precipices. On certain days there is a view of the Angad plain, where the town of Oujda was built.

El-Ma Souk (Water Market) and the Attarine Souk take place contain trees and fountains, and are the living centre of the medina.

The **Musée Ethnographique**, outside the ramparts, contains local costumes and items relating to daily life.

🏛 **Musée Ethnographique**
Parc Lalla Meriem. 📞 (056) 68 56 31. ◻ daily. 🚫

ENVIRONS: Sidi Yahia, 6 km (4 miles) east of Oujda, is an oasis with abundant springs. Nearby is the tomb of Sidi Yahia ben Younes, patron

Doorway in the medina at Oujda

saint of Oujda. Venerated by Muslims, Jews and Christians alike, he is sometimes equated with St John the Baptist.

Figuig ㉑

Road map F3, 368 km (229 miles) south of Oujda. 🚶 14,600. 🚌 from Oujda. 🛈 Oujda; (056) 79 80 75. 🎪 Tue & Sun.

A N OASIS located at an altitude of 900 m (2,955 ft), Figuig consists of seven villages, or *ksour*, spread out in a vast palm plantation that covers almost

20 sq km (8 sq miles). The water provided by the artesian springs irrigates a large number of gardens, which lie behind clay walls. **Zenaga**, a typical *ksar*, is the largest of the villages, while El-Oudaghir is the administrative centre. The top of its minaret offers a view of the palm grove.

Figuig, at the crossroads of major caravan routes, was a busy caravanserai during the Middle Ages but lost its importance over the following centuries. More recently, the closure of the border with Algeria deprived it of its role as a border post, which it once shared with Oujda.

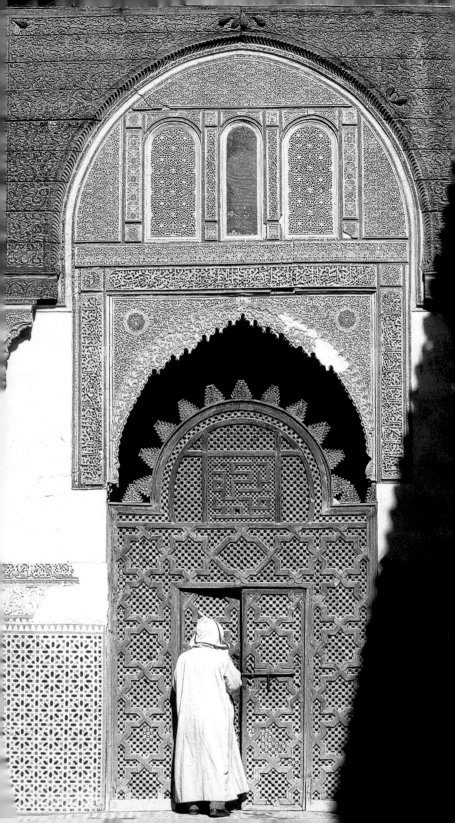

FÈS

....

L OCATED BETWEEN *the fertile lands of the Saïs and the forests of the Middle Atlas, Fès is the oldest of Morocco's imperial cities. It is the embodiment of the country's history and its spiritual and religious capital, and has been declared a World Heritage Site by UNESCO. Morocco's third-largest city, it consists of Fès el-Bali, the historic centre; Fès el-Jedid, the imperial city of the Merinids; and, located further south, the modern districts created under the Protectorate.*

Idriss I founded Madinat Fas, on the right bank of the River Fès, in 789. In 808, his son, Idriss II, built another town on the left bank, which was known as El-Alya (High Town). In 818, these two cities, each within their own walls, received hundreds of Muslim families who had been expelled from Córdoba. Soon afterwards, some 300 refugee families from Kairouan, in Tunisia, found asylum in El-Alya, which then became known as Karaouiyine, after them. Within a few years, the two towns became the centre of the Arabization and Islamization of Morocco.

In the mid-11th century, the Almoravids united the two towns, building a wall around them. The Almohads took the city in 1145, after a long siege. Fès then became the country's foremost cultural and economic metropolis, thanks in large part to its recently founded university. In 1250, the Merinids raised Fès to the status of imperial capital and endowed it with prestigious buildings. To the west of the old town they established a new royal city, Fès el-Jedid (New Fès). Conquered by the Alaouites in 1666, Fès was spurned by Moulay Ismaïl, who chose Meknès as his capital. The city's decline continued until the early 20th century.

When the Protectorate was established in 1912, a Ville Nouvelle (New Town) was built. After independence this was filled by the prosperous citizens of the old medina, while the country people, rootless and poor, crowded into the old town. However, UNESCO's ongoing restoration programme has saved the historic city of Fès el-Bali.

The rooftops of the Karaouiyine Quarter, Fès el-Bali

◁ The entrance to the Bou Inania Medersa in the Karaouiyine Quarter, Fès el-Bali

Exploring Fès

SEEN FROM THE SUMMIT of the hill of the Merinid Tombs, Fès appears as a compact and tightly woven urban fabric. Enclosed within its defensive walls, Fès el-Bali, the historic medina, is a sea of rooftops from which emerge minarets and domes. Wadi Fès separates the two historic entities: the Andalusian Quarter to the east, and the Karaouiyine Quarter to the west. Fès el-Jedid *(see pp180–83)* is built on a height south of the medina. Notable features here include the royal palace and the former Jewish quarter. The Ville Nouvelle (New Town), dating from the Protectorate, lies further south.

Rue Talaa Kebira, Fès el-Bali

KEY

	Medina
	Historic building
—	Ramparts
	Bus station
P	Parking
⊠	Post office
✚	Hospital
C	Mosque
✡	Synagogue
⚑	Muslim cemetery
▪	Jewish cemetery

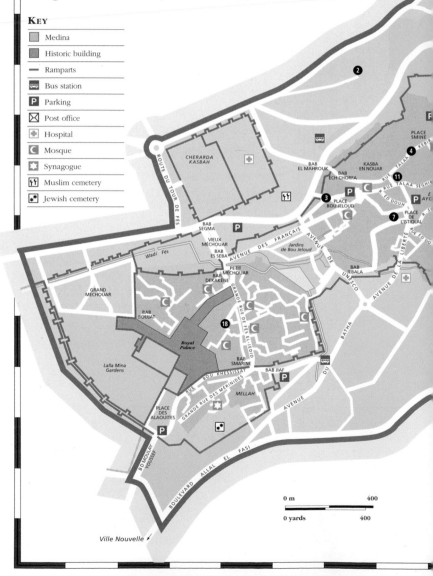

0 m 400
0 yards 400

Ville Nouvelle

GETTING AROUND
Both Fès el-Bali and Fès el-Jedid can be explored only on foot since the labyrinthine layout of these quarters is unsuitable for motorized traffic. Parking is available near Bab Boujeloud or Bab el-Ftouh, or on Place des Alaouites. Buses (often very crowded) run between Ville Nouvelle and both Fès el-Bali and Fès el-Jedid. It is best to take a *petit taxi (see p366)*. *Petits taxis* can be found near the post office, at Bab Boujeloud and in the vicinity of the large hotels.

Carpets spread out on a terrace in the medina

SEE ALSO

• *Where to Stay* pp308–9

• *Where to Eat* pp327–8

SIGHTS AT A GLANCE

Historic Buildings
Fondouk el-Nejjarine ⑥
Merinid Tombs ①
Zaouia of Moulay Idriss II ⑧

Streets, Squares and Historic Quarters
Andalusian Quarter ⑮
Fès el-Jedid pp180–83 ⑱
Place el-Seffarine ⑬
Rue Talaa Kebira ④
The Souks ⑤
Tanners' Quarter ⑫

Mosques
Andalusian Mosque ⑭
Karaouiyine Mosque pp176–7 ⑰

Medersas
Bou Inania Medersa pp172–3 ⑪
El-Attarine Medersa ⑨
El-Cherratine Medersa ⑩

Museums
Musée des Armes ②
Musée Dar el-Batha pp168–9 ⑦

Gates
Bab Boujeloud ③
Bab el-Ftouh ⑯

The Merinid tombs, overlooking the medina of Fès

Merinid Tombs ❶

North of the medina, on the hill of the Merinid tombs.

STANDING AMONG olive trees, cacti and blue agaves, the 16th-century ruins that overlook Fès el-Bali are those of a Merinid palace and necropolis. Ancient chroniclers recorded that these tombs elicited wonderment because of their magnificent marble and the splendour of their coloured epitaphs. Today, the tombs are very dilapidated, and the area is popular with petty thieves, but it offers an impressive view of the city. The view from the terrace of the Hôtel Les Mérinides (see p308) is equally fine.

The stretch of wall immediately beneath the hill is the oldest part of the medina's defences. Parts of the curtain wall date from the Almohad period (12th century), notably Borj Kaoukeb, near which the lepers' quarter was once located. The tombs overlook a tiered cemetery which stretches as far as Bab Guissa, an Almohad gateway dating from the 13th century.

Silver dagger, Musée des Armes

Musée des Armes ❷

Borj Nord. ☎ (055) 64 52 41.
⬛ for renovation. Call (055) 63 56 26 for details.

BORJ NORD WAS BUILT in 1582, on the orders of the Saadian sultan Ahmed el-Mansour (1578–1603). From its vantage point over the city, the fortress both defended and controlled Fès el-Bali. In 1963 the collection of weapons from the Musée Dar el-Batha (see pp168–9) was transferred here to create the Museum of Arms. Much of the collection, comprising over 8,000 pieces, comes from the Makina, the arsenal built by Moulay Hassan I at the end of the 19th century, although it was enriched by donations from various Alaouite sultans.

Some 1,000 pieces of weaponry are exhibited in 16 rooms, in a chronological display running from prehistory to the first half of the 20th century. Moroccan weapons are well represented and demonstrate the technical knowledge of Moroccan craftsmen. There is also an interesting collection of weapons from all over the world.

Bab Boujeloud ❸

Place du Pacha el-Baghdadi.

ENCLOSED WITHIN high walls, the large Place Pacha el-Baghdadi links the medina and Fès el-Jedid. On one side of the square stands Bab Boujeloud. Built in 1913, this fine monumental gate is the principal entrance into Fès el-Bali.

With the development of heavy artillery, the fortified gates of Fès lost their effectiveness as defences and came to be seen as decorative buildings, contributing to the city's prestige and helping to justify the levy of city taxes.

Bab Boujeloud, built in the Moorish style, consists of three perfectly symmetrical horseshoe arches. A rich decorative scheme consisting of geometric patterns, calligraphy, interlaced floral motifs and glazed tilework of many colours, with blue predominating, graces the façade. From this entranceway the silhouette of the minaret of the Bou Inania Medersa can be glimpsed on the left.

The Musée des Armes, housed in a 16th-century fortress

Rue Talaa Kebira ❹

Reached via Bab Boujeloud.

THIS THOROUGHFARE, whose name means "Great Climb" and which is partly covered by a cane canopy, is lined with small shops along almost its entire length. It is continued by the Ras Tiyalin and Aïn Allou souks and by spice markets. The street passes the *kissaria* and ends

Rue Talaa Kebira, the main thoroughfare in the medina of Fès

at the Karaouiyine Mosque *(see pp176–7)*. Running parallel to it at its southern end is another important street, Rue Talaa Seghira ("Short Climb"), which joins up with Rue Talaa Kebira at Aïn Allou. These streets are the two principal cultural and economic thoroughfares of Fès el-Bali. The city's most important buildings are located here.

Opposite the Bou Inania Medersa *(see pp172–3)* stands **Dar el-Magana** (House of the Clock), built by the ruler Abou Inan in 1357. It contains a water-clock built by Fassi craftsmen during the Merinid period. It is currently undergoing restoration.

Not far from here, level with a covered passage in the Blida Quarter, is the **Zaouia el-Tijaniya**, containing the tomb of Ahmed el-Tijani, master of *Tariqa el-Tijaniya* (The Way), a doctrine that spread widely throughout the Maghreb and sub-Saharan Africa. Further on are three musical instrument workshops. Makers of stringed instruments have almost completely disappeared from Fès; the only remaining practitioner is a craftsman in Rue Talaa Seghira, opposite Dar Mnebhi, who still makes *ouds* (lutes) by traditional methods. Beyond is the skindressers' *fondouk*, which contains leather workshops.

Across the Bou Rous bridge stands the **Ech Cherabliyine Mosque** (Mosque of the Slipper-Makers). Built by the Merinid sultan Abou el-Hassan, it is distinguished by its elegant minaret.

The Souks ❺

THE SOUKS OF Fès el-Bali spread out beyond the Ech Cherabliyine Mosque.

The location of each souk reflects a hierarchy dictated by the value placed on the various goods on offer in each of them. Makers and sellers are grouped together according to the products that they offer. Every type of craft has its own street, or part of a street, around the Karaouiyine Mosque, which has resulted in a logical but relatively complex layout. While the **El-Attarine Souk** sells spices, there is also a **Slipper Souk** and a **Henna Souk**, which is laid out in an attractive shaded square planted with arbuses. A plaque records that the Sidi Frijthe *maristan*, which was the largest mental asylum in the Merinid empire, once stood on this square. Built by Abou Yacoub Youssef (1286–1307), it also functioned as a hospital for storks. It was still in existence

Skin-dressing workshops, unchanged since the Middle Ages

in 1944. In the 16th century, Leo Africanus, known today for his accounts of his travels, worked there as a clerk for two years.

The *kissaria*, near the Zaouia of Moulay Idriss, marks the exact centre of the souks. This is a gridwork of covered streets where shops selling luxury goods are especially conspicuous. Some of the fine silks and brocades, high-quality kaftans and jewellery on offer here supply the international market.

Fondouk el-Nejjarine, a UNESCO World Heritage Site

Fondouk el-Nejjarine ❻

Place el-Nejjarine. **(** (055) 74 05 80. **Musée du Bois** ◯ 9:30am–6pm daily.

NOT FAR FROM the Henna Souk, the impressive Fondouk el-Nejjarine, with an elegant fountain, is one of the most renowned buildings in Fès. Built by the *amine* (provost) Adeyel in the 18th century, this former caravanserai provided food, rest and shelter to the traders in luxury goods arriving from the interior. Classed as a historic monument in 1916, it is now one of UNESCO's World Heritage Sites. Its restoration (completed in 1998) formed part of the preservation programme carried out on the whole medina. The *fondouk*'s three floors house the privately run **Musée du Bois** (Museum of Wood). The displays include carved doors from the Bou Inania Medersa *(see pp172–3)*.

Musée Dar el-Batha ⓐ

Dish with calligraphy, 14th century

THE PALACE OF DAR EL-BATHA was begun between 1873 and 1875 by Moulay el-Hassan, and was completed by Moulay Abdel Aziz in 1897. The location of the palace was an area of neglected gardens, which had been irrigated by a river. The sultan, who wanted to make the palace a residence worthy of being used for official receptions, added an imposing courtyard covered with coloured tiles and featuring a large fountain. He also laid out a large and very fine Andalusian garden. Despite many later alterations, the traditional Moorish features of this relatively recent building have survived.

EXPLORING THE COLLECTIONS OF THE MUSÉE DAR EL-BATHA

IN 1914, the Orientalist Alfred Bel made the first bequest to the future ethnographic musem which, by royal decree, became the museum of local crafts (Musée des Arts et des Traditions) in 1915.

Today, the permanent exhibition, which fills 12 rooms, consists of more than 500 objects selected from the 5,000 that the museum has acquired. They are shown in two large sections. The ethnographic section, featuring the arts and crafts of Fès and the rural crafts of neighbouring areas, fills the first eight rooms. The archaeological section is laid out in the four remaining rooms. Particularly notable is the display tracing the development of architecture in Fès, from the Idrissid period to that of the Alaouites.

BOOKS AND MANUSCRIPTS

ROOM 1 CONTAINS some extremely fine leather-bound books dating from the 11th century. Their embossed and gold-painted decoration is a tradition peculiar to Fès that stayed alive until the 17th century. Also on display are manuscript copies of the

Koran made on parchment in the 16th to 18th centuries; prayer books by the Sufi scholar El-Jazouli; and important manuscripts written in the Andalusian cursive style of calligraphy, which was widely used in Morocco in the 8th and 9th centuries. Examples of illuminated calligraphy with geometric decorative motifs, as well as other exhibits, highlight the role that Fès played in the development and diffusion of learning.

A soup tureen with blue and white decoration

CERAMICS

THE ORIGINAL LOCATION of the potters' souk, next to the Karaouiyine Mosque, is proof of the respect and repute in which the makers of the famous Fès blue and white ware were held. As well as this pottery, Room 2 contains dishes and *jebbana* (traditional earthenware vessels) with polychrome decoration in blue, green, yellow and brown over a white tin glaze, or with *sboula* (herringbone)

or *chebka* (scale) motifs. Some of the dishes with green motifs displayed in Case 11 are examples of *zargbmil*, the famous "centipede" style of decoration characteristic of Fès.

LEATHERWORK

EXHIBITS IN ROOM 3 include a fragment of a 13th-century candelabra from the Karaouiyine Mosque, alms measures made in Fès in the 14th to 18th centuries, some fine astrolabes and various instruments for determining the times of day at which prayers are to be said, for indicating the direction of Mecca and for tracking the lunar calendar.

Alms measur (18th century

There are also lamps, writing tables and a medicine bowl with verses from the Koran and formulae; equipment for use in the hammam and for brewing and drinking tea; and a fine 18th-century tray decorated with a complex geometric pattern. Each of these pieces demonstrates the consummate skill and exceptional creativity of the craftsmen of Fès, who in making them fulfilled the religious, scientific and symbolic needs of their time.

WOOD, EMBROIDERY AND WEAVING

THE FURNITURE in Room 4, including chests, sets of shelves and other pieces, show both the range of woods used (cedar, thuya, almond, walnut, ebony, mahogany and citron) and a range of cabinet-making

Lintel from the Andalusian Mosque, carved in 980

Detail of 19th-century embroidery from Fès

cabinet-making skills. Shown here are carved and painted or leather-covered furniture, and furniture with iron fittings, marquetry decoration and mother-of-pearl and ivory inlay. There is also a fine 14th-century Moorish chest, made to hold the most valuable pieces of a bride's trousseau as they were carried to her new home.

Double pitcher from the Rif (19th century)

The exhibits in Room 5 consist of examples of the different types of Fassi embroidery. These include exquisite examples of *terz sqalli*, lamé embroidery in which gold thread and gold dust are used; *al-aleuj* embroidery, a technique very similar to Persian stitch; and *erz alghorza*, counted-thread embroidery, the most famous type of Fassi embroidery, usually in red, blue, purple and green silk. Women's costumes, headdresses and accessories in embroidered silk decorated with trimmings demonstrate the high degree of refinement in traditional Fassi dress.

RURAL CRAFTS

OBJECTS OF everyday life from various regions of Morocco are exhibited in Room 6: pottery made by the women of the Rif, carpets from the Middle Atlas, and fine Berber jewellery, such as brooches, pectorals, necklaces, finger rings and bracelets. All these show the skills and inventiveness of Moroccan craftsmen and craftswomen.

DOORS

A DISPLAY OF doors fills Room 7. Doors from ordinary houses and large palace doors carved and decorated with patterns of nails are shown with a selection of door locks from houses in Fès.

THE ART OF ZELLIJ

ROOM 9 IS DEVOTED to *zellij* tilework made in Fès from the 14th to the 18th centuries and among the finest of its kind.

One of the exhibits, a remarkable panel from the Bou Inania Medersa, perfectly exemplifies this brilliant tradition of architectural decoration in Morocco. The rich aesthetic vocabulary of this art form brings to life plain surfaces with a lively play of patterns and colours.

MONUMENTAL WOODCARVING

THE DISPLAYS IN Rooms 10 and 11 trace the evolution of monumental woodcarving in Fès from the 9th century to the present day. Among the most interesting pieces are a lintel from the Karaouiyine Mosque (877) and the monumental door from the El-Attarine Medersa (1325). The splendid lintel from the Andalusian

Minbar dating from 1350, from the Bou Inania Medersa

Mosque, made in 980, is a masterpiece of religious art of the early years of Islam in Morocco. The museum's collection also includes the minbar from the Andalusian Mosque, which is exhibited alternately with that from the Bou Inania Medersa (1350).

FUNERARY ARCHITECTURE

VARIOUS PIECES of Muslim funerary architecture and a selection of tombstones from Volubilis end the museum's displays.

Arabic Calligraphy

ISLAM TRADITIONALLY FORBIDS all figurative representation, and since the 8th century this prohibition has encouraged the use of calligraphy in Arabic civilization. Decorative writing became an art form that was used not only for manuscripts but also to decorate buildings. Islamic calligraphy is closely connected to the revelation of the Koran: the word of God is to be transcribed in a beautiful script far finer than secular writing. Writing out not only the Koran, but also the 99 names of Allah is considered to be a very pious

Calligraphic manuscript

undertaking. The importance of this art form in Islamic civilization is shown by the carved, painted or tiled friezes that decorate the walls and domes of mosques and medersas, as well as by the thousands of scientific, literary and religious calligraphic manuscripts preserved in public and private libraries. Maghrebi script, used in the Maghreb, in Andalusia and in the Sudan, is derived from Kufic script, which is named after the town of Kufa, in Iraq, where this style of writing originated.

MANUSCRIPTS AND FRIEZES

Quotations from the Koran are omnipresent in manuscripts and calligraphic friezes. Calligraphy appears in all dimensions and on a great variety of surfaces. Maghrebi script is characterized by rounded letters combined with slender descenders and ascenders.

This detail from an illuminated manuscript in Maghrebi script, produced in Rabat in the 8th century, features plant motifs.

This illuminated manuscript *of a hadih, recording the words and deeds of the Prophet Mohammed, is in Maghrebi script. With gold and bright colours, illumination enriches both religious and secular manuscripts. The finest illuminated manuscripts are preserved in the Royal Library in Rabat.*

Cursive script, *like this example from the Bou Inania Medersa, may appear in the form of carved zellij work. Calligraphic friezes, often with a religious content, were made both for public buildings and private houses.*

Decorative details, *like this one from an anonymous manuscript of a musical score, shows that calligraphy was sometimes more ornamental than purely functional.*

Calligraphy on marble, *Mosque of Hassan II.*

INKWELLS

Used for calligraphy and for illumination, inkwells were made in the shape of a *koubba*, the shrine of a Muslim saint.

The compartments in *these* mejma *inkwells were designed to hold the inks of different colours that were used for illumination.*

Fountain for ablutions at the Zaouia of Moulay Idriss II

Zaouia of Moulay Idriss II **8**

🚫 to non-Muslims. Glimpses possible through the open doors.

THE ZAOUIA of Moulay Idriss II, containing the tomb of the second Idrissid ruler (considered to be the founder of Fès) is the most venerated shrine in Morocco. Built in the centre of the city at the beginning of the 18th century, during the reign of Moulay Ismaïl, the building was restored in the mid-19th century. The pyramidal dome that covers the saint's tomb and its polychrome minaret give it a majestic silhouette. The courtyard of the mosque contains a fountain which consists of a white marble basin on a shaft, richly decorated with *zellij* tilework.

The *borm*, the perimeter wall around the *zaouia*, is also holy. The narrow streets leading to the shrine are barred at mid-height by a wooden beam that is supposed to prevent the passage of beasts of burden. The *borm* also made the shrine an inviolable place, so that in the past outlaws would find sanctuary here.

At the end of each summer, during a *moussem* lasting two to three days, this place of pilgrimage attracts not only the inhabitants of Fès but also people from the surrounding countryside and mountain-dwellers from distant tribes. They all come to receive a

blessing and *baraka* ("bene-ficient force"). The motley crowd of the faithful is made up of pilgrims and beggars, as well as nougat, candle and incense sellers whose goods are used as tomb offerings.

Decorative column in the El-Attarine Medersa

El-Attarine Medersa **9**

Opposite the Karaouiyine Mosque.
📞 (055) 62 34 60. 🕐 8:30am–5:30pm daily. 🕐 11:30am–3pm Fri. 🈳

THE EL-ATTARINE Medersa (Medersa of the Spice Sellers) stands in the neigh-bourhood of the Karaouiyine Mosque and the El-Attarine Souk. With the Bou Inania Medersa *(see pp172–3)*, it is considered to be one of the wonders of Moorish architecture. It was built between 1323 and 1325 by the Merinid sultan Abou Saïd Othman, and has all the elements specific to a medieval Muslim school.

The highly decorated entrance leads through to a courtyard paved with *zellij* tilework in a two-colour pattern of brown and white, and enclosing an ablutions fountain. A cladding of polychrome tiles covers the base of the courtyard's four interior walls and its columns. A door with fine decoration and exquisite fittings leads from the courtyard to the prayer hall, which contains a mihrab. The prayer hall has a highly decorated ceiling, walls featuring luxuriant stuccowork and *zellij* work, and lintels with epigraphic decoration.

The students' rooms, look-ing onto the courtyard from the upper floor, have wind-ows fronted by turned wood-en railings. The terrace offers a view of the rooftops of Fès el-Bali and the courtyard of the Karaouiyine Mosque.

El-Cherratine Medersa **10**

Rue El-Cherratine. 🈳

LOCATED SOUTHEAST of the Karaouiyine Mosque, in Rue el-Cherratine (Street of the Ropemakers), this medersa was built by Moulay Rachid, the first Alaouite sultan, in 1670. Although it is structurally similar to the Merinid medersas, it is less elaborately decorated. Adding to the building's austerity are the high, narrow residential units known as *douiras*, which stand in three corners of the courtyard. The tiny cells inside were for the use of students.

Entry into the medersa is through beautiful double doors cased in engraved bronze. The doors open onto a passageway with a fine carved and painted wooden ceiling, which in turn leads to the Moorish courtyard.

The El-Cherratine Souk, where ropemakers sell their wares

Bou Inania Medersa ⓫

Glazed tiles on the medersa's roof

'T̲his is the largest and most sumptuously decorated medersa ever built by the Merinids. Constructed between 1350 and 1355 by the sultan Abou Inan, it is the only medersa in Morocco that has a minbar (pulpit) and a minaret. A mosque, cathedral, students' residence and school combined, its functions have determined its architectural complexity. The one-storey building, on a rectangular plan, is arranged around a square Moorish courtyard paved with marble and onyx, and surrounded on three sides by a cloister. It is one of the few Islamic religious buildings that is open to non-Muslims.

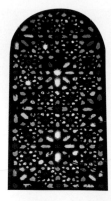

Stained-glass Windows
The windows of the prayer hall feature old stained-glass panels.

Capitals
The carved motifs on the capitals in the medersa show Moorish influence.

Pitched roofs over the mosque

★ Prayer Hall
The mihrab (above) is surmounted by stained-glass windows. The minbar (1350) is now in the Musée Dar el-Batha (see pp168–9).

Zellij Tilework
In the medersa, the three decorative bands always appear in the same order: geometric tilework below, cursive script carved into tiles in the centre, and stuccowork above.

STAR FEATURES

★ Façade

★ Prayer Hall

THE MOROCCAN MEDERSA

**Student at
a medersa**

The medersa was both a cultural and a religious establishment. It was primarily a residential college, designed for local students from the town or city and especially for those from the immediate or more distant rural areas, but also for anyone who came in search of learning. It was an extension of the great university-mosque, an institution once restricted to the study of religion, law, science and even the arts. It was finally a place of prayer and reflection. The medersas of Fès, home to the greatest scholars in the country, were the most highly esteemed in Morocco.

VISITORS' CHECKLIST

Rue Talaa Kebira. ☐ (to non-Muslims) 8:30am–6:30pm Wed–Mon.

Windows
The ornate windows of the students' rooms on the upper floor are framed by stuccowork surmounted by muqarnas.

★ Façade
Richly decorated with zellij *tilework, stuccowork and sculpted wood, the façade runs the gamut of the Moorish decorative repertoire.*

The minaret, one of the finest in Fès, is decorated with a frieze featuring merlons. The lantern is topped by a similar frieze.

Shops

Beggars' Gate

Main entrance

Student's cell

Courtyard paved with marble and onyx

Wooden Screen
The magnificent carved wooden screen of the main entrance is framed by sturdy pillars. The adjoining door, of much plainer design, was known as Beggars' Gate.

The Tanneries of Fès

OFTEN LOCATED NEAR water-courses, and usually some distance from residential quarters because of the unpleasant odours that they produced, tanneries made a substantial contribution to

Blue leather bag

a city's economy. Tanning is a craft with traditions that go back thousands of years. The process turns animal hides into soft, rot-proof leather. Once tanned, the hides are passed on to leatherworkers.

Vats, some of which have been in use for centuries, are used for soaking skins after the hair and flesh have been removed. The tanning solution that turns them into leather is obtained from the bark of pomegranate or mimosa.

The tanned hides are hung out to dry on the terraces of the medina, as here, or in other parts of Fès, such as the Bab el-Guissa cemetery. The roofs of houses and the hillsides around the city may also be used as drying areas.

STAGES IN THE TANNING PROCESS

In Fès, the tanneries *(chouaras)* are located near Wadi Fès. The hides of sheep, goats, cows and camels undergo several processes – including the removal of hair and flesh, followed by soaking in vats, then by drying and rinsing – before they are ready to be dyed and handed over to leatherworkers.

The dried hides are rinsed in generous quantities of water. They are then softened by being steeped in baths of fatty solutions.

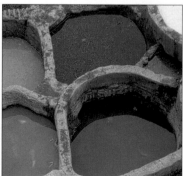

Natural pigments, obtained from certain plants and minerals, are still used by Moroccan craftsmen to colour the hides. However, chemical dyes are also used today.

Dyed leather is used to make many types of useful and decorative objects, such as embroidered bags, babouches, pouffes and clothing. These goods are offered for sale in the numerous souks in the medina of Fès.

Tanners' Quarter ⑫

North of Place el-Seffarine.

THE CHOUARA, or Tanners' Quarter, has been located near Wadi Fès since the Middle Ages. Its dyeing vats, in the midst of houses in the Blida quarter, are best seen from neighbouring terraces. Although pervaded by an unpleasantly strong smell, this is the most lively and picturesque of all the souks in Fès.

Place el-Seffarine ⑬

FÈS IS THE MOST important centre for the production of brassware and silverware in Morocco. The workshops of brass-workers and coppersmiths that line Place el-Seffarine have been here for centuries. The pretty fountain with fleur-de-lis decoration is worth a look. It was probably built by French convicts in the 16th century.

North of the square is the 14th-century **Karaouiyine Library**, which was set up on the orders of the sultan Abou Inan. It was used by the greatest Moorish men of learning, including the philosopher and doctor Ibn Rushd, known as Averroës (*see p231*), the philosopher Ibn Tufayl, the historian Ibn Khaldoun and the 16th-century traveller Leo Africanus. The manuscripts that once formed part of the library's collection have been transferred to the Royal Library in Rabat.

Brassworker making trays in Place el-Seffarine

The **El-Seffarine Medersa**, opposite the Karaouiyine Library, was built in 1280 and is the oldest medersa in Morocco that is still in use. The **El-Mesbahiya Medersa**, also north of the square, was built by the Merinid sultan Abou el Hassan in 1346. Further on, on the right, is the 16th-century **Tetouani Fondouk**, which accommodated traders and students from Tetouan.

Place el-Seffarine leads to **Rue des Teinturiers** (Dyers' Street), which runs parallel to the *wadi* and where skeins are hung out to dry.

Karaouiyine Library
Place el-Seffarine. ☎ (055) 62 34 60. ◯ 9am–noon Sat–Thu, 8:30–11am Fri.

The north entrance of the Andalusian Mosque

Andalusian Mosque ⑭

Accessible via Rue el-Nekhaline or Bab Ftouh and Rue Sidi Bou Ghaleb. ● to non-Muslims.

ACCORDING TO LEGEND, this mosque was established by a religious woman, Mariam el-Fihri, sister of the founder of the Karaouiyine Mosque, and by the Andalusians who lived in the Karaouiyine Quarter. Its present appearance dates from the reign of the Almohad ruler Mohammed el-Nasser (13th century). The Merinids added a fountain in 1306 and funded the establishment of a library here in 1416. Non-Muslims can only admire the building from the exterior; notable are the great north entrance, with a carved cedar awning, and the domed Zenet minaret.

Andalusian Quarter ⑮

THE ANDALUSIAN QUARTER did not undergo the same development as the Kairaouiyine Quarter, located on the opposite bank of Wadi Fès and better provided with water. Nevertheless, this part of the city, which is quieter and more residential, has monuments that are worth a visit.

The **El-Sahrij Medersa**, built in 1321 takes its name from the large water basin in one of the courtyards. This is considered to be the third-finest medersa in Fès after the Bou Inania and the El-Attarine medersas. The **Mausoleum of Sidi Bou Ghaleb**, in the street of that name, is that of a holy man from Andalusia who lived and taught in Fès in the 12th century.

El-Sahrij Medersa
Rue Sidi Bou Ghaled. ☎ (055) 62 34 60 (information). ◯ 9:30am–12:30pm daily (9:30–11:30am Fri) & 2:30–6pm daily. ◪

Bab el-Ftouh ⑯

Southeast of the medina.

LITERALLY MEANING "Gate of the Aperture", the huge Bab el-Ftouh is also known as the Gate of Victory. It leads through to the Andalusian Quarter. The gate was built in the 10th century by a Zenet emir, and was altered in the 18th century, during the reign of the Alaouite ruler Sidi Mohammed ben Abdallah. Outside the ramparts, on a hill opposite the city, is the Bab el-Ftouh cemetery, where some of the most illustrious inhabitants of Fès are buried.

Bab el-Ftouh cemetery, resting place of some renowned teachers

Karaouiyine Mosque ⑰

ESTABLISHED IN 859, the Karaouiyine Mosque is one of the oldest and most illustrious mosques in the western Muslim world. The first university to be established in Morocco, it was frequented by such learned men as as Ibn Khaldoun *(see p181)*, Ibn el-Khatib, Averroës *(see p231)* and even Pope Sylvester II (909–1003). Named after the quarter in which it was built – that of refugees from Kairouan, in Tunisia – it was founded by Fatima bint Mohammed el-Fihri, a religious woman from Kairouan, who donated her worldly riches for its construction. It is still considered to be one of the main spiritual and intellectual centres of Islam and remains the seat of the Muslim university of Fès.

Pitched Roof
The roof of the mosque is covered in emerald-green tiles.

The prayer hall can hold 20,000 people.

★ The Prayer Hall
The hall is divided into 16 aisles by 270 columns, parallel to the qibla wall (indicating the direction of Mecca). It is lit by a magnificent 12th-century Almohad candelabra.

This door is one of 14 entrances to the mosque.

★ The Courtyard
The courtyard, or sahn, is paved with zellij tilework consisting of 50,000 pieces that were made especially for the floor of the mosque.

STAR FEATURES

★ **Courtyard**

★ **Prayer Hall**

Women's mosque

Ablutions Basin
This basin, in the centre of the courtyard, is carved from a single block of marble. It rests on a marble fountain to which the faithful come to carry out their ablutions, an essential preparation for prayer.

The minaret, in an early Almoravid style, is very similar in shape to a lookout tower.

THE ROLE OF THE MOSQUE

Each quarter of Fès has one or more mosques and other places of worship. Friday prayers take place in both large and small mosques. *Msids*, small oratories without a minaret, are designed for prayer and for teaching the Koran. *Zaouias* are sanctuaries where religious brotherhoods gather. The mosque, which stands both as a civic and a social symbol, is simultaneously a place of worship, a university, a tribunal, an inviolable place of asylum and a friendly meeting place. The call to prayer is given by the muezzin five times a day.

Saadian pavilion

Dome Over the Entrance
The main entrance into the courtyard of the mosque faces Rue Bou Touil. The monumental doorway is surmounted by a small striated dome.

Mashrabiyya
The main doorway has a mashrabiyya *screen to protect worshippers from prying eyes.*

Fès el-Jedid 🔞

FÈS EL-JEDID, meaning New Fès or White Fès, was built in 1276 by Merinid princes as a stronghold against the permanent threat of the rebellious Fassis, and as a vantage point from which to survey their activities in the old town. Surrounded by ramparts, Fès el-Jedid was primarily a kasbah and its political and military role predominated over the civic functions of a true Islamic town. It was the administrative centre of Morocco up to 1912.

Fès el-Jedid consists of several distinct units. In the west is the royal palace, and other buildings associated with it, and the Moulay Abdallah Quarter. In the south is the mellah, or Jewish quarter, a maze of dark, narrow streets. In the east are the Muslim quarters.

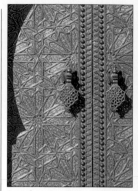

Brass doors into the Dar el-Makhzen engraved with a geometric pattern

Dar el-Makhzen, the royal palace in Fès

🏛 Dar el-Makhzen
🚫 *to the public.*

This palatial complex in the centre of Fès el-Jedid is surrounded by high walls and covers more than 80 ha (195 acres). It was the main residence of the sultan, together with his guard and his retinue of servants. Until relatively recent times, it was also where dignitaries of the *makhzen* (central government) came to carry out their duties. The palace is still used by the king of Morocco when he comes to Fès.

The main entrance to the complex, on the huge Place des Alaouites, is particularly imposing. Its magnificent Moorish gateway, which is permanently closed, is richly ornamented. The exquisitely engraved bronze doors are fitted with fine bronze knockers.

The walls enclose a disparate ensemble of buildings: palaces arranged around courtyards or large patios, as well as official buildings, notably the Dar el-Bahia, where Arab summit meetings are held; the Dar Ayad el-Kebira, built in the 18th century by Sidi Mohammed ben Abdallah; administrative and military buildings; and gardens, including the enclosed garden of Lalla Mina.

The complex also includes a mosque and a medersa, which was built in 1320 by the Merinid prince Abou Saïd Othman. There is also a menagerie.

🏛 Moulay Abdallah Quarter
Accessible via Bab Boujat or Bab Dekaken.

This district is completely closed off on its western side by the palace walls and the ramparts of Fès

el-Jedid. The quarter has two gateways linked by a central thoroughfare with a lattice-work of narrow streets leading off it. Bab Dekaken, the east gate, leads to the former *méchouar* (parade ground) and Bab Boujat, the west gate, pierces the city's walls. Nearby, in the main street, stands the Grand Mosque, a Merinid building dating from the 13th century that houses the necropolis of the sultan Abou Inan. Also on this street, in the direction of Bab Boujat, stands the Mosque of Moulay Abdallah, which was built in the mid-18th century.

🏛 Grande Rue de Fès el-Jedid and the Muslim Quarters
Accessible via Bab el-Semarine to the south and Bab Dekaken to the north.

The Muslim quarters – Lalla Btatha, Lalla Ghriba, Zebbala, Sidi Bounafaa, Boutouil and Blaghma – are the principal components of the urban agglomeration that Fassis know as Fès el-Jedid. The quarters are enclosed by the walls of Dar el-Makhzen to the west, and by a double line of walls to the east. Two gateways lead into the Muslim quarters; that on the northern side is Bab Dekaken, a simple opening in the fortifications

A tower set in the walls of the *méchouar*

◁ **Courtyard of the Es Sahrij Medersa, in the Andalusian Quarter**

IBN KHALDOUN

Abder Rahman Ibn Khaldoun was born in Tunis in 1332 into a family of great scholars. In about 1350 he came to Fès, which at the time was the leading intellectual centre in the Maghreb, and became diplomatic secretary to the sultan Abou Inan. He taught in Cairo, where he died in 1406. His extensive writings include *Discourse on Universal History*. He is considered to be the founder of sociology, and is without

a doubt one of the greatest historians of all time.

Modern-day portrait of Ibn Khaldoun

that once led to the former *méchouar*. On the southern side is the monumental **Bab el-Semarine** (Gate of the Farriers). This monumental vaulted gateway, beneath which a souk for all sorts of food takes place; the stalls are laid out in the old Merinid grain stores.

The two gates are connected by **Grande Rue de Fès el-Jedid**, the main north–south artery through the city. The street, covered by a cane canopy at its northern extremity, is lined with an almost continuous succession of shops. This congested thoroughfare is the economic centre of the royal city. At intervals it is flanked by quiet residential quarters with a maze-like layout like that of all Muslim towns.

On the western side of the street, a small quarter huddles around the **Lalla el-Azhar Mosque** (Mosque of

Detail of Bab Segma, north of the old *méchouar*

the Lady Flower), which was built by the Merinid sultan Abou Inan in 1357. On the eastern side are the humble quarters inhabited by the families of old warrior tribes. There are two important mosques here: Jama el-Hamra (Red Mosque) with a 14th-century minaret, and Jama el-Beïda (White Mosque).

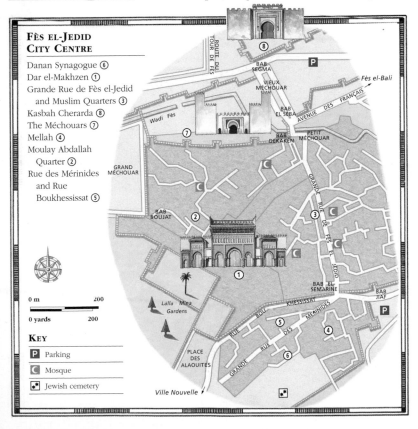

FÈS EL-JEDID CITY CENTRE

Danan Synagogue ⑥
Dar el-Makhzen ①
Grande Rue de Fès el-Jedid and Muslim Quarters ③
Kasbah Cherarda ⑧
The Méchouars ⑦
Mellah ④
Moulay Abdallah Quarter ②
Rue des Mérinides and Rue Boukhessissat ⑤

ROUTE DU TOUR DE FÈS

BAB SEGMA

VIEUX MÉCHOUAR

Fès el-Bali

Wadi Fès

BAB EL SEBA

AVENUE DES FRANÇAIS

BAB DEKAKEN

PETIT MÉCHOUAR

⑦

GRAND MÉCHOUAR

GRANDE RUE DE FÈS EL JEDID

BAB BOUJAT

②

③

①

BAB EL SEMARINE

BAB JIAF

RUE BOU

KHESSISSAT

RUE DES MÉRINIDES

⑤

④

⑥

Lalla Mina Gardens

PLACE DES ALAOUITES

GRANDE RUE

Ville Nouvelle

0 m   200
0 yards   200

KEY

🅿 Parking

Ⓒ Mosque

Jewish cemetery

Richly ornamented door to a house in the mellah

⊞ Mellah
Accessible via Place des Alaouites or Bab el-Mellah.

Bab el-Semarine, then Bab el-Mellah leads into the mellah, the Jewish quarter of Fès. The name *mellah* probably comes from the Arabic word for "salt", the terrain on which the quarter grew up.

This quarter, thought to be the first Jewish enclave to be established in Morocco, was originally located in the northern part of Fès el-Bali, in the El-Yahoudi Quarter next to the Karaouiyine district. In the early 13th century the Merinid rulers moved it near the palace, to the site of a former kasbah that was once occupied by the sultan's Syrian archers. The rulers of Fès had undertaken to protect the Jewish community, in return for an annual levy collected by the state treasury. The Jewish quarter's new location afforded the inhabitants greater security.

With its souks, workshops, schools, synagogues and a cemetery, the quarter flourished, providing the Jewish community with strong social cohesion and unrivalled opportunities for social advancement. Like the Muslims elsewhere, most of the Jews in the district were grouped according to their craft speciality. Thus Leo Africanus mentioned metalworking, recording that only the Jews worked with gold and silver. Today, the Jews of Fès have left to settle in Casablanca or have emigrated abroad, to Israel in particular.

Exploring the mellah reveals a striking contrast with the Muslim quarters. In architectural terms it is another world, the buildings being higher, narrower and more closely spaced. The present boundaries of the Jewish quarter were established only at the end of the 18th century, during the time of the Alaouite sultan Moulay Yazid, and the space available was small. As a result, the inhabitants were forced to build two-storey houses around tiny courtyards, and space to move around in is very restricted.

⊞ Rue des Mérinides and Rue Boukhessissat
Accessible via Bab el-Semarine or Place des Alaouites. **Jewellery Souk** ◯ *from 9am Sat–Thu.*

A central rectilinear axis, lined with various workshops and a *kissaria*, divides the mellah into two. All the commercial activity in the quarter takes place in this street, which was once the economic and spiritual centre of the mellah.

Rue des Mérinides cuts through the jewellery souk, where Jewish goldsmiths could once be seen at work.

Rue Boukhessissat separates the mellah from the Dar el-Makhzen. With some luxury residences, this was once the aristocratic area. The design of the houses here is the most unified and harmonious in the mellah. The rows of houses open onto the street, each house having a workshop on the ground floor. The upper storeys are fronted by the generously proportioned, finely carved wooden balconies that are characteristic of the Jewish architecture of Fès.

The Danan Synagogue, nestling between houses in the mellah

✦ Danan Synagogue
Rue Der el-Feran Teati. ◯ 9am–5pm daily. No entrance fee but a small contribution is requested. **Jewish Cemetery** ● *Sat.*

The 17th-century synagogue, the property of a family of rabbis from Andalusia, looks as if it has been squeezed in between the houses in the mellah. The interior is divided into four aisles. A trap door in the aisle on the far right opens onto a stairway that leads down to a *mikve* – a bath for ritual purification where the faithful were cleansed of their sins. Above this fourth aisle is the *azara*, the women's gallery, which

Tombs in the Jewish cemetery

The Vieux Méchouar, accessible via Bab el-Seba

offers an overall view of the synagogue. It is worth going out onto the terrace for a sweeping view of the mellah, and of the white tombs of the Jewish cemetery below.

The Méchouars
Méchouars are wide, walled parade grounds used on ceremonial military occasions. Processions and ceremonies, such as acts of allegiance and the acknowledgment of the royal right to rule, are also performed here. There are three such esplanades in Fès. The **Grand Méchouar,** in the northwest, also known as the Méchouar de Bab Boujat, is an extensive parade ground. The **Méchouar de Bab Dekaken** (Gate of the Benches), or **Vieux Méchouar**, in the northeast, is a rectangular esplanade with the high ramparts of the Makina on one side. It links

Bab Segma, the Merinid gate, and Bab el-Seba. It is here that the population gathered at sunset to watch dancers, musicians and storytellers. The **Petit Méchouar**, the smallest of the three, links the Méchouar de Bab Dekaken and Dar el-Makhzen. It can be reached through **Bab el-Seba** (Gate of the Lion), which once defended the entrance to the palace.

On Avenue des Français, just south of Bab el-Seba, a narrow street on the right, reachable through an opening in the wall, leads, after about 150 m (165 yards), to a large *noria* (waterwheel) built in 1287 by the Andalusians. The **Makina** was an arsenal, established by Moulay el-Hassan in 1855 with the help of Italian officers. It was built on the west side of the Méchouar de Bab Dekaken. Having fallen into disuse, the Makina

was restored. It is now used as a concert hall and conference venue.

Kasbah Cherarda
North of the town, accessible via Bab Segma.

Once known as the Kasbah el-Khmis (Thursday Fort), after the El-Khmis Souk which took place along the northern and eastern walls, this kasbah was built by Moulay Rachid in the 17th century. Its present name is derived from a former kasbah built nearby by a Cherarda *caid* (chief) to defend his tribe's grain stores. With Bab Segma and Bab Dekaken, the kasbah formed a system of fortifications that controlled the road to Meknès and Tangier, and protected Fès el-Jedid along the intersection with Fès el-Bali.

Enclosed within crenellated walls set with sturdy square towers, the kasbah has two monumental gateways, one on the western and the other on the eastern side. The kasbah now contains a hospital and an annexe of the Karaouiyine university. Beneath the walls on the southern and western sides, in an area where Almoravid and Almohad grain stores once stood, are the tombs of the Bab el-Mahrouk cemetery. Among the small Mausoleum of Sidi Boubker el-Arabi can be seen.

Walls of the Kasbah Cherarda, built by Moulay Rachid in the 17th century

MEKNÈS & VOLUBILIS

LOCATED BETWEEN the fertile plain of the Rarb and the Middle Atlas, Meknès and Volubilis lie at the heart of an agricultural area that has been Morocco's grain store since ancient times. The historical importance of the two cities can be clearly seen in the ruins of Volubilis, capital of Mauretania Tingitana and the most important archaeological site in Morocco, as well as in the grandeur of the Moorish buildings in Meknès.

From the time of its foundation in the tenth century to the arrival of the Alaouites in the 17th century, Meknès was no more than a small town overshadowed by Fès, its neighbour and rival. It was not until the reign of Moulay Ismaïl *(see pp54–5)*, which began in 1672, that Meknès first rose to the rank of imperial city. With tireless energy, the sultan set about building gates, ramparts, mosques and palaces. This ambitious building programme continued throughout his reign and involved robbing the ruins of Volubilis *(see pp 202–5)* and the Palais el-Badi in Marrakech *(see p235)*. After 50 years, work was still not completed. Although the sultan's impatience was often a hindrance, he reinvigorated palace architecture.

Today, Meknès is the fifth-largest city in Morocco, with a population of 450,000. It is a dynamic economic centre, renowned for its olives, wine and mint tea. The imperial city stands alongside the new town, on the banks of Wadi Boufekrane.

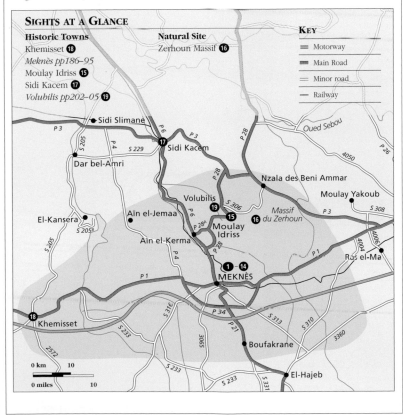

◁ **Mosaic of Bacchus, from the House of Dionysus and the Four Seasons in Volubilis**

Exploring Meknès

THREE WELL-DEFINED quarters – the medina, the imperial city and Ville Nouvelle (the New Town) – make up the city of Meknès. The medina is a densely packed quarter. The kasbah, or imperial city, contains the finest of the buildings constructed by Moulay Ismaïl. Ville Nouvelle is located on the east bank of Wadi Boufekrane.

SEE ALSO

• *Where to Stay* p309

• *Where to Eat* pp328–9

A Moroccan in Place el-Hedime, "Square of Ruins"

GETTING AROUND

Place El-Hedime is a good starting point for exploring the medina and the imperial city. Parking is available not far from this square. From here, it is an easy walk to the area around Bab Mansour and to the Mausoleum of Moulay Ismail. To see the rest of the imperial city, particularly Dar el-Ma, a car is needed.

VISITORS' CHECKLIST

🏛 450,000. 🚉 🚌
🛈 Place Administrative; (055)-52 44 26. Esplanade de la Foire (055-52 01 91).

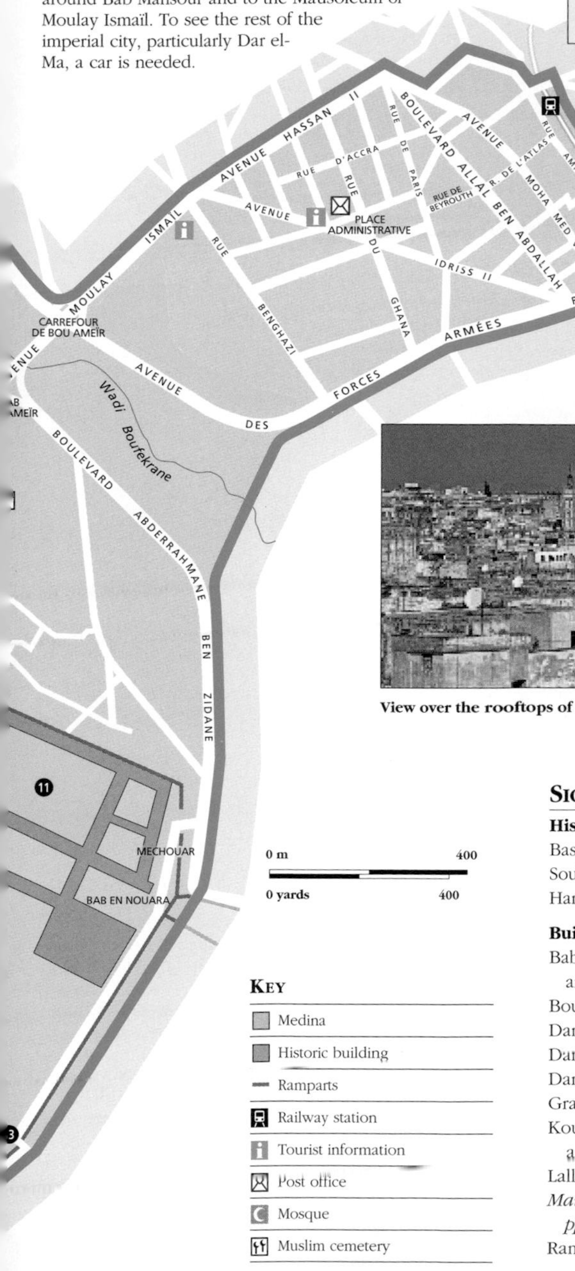

View over the rooftops of the medina in Meknès

SIGHTS AT A GLANCE

Historic Sites and Quarters
Bassin de l'Aguedal ⑫
Souks and Kissaria ②
Haras de Meknès ⑭

Buildings and Monuments
Bab Mansour el-Aleuj
   and Place el-Hedime ⑥
Bou Inania Medersa ④
Dar el-Kebira Quarter ⑦
Dar el-Ma and Heri es-Souani ⑬
Dar el-Makhzen ⑪
Grand Mosque ③
Koubba el-Khayatine
   and Habs Qara ⑨
Lalla Aouda Mosque ⑧
*Mausoleum of Moulay Ismaïl
   pp194–5* ⑩
Ramparts ①

Museum
Musée Dar Jamaï pp190–91 ⑤

KEY

🟦	Medina
🟦	Historic building
—	Ramparts
🚉	Railway station
🛈	Tourist information
✉	Post office
☪	Mosque
⚊	Muslim cemetery

0 m ———————— 400
0 yards ———————— 400

Bab el-Berdaïne, one of the gates into the medina of Meknès

Ramparts ❶

Encircling the medina, Meknès.

PROTECTED BY three stretches of wall that together amount to about 40 km (25 miles), the medina has the appearance of a sturdy fortress set with elegant gates. **Bab el-Berdaïne** (Gate of the Pack-Saddle-Makers), on the northern side, was built by Moulay Ismaïl. It is flanked by protruding square towers crowned by merlons, and stylized flowers in *zellij* tilework decorate its exterior façade. West of the gate, the walled cemetery contains one of the most highly venerated mausoleums in Morocco – that of Sidi Mohammed ben Aïssa, founder of the brotherhood of the Aïssaoua *(see p198)*.

On the southern side of the cemetery stands **Bab el-Siba** (Gate of Anarchy) and **Bab el-Jedid** (New Gate, although in fact it is one of the oldest in Meknès). Further south is **Bab Berrima**, which leads into the medina's principal souks. To the west stands **Bab el-Khemis** (Gate of Thursday), which once led into the mellah, now non-existent. The remarkable decoration of the gate's façade is on a par with that of Bab el-Berdaïne.

The layout of the medina, a medieval labyrinth, is identical to that of the other imperial cities. There are a few main thoroughfares. Rue Karmouni, which runs through the quarter from north to south links Bab el-Berdaïne with the spiritual and economic heart of the medina. Rue des Souks runs from Bab Berrima, in the west, also to the heart of the medina. Several smaller streets radiate from this centre, which is marked by the Grand Mosque and the Bou Inania Medersa.

Souks and Kissaria ❷

Rue des Souks, Meknès. ◻ *daily.*

A NETWORK OF SMALL covered or open streets lined with shops and workshops, the souks are a fascinating encapsulation of the 17th- and 18th-century Moroccan urban environment. Rue des Souks, near Bab Berrima, is filled with hardware merchants *(akarir)*, corn chandlers *(bezzazine)*, and fabric sellers *(serrayriya)*, while metalsmiths *(haddadin)* are to be found in the old Rue des Armuriers.

Minaret of the En-Nejjarine Mosque, the Mosque of the Carpenters

Bab Berrima leads through to Souk En-Nejjarine, the Carpenters' Souk, which is next to that of the brass and coppersmiths, and to the Cobblers' Souk *(sebbat)*.

The **En-Nejjarine Mosque**, built by the Almohads in the 12th century, was restored by Mohammed ben Abdallah in about 1756, when it was given a new minaret. Set back from the En-Nejjarine Souk, in the **Ed-Dlala Kissaria**, is the location of a Berber souk. Every day from 3pm to 4pm, the mountain-dwellers of the Middle Atlas come to sell carpets and blankets here at auction.

Ablutions fountain in the Grand Mosque in Meknès

Grand Mosque ❸

Rue des Souk es Sebbat, Meknès. ◻ *daily.* ⬤ *to non-Muslims.*

THE GRAND MOSQUE, which stands near the souks and the Bou Inania Medersa, was established in the 12th century during the reign of the Almoravids. It was remodelled in the 14th century. The main façade is pierced by an imposing doorway with a carved awning. The green-glazed terracotta tiles of the roof and of the 18th-century minaret are particularly striking, the bright sunlight giving them an almost translucent appearance.

The **Palais el-Mansour**, a sumptuous 19th-century residence in Rue Karmouni, has been converted into a carpet and souvenir bazaar.

Bou Inania Medersa

Rue des Souks es Sebbat, Meknès.
☐ *8am–noon, 3–6pm daily.* 📷

THIS KORANIC SCHOOL oppo-
site the Grand Mosque
was established by the Merinid
sultans in the 14th century.
The building is divided into
two unequal parts with a long
corridor between them. On
the eastern side is the
medersa proper, while on the
western side is an annexe for
ablutions (now no longer in
use). The main entrance is
crowned by a flat-sided dome
and faced with horseshoe
arches with delicate stuccowork decoration.

A corridor leads to a beautiful courtyard in the centre of
which is a pool. While three
sides of the courtyard are
lined with a gallery, the
fourth opens onto the prayer
hall. The green-tiled awnings,
the sophisticated decoration
of carved wood, stuccowork
and colourful *zellij* tilework,
as well as the mosaic-
like tiled floor make
the whole courtyard
an entrancing sight.

The prayer hall,
with carved stucco
decoration and an
elegant mihrab within
a horseshoe arch,
remains unaltered.
Students' cells fill the
rest of the ground
floor and the upper floor. The
terrace offers a fine view of
the medina and the Grand
Mosque next to the medersa.

Place el-Hedime, once the grand entrance to the imperial city of Meknès

Zellij tilework
in the Bou Inania
Medersa

before the imperial city, it
pierces the walls of the
kasbah and leads through to
Place Lalla Aouda and the Dar
el-Kebira Quarter *(see p192)*.

Of monumental proportions
and distinguished for its
decoration, Bab Mansour el-
Aleuj is held to be the finest
gate in Meknès, or even in
Morocco. It was begun
by the sultan
Moulay Ismaïl in
about 1672, when
the building of the
kasbah, his first
project, was under
way. The gate was
completed during the
reign of his son,
Moulay Abdallah, in
1732. The gate stands
about 16 m (52 ft) high, while
the arch has a span of 8 m
(26 ft) wide and is surmounted
by a pointed horseshoe arch.
An intricate pattern of inter-

lacing motifs is carved in
relief on a background of
predominantly green mosaics
and tiles. The cornerpieces
are filled with sgraffito floral
decoration incised into dark-
glazed terracotta. The gate is
framed by protruding towers
built in the style of loggias.
Temporary exhibitions are
sometimes held here.

Place el-Hedime (Square
of Ruins) links the medina
and the kasbah. It was laid out
on the ruins of the Merinid
kasbah that Moulay Ismaïl
razed to make space for the
palaces, water tanks, gardens,
stables, arsenals and forts with
which he planned to surround
himself. Recently restored, the
square is now lined with
modern residential buildings
that are not in keeping with
its historic character. Nearby,
to the left of the square, is a
covered food market.

Musée Dar Jamaï

See pp190–91.

Bab Mansour el-Aleuj and Place el-Hedime

South of the medina, Meknès.

BAB MANSOUR EL-ALEUJ (Gate
of the Victorius Renegade)
is named after the Christian
who designed and built it.
Standing like a triumphal arch

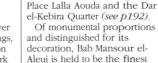

SACRED SNAKES

Expelled from Meknès by the sultan in the 16th century, Sidi
Mohammed ben Aïssa, founder of the Aïssaoua brotherhood
(see p198), and his disciples fled to the desert. Famished,
they ate whatever they could find – snakes, scorpions and
cactus leaves. Ever since, the
cobra has been the Aïssaoua's
mascot, and no member ever
kills one. Being immune to
their venom, the Aïssaoua
are often called upon to rid
villages of the dangerous
reptiles. Cobras also feature
in the Aïssaouas' religious
rituals, in which participants
fall into a trance-like state.

An Aïssaoua in a trance

Musée Dar Jamaï ❺

Painted wood, museum door

THIS MUSEUM, in which Moroccan arts are displayed, is laid out in a delightful residence built in about 1882 by Mohammed Belarbi el-Jamaï, who was a grand vizier of Moulay el-Hassan in 1873–4. The sophisticated architecture of the palace includes painted wooden cornices. a green-tiled roof and a courtyard with two pools and *zellij* tilework. There is also an Andalusian garden planted with tall cypresses. Covering 2,845 sq m (30,600 sq ft), the palace also has several annexes and outbuildings.

The Museum of Moroccan Arts, occupying a large and elegant 19th-century palace

EXPLORING THE MUSEUM OF MOROCCAN ARTS

BEFORE IT WAS converted into a regional ethnographic museum, this palace incorporated a mosque, a garden, a *menzah* (pavilion), a courtyard, a small house, a kitchen and a hammam. Of the 2,000-plus objects in the museum's collection, some 670 are on display.

Perfume bottle from Tamegroute
(late 18th century)

WOODWORK

ROOM 1, on the ground floor, contains examples of architectural features in wood – pieces of carved and painted wood that were used in the building or decoration of the palaces and town houses of Meknès.

The exhibits also include a 17th-century minbar (pulpit) that originally stood in the Grand Mosque in Meknès.

CERAMICS

CERAMICS FROM Fès and Meknès are displayed in Room 2. Fassi potters attained unprecedented renown for their famous blue and white ware. Two kinds of blue pigment were used: a pale blueish-grey, which was in use up until the mid-19th century, and a clear blue with a violet tinge that was obtained by more recent industrial means.

The Fassi potting industry probably goes back to the 10th or 11th century. That of Meknès, by contrast, is much more recent, having been imported from Fès in about the 18th century. Three colours – brown, green and yellow – were used.

Before the pottery was decorated, it was fired in a kiln and was then covered in white glaze. The potter would decorate this surface with elegant motifs of Moorish inspiration.

Painted wooden door from a house in Meknès

CARPETS

THE MUSEUM'S RICHEST section is that devoted to carpets, which fill Room 4. Most of the carpets and kilims on display come from the High and Middle Atlas. Among the latter, the most noteworthy pieces are those made by two Berber tribes, the Zemmour and the Beni M'Guild. Traditions of craftsmanship are still alive among these tribes today – a relatively rare phenomenon in Morocco – and carpets similar to those on display here are still being made.

Brass and painted wood coffer from Fès (19th century)

Meknès carpets are characterized by a mixture of bright colours forming geometric patterns. This section of the museum also includes a fine collection of beautiful gold-thread embroidery, another craft speciality that has brought Meknès renown.

GALLERY GUIDE

The eight exhibition rooms on the ground floor are arranged around the garden. Room 1 contains a display of carved and painted wood; Rooms 2 and 3 are devoted to ceramics; Room 4 to carpets and embroidery; Room 5 to kaftans and belts; Room 6 to jewellery; and Rooms 7 and 8 to the art of damascening (see p191). On the upper floor, the reconstruction of a traditional Moroccan room can be seen. The museum has undergone renovation and its collections are now effectively displayed.

COSTUMES

THE COSTUMES of town- and city-dwellers, especially the kaftan (see pp36–7), is the theme of Room 5. The brightly coloured kaftan, a long robe worn by women on special occasions, is the quintessential garment of city-dwellers. Kaftans were often embroidered with silk, silver or gold thread, as was the belt (mdamma) worn with the kaftan. Wealthy women might even wear a belt made of silver or solid gold. The mdamma now forms part of a young townswoman's dowry.

JEWELLERY

JEWELLERY FROM several regions of Morocco is displayed in Room 6. Particular prominence is given to Berber jewellery.

Metalworking is a traditional craft that was once widespread throughout the country, and was particularly associated with Jewish craftsmen. Moroccan jewellery, which is typically made of gold or silver and sometimes set with precious or semi-precious stones, is made by age-old techniques. It forms an integral part of different types of dress (see pp36–7) and the way that it is worn is

Vase in damascened metal

highly significant. Jewellery also once indicated the wearer's geographical origin or tribal identity.

Modern copies of Berber jewellery can be seen today on offer in the souks.

METALWORK

WHILE CERAMICS reached their apogee in Fès, the craftsmen of Meknès were distinguished masters of the art of damascening. The technique consists of covering a metallic surface with a patterned filigree of gold, silver or copper. There are some particularly fine damascened vases in Rooms 7 and 8. The craft is still very much alive in Meknès today, and some exquisite damascened pieces can be found in the souks of the old town.

VISITORS' CHECKLIST

Place el-Hedime.
((055) 53 08 63.
9am–noon & 3–6:30pm Wed–Mon.

This section of the museum also includes an interesting collection of keys decorated with the stylized names of their former owners.

THE MOROCCAN ROOM

AS IN OTHER ethnographic museums in the country, this museum features a reconstruction of a traditional Moroccan room. On the upper floor, it has walls covered with zellij tilework and a carved wooden domed ceiling. It is furnished with pieces from various houses and palaces in Meknès.

Reconstruction of a traditional Moroccan room, sumptuously decorated

EMBROIDERY

Embroidery is a time-honoured craft practised by the townswomen of Morocco. Young girls start to learn embroidery from childhood, being taught either in their homes or in a workshop, and always under the supervision of a teacher (maalma). Fès, Meknès, Marrakech, Rabat, Salé, Tetouan, Chefchaouen and Azemmour are the main centres of embroidery. Each town has its own characteristic colours, stitches and repertoire of motifs. Fès embroidery is characterized by tree-like motifs, often depicted in a single colour. That of Salé alternates cross stitch and satin stitch. In Meknès embroidery (terz el-meknassi), motifs are peppered over the fabric, and bright colours are used to decorate tablecloths and scarves.

Cotton and silk embroidery from Rabat (19th century)

Chefchaouen gold-thread embroidery

Place Lalla Aouda and the minaret of the Lalla Aouda Mosque

Dar el-Kebira Quarter **7**

Behind Place Lalla Aouda (between Bab Moulay and the Lalla Aouda Mosque), Meknès.

THIS QUARTER forms part of what is known as the **Imperial City**, or the Kasbah of Moulay Ismaïl. Covering an area four times as large as that of the medina, the whole quarter is in keeping with the grand ambitions of this enterprising sultan. Protected by a double line of walls and monumental angled gates, the Imperial City has the appearance of an impregnable *ksar* (fortified village). It contains wide avenues and large squares, palaces with attractive pools and extensive gardens, as well as administrative buildings enclosed within their own ramparts.

The Imperial City comprises three palatial complexes: Dar el-Kebira, Dar el-Medrasa and Ksar el-Mhanncha. Dar el-Kebira, the Quarter of the Large House, is located southeast of the medina. It was the first palatial complex of the Imperial City that Moulay Ismaïl ordered to be built, in about 1672. It stands near Place Lalla Aouda, probably on the site of the former Almohad kasbah. The complex was cut off from the urban bustle by a double wall and by Place el-Hedime *(see p189)*.

Each palace in Dar el-Kebira contained a harem, reception rooms, hammams, kitchens, armouries, ovens and mosques. They were interlinked by a somewhat haphazard network of open or partially covered alleys. Today, the ancient heart of the Imperial City, which is partly in ruins, has become a poor district that has been filled with shanty dwellings.

The Mausoleum of Moulay Ismaïl, the Lalla Aouda Mosque and a monumental gate near Bab Bou Ameïr are the last surviving vestiges of the ostentatiously grand complex that the sultan had envisaged.

The second complex, which is now in complete ruins, was the Dar el-Medrasa. The palace comprised suites of residential rooms, some of which were used exclusively by the sultan and his harem.

Lalla Aouda Mosque **8**

Place Lalla Aouda, Meknès. ☐ daily. ● to non-Muslims.

THE FIRST MAJOR place of worship to be built by Moulay Ismaïl, in 1680, this mosque is one of the few of the sultan's projects to have survived intact. The building has three doorways. Two on the northwestern side open onto the former *méchouar* (parade ground) and a smaller one, on the side of the mosque where the mihrab is located, leads to a corridor running behind the mosque. It was probably the sultan's private entrance. The pitched roof is covered with green tiles.

Koubba el-Khayatine and Habs Qara **9**

Place Habs Qara. ☐ 9am–noon, 3–6pm daily. ● public holidays. 📷

THIS IMPERIAL PAVILION, also known as the Pavilion of the Ambassadors, was used originally to receive diplomats who came to negotiate, among other things, the ransom of Christian prisoners. In more recent times, the building was used by tailors *(khiyatine)*, who made military uniforms here. The building is crowned by a conical dome decorated with geometric and floral motifs.

Behind the pavilion are the former underground storage areas that were converted into the **Christian Prison**, or Habs Qara. The prisoners – probably Europeans captured by the corsairs of Rabat – were made to work on the sultan's herculean building projects. Chroniclers recorded that thousands of convicts were incarcerated in these underground galleries, which were later partly destroyed by an earthquake.

Mausoleum of Moulay Ismaïl **10**

See pp194–5.

Dar el-Makhzen **11**

Place Bab el-Mechouar, Meknès. ● to the public.

THIS ROYAL COMPLEX was formerly known as the Palace of the Labyrinth, after a white marble pool fashioned as a labyrinth. In contrast to Dar el-Kebira and Koubbet el-Khiriyatine, the complex has a neat and compact layout. It is divided into eight parts and is surrounded by walls set with bastions. In the centre stands a monumental gate, the

Gate of the Kasbah Hedrach, Dar el-Makhzen

The Bassin de l'Aguedal, a water tank created by Moulay Ismaïl

fulsomely decorated **Bab el-Makhzen** (Gate of the Warehouse), built by Moulay el-Hassan in 1888. A second gate, **Bab el-Jedid** (New Gate), was made on the northwestern side. Features of the complex include a *méchouar* and **Kasbah Hadrach**, the former barracks of the sultan's army of black slaves.

Bassin de l'Aguedal ⑫

Aguedal Quarter, Meknès.

THIS WATER TANK *(sahrij)* was built within the kasbah by Moulay Ismaïl. It has a surface area of 40,000 sq m (430,000 sq ft) and its purpose was to supply water to the palace and the Imperial City, including its mosques, hammams, gardens and orchards. The women of the harem, so it is said, would sail on it in their pleasure boats. Only a few stretches of its crenellated walls survive.

The spot has suffered some unfortunate alterations carried out in an effort to create a place where the people of Meknès could come to walk.

Dar el-Ma and Heri es-Souani ⑬

L'Agdal Quarter, Meknès.
◯ 9am–noon, 3–6pm daily.

DAR EL-MA, the Water House, held the town's water reserves and was another of Moulay Ismaïl's grandiose projects. The huge barrel-vaulted building contains 15 rooms, each with a *noria* (water wheel) once worked by horses to draw underground water by means of scoops. The terraces offer a fine view of the city.

Dar el-Ma gives access to **Heri es-Souani**, the so-called

Horsemen in Heri es-Souani

Grainstore Stables, which are considered to be one of the sultan's finest creations. This monumental building, with 29 aisles, was designed for storing grain. The thick walls, as well as a network of underground passages, maintained the temperature inside the grainstore at a low and constant level. The ceilings collapsed during the earthquake of 1755.

Haras de Meknès ⑭

Zitoune Quarter of Meknès, southwest of the town. *From Dar el-Ma, 1 km (0.6 mile) towards Dar el-Beïda, turning right 400 m (440 yds) beyond Dar el-Beïda and continuing for 2 km (1 mile) to the stud.* ◯ *9am–noon, 2–5pm Mon–Fri.*

ALTHOUGH IT CANNOT rival the modern studs in Rabat and Marrakech, the Haras de Meknès is well known in Morocco. The stud was established in 1912 with the aim of improving blood lines and promoting various Moroccan breeds of horse for use in racing, competitive riding and fantasias *(see p35)*.

The stud can accommodate 231 horses, ranging from pure-bred Arabs and Barbs to English thoroughbreds and Anglo-Arabs. A visit here may include seeing horses being put through their paces.

THE ROYAL CITIES

The creation of royal cities in the Islamic world dates from the late 8th century. The Almohads, the Merinids and the Alaouites under Moulay Ismaïl continued this tradition, and it spread throughout the Maghreb, where it survived until recently. The royal city is an architectural complex built to protect the king and his courtiers. Several palaces and other buildings were needed to accommodate all the members of the royal household. Water tanks were built to irrigate the many gardens and to supply the baths and hammams of the harem. Designed both for royal receptions and for the king's private life, the royal city was architecturally the most sophisticated and most sumptuous component of a great urban centre.

Bab el-Makhzen, gateway of Dar el-Makhzen, Meknès

Mausoleum of Moulay Ismaïl ⑩

Fᴇᴀᴛᴜʀɪɴɢ ᴀ sᴜɪᴛᴇ of three rooms, 12 columns and a central sanctuary where the great sultan *(see pp54–5)* lies, the Mausoleum of Moulay Ismaïl is in some aspects reminiscent of the Saadian Tombs in Marrakech *(see pp238–9)*. The mausoleum was built in the 17th century and was remodelled in the 18th and 20th centuries. The wife of Moulay Ismaïl and his son, Moulay Ahmed al-Dahbi, as well as the sultan Moulay Abder Rahman (1822–59), are laid to rest in the burial chamber, which is decorated with stuccowork and mosaics.

View of Meknès and the mausoleum

Mihrab
The mausoleum's mihrab is located in the open courtyard. This unusual position differs from the arrangement at the Saadian Tombs in Marrakech (see pp238–9).

Finials
The roof of the mausoleum is topped with five brass spheres indentifying the building as a shrine or sacred place.

Prayer Hall
The floor of the prayer hall is covered with mats on which worshippers kneel to pray or to reflect before going into the burial chamber.

Cemetery

Clock presented by Louis XIV (see pp54–5)

Tomb of Moulay Ismaïl

Decorated Door
This carved and painted wooden door between the ablutions room and the second room of the burial chamber is similar to those of the palaces and fine town houses of Meknès.

★ Burial Chamber
This consists of a suite of three rooms, including the ablutions room with central fountain (above) and the room containing the tomb of Moulay Ismaïl, and those of his wife and sons.

Entrance to Mausoleum
This imposing carved stone doorway, surmounted by an awning and a pyramidal roof, indicates the importance of the royal building to which it gives access.

VISITORS' CHECKLIST

Rue Sarag, Meknès.
🕘 9am–noon & 3–6pm daily.

Small Courtyards
En route to the burial chamber you pass through several empty courtyards, which are decorated in a sober style. This allows visitors to leave behind them the noise and bustle of the city.

Open
courtyard

★ **Zellij Tilework**
The lower part of the walls of the rooms leading into the burial chamber is covered with traditional zellij tilework, mosaics of glazed polychrome tiles.

STAR FEATURES

★ Burial Chamber

★ Courtyard & Fountain

★ Zellij Tilework

★ **Courtyard & Fountain**
The ablutions room, paved with green glazed tiles, is a square courtyard with a star-shaped fountain and bowl. The 12 columns surrounding it come from Volubilis.

The ruins of Volubilis, seen from the triumphal arch ▷

Holy Men and Mystics

IN MOROCCO, the Islamic faith of law-makers *(fkihs)* and learned men *(ulema)* coexists with popular forms of religion, in which the cult of saints and the role of brotherhoods (known as *tariqas*, meaning "ways") are prominent. Many followers of these religions are craftsmen and traders, who gather to perform spiritualist rites *(zikrs)*, involving singing, dancing and music, according to the teaching of their respective founder. These religions are connected to those of Eastern mystics, and they have spread well beyond the boundaries of Morocco. This spiritualist branch of Islam is widely known as Sufism, after the rough woollen garment *(suf)* worn by certain ascetics.

The pilgrimage to Sidi Ahmed Ou Mghanni *takes place near Imilchil, in the territory of the Aït Haddidou. It is known as the Marriage Fair, as many betrothals are made on this occasion.*

THE AÏSSAOUA

This brotherhood came into being in the 16th century. Its beliefs are based on the teachings of Sidi Mohammed ben Aïssa, a mystic who was born in the 15th century. Through El-Jazouli, the holy man of Marrakech, it is connected to Chadhiliya, the great Sufi "way" that spread throughout the Muslim world. The Aïssaoua brotherhood exists in Meknès *(see p189)* and Fès, and also in Algeria.

The Mausoleum of Sidi Mohammed ben Aïssa, *in Meknès, contains the tomb of the holy man who founded the Aïssaoua "way".*

The spectacular ceremonies of the Aïssaoua, involving banners, drums and incense, have always made a deep impression on foreigners in Morocco. This scene, entitled *Les Aïssaouas,* was painted by Georges Clairin (1843–1919).

The Aïssaoua are always dressed in white. They hav a fear of black.

Like the Hamadcha, the Aïssaoua are a popular brotherhood because of some of their practices. During their moussem *(festival) they perform long-drawn-out and impressive rituals, called* hadras, *which are accompanied by singing, dancing and drumming. These rituals may send them into a trance or lead followers to perform orgies of self-mutilation.*

The moussem *of Moulay Abdallah*, near
El-Jadida, can draw up to 150,000 visitors and
a huge tent city springs up on the site.

The moussem *in Guelmim*, a town on the
caravan route on the edge of the Sahara (see
p294), takes place each June in honour of the
holy man Sidi el-Ghazi. Attended by the
Reguibat, nomads known as the "blue men",
this is also when a major camel fair takes place.

During the moussem *of Moulay Idriss II*
in Fès, the various guilds of craftsmen, such as
tanners, shoemakers, blacksmiths, brass-founders
and coppersmiths, as here, process through the
medina, bringing gifts and sacrifices to the
zaouia (shrine) of this highly venerated holy man.

TOMBS OF HOLY MEN

Followers gather eagerly in order to make pilgrimages to the
many tombs of holy men *(marabouts)* so as to seek a
blessing *(haraka)*. These small mausoleums, which are often
covered with a white dome known as a *koubba*,
can be seen throughout the country. Some of
the more important shrines – or *zaouias*
– are the seat of a religious brotherhood and, besides the tomb of the
holy man, consist of buildings in
which pilgrims are accommodated and religious instruction given.
Once a year, certain pilgrimages take the form of *moussems*, great
gatherings that are simultaneously joyous occasions, festivals for the
performance of traditional shows and commercial fairs.

Marabout of Sidi Ahmad Ou Mghanni

Moussem in Guelmim

Moulay Idriss

Road map D2. 27 km (38 miles) north
of Meknès. 🕌 *12,600.* 🚌 *from
Meknès.* 🛒 *Sat.* 🎪 *last Thu in Aug.*

THE MOST SPECTACULAR sight
of Moulay Idriss is from
the scenic route S306 from
Volubilis, which runs above
the more frequently used P28.
In a superb setting, the bright
white town clings to two
rocky outcrops between
which rises the **Tomb of
Idriss I**, conspicuous with its
green-tiled roof.

Fleeing the persecution of
the Abbassid caliphs of
Baghdad, Idriss found a
haven in Oualili (Volubilis). A
descendant of Ali, son-in-law
of the Prophet Mohammed,
he founded the first Arab-
Muslim dynasty in Morocco.
He died in 791 and was
buried in the town that now
bears his name. It was not
until the 16th century that the
town began to prosper, and it
was still in the process of developing in the 17th century,
during the reign of Moulay
Ismaïl *(see pp54–5)*. The latter
endowed it with defensive
walls and a monumental gate,
as well as Koranic schools,
fountains and a new dome for
the mausoleum.

The Tomb of Idriss I is closed
to non-Muslims, and a wooden
beam across the entrance
marks this as sacred ground,
or *horm*. However, from the
terrace, near the Mosque of
Sidi Abdallah el-Hajjam,
which perches above the
town, there is a splendid view
of the town and the mausoleum. The minaret (1939),
whose cylindrical shape is
unusual in the Maghreb, is
covered with green tiles with
verses from the Koran.

The grand entrance to the Tomb of Idriss I in Moulay Idriss

Zerhoun Massif

Road map D2. About 50 km
(31 miles) northwest of Meknès.

CULMINATING IN Jbel Zerhoun,
which rises to a height of
1,118 m (3,670 ft), the massif
forms part of an extensive
range of hills bordering the
southern side of the Rif and
running from the region of
Meknès to the environs of
Taza in the east.

This pre-Riffian terrain,
consisting mostly of clay and
marl, is very susceptible to
fluvial erosion. As a result, a
few outcrops of harder
limestone and sandstone have
emerged, one of which is Jbel
Zerhoun, whose gorges,
peaks and cliffs have all been
created by erosion.

Water is abundant here, and
the Romans tapped the springs
to supply Volubilis. Large
villages grew up on the hillsides, along the line of springs
and at the foot of the massif.
While fig trees, orange trees
and olive trees grow on the
higher slopes, corn and
barley thrive in the valleys
and on the lower hillsides.
Enclosures *(zriba)* made of
loose stones or thorny
branches, for small herds of
cattle, sheep and goats, can
be seen near the villages.

Moulay Idriss, clinging to an outcrop of rock

For Moroccans, Zehroun is a holy mountain, the home of many religious men, and the setting of numerous stories and legends.

The verdant Zerhoun Massif, where water is plentiful

Sidi Kacem ⑰

Road map D2. 46 km (29 miles) northwest of Meknès. 🏠 *70,000.* 🚉 🚌 *from Meknès.* 🛒 *Thu.*

SIDI KACEM grew out of a military outpost that was set up in 1915 near a *zaouia* and the souk of the local Cherarda tribe. It is now an important agricultural and industrial centre on the plain of the eastern Rharb.

The three building complexes that dominate the town bear witness to the history and economic activity of Sidi Kacem. One is the railway station, at the intersection of lines running between Rabat and Fès and between Tangier and Fès. The second is the oil refinery (initially for local, then for imported fuel). Thirdly, there are the grain silos, at the heart of a well-watered and productive region.

Sidi Kacem is a major centre of agricultural food production and of brick-making. These industries have made the town an important banking and commercial hub.

Khemisset ⑱

Road map D2. 🏠 *90,000.* 🚌 *from Meknès.* 🛒 *Tue.*

THIS TOWN was founded in 1924, on the site of a military outpost on the road from Rabat to Fès. Now a provincial capital, Khemisset is also the

Carpet made by the Zemmour, with graphic geometric motifs

"capital" of the confederation of the Berber-speaking Zemmour tribes.

This is a good place to stop, since there are many cafés and restaurants. The town also has a crafts cooperative where you can buy regional specialities, such as carpets and mats woven in palm fibre or wool. Every Tuesday, Khemisset is the venue for one of the most important country souks in Morocco, with almost 1,900 stalls.

COUNTRY SOUKS

At daybreak, hundreds of country people travelling on foot, on donkeys or in heavily laden trucks make their way to a site where tents and stalls are being set up. Around 850 country souks – named after the day on which they take place – are held every week in Morocco, drawing people from up to 10 km (6 miles) around. On an area of open ground, alleys between the stalls form according to a well-defined plan. The pattern on which the goods are laid out is similar to that of the economic layout of a medina. In the centre are such prized goods as fabric and clothing, followed by basketwork, carpets and blankets; on the periphery are second-hand items, scrap metal, humble traders such as cobblers and hair-dressers, and also food stalls. Beyond, various livestock markets are laid out in separate areas.

Returning from the souk

Souks allow townspeople to buy agricultural produce and craft items brought in by country people, who in turn stock up with groceries, sugar, tea and fruit. They provide services, entertainment and food, but also attract charlatans and storytellers. The civic authorities also use souks to set up temporary registry offices, post offices and health centres. Permanent shops that may appear on the site of a weekly souk sometimes lead to the establishment of a new town.

A country souk, with tents set up for a day

Volubilis ⑲

THE ANCIENT TOWN of Volubilis backs on to a triangular spur jutting out from the Zerhoun Massif. The site was settled and began to prosper under the Mauretanian kings, from the 3rd century BC to AD 40. Temples from this period, as well as a strange tumulus, have been uncovered. When Mauretania was annexed by the Roman emperor Claudius in AD 45, Volubilis was raised to the status of *municipia* (free town), becoming one of the most important cities in Tingitana. The public buildings in the northeastern quarter date from the 1st century, and those around the forum from the 2nd century. After Rome withdrew from Mauretania in the 3rd century, the city declined. It was inhabited by Christians but had been Islamicized when Idriss I arrived in 788.

Mosaic from the House of Dionysus and the Four Seasons

Gordian Palace

House of the Bathing Nymphs

House of Dionysus and the Four Seasons

Decumanus maximus

The House of the Labours of Hercules is named after a mosaic depicting the Greek hero's 12 labours.

Knight's House

House of the Columns
This house is arranged around a huge peristyle courtyard with a circular pool. Columns with twisted fluting and composite capitals front the grand reception room.

House of the Dog

House of the Athlete

Macellum (market)

★ **Triumphal Arch**
Bestriding the decumanus maximus, *the triumphal arch overlooks plantations of cereals and olive trees. The fertile plain to the west of Volubilis has provided the area with grain and oil since antiquity.*

STAR FEATURES

★ **Basilica**

★ **Diana and the Bathing Nymphs**

★ **Triumphal Arch**

Tangier Gate

THE SITE OF VOLUBILIS TODAY

The forum, basilica and capitol were built in the 2nd century, under the Severi dynasty. Richly appointed residences paved with mosaics also graced the city. These buildings are still easily identifiable today. Recent excavations have shown that the site was still inhabited during the Almoravid period *(see pp46–47)*.

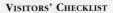

VISITORS' CHECKLIST

Road map D2. 31 km (19 miles) northwest of Meknès; 5 km (3 miles) from Moulay Idriss. ▭ *from Meknès to Moulay Idriss, then by grand taxi to the site.* ○ *8am–one hour before sunset daily.*

House of the Golden Coins

★ Diana and the Bathing Nymphs

In this mosaic in the House of the Cortège of Venus, the nymphs admire Diana as she receives water from Pegasus, the winged horse. A similar scene is depicted in a mosaic in the House of the Bathing Nymphs.

Aqueduct

Artisans' quarters

★ Basilica

Apart from the triumphal arch, this was the only building whose ruins were still impressive when excavations began. The interior is divided into three aisles and two apses.

Visitors' entrance

The Capitol

Of the original building (dating from the early 3rd century) only the foundations remain. The sacrificial altar, identifiable by its moulded base, stood in front of the steps.

House of Orpheus

Exploring Volubilis

THE ANCIENT SITE OF VOLUBILIS was known from the 18th century, but it was not until the late 19th century that it was first investigated. Excavations resumed in 1915, and have continued almost uninterrupted since, although extensive areas still remain to be investigated. Although Volubilis is not as large as some other Roman towns, it shows how thoroughly romanized Mauretania Tingitana had become. This is seen in the public buildings and sophisticated town houses within the 2nd-century walls, which enclose an area of more than 400,000 sq m (99 acres). The site, a pre-existing settlement on which the Romans imposed their way of life, features baths, oil presses, bakeries, aqueducts, drains and shops that evoke the inhabitants' daily lives. Well signposted, Volubilis is easy to explore.

Reconstruction of an oil press, showing the baskets used for pressing the olive

The House of Orpheus

Located in the southern quarter of the city, the House of Orpheus is remarkable not only for its size but for the rooms that it contains. Opposite the entrance is a large peristyle courtyard, with a slightly sunken square pool that is decorated with a mosaic of tritons, cuttlefish, dolphins and other sea creatures. The *tablinum*, looking onto the courtyard, is the main reception room; the centre is paved with the Orpheus Mosaic, the largest of the circular mosaics that have been discovered in Volubilis. A richly dressed Orpheus is depicted charming a lion, an elephant and other animals with his lyre. The house also has an oil press with purification tanks, as well as private areas. These have further rooms paved with mosaics in geometric patterns and bath suites with hypocausts (underfloor heating).

Oil Press

The reconstruction of an oil press near the House of Orpheus shows how this device worked in Roman times. The olives were crushed in a cylindrical vat by the action of a millstone fixed to a vertical axis. The resulting pulp was emptied into rush or esparto baskets laid beneath planks of wood on which pressure was exerted by means of a beam that acted as a lever. The oil ran out along channels and into purification tanks set up outside. Water poured into the tanks forced the

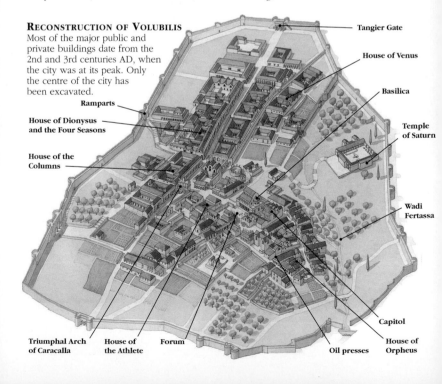

RECONSTRUCTION OF VOLUBILIS
Most of the major public and private buildings date from the 2nd and 3rd centuries AD, when the city was at its peak. Only the centre of the city has been excavated.

Ramparts

House of Dionysus and the Four Seasons

House of the Columns

Triumphal Arch of Caracalla

House of the Athlete

Forum

Oil presses

House of Orpheus

Capitol

Wadi Fertassa

Temple of Saturn

Basilica

House of Venus

Tangier Gate

better-quality oil to float to the surface. It was then poured off into large earthenware jars for local use or for export.

The Forum, Basilica and Capitol

Like the other major public buildings in the heart of the city, the unusually small forum dates from the early 3rd century. It was the focal point of public life and administration, as well as a meeting place where business was done. It is continued on its western side by the *macellum,* a market that was originally covered.

On the left of the entrance, from the direction of the oil press, stands the stele of Marcus Valerius Servus, which lists the territory that the citizens of Volubilis possessed in the hinterland.

The *decumanus,* linking Tangier Gate and the triumphal arch

On the eastern side of the forum, a short flight of steps and three semicircular arches leads into the basilica. This was the meeting place of the curia (senate), as well as the commercial exchange and tribunal, and somewhere to take a stroll. On the capitol, south of the basilica, public rites in honour of Jupiter, Juno and Minerva were performed.

House of the Athlete

The athlete that gives this house its name is the *desultor,* or chariot jumper, who took part in the Olympic Games. He would leap from his horse or his chariot in the

The Chariot Jumper, parodied in this mosaic

middle of a race and remount or get back in immediately.

The mosaic here depicts the *desultor* as a parody. The naked athlete is shown be-striding a donkey backwards, and holding a *cantharus,* a drinking vessel given as a prize. The scarf, another emblem of victory, flutters in the background, behind the horseman.

House of the Dog and House of the Ephebe

The House of the Dog, behind the triumphal arch on the western side, is laid out to a typical Roman plan. A double doorway opens onto a lobby leading through to the atrium. This room, which is lined on three sides by a colonnade, contains a pool and leads in turn to a large dining room, or *triclinium.* In 1916, a bronze statue of a dog *(see p79)* was discovered in one of the rooms off the *triclinium.*

Opposite the House of the Dog stands the House of the Ephebe, where a beautiful statue of an ivy-wreathed ephebe (youth in military training) was found in 1932. It is now in the Musée Archéologique in Rabat *(see pp78–9).*

Triumphal Arch and Decumanus Maximus

According to the inscription that it bears, the triumphal arch was erected in AD 217 by the governor Marcus Aurelius Sebastenus in honour of Caracalla and his mother Julia Domna. The statues that originally filled the niches in the arch were surmounted by busts of Caracalla and his mother within medallions. Above the inscription, at the

top of the monument, ran a frieze and a band, and the whole was crowned by a chariot drawn by six horses.

The arch, which stands over 8 m (26 ft) high, was reconstructed in 1933. It faces west onto the plain and east onto the *decumanus maximus.* This main axis through the city, 400 m (1,312 ft) long and 12 m (39 ft) wide, leads from the triumphal arch in the southwest to the gateway known as Tangier Gate in the northeast.

Parallel with the *decumanus maximus,* and a few metres away on its southern side, ran an aqueduct, substantial parts of which survive. This brought water from the Aïn Ferhana, a spring 1 km (0.6 mile) east-southeast of Volubilis, on Jbel Zerhoun, to the city's baths and fountains. The largest of these fountains can be seen between the basilica and the triumphal arch.

Aristocratic Quarter

Fine houses, such as the elegant House of the Columns, House of the Knight and House of the Labours of Hercules, constituted the aristocratic quarter. The House of Dionysus and the Four Seasons, and the House of the Bathing Nymphs, have high-quality mosaics. The Gordian Palace, named after Emperor Gordian III (238–44) and probably the residence of the Roman governor, is notable for the 12 columns that front it and the horseshoe-shaped pool with almost perfectly semicircular outlines.

Autumn, from the Four Seasons

Cortège of Venus

Busts of Cato the Younger *(see p79)* and Juba II were found south of the *decumanus.* The mosaic depicting the Cortège of Venus, which paved the *triclinium,* is displayed in the Museum of Moroccan Crafts and Antiquities in Tangier *(see pp132–3).* Some of the mosaics have motifs very similar to those seen in Berber carpets today.

MIDDLE ATLAS

A WILD REGION OF RARE BEAUTY, *the Middle Atlas is surprisingly little visited. The great cedar forests that cover the mountainsides between deep valleys stretch as far as the eye can see. Bordered by the fertile plain of the Saïs and the cities of Fès and Meknès, the mountainous heights of the Middle Atlas are the territory of Berber tribes, whose population is thinly scattered in the area.*

The mountains of the Middle Atlas are traversed by one of the main routes through to southern Morocco, running from Fès to the Tafilalt. Unless they take their time, travellers on this road will remain sadly ignorant of the beauty and serenity of the region's landscapes.

This mountain chain northeast of the Atlas is 350 km (217 miles) long, and is delimited on its eastern side by Tazzeka National Park, whose terrain is scarred with caves and gorges. South of Sefrou, forests of cedar, holm-oak and cork oak form a patchwork with the bare volcanic plateaux and small lakes brimming with fish.

The Oum er-Rbia rises in the heart of the mountains. The longest river in Morocco, it runs for 600 km (375 miles) before reaching the Atlantic.

To the west, the Middle Atlas abuts the foothills of the High Atlas. Here, the Cascades d' Ouzoud crash down 100 m (328 ft) to the bottom of a natural chasm wreathed in luxuriant vegetation. Nicknamed the Switzerland of Morocco, the Middle Atlas also features some exquisitely scenic small towns at mid-altitude. Ifrane, which has stone-built chalets with red-tiled roofs, Azrou, a resort on the slopes of a cedar plantation, and Imouzzer du Kandar are among the most attractive; they also serve as bases for hikes and tours in the mountains. A tour of the lakes takes in the wild and arid mountain landscape, which is populated only by Berbers. Forest roads darkened by towering stands of cedar are patrolled by peaceable macaques.

Berber shepherd with his flock of sheep in the lakes region of the Middle Atlas

◁ The Cascades d'Ouzoud, a spectacular waterfall in the Middle Atlas

Exploring the Middle Atlas

A VARIED LANDSCAPE characterizes the Middle Atlas. The eastern part receives scant rainfall and is thus only sparsely covered with vegetation, but above the deep valleys rise Jbel Bou Naceur and Jbel Bou Iblane: reaching a height of 3,340 m (10,962 ft) and 3,190 m (10,470 ft) respectively, these are the highest peaks of the Middle Atlas. In the thinly populated central high plateaux between Azrou and Timhadit, lakes (known as *dayet* or *aguelmame*) fill the craters of extinct volcanoes and are surrounded by forests. The western part receives the highest rainfall and arable areas have attracted denser populations. Here, plateaux and valleys are covered in forests of cedar, cork oak and maritime pine. From December, peaks over 2,000 m (6,564 ft) are covered with snow. The Middle Atlas is the territory of the semi-nomadic Beni M'Guild and Zaïana.

The desert-like shores of Sidi Ali Lake

SEE ALSO

- *Where to Stay* pp309–10
- *Where to Eat* p329

0 km   10

0 miles   10

Rommani, Rabat

OUED ZEM

Casablanca

S 133

P 22

15 BOUJAD

P 13

KASBA TADLA

1659

14

EL-KSIBA

FKIH BEN SALAH

P 22

S 133

P 24

16 BENI MELLAL

Marrakech

P 24

S 508

D

1811

M

BIN EL-OUIDANE DAM

17

CASCADES D'OUZOUD

18

Khemisset, Rabat

MEKNÈS

Ouez

Sidi Kac

EL-HAJ

S 331

AÏN LI

P 24

S 209

2516

SOURCES OF T OUM ER-RBIA

KHENIFRA 13

3485 AGUEL AZIC

EL-K

P 33

P 24

KEY

▬ Motorway

▬ Major road

═ Minor road

═ Track

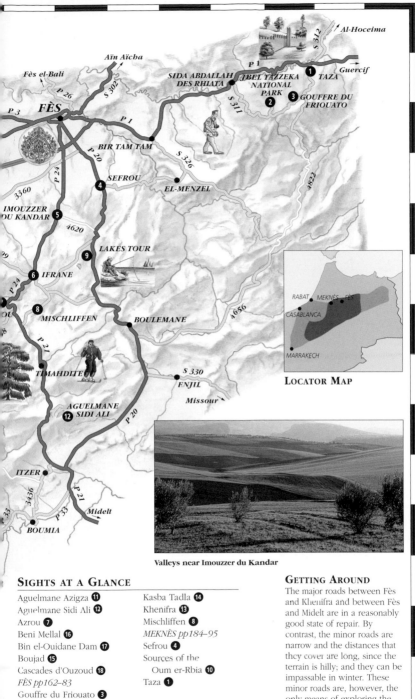

Valleys near Imouzzer du Kandar

LOCATOR MAP

SIGHTS AT A GLANCE

GETTING AROUND

The major roads between Fès and Khenifra and between Fès and Midelt are in a reasonably good state of repair. By contrast, the minor roads are narrow and the distances that they cover are long, since the terrain is hilly; and they can be impassable in winter. These minor roads are, however, the only means of exploring the Middle Atlas. In the eastern part of the mountains, many tracks lead to small isolated lakes.

Taza, between the Rif and the Middle Atlas, on the route towards eastern Morocco

Taza ❶

Road map E2. 👥 *120,000.* 🚉 *from Oujda, Fès and Meknès.* 🚌 *from Nador, El-Hoceima, Fès and Oujda.* 🛈 *56 Avenue Mohammed V.* 📅 *Moussem of Sidi Zerrouk (Sep).*

L OCATED ON THE ROUTE between Fès and Oujda, in the lower foothills of the Rif and the Middle Atlas, the town of Taza is a stopping-place that seldom figures on the tourist route. It is, however, one of the oldest towns in Morocco.

Taza was founded in the 8th century by the Meknassa, a Berber tribe, and was regularly seized by sultans who wished to establish their authority before going on to take Fès. The old town, built on a rocky hill, overlooks the new town, 3 km (2 miles) below, which the French began to build in 1920. The 3-km (2-mile) walls surrounding the medina date mostly from the 12th century, the Almohad period, and were restored on several occasions, notably by the Merinids in the 14th century. Moulay Ismaïl, of the Alaouite dynasty, embellished the town and heightened its role as a military stronghold on the eastern frontier.

The Andalusian Mosque, with a 12th-century minaret, stands at the entrance of the medina, from where the main street runs through to the **Grand Mosque**. Founded by the Almohad sultan Abd el-Moumen in 1135, this is one of the oldest mosques in

Morocco. It is closed to non-Muslims, who are therefore unable to see the interior of the magnificent pierced dome or the fine bronze candelabrum.

There is a lively souk in the medina, as well as an unusual minaret whose summit is wider than the base of Djemma Es Souk, the Market Mosque. Bab er-Rih, in the north of the town, offers a splendid view of the orchards and olive trees below, the hills of the Rif and the slopes of Jbel Tazzeka.

Jbel Tazzeka National Park ❷

Road map E2. 🌳 *76-km (47-mile) tour on road S311 starting from Taza.* 🏪 *Sun, at Es-Sebt.*

E STABLISHED IN 1950 to protect the cedar forests of Jbel Tazzeka, this national park offers a spectacular tour southwest of Taza.

In the middle of a valley of almond, cherry and fig trees are the **Cascades de Ras el-Oued** (falls which only flow between November and April). The winding road crosses the fertile plateau of the **Chiker**, a punch-bowl which at certain times of year becomes a small lake (*dayet*) fed by underground water.

Beyond Bab Taka, a mountain pass at an altitude of 1,540 m (5,054 ft), a narrow track leads over 9 km (5.5 miles) to the summit of Jbel Tazzeka. The peak, at an altitude of 1,980 m (6,498 ft), supports a television mast. There is a fine view north over the mountains of the Rif, west over the plain of Fès and south to the higher foothills of the Middle Atlas and the snow peaks of the Jbel Boulblanc. The road then winds through the Wadi Zireg gorge. Caves in the cliffs here are used by local shepherds.

A single-storey house in the foothills of Jbel Tazzeka

Gouffre du Friouato ❸

Road map E2. 22 km (13.5 miles) southwest of Taza on road S311.

THIS NATURAL CHASM, which was first explored in 1934, is open to visitors, although sturdy walking boots are necessary. A flight of 500 slippery steps leads down to the cave. It is 180 m (590 ft) deep and contains galleries and halls filled with fascinating stalactites, stalagmites and other curious formations. The adjacent **Chiker Caves** are open only to speleologists.

The canyons of the Sebou gorge

Sefrou ❹

Road map D2. 🏯 230,000. 🚌 from Fès and Midelt. 🅰 Thu. 🎪 Cherry Festival (Jun); Moussem of Sidi Lahcen Lyoussi (Aug).

THIS ANCIENT TOWN has always stood in the shadow of Fès, the imperial capital. It takes its name from the Ahel Sefrou, a Berber tribe that was converted to Judaism 2,000 years ago, and that was then Islamicized by Idriss I in the 8th century. In the 12th century, trade with the Sahara brought Sefrou prosperity. A century later, it became home to a large colony of Jews who had fled from the Tafilalt and southern Algeria. In 1950, a third of Sefrou's population was Jewish. The majority of Jews emigrated to Israel in 1967, and the town's population is now mostly Muslim.

Sefrou is surrounded by crenellated ramparts pierced by nine gates. These ochre pisé walls have been restored on several occasions.

The town is bisected by Wadi Aggaï, which irrigates the surrounding fertile plain. Four bridges link the two parts of the town. South of the *wadi* is the mellah, the former Jewish quarter, a district of narrow winding streets. North of the *wadi* is the old medina, with its souks centred around the Grand Mosque and the *zaouia* of Sidi Lahcen Lyoussi, who became patron saint of Sefrou in the 18th century. On the north side of the town, outside the ramparts, is a crafts centre where leather goods, pottery and wrought-iron items are made.

The Cherry Festival, marking the end of the cherry harvest in June, is a major event in the town, which is surrounded by cherry orchards. The festival goes on for several days, and the major event is a grand procession marked by the coronation of the Cherry Queen. Folk dancers and musicians from the Middle Atlas, Fès and the Rif perform and there are sometimes fantasias.

The road following the river upstream for 1 km (0.6 mile) west of Sefrou leads to the **Kef el-Moumen Caves**, natural caves in the cliff face containing tombs that are venerated by Muslims and Jews. One of them is said to be that of the prophet Daniel. The **Wadi Aggaï Falls** here bring a welcome freshness to the surrounding hills.

The green-roofed **Koubba of Sidi bou Ali Serghine**, 2 km (1 mile) west of Sefrou, offers a scenic view over Sefrou and the Kandar hills. Nearby is the miraculous spring of **Lalla Rekia**, which is reputed to cure madness.

The village of **Bhalil**, 7 km (4 miles) north of Sefrou, has troglodytic dwellings. Its population, Christian during the Roman period, was converted to Islam by Idriss II.

A minor road east of Sefrou leads to the small town of El-Menzel. The kasbah here overlooks the **Sebou Gorge**, which has impressively sheer cliffs.

Fortified gateway into the mellah in Sefrou

Imouzzer du Kandar ❺

Road map D2. 🏯 12,000. 🅰 Mon. 🎪 Apple Festival (Jul).

BUILT BY THE FRENCH, the small hillside town of Imouzzer du Kandar overlooks the Saïss plain, which abuts the plateaux of the Middle Atlas. At an altitude of 1,345 m (4,414 ft), the town is pleasantly cool in summer, providing a welcome respite from the heat of Fès and Meknès. Many Moroccans come here for the weekend.

The dilapidated kasbah of the Aït Serchouchène, where the souk takes place, contains troglodytic dwellings, of which there are many in the region. The caves were dug into the hillside and, in times gone by, protected Berbers from attacks by their enemies. Some are still inhabited. Steps or just a slope lead up to the entrance. The openings – no more than a small door and a few ventilation holes – are small so as to keep out the cold, and the spartan interiors have neither water nor electricity.

Troglodytic dwelling in the kasbah of Imouzzer du Kandar

The King's summer residence at Ifrane, set in a dense cedar forest

Ifrane ❻

63 km (39 miles) south of Fès on road P24. 👥 10,000. 🚌 from Fès and Azrou. 🛈 Avenue Mohammed V; (055) 56 68 21.

Established in 1929 during the Protectorate, Ifrane is a small, noticeably clean town with a European rather than a Moroccan character. Located at an altitude of 1,650 m (5,415 ft), it is cool in summer and may be snow-bound from December to March. On the descent into the valley, a green-roofed palace, the King's summer residence, comes into view. Al-Akhawaya University, inaugurated by Hassan II in 1995, has contributed considerably to the town's development.

Ifrane serves as the departure point for many tours, including a trip to the waterfalls known as the **Cascades des Vierges**, 3 km (2 miles) west (follow the signs to Source Vittel), and north to the **zaouia** of Ifrane, which is surrounded by caves and *koubbas*.

Wooden chalet in Ifrane

Holm-oak in the forests surrounding Azrou

Environs: Road S309 out of Ifrane, going up to the Tizi-n-Tretten Pass, leads to the **Forêt de Cèdres**. After running along the Mischliffen and Jbel Hebri, it reaches a legendary 900-year-old cedar known as Cèdre Gouraud.

Azrou ❼

48 km (30 miles) south of Ifrane on road P24. 👥 45,000. 🚌 from Meknès, Fès, Marrakech and Er-Rachidia; Grands taxis. 🛈 Ifrane; (055) 56 68 21. 🗓 Tue.

A large outcrop of volcanic rock at the entrance to the town gave Azrou (meaning "rock" in Berber) its name. At an altitude of 1,250 m (4102 ft), it is located at the crossroads of routes linking Meknès and Erfoud, and Fès and Marrakech.

The town nestles in the centre of a geological basin, with Jbel Hebri to the southeast. It is circled by a dense belt of cedar and holm-oak, where the Beni M'Gid, the most prominent Berber tribe in the region, once came to spend their summers. These nomadic pastoralists from the Sahara gradually adopted a sedentary lifestyle and founded the town.

Azrou is still a regional market town, with a large weekly souk. At the **crafts centre** (opposite the police station) items made of cedar, thuya, walnut and juniper are on sale, as are wrought-iron objects and the renowned carpets, with geometric motifs on a red background, made by the Beni M'Gid.

During the Protectorate the town became a health resort, and highly reputed treatment centres are still found here. It is also the departure point for tours of the cedar forests and plateaux. The lakes in the vicinity offer fishing for trout, pike and roach (a permit is compulsory).

Environs: North of Azrou, the road to El-Hajeb runs along the edge of a plateau, the **Balcon d'Ito**, offering good views of the lunar lansdcape. The Berber hill village of **Aïn Leuh**, 32 km (20 miles) south of Azrou, is the venue for the Middle Atlas Arts Festival in July. There is a souk here on Mondays and Thursdays.

The ski resort on the Mischliffen, located in a volcanic crater

Mischliffen ❽

Road map D2.

A shallow bowl surrounded by cedar forests, the Mischliffen is the crater of an extinct volcano. The villages here are outnumbered by the tents of the shepherds who bring their flocks for summer grazing. A small winter sports resort (also called Mischliffen) has also been set up, at an altitude of 2,000 m (6,564 ft), among the trees. The resort's facilites, which consist of just two ski-lifts, are, however, relatively basic.

Lakes Tour ❾

THREE ATTRACTIVE LAKES – Dayet Aoua, Dayet Ifrah and Dayet Hachlaf – lie 9 km (6.5 miles) south of Imouzzer du Kandar. A turning off road P24 leads to Dayet Aoua, which formed in a natural depression. The narrow road running along it leads to Dayet Ifrah, surrounded by a cirque of mountains, and on to Dayet Hachlaf. Beyond a forestry hut, a track on the right leads to the Vallée des Roches (Valley of the Rocks). Ducks, grey herons, cranes, egrets, birds of prey and dragonflies populate these arid expanses.

Bird sanctuary ②
When the lakes are full, the area becomes a nature reserve for many species of birds. It attracts waders – such as avocets, cattle egrets, grey herons and crested coots – wildfowl, birds of prey – such as red kites and kestrels – and swallows.

Dayet Aoua ①
This lake sits in a natural depression surrounded by hills. It sometimes remains dry for several years in a row and this is due to persistent drought and the fact that the water table has been tapped to irrigate orchards in the area.

Dayet Ifrah ③
Surrounded by a natural amphitheatre of hills, this is one of the largest lakes in the area. Shepherds set up their tents on the lakeshore, and two hamlets face each other across the water, their white minarets rising up into the sky.

Rock formations ⑤
Continuing along track 3325 in the direction of the Ifrane-Mischliffen road, a rough track branching off to the right leads to this circle of rocks which, shaped by natural forces, have the appearance of ruins.

Vallée des Roches ④
A track on the right, beyond the forestry hut, leads to these outcrops of limestone, strangely shaped by erosion, and to caves inhabited by bats.

KEY

▪▪ Tour route (track)

═ Road

‗‗ Track

0 km ——————— 5

0 miles ——————— 5

TIPS FOR DRIVERS

Tour length: about 60 km (37 miles).
Departure point: 16 km (10 miles) north of Ifrane on the P24, forking left to Dayet Aoua.
Duration: one day.
Stopping place: Chalet du Lac, on the shores of Dayet Aoua.

The sources of the Oum er-Rbia, the "Mother of Spring"

Sources of the Oum er-Rbia ⑩

Accessible via road 3485, then road 3211 from Khenifra or road S303 from Aïn Leuh. There are no hotels or petrol stations between Azrou and Khenifra.

A WINDING ROAD runs above the valley of the Oum er-Rbia, then leads down to the *wadi*. The river's sources – over 40 springs – form cascades that crash down the limestone cliffs, joining to form the Oum er-Rbia, the longest river in Morocco. The springs can be explored via a footpath.

Aguelmane Azigza, a lake in a verdant setting

Aguelmane Azigza ⑪

12 km (7.5 miles) south of the sources of the Oum er-Rbia.

T HE RIVERS whose sources lie in the heart of the Middle Atlas have formed lakes in the craters of extinct volcanoes. One such is Aguelmane Azigza. It is enclosed by cliffs and forests of cedar and holm-oak and contains plenty of fish.

Aguelmane Sidi Ali ⑫

Junction with P21.

A RIGHT TURN off road P21 from Azrou to Midelt leads to Aguelmane Sidi Ali, a deep, fish-filled lake that is 3 km (2 miles) long and lies at an altitude of 2,000 m (6564 ft). With Jbel Hayane rising above, it is surrounded by rugged hills and desolate pasture where the Beni M'Guild's flocks are brought for summer grazing.

Continuing towards Midelt, this very scenic road climbs up to the Zad Pass, which at 2,178 m (7,148 ft), is the highest in the Middle Atlas.

Khenifra ⑬

160 km (99 miles) from Fès; 130 km (81 miles) from Beni Mellal. 15,000, from Fès and Marrakech. Sun & Wed.

I N THE FOLDS of the arid hills and on the banks of the Oum er-Rbia stand houses painted in the carmine red that is typical of Khenifra. Until the 17th century, the town was the rallying point of the Zaïane tribe, which resisted attempts by the French to pacify the region. In the 18th century Moulay Ismaïl asserted his authority by building imposing kasbahs in which armies were garrisoned. The livestock market here is one of the few interesting aspects of the town.

An elegant gate in Khenifra

THE LIONS OF THE ATLAS

Before World War I, the roaring of lions in the Moroccan Atlas could be heard at dusk and during the night. The last Atlas lion was killed in 1922. During the Roman period, lions were plentiful in North Africa. They flourished in Tunisia as recently as the 17th century, although by 1891 not one remained. In Algeria, the last lion was killed in 1893, about 100 km (60 miles) south of Constantine. The lions of the Atlas were large, with a thick mane, which was very dark or almost black. Because the genetic make-up of the Atlas lion is known, it should be possible to bring this extinct sub-species back to life. With this end in view, a breeding programme is under way, using lions bred in circuses and in zoos, most particularly the zoo in Rabat.

The Atlas lion, portrayed by Eugène Delacroix (Musée Bonnat, Bayonne)

◁ A beautiful olive grove in the Taza area *(see p210)*

OLIVES AND OLIVE OIL

Olive groves are a common sight around Meknès and Beni Mellal and in the Rif. The gnarled and knotty olive tree survives in poor soil, taking root in rough and uneven ground. Olive oil is extracted by time-honoured methods. In the autumn, the green, black and violet-tinged olives are harvested, the mixture of all three determining the flavour and aroma of the oil. A heavy grindstone turned by donkeys grinds the olives, crushing both the flesh and the kernel. The resulting dark-hued pulp is emptied into large, shallow, circular porous containers placed beneath the oil press. The oil seeps out

Piles of olives set out for sale in the souk

Grindstones, carved from a single block

and runs into vats, where, mixed with water, it floats to the surface, free of debris. A whole 5 kg (11 lb) of olives makes just 1 litre (1.76 pints) of oil. On the colourful stalls in the souks, the different kinds of olives are piled up into pyramids; there are green olives with herbs, violet-hued olives with a sharp taste, piquant olives spiced with red peppers, olives with bitter orange, crushed black olives that have been sun-dried and steeped in oil, and olives for making *tajine*.

ENVIRONS: The village of **El-Kebab** clings to a hillside southeast of Khenifra. Here craftsmen make pottery and carpets. Above the village is the hermitage where Father Albert Peyriguère, a doctor and companion to the French ascetic Charles de Foucauld, lived from 1928 to 1959. A souk is held on Mondays.

Kasba Tadla ⑭

82 km (51 miles) southwest of Khenifra on the P24. 🏠 36,000. 🚌 from Beni Mellal and Khenifra. 🛈 Beni Mellal. 🛒 Mon.

THE FOCAL POINT of this former garrison town is, not surprisingly, the kasbah, which was built by Moulay Ismaïl in the 17th century. So as to subdue rebellious tribes, Moulay Ismaïl made his son governor of the province. The latter built a second kasbah, contiguous with the one that his father had built. A double line of walls thus surrounds the town, enclosing two dilapidated mosques, the former governor's palace and grain stores. Below the town, a ten-span bridge crosses Wadi Oum er-Rbia.

ENVIRONS: Plantations of olive trees cover the Tadla plain between Kasba Tadla and Khenifra, and many traditional olive mills line the road at **Tirhboula**, about 10 km (6 miles) from Khenifra. In the autumn, visitors can see the various stages in the oil-producing process and buy

olive oil here. **El-Ksiba** is an attractive village on the edge of the forest 22 km (13.5 miles) east of Kasba Tadla. It has a souk, which is very busy on Sundays. Beyond El-Ksiba, the road becomes a track that crosses the High Atlas via Imilchil, descending to Tinerhir, in the southern foothills.

The ten-span bridge over the Oum er-Rbia at Kasba Tadla

The Mountains of Morocco

Lammergeier

Fʀᴏᴍ ᴛʜᴇ ʜɪɢʜ ᴘᴇᴀᴋs down to altitudes above 600 m (1,970 ft), the climate is permanently moist. Annual precipitation ranges from 650 mm (25 in) in the eastern Grand Atlas to over 2 m (80 in) in the Rif, and snowfall is often heavy. The vegetation in this band is particularly luxuriant, and many forests thrive in this well-watered environment. These consist mostly of cedar, cork oak, deciduous oak, evergreen holm-oak and, in the Rif, Moroccan pine.

Holm-oak grows at altitudes of 600 to 2,700 m (1,970 to 8,860 ft) and makes up a quarter of all Morocco's forested areas.

Aleppo pine, which grows naturally in the mountains, is planted almost everywhere since its timber is used for a wide range of purposes.

Forests of Atlas cedar are impressive for their sheer size, and the trees for their beauty, their majestic appearance and their height, which can exceed 50 m (164 ft).

Atlas cedar

The carob produces sugar-rich pods that are a nutritious food for both humans and animals.

Aleppo pine can grow to a height of 25 m (82 ft).

Barbary thuya

Holm-oak

Argan

Kermes oak

Wild olive can be used as grafting stock. Its timber is suitable for carpentry and is also used as firewood.

The argan (see p127) is a small tree that grows exclusively in southwestern Morocco. Argan nuts are a favourite food of goats, which climb up into the branches to reach them. Oil extracted from the kernels is used in foods, in cosmetics and as a tonic.

HIGH-ALTITUDE VEGETATION

At altitudes above 2,700 m (8,860 ft), the mountains consist of cold and arid steppe, which is often covered in snow. No trees grow here but there are abundant streams. The low-growing vegetation, including some endemic species, is varied and forms a covering of spiny, cushion-like clumps.

Juniper

The Tizi-n-Test Pass commands a view of the snowy heights of the Atlas and the Souss valley, 2,000 m (6,564 ft) below.

MOUNTAIN FAUNA

The Barbary sheep, Africa's only wild sheep, inhabits the High and Middle Atlas. It can also be seen in Jbel Toubkal National Park *(see p249)*, which was created especially to ensure its survival. Three-quarters of the country's population of macaques live in the cedar forests of the Middle Atlas. Wild boar is found in all mountain-ous areas and the Barbary stag was reintroduced in 1990. Birds are plentiful at altitudes between 2,200 and 3,600 m (7,220 and 11,815 ft). They include the golden eagle, Bonelli's eagle, bald eagle, the huge lammergeier, Egyptian vulture, partridge, Moussier's redstart and the rare crimson-winged finch, which nests only at altitudes above 2,800 m (9,190 ft).

Barbary sheep

Adult booted eagle, feeding chicks in the nest

Female macaque carrying her newborn on her back

M'Goun, which rises to a height of more than 4,000 m (13,128 ft), is the second-highest peak in the High Atlas.

The Aïn-Asserdoun springs, "Springs of the Mule"

Boujad ⑮

24 km (15 miles) north of Kasba Tadla on road P13. 🏛 15,000. 🚌 Thu.

THE HOLY TOWN of Boujad, which is filled with *koubbas* (tombs) and shrines, is set in the Tadla plain, on the caravan route that once ran between Marrakech and Fès. It was established in the 16th century by Sidi Mohammed ech-Cherki, patron saint of Tadla, who built an important *zaouia* here. The saint and his descendants, bearers of *baraka* (blessing, luck or good fortune) from one generation to the next, have always been highly venerated by the Beni Meskin and Seguibat, local Berber tribespeople. In 1785, sultan Sidi Mohammed ben Abdallah, who was resentful of this power, razed the town, including the *zaouia*. The latter was rebuilt in the 19th century and is still inhabited by the saint's descendants.

The tombs of the saintly dynasty can be seen around the market square in the north of the town. The largest, the **Koubba of Sidi Othman**, is open to visitors. There are many other mausoleums here, most notably that of the sheik Mohammed ech-Cherki, which is closed to non-Muslims. On a promontory outside Boujad, in the direction of Oued Zem on the northern side of the town, stand five white *koubbas*, to which crowds of pilgrims come for annual gatherings.

Beni Mellal ⑯

30 km (18.5 miles) southwest of Kaṣba Tadla on road P24. 🏛 140,000. 🚌 from Khenifra, Marrakech and Demnate. 🛈 Avenue Hassan II; (023) 48 86 63. 🚌 Tue; Sun in Sebt-Oulad-Nemaa 35 km (22 miles) to the west.

THE MODERN TOWN of Beni Mellal lies at the foot of the Middle Atlas, on the edge of the great Tadla plain, where cereals are extensively cultivated. Although it is devoid of any obvious appeal, it is still a convenient stopping-place.

Inhabited by Berbers and Jews well before the arrival of Islam, the town was known successively as Day, Kasba Belkouche and Beni Mellal. In the 13th century, it stood on the border between the kingdoms of Fès and Marrakech, which were the object of bitter dispute between the Merinid and Almohad dynasties. In 1680 Moulay Ismaïl built a kasbah here, which was restored on several occasions.

The town is surrounded by orange groves (oranges from Beni Mellal are renowned), and olive groves stretch to the horizon. Beetroot and sugarcane have replaced bananas as cultivated crops. All are unusually well watered thanks to the Bin el-Ouidane dam.

South of the town, in the lower foothills of the Middle

Cedar-dwelling macaque

Atlas, a road marked "Circuit touristique" leads to the **Aïn Asserdoun springs**, which run between trees and small gardens. It is worth making the short detour to **Ras el-Aïn**, a little further up. This stone and pisé *borj* (tower) offers a picturesque view of Beni Mellal and its orchards.

ENVIRONS: The area around Beni Mellal has many waterfalls, springs, caves and wooded gorges populated by monkeys. About 10 km (6 miles) east, a road leads to **Foum el-Anser**, where a waterfall crashes into a gorge. The rockface here is marked by artificial caves, access to which is difficult. South of Beni Mellal, a hillside track leads up to **Jbel Tassemit** (2,248 m/7,378 ft), which is the departure point for scenic mountain hikes. Hikers can also reach the **Tarhzirte Gorge** and the Wadi Derna valley, 20 km (12 miles) northeast of Beni Mellal.

Bin el-Ouidane Dam ⑰

43 km (27 miles) southwest of Beni Mellal on road P24, branching left to Ouaouizarht on road 1802 or via Afourer on road S508. 🛈 Beni Mellal.

FROM BENI MELLAL the road climbs through wooded hills to reach the grandiose site of an artificial lake, the

The *borj* of Ras el-Aïn, offering a spectacular view over the Tadla plain

The Bin el-Ouidane reservoir, at the foot of the High Atlas

Bin el-Ouidane reservoir. The dam here is 285 m (935 ft) long and 133 m (436 ft) high and the reservoir, with a surface area of 380,000 sq m (94 acres), is the largest lake in Morocco. Fed by Wadi el-Abid and Wadi Ahansalt, it irrigates the intensively cultivated Tadla plain, while the hydroelectric generator provides a quarter of Morocco's electricity. The turquoise waters of the lake, which are broken by spits of land and small islands, are surrounded by red hills, and the lakeshore is dotted with a few isolated houses.

Watersports and fishing are permitted on the lake and Wadi el-Abid is suitable for kayaking and rafting in spring, when the water level is sufficiently high. A track leading from the lake ends at a rock formation known as La Cathédrale. This rock, with a covering of red soil and a setting among Aleppo pines, is well known to abseilers.

From the dam, Azilal and the Aït Bouguemez valley (see pp254–7) can be reached on road S508.

Cascades d'Ouzoud ⓲

65 km (40 miles) southwest of Bin el-Ouidane on roads S508 and 1811, or 156 km (97 miles) from Marrakech via Demnate. 🚌 for Beni Mellal-Azilal then grand taxi.

ONE OF THE MOST spectacular sights in Morocco, the Cascades d'Ouzoud attract large numbers of visitors. The waterfall is particularly impressive in spring, when the waters pour down from the top of reddish cliffs, crashing off a succession of rocky ledges to fall into the canyon of Wadi el-Abid 100 m (328 ft) below.

The road to the site leads to a spot above the waterfall, which can be reached along a footpath with steps cut into the earth. From platforms set at intervals on the path, visitors can marvel at the majestic succession of cascades and admire the permanent rainbow created by the mist thrown up by the water. Mills, whose only vestiges are small rectangular recesses, once worked a grindstone on which corn and barley were ground to make flour. The fig trees and carobs that grow beside the path are often full of monkeys – the beige-coated macaques with eyes outlined in black. Bathing is permitted in the natural pools.

Starting from the bottom of the waterfall, energetic visitors wearing strong walking boots can hike to the Wadi el-Abid gorge.

ENVIRONS: 6 km (4 miles) southwest of Demnate, on road S508, is **Imi-n-Ifri**, a natural bridge that has been partly carved out by the *wadi*. A track leads down to the bottom of the chasm.

The Cascades d'Ouzoud in spring, at their most spectacular

MARRAKECH

SUCH IS THE IMPORTANCE *of Marrakech that it gave its nam.*
Morocco. For more than two centuries, this Berber city at t.
point of interchange between the Sahara, the Atlas and the Anti-
Atlas was the hub of a great empire, and the achievements of illustrious
builders can be seen within the city's walls. It is the capital of the great
South and, although it is now only Morocco's third city after
Casablanca and Rabat, its fabulous palaces and luxuriant palm grove
continue to hold a powerful fascination for visitors.

Marrakech was founded in 1062 by Almoravids from the Sahara. These warrior monks soon carved out an empire that stretched from Algiers to Spain. In 1106, Ali ben Youssef hired craftsmen from Andalusia to build a palace and a mosque in the capital. He also raised ramparts around the city and installed *khettaras* (underground canals), an ingenious irrigation system that brought water to its great palm grove.

The Almohads took the city in 1147. Abd el-Moumen built the Koutoubia, a masterpiece of Moorish architecture, and his successor was responsible for building the kasbah. But the Almohad dynasty collapsed, to the benefit of the Merinids of Fès, and for over 200 years Marrakech stagnated. It was not until the 16th century that the city was reinvigorated by the arrival of the Saadians, most notably by the wealthy Ahmed el-Mansour. The Saadian Tombs, the Ben Youssef Medersa and the remains of the Palais el-Badi mark this golden age. In 1668, Marrakech fell to the Alaouites, who made Fès, then Meknès, their capital.

In the 20th century, Marrakech embraced the modern age with the creation of the Quartier Gueliz, built during the Protectorate. Visitors continue to flock to this magical city, and tourism is central to its economy today.

A woman leaving the *zaouia* of Sidi bel Abbès

◁ The garden of the Villa Majorelle

...ring Marrakech

...RICH HISTORY of Marrakech is reflected in ... various quarters. The medina, above which ... the minaret of the Koutoubia Mosque, the ...blem of the city, corresponds to the old town. ...ace Jemaa el-Fna, the hub of all activity, is ...ts heart. Within the ramparts are the souks (north of Place Jemaa el-Fna), the kasbah and the mellah (the Jewish quarter). Gueliz, in the northwest, is the new town laid out by Marshal Lyautey under the Protectorate. It is filled with Western-style offices, businesses and a residential area. Avenue Mohammed V is the district's main thoroughfare. Extending Gueliz in the southwest is Hivernage, a verdant quarter with many hotels that also dates from the Protectorate. The district is bordered on its western side by the Menara Gardens, and on its eastern side by the walls of the medina.

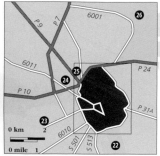

LOCATOR MAP

KEY

	Medina
	Historic building
—	Ramparts
	Bus stations
P	Parking
⊠	Post office
✚	Hospital
C	Mosque
	Jewish cemetery
⛛	Muslim cemetery
—	Major road
=	Minor road

0 m   400

0 yards   400

SEE ALSO

• **Where to Stay** pp310–12

• **Where to Eat** pp329–31

SIGHTS AT A GLANCE

Squares and Historic Quarters
Gueliz ㉔
Méchouars ⑳
Mellah ⑭
Place Jemaa el-Fna ⑩
The Souks pp228–9 ⑧

Historic Buildings
Bab Agnaou ⑱
Chrob ou Chouf Fountain ③
Dar el-Makhzen ⑲
Koubba Ba'Adiyn ⑥
La Mamounia Hotel ⑫

Palais el-Badi ⑮
Palais Bahia ⑬
Saadian Tombs ⑰

Mosques and Religious Buildings
Bab Doukkala Mosque ⑦
Ben Youssef Medersa ④
Kasbah Mosque ⑯
Koutoubia Mosque pp236–7 ⑪
Mouassine Mosque ⑨
Zaouia of Sidi bel Abbès ①
Zaouia of Sidi ben Slimane el-Jazouli ②

Museums
Dar Si Saïd Museum ㉑
Musée de Marrakech ⑤

Gardens
Aguedal Gardens ㉒
La Palmeraie ㉖
Majorelle Garden ㉕
Menara ㉓

GETTING AROUND
The only way to explore the souks and the medina is on foot. The ramparts and most other features of interest to visitors can be reached by car, though parking can be difficult. A very pleasant and inexpensive way of travelling around the city is by yellow *petit taxi* or horse-drawn carriage. It is wise to agree in advance the fare for your journey. *Petit taxis* and carriages can be hired mainly in Gueliz (on Avenue Mohammed V, near the central market and the large hotels) and around Place Jemaa el-Fna, near the central police station.

...ouia of
...di bel Abbès ❶

Sidi bel Abbès quarter (north of the
medina). ◐ to non-Muslims.
Pilgrimage on Thu.

FROM BAB EL-KHEMIS, Rue
Sidi Rhalem leads to the
Zaouia of Sidi bel Abbès. The
sanctuary is a focal point for
the pilgrimage of the Regraga
(the Seven Saints), which was
instituted by Moulay Ismaïl so
as to obtain forgiveness for
his depredations in Marrakech.
    Sidi bel Abbès (1130–1205)
is the city's most highly
venerated patron saint. A
disciple of the famous Cadi
Ayad, he devoted his life to
preaching and to caring for

**The monumental entrance to the
Zaouia of Sidi bel Abbès**

and defending the weak and
the blind. Because of him, it
was said throughout Morocco
that Marrakech was the only
city where a blind man could
eat his fill. To this day, the
gifts of pilgrims are distributed
to the poor and the blind.
    In 1605, the Saadian sultan
Abou Faris raised a mausoleum for the saint in the hope
of curing his epilepsy. Moulay
Ismaïl added a dome in the
18th century and the
mausoleum was given its
present appearance by Sidi
Mohammed ben Abdallah a
few years later.
    The *zaouia* also includes a
mosque, a hammam, a home
for the blind, a small market,
an abattoir and a cemetery.

South of the *zaouia* is the
El-Mjadlia Souk, the Passementerie Souk, built in a
covered alley during the reign
of Sidi Mohammed ben
Abderrahman, at the end of
the 19th century. Going from
here towards the centre of the
medina, you will pass **Bab
Taghzout**, an Almoravid gate
that has been integrated into
the surrounding architecture.

Zaouia of
Sidi ben Slimane
el-Jazouli ❷

North of the medina (near Rue Dar
el-Glaoui). ◐ to non-Muslims.
Pilgrimage on Fri.

AFTER BAB TAGHZOUT, if
you follow Rue de Bab
Taghzout, then take the
first right, and then go right
again, you will reach this
zaouia, which also features
in the Regraga pilgrimage
(see p38). The mausoleum
dates from the Saadian
period and was remodelled
in the late 18th century
during the reign of Sidi
Mohammed ben Abdallah.
    Sidi Mohammed ben
Slimane el-Jazouli, another
venerated mystic, founded
Moroccan Sufism in the
15th century. Under the
Wattasids, this religion
spread to every level of the
population. A champion of
the holy war against the
Portuguese and a politically
influential figure, this holy
man attracted thousands of
followers; his reputedly occult
powers even worried the sultan.

**Interior of the Zaouia of Sidi
ben Slimane**

Chrob ou Chouf
Fountain ❸

Rue Amesfah, near the Mosque of
Ben Youssef.

AS ITS NAME – meaning
"Drink and Admire" –
suggests, this Saadian fountain is one of the most beautiful in the medina. It was built
during the reign of Ahmed
el-Mansour (1578–1603), and
it is shaded by a carved cedar
awning with coloured *zellij*
tilework and inscriptions in
cursive and Kufic script
engraved into the wood.
    In a town like Marrakech,
located at the head of pre-
Saharan valleys, water was a
very precious commodity. An
underground network of
channels supplied the
mosques and the houses and
fed the fountains. Obeying
the precepts of the Koran,
according to which water
must be given to the thirsty,
many of the leading citizens
of Marrakech financed the
building of fountains.

Detail of the cedar awning over the Chrob ou Chouf Fountain

The Ramparts of Marrakech

SKIRTING THE GUELIZ and Hivernage quarters on their eastern side, the ramparts completely encircle the medina. From the time of its foundation, Marrakech was defended by sturdy walls set with forts. Although their outline has hardly altered from the time of the Almoravids, they were extended to the south by the Almohads and to the north by the Saadians in the 16th century. These pisé walls are 19 km (12 miles) long, up to 2 m (6 ft) thick and up to 9 m (30 ft) high. Some of the monumental gates that pierce them are very fine examples of Moorish architecture. The best time to walk around the ramparts is in the early morning or just before sunset. Their warm ochre colour changes according to the time of day and the intensity of the light. In the evening, they take on an almost rust-coloured hue.

THE GATES

Bab Aghmat and Bab Aylen, on the eastern side of the ramparts, date from the 12th century, and are relatively plain. Bab ed-Debbagh, dating from the same period, opens onto the tanners' quarter. On the northern side stands Bab el-Khemis and on the southern, Bab el-Robb (1308). The latter takes its name from a grape liqueur in which the city once did a brisk trade. Bab el-Jedid, on the western side, leads to La Mamounia hotel (see p234).

Bab el-Khemis *was remodelled after the Almoravid period (1147–1269). An open-air market is held outside the gate on Thursdays. The tomb of the Seven Saints is a small dome-topped building dedicated to a marabout.*

Bab Agnaou (see p239), *whose name is derived from the Berber for "horn-less black ram", is one of the finest gates in Marrakech. It is carved in an ochre stone with tinges of pink. It once led into the Almohad palace.*

These lower pisé walls, *which are just high enough to close a harem off from a house or a garden, or to shield a sanctuary from prying eyes, were not built for defensive purposes.*

The ramparts of Marrakech, *which date from the 12th century, are the most impressive city walls in Morocco. The well-preserved defences encircle the old town, with its palaces and gardens.*

The Souks **8**

Olives

THE SOUKS OF MARRAKECH are among the most fascinating in the Maghreb. Arranged according to the individual nature of the goods on offer, they are laid out in the narrow streets north and east of Place Jemaa el-Fna. On the map shown here, the area marked in orange denotes the historic heart of the souks, which stretches from the Ben Youssef Mosque in the north to the Souk Smarine in the south. Many of the souks are known by the name of whatever is sold here. Today a very wide range of goods, from fabric to jewellery and slippers, is on offer. Leatherwork is particularly prominent. Around this commercial hub are the crafts traditionally associated with country people, such as blacksmithing, saddle-making and basketry. Because of rank odours, the tanneries are banished to the edge of the city.

KEY

- Historic souk
- Historic monument

0 m ———————— 100
0 yards ———————— 100

Souk Kimakhin (stringed instruments)

Souk Addadine (metalwork)
Amid a deafening clatter, brass and copper workers tirelessly hammer hot metal, shaping it into a range of everyday items such as trays, ashtrays, lanterns, wrought-iron grilles, locks and keys.

Souk El-Bradiia (pitchers)

Souk Nahhasin (brass and copper)

Souk Chouari (basketry and woodturning)
The chouari is the double pannier that is put on the backs of donkeys. These baskets are woven from palm fibre.

Dyers' Souk
Skeins of wool or silk, freshly dyed and still wet, are hung out to dry in the sun and warm air.

Souk Smarine (clothing)

Souk Smata (slippers and belts)

The craftsmen of Marrakech are master-leatherworkers. The craft of leatherworking is said to have originated in the city.

Kissarias

Clothing, fabric, leather goods and passementerie are on sale in these lit and covered galleries. This was once where the most highly prized goods, some of them imported, were sold.

Souk Siyyaghin (jewellery)

Souk Fakharina

Souk El-Kebir (leatherwork)

Souk Zrabia (the Criée Berbère, the main carpet market)

Souk El-Maazi (goatskin)

BEN YOUSSEF MOSQUE

BEN YOUSSEF MEDERSA

MUSÉE DE MARRAKECH

KOUBBA BA'ADIYN

RUE SOUK EL KEBIR

RAHBA KEDIMA

Former slave market

Souk el-Batna (skins)

Thousands of skins for use in leatherwork are sold in the skinners' souk.

Rahba Kedima, "Old Square"

Magicians and healers buy their supplies here, and country people sell fruit, vegetables and live chickens.

Zellij tilework in the Ben Youssef Medersa

Ben Youssef Medersa ❹

Place ben Youssef *(in the medina).*
📞 *(044) 39 09 11.* ⏱ *9am–6pm daily.* 📷

THIS KORANIC SCHOOL is not only one of the finest but also one of the largest in the Maghreb, with a capacity for up to 900 students.

It was founded by the Merinid sultan Abou el-Hassan in the mid-14th century, and was rebuilt by the Saadian sultan Moulay Abdallah in the 16th century. This fact is recorded by the inscriptions carved into the lintel above the entrance, together with the date, 1564.

Bronze door of the Ben Youssef Medersa

The medersa takes its name from the Almoravid mosque of Ali ben Youssef to which it was once attached. For four centuries this mosque was the focal point of worship in the medina, and with the medersa it constituted an important centre of religion.

Architecturally, and with its sumptous decoration, it is on a par with the Merinid medersas, particularly the Bou Inania Medersa of Fès *(see pp172–3).* By building it, Moulay Abdallah was expressing his desire to restore to Marrakech the

prestige of an imperial capital and simultaneously to affirm his devotion to Allah.

Covering an area of some 1,720 sq m (18,514 sq ft), this harmoniously proportioned medersa appears as it was originally designed, with no later alteration. The dome, decorated with exquisite stalactites within, can be seen from the street. The main entrance, a bronze door topped by a carved cedar lintel, opens onto a mosaic-paved corridor, which in turn leads to the courtyard. This masterpiece of Moorish design is paved with white marble and has an ablutions pool in the centre. The walls are decorated with *zellij* tilework below and carved plaster above. A double tier of galleries supported on thick columns lines both sides of the courtyard. The students' cells on the ground and upper floors opened onto the courtyard. Those that are shielded from daylight are arranged around seven smaller interior courtyards.

A magnificently ornate doorway leads through to the large prayer hall. The room is crowned by a pyramidal cedar dome and divided into three by marble columns with capitals with calligraphy

praising Moulay Abdallah. The mihrab is decorated with verses from the Koran in calligraphic script and is lit by 24 windows decorated with a tracery of plasterwork.

Musée de Marrakech ❺

Place ben Youssef. 📞 *(044) 39 09 11.*
⏱ *9am–6pm daily.* 📷

THIS MUSEUM is laid out in the Dar Menebhi, a palace built at the end of the 19th century by the grand vizier of Sultan Moulay Mehdi Hassan. The building is in the style of a traditional Moorish house.

The decorated door – which, as in many Moorish houses, is the only opening in the otherwise featureless external walls – leads through to an open courtyard with *zellij* tilework and three marble basins in the centre. The courtyard gives access to the rooms on the ground and upper floors.

The museum's collection is displayed in two wings. One contains contemporary art, Orientalist paintings and a series of original engravings of Moroccan subjects.

The second wing contains a rather haphazard display of objects: coins from the Idrissid period of the 9th century to that of the Alaouites in the present day; illuminated copies of the Koran, including a 12th-century Chinese example and a 19th-century book of Sufi prayers; southern Moroccan jewellery; Tibetan dress, 17th- and 18th-century ceramics; and some fine decorated Berber doors.

Zellij tilework in the courtyard of the Musée de Marrakech

The Koubba Ba'Adiyn, the only vestige of the Almoravid mosque

Koubba Ba'Adiyn 6

Place ben Youssef. **C** *(044) 39 09 11.*
O *9am–12:30pm & 2–6pm daily.*

THIS BRICK-BUILT DOME is the only example of Almoravid architecture in Marrakech. Built by Ali ben Youssef in 1106, originally it formed part of a richly decorated mosque that was demolished by the Almohads. Miraculously spared, the rectangular pavilion was rediscovered in 1948. It contained an ablutions pool fed by three reservoirs. While the exterior is decorated with chevrons and pointed arches in relief, the interior is graced by scalloped and horseshoe arches and floral ornamentation. These elements anticipate the full-blown artistic creativity of Islamic architecture.

Bab Doukkala Mosque 7

Rue de Bab Doukkala. *to non-Muslims.* **Dar el-Glaoui** *to visitors.*

THIS PLACE OF WORSHIP was built in the mid-16th century by the mother of the Saadian ruler Ahmed el-Mansour. Its slender minaret, crowned by four golden orbs, and its refined decoration are reminiscent of the Kasbah Mosque *(see p238)*. Next to the building stands an ornate fountain with a bowl surmounted by three domes.

From here, Rue de Bab Doukkala, going towards the centre of the medina, leads to **Dar el-Glaoui**,

AVERROËS

Born in Córdoba in 1126, Averroës (Ibn Rushd) was one of the most renowned Muslim scholars of his day. Like other men of learning at the time, his knowledge encompassed medicine, law, philosophy, astronomy and theology. Born into an important Cordoban family, he was the grandson of an imam at the Great Mosque in Granada. Under the patronage of Abou Yacoub Youssef, Averroës divided his time between Seville, Córdoba and Marrakech. He took the place of his friend and teacher, the famous physician Abubacer (Ibn Tufayl). Basing his approach on his own reading of Aristotle, he promoted a rationalist, rather than an esoteric, interpretation of the Koran. This brought him condemnation from Córdoba. However, he was soon rehabilitated by the Almohad ruler Yacoub el-Mansour, who gave him asylum in Marrakech until his death in December 1198.

Averroës, the great 12th-century philosopher

the palace built by El-Glaoui, the famous pasha of Marrakech *(see p57),* at the beginning of the 20th century. While one part of the building contains a library, another is used to receive heads of state during official visits.

The palace has several beautifully decorated courtyards lined with *zellij* tilework, stuccowork, painted wood and *muqarnas* (stalactites). It also features a fine Andalusian garden planted with fruit trees. The palace is reputed to have been the venue for some wild and extravagant parties.

The Souks 8

See pp228–9.

Mouassine Mosque 9

Mouassine Quarter.
to non-Muslims.

THE SAADIAN SULTAN Moulay Abdallah established this place of worship, which was built between 1562 and 1573 on what is thought to be a former Jewish quarter. Its design as well as its decoration

bear certain similarities to the Koutoubia Mosque *(see pp236–7)* and the Kasbah Mosque *(see p238).*

The minaret, which is crowned by a gallery with merlons, is of strikingly simple design. The adjacent Mouassine Fountain consists of three large drinking troughs for animals and a fourth for people. The fountain is enclosed within a portico with decorative stuccowork and carved wooden lintels.

Dar el-Glaoui, palace of the extravagantly hospitable pasha of Marrakech

Small open-air restaurants on Place Jemaa el-Fna

The hotel, in a restrained and unified style, was designed by Henri Prost and Antoine Marchisio, who achieved a pleasing combination of Art Deco and Moorish styles. Many famous people, including Winston Churchill, Richard Nixon and Orson Welles, have stayed here.

Palais Bahia ⑬

Riad Zitoun Jedid (medina). ☎ (044) 38 932:45pm daily. ◯ 8:45am–11:45am & 2:30–5:45pm. 🎦

THIS PALACE, whose name means "Palace of the Favourite", was built by two powerful grand viziers – Si Moussa, vizier of Sultan Sidi Mohammed ben Abderrahman, and his son Ba Ahmed, vizier of Moulay Abdelaziz – at the end of the 19th century.

The palace complex consists of two parts, each built at different times. The older part, built by Si Moussa, contains apartments arranged around a marble-paved courtyard. It also has an open courtyard with cypressses, orange trees and jasmine, with two star-shaped pools.

The newer part, built by Ba Ahmed, is a huge palace without a unified plan. It consists of luxurious apartments looking onto courtyards planted with trees. So as to make it easier for the obese master of the house to move around, almost all the apartments were located on the ground floor. The main

Place Jemaa el-Fna ⑩

East of Gueliz (off the southern extremity of Avenue Mohammed V).

FOR CENTURIES, this unique and extraordinary square has been the nerve centre of Marrakech and the symbol of the city. Although it is in fact no more than an irregular space devoid of a harmonious ensemble of buildings, it is of interest to visitors mainly because it is a showcase of traditional Morocco. UNESCO has declared it a World Heritage Site.

It has a gruesome past: until the 19th century, criminals on whom the death sentence had been passed were beheaded here. Sometimes up to 45 people were executed on a single day, their heads being pickled and suspended from the city gates.

No traces are left of this today. A large market is held in the mornings, and medicinal plants, freshly squeezed orange juice as well as all kinds of nuts and confectionery.

From sunset, the life and bustle on the square reaches its peak. It becomes the arena of a gigantic, multifaceted open-air show. As the air fills with smoke from grilling meat and the aroma of spices, the square fills with musicians, dancers, storytellers, showmen, tooth-pullers, fortune-tellers and snake-charmers, who each draw a crowd of astonished onlookers.

A monkey-handler on Place Jemaa el-Fna

Koutoubia Mosque ⑪

See pp236–7.

La Mamounia Hotel ⑫

Avenue Bab el-Jedid. ☎ (044) 44 44 09. See also p310.

OPENED IN 1929, the legendary La Mamounia Hotel stands on the site of a residence that, in the 18th century, belonged to the son of the Alaouite sultan Sidi Mohammed. All that remains of that residence is the magnificent 130,000-sq-m (32-acre) garden, planted with olive and orange trees and containing a pavilion that was probably built by a Saadian ruler in the 16th century.

The entrance to La Mamounia Hotel (see p310)

◁ **La Palmeraie, the famous palm grove in Marrakech, with the High Atlas in the background**

Intricately decorated arch leading to the main courtyard in Palais Bahia

courtyard is paved with marble and *zellij* tilework. It is surrounded by a gallery of finely fluted columns, while three fountains with bowls stand in the centre. This courtyard, once used by the viziers' concubines, faces the main reception room. It has a cedar ceiling painted with arabesques. The decoration of the palace apartments and of the council chamber is equally splendid.

Ba Ahmed hired the best craftsmen in the kingdom to build and decorate this palace. It is decked out with highly prized materials, such as marble from Meknès, cedar from the Middle Atlas and tiles from Tetouan. Not surprisingly, Marshal Lyautey chose to live here during the Protectorate.

Maison Tiskiwin, at No. 8 Rue de la Bahia, houses the **Bert Flint Museum**. This charming residence with a courtyard is an example of a traditional 19th-century Marrakech house. Here, Bert Flint, a Dutch professor who fell in love with Morocco and settled here in the 1950s, amassed a collection of folk art and artifacts from the Souss valley and the Saharan region *(see pp283–96)*. Exhibits include jewellery and daggers from the Anti-Atlas, pottery from the Rif and carpets from the Middle Atlas. The museum is close to another museum, the Dar Si Saïd *(see pp240–41)*.

🏛 **Bert Flint Museum**
8 Rue de la Bahia, Riad Zitoun Jedid. 📞 *(044) 38 91 92.*
⏰ *9am–noon & 3–6pm Wed–Mon.* 🖼

Mellah ⑭

East of Palais el-Badi and south of Palais Bahia.

ONCE ACOMMODATING some 16,000 inhabitants, the former Jewish quarter of Marrakech was the largest mellah in Morocco until the country's independence. Previously located on what became the site of the Mouassine Mosque, the mellah was established in the mid-16th century by the Saadian sultan Moulay Abdallah, and it was almost identical to the mellah in Fès *(see p182)*. Until 1936, it was surrounded by a wall pierced by two gates, one opening east onto the cemetery and the other leading into the city. The jewellers' souk that is held opposite the Palais Bahia.

Palais el-Badi ⑮

Hay Salam, Rue Berrima.
⏰ *9am–noon & 2:30–5:45pm daily.* 🖼

FIVE MONTHS after acceding to the throne, Ahmed el-Mansour decided to consolidate his rule and banish the memory of earlier dynasties. Having emerged victorious over the Portuguese at the Battle of the Three Kings on 4 August 1578 *(see p52)*, Ahmed el-Mansour, "the Golden", ordered a luxurious palace to be built near his private apartments. It was to be used for receptions and audiences with foreign embassies. Its construction was financed by the Portuguese whom he had defeated in battle, and work continued until his death in 1603.

El-Badi, "the Incomparable", is one of the 99 names of Allah. For a time, the palace was indeed considered to be one of the wonders of the Muslim world. Italian marble,

Door opening onto a narrow street in the mellah of Marrakech

Irish granite, Indian onyx and coverings of gold leaf decorated the walls and the ceilings of the 360 rooms.

In 1683, Moulay Ismaïl demolished the Palais el-Badi and salvaged the materials to embellish his own imperial city of Meknès *(see p192)*. Today, all that remains of the palace are empty rooms.

The remains of the Palais el-Badi, built in the 16th century

Koutoubia Mosque ⓫

IN ABOUT 1147, to mark his victory over the Almoravids, the Almohad sultan Abd el-Moumen set about building one of the largest mosques in the Western Muslim world. The minaret, a masterpiece of Islamic architecture, was completed during the reign of Yacoub el-Mansour, grandson of Abd el-Moumen. It later served as the model for the Giralda in Seville, as well as for the Hassan Tower in Rabat *(see p76)*. The "Booksellers' Mosque" takes its name from the manuscripts souk that once took place around it. The interior of the minaret contains a ramp used to carry building materials up to the summit. The mosque has been restored to reveal the original pink colour of the brickwork.

Four gilt-bronze spheres surmount the lantern.

Denticulate merlons

★ Minaret
This splendid tower in pink Gueliz stone stands likes a sentinel above the city. It is 70 m (230 ft) high and its proportions obey the canons of Almohad architecture: its height equals five times its width.

The interior of the minaret contains six superimposed rooms.

Entrance to the Koutoubia Courtyard
This restrained and simple entrance follows the design of most gateways to important Moroccan buildings: a horseshoe arch with moulded arcature.

Detail of the East Side of the Minaret
Each side of the minaret has a different decorative scheme. Common to all, with variations, are floral motifs, inscriptions, bands of moulded terracotta and, as here, windows with festooned arches.

West View of the Minaret
The minaret is the highest building in the city and it stands as a landmark for many miles around. Only Muslims may enjoy the unforgettable view from the top of the building.

VISITORS' CHECKLIST

Place de la Koutoubia.
🛈 (044) 43 62 39.
⊘ to non-Muslims.

Eastern Entrance to the Prayer Hall
This is the main entrance for the faithful. The design of the doorway is relatively plain, with minimal ornamentation.

Roof of green tiles

Courtyard and pool

The interior of the mosque consists of 16 parallel aisles of equal width bisected by a wider nave.

The original mosque was superseded by another, built on the orders of the Almohad ruler Abd el-Moumen. This was because the *qibla* wall of the earlier mosque was not accurately oriented towards Mecca. Its foundations can still be seen today.

STAR FEATURES

★ Minaret

★ Prayer Hall

★ Prayer Hall
This can accommodate some 20,000 faithful. The white columns supporting horseshoe arches and the braided pattern of the floor create a striking perspective.

Detail of the minaret of the Kasbah Mosque

Kasbah Mosque ⑯

Rue de la Kasba, near Bab Agnaou.
⬤ to non-Muslims.

UILT BY YACOUB EL-MANSOUR
B(1184–99), the Kasbah
Mosque is the only other
Almohad building besides
Bab Agnaou to survive in
Marrakech. Its distinctive
minaret, a beautiful stone and
brick construction in shades
of ochre, was used as a
model by later builders.
Successive remodelling in the
16th and 17th centuries has
robbed the mosque of its
original appearance. Even so,
it is not without interest.

Built to a rectangular plan,
77m (253 ft) long by 71 m
(233 ft) wide, the mosque
consists of a prayer hall and
five interior courtyards separated by arcades. The 80-m
(263-ft) long façade is topped
by crenellations and denticulate merlons. According to
Almohad custom, the minaret
is devoid of ornamentation
up to the height of the walls.
Above this, it has restrained
decoration and is crowned by
an attractive terracotta frieze.
Turquoise tiles moulded with
a magnificent pattern of
interlaced lozenges almost
completely cover the four
faces of the minaret.

Two-fifths of the tower are
taken up by the lantern,
which is crowned by three
spheres. These are made of
brass, but legend has it that
they are made of gold, hence
their popular name, the
Golden Apples.

Saadian Tombs ⑰

Rue de la Kasba. ☎ (044) 43 62 39.
◯ 9am–noon & 2–6pm Wed–Mon. ◪

LTHOUGH THEY WERE
Aneglected for more than
two centuries, the tombs of
the Saadian dynasty constitute
some of the finest examples
of Islamic architecture in
Morocco. Their style is in
complete contrast to the
simplicity of Almohad architecture, as the Saadian
princes lavished on funerary
architecture the same ostenta-
tion and magnificence that
they gave to other buildings.

A necropolis existed here
during the Almohad period
(1145–1248), continuing in
use during the reign of the
Merinid sultan Abou el-Hassan
(1331–51). The Saadian Tombs
themselves date from the late
16th to the 18th centuries. Out
of respect for the dead, and
even though he had been at
pains to erase all traces of his
predecessors, the Alaouite
sultan Moulay Ismaïl raised a
wall round the main entrance.

It was not until 1917 that
the tombs were made accessible to the public. They

Mausoleum of Ahmed el-Mansour, with marble-columned mihrab

consist of two mausoleums
which are set in a garden
planted with flowers
symbolizing Allah's paradise.

The central mausoleum is
that of Ahmed el-Mansour
(1578–1603). It consists of
three funerary rooms laid out
to a plan reminiscent of that
of the Rawda in Granada. The
first room is a prayer hall
divided into three aisles by
white marble columns. The
mihrab is decorated with
stalactites and framed by a
pointed horseshoe arch
supported by grey marble

Ornate capitals on the columns in the Saadian Tombs

pilasters. The prayer hall is lit by the three windows of the lantern, which rests on a cedar base decorated with inscriptions.

The central room, a great masterpiece of Moorish architecture, is crowned by a remarkable dome with stalactites. Of carved cedar with gold-leaf decoration, it is supported by 12 columns of Carrara marble. The walls are completely covered – the lower part by a graceful interlacing pattern of glazed tiles, and the upper part by a profusion of stuccowork.

In the centre of the room lie Ahmed el-Mansour and his successors. The ivory-coloured marble tombstones are covered with arabesques and inscriptions arranged on two levels: above are verses from the Koran, and below a framed epitaph in verse. The third room, known as the Hall of the Three Niches, has an equally sumptuous decorative scheme. It contains the tombs of young princes.

The second mausoleum, a green-roofed building, has more modest proportions. It consists of a room with two loggias and a prayer hall. A cedar lintel carved with inscriptions links the columns of the loggias. In the prayer hall, the dome hung with stalactites is a splendid sight.

In the burial chamber the tomb of Lalla Messaouda, mother of Ahmed "the Golden", who died in 1591, fills a honeycombed niche.

Bab Agnaou ⓲

Rue de la Kasba, opposite the Kasbah Mosque.

LIKE ITS TWIN, Bab Oudaïa in Rabat *(see pp68–9)*, this monumental gate was built by Yacoub el-Mansour. Its name means "horn-less black ram" in Berber.

Protected by Bab el-Robb *(see p227)*, the outer defensive gate, Bab Agnaou marked the main entrance to the Almohad palace, and its function was thus primarily decorative.

Although the gate no longer has its two towers, the façade

Bab Agnaou, the royal entrance to the old Almohad palace

still makes for an impressive sight. In the carved sandstone tinges of red meld with tones of greyish-blue.

The sculpted façade consists of alternating layers of stone and brick surrounding a horseshoe arch. The floral motifs in the cornerpieces and the frieze with Kufic script framing the arch are unusually delicate.

This is another example of the sober, monochrome style of decoration that is typical of Almohad architecture and that gives the gate a dignified and majestic appearance.

Dar el-Makhzen ⓳

Southeast of the Saadian Tombs. ● to the public.

WHEN SIDI MOHAMMED ben Abdallah arrived in Marrakech in the 18th century, he found the Almohad and Saadian palaces in a state of ruin. On an extensive area within the kasbah that he enclosed within bastioned walls, he ordered a royal palace, Dar el-Makhzen, to be built, next to the ruins of the Palais el-Badi.

Sidi Mohammed's building project is notable because, unlike the design of other palaces in Marrakech, it took into account the perspective and dimensions of the terrain.

Restored countless times, Dar el-Makhzen consists of several groups of buildings: the Green Palace (el-Qasr el-Akhdar), the Nile Garden (Gharsat el-Nil) and the main

house (el-Dar el-Kubra), as well as outbuildings and several pavilions *(menzah)* set in the park. The palace is still a royal residence today.

Méchouars ⓴

Near Dar el-Makhzen.

DAR EL-MAKHZEN has three large parade grounds, known as *méchouars*. where royal ceremonies are held.

The inner *méchouar*, located south of the palace, is connected to it by Bab el-Akhdar and is linked to the Aguedal Gardens. The outer *méchouar*, east of the palace, is connected to the Berrima quarter by Bab el-Harri. The large *méchouar* south of the inner *méchouar* is outlined by a wall set with merlons.

procession gathering on one of the *méchouars* at Dar el-Makhzen

Si Saïd Museum ㉑

STONE'S THROW from the Palais Bahia *(see pp234–5)* is the contemporary Dar Si Saïd. This delightful palace, now a museum, was built in the late 19th century by Si Saïd ben Moussa, brother of Ba Ahmed and a vizier of Moulay Abdel Aziz. Consisting of *zellij* tilework, intricate plasterwork and carved or painted wooden domes, the decoration alone is worth the visit.

THE PALACE

FOLLOWING ISLAMIC tradition, the palace is enclosed within solid walls and consists of a two-storey central building arranged around courtyards with graceful arcades. It also has an Andalusian garden, with a pavilion and fountain in the centre.

The sumptuous **Reception Room** on the upper floor is a jewel of Moorish design. The cedar dome and the walls, with *zellij* tilework and a stuccowork frieze, are a mesmerizing sight.

The room contains a wooden candelabrum, a cedar sofa and benches covered with colourful fabric. From the topmost floor there is a view over the medina and towards the High Atlas.

THE COLLECTIONS

CONVERTED INTO a museum in 1932, Dar Si Saïd houses a fine collection of carpets, doors, chests, weapons, ceramics, costume and jewellery illustrating the skill of the craftsmen of southern Morocco, particularly of the High Atlas, the Tafilalt, the Anti-Atlas, the Souss and the Tensift.

Also on display are a few archaeological pieces and architectural fragments from Fès. The museum's collections are laid out thematically on three levels.

DOORS AND CARRIAGES

ENTRY TO the museum is through an imposing door studded with nails and fitted with locks. A map at the entrance shows the geographical location of the main centres of craft production in southern Morocco.

Arranged along the walls are a cedar chest and some interesting old doors from the region's kasbahs and *ksour* (fortified villages). These unusual and finely worked

Detail of the door of the reception room

Marble basin for ritual ablutions

doors consist of a single panel of oak, almond wood, poplar or walnut. Some of them are decorated with applied relief patterns of wood cut to geometrical shapes. Others are decorated with engraved or painted motifs.

As these doors were made by craftsmen working in isolation in a rural environment, they are unique pieces, each one different from the next.

At the end of the corridor a splendid basin for ritual ablutions is on display. The basin was carved from a single block of marble in Andalusia in the late 10th or early 11th century. The decoration features three tiers of ornament: floral motifs, four-legged creatures and heraldic eagles.

The next room contains a display of antique children's carriages and swings.

JEWELLERY

LOCATED TO THE LEFT of the entrance, the room in which jewellery is displayed contains a collection of headdresses typical of southern Morocco as well as earrings, diadems, finger rings, necklaces, fibulas (pin-like brooches), bracelets and anklets.

These pieces are engraved, inlaid with niello (a black

The pavilion and fountain of the *riad* (Andalusian garden)

compound) or enamelled, and are set with polished gems, shells, coral, amber or coins.

Geometric shapes such as rectangles, triangles, lozenges, circles, crosses and zigzags are the principal Berber motifs. Some have a symbolic meaning: for example, motifs arranged in sets of five refer to the fingers of one hand, symbolizing life, creativity and representing a lucky charm. Arabesques and floral motifs, by contrast, belong to the Moorish canon of decorative motifs.

Silver pendant from the Tafilalt

Mastered by Jewish metal-workers, these various styles led to the creation of jewellery inspired both by city and rural traditions.

Cedar dome on the ceiling of the reception room

POTTERY

THE ROOM on the right of the entrance contains a display of everyday objects consisting mostly of pottery from Amizmiz, stone oil lamps from Taroudannt, amphorae, pitchers, storage jars, churns, cooking pots and various dishes. These pieces, most of which are made of terracotta, have incised, relief or painted decoration.

Two major regional types of pottery can be seen in this room. One is from Safi *(see p118)*, a continuation of the Fassi tradition and characterized by restrained polychrome decoration, often on a white ground. The other is from Tamegroute *(see p269)*, south of Zagora, typified by glazed monochrome ware in which green predominates.

CARPETS

THE UPPER FLOOR is devoted to village carpets, most notably those from the Tensift and Boujad. The display includes antique carpets and thick woollen blankets *(hanbel)* in which madder-red predominates. The latter are loosely woven so as to retain more warmth.

The display continues in the second courtyard with carpets from the High Atlas. These include Glaoula and Ouaouzguite carpets, which are both embroidered, woven and knotted and which feature bright colours. Carpets from Chichaoua, with a red or rosewood background, display a variety of motifs: geometric patterns including zigzags, chevrons and squares; animal motifs depictings snakes, scorpions and camels; and motifs derived from everyday objects such as teapots and combs. Certain motifs are based on tribal tattoos.

The more unusual figure of a horseman was brought from the Sudan by slaves who worked in local plantations.

VISITORS' CHECKLIST

Riad Zitoune Jedid.
(*(044) 38 95 64.*
9am–12.15pm & 3–6pm Wed–Mon.

WOODWORK

THE INTERESTING collection of woodwork displayed in the second courtyard includes house doors, house frontages and delicate *mashrabiyya* (screenwork), some of it painted in bright colours. These architectural elements, most of them carved in cedar, originate from old houses and shops in Marrakech. The beautiful pieces in wood and marble dating from the Saadian period (16th century) are not to be missed.

A room in the richly decorated former palace

COSTUME

THE CORRIDOR leading to the exit contains a display of boots and burnouses worn by the shepherds of the Siroua mountains. Made of black wool, they are decorated with motifs worked in cotton or in silk. Such garments are still worn today, although the workmanship is less refined.

GALLERY GUIDE

The building has three storeys. The exhibition rooms on the ground floor open onto the riad. Beyond the entrance, large-scale pieces such as wooden doors and chests are displayed. Left of the entrance is the jewellery room, and on the right of it are displays of everyday objects. Next comes the pottery room. The room at the far end of the garden contains brass and copper, and in the second courtyard is a display of woodwork. The reception room is on the first floor and village carpets on the second. The corridor leading to the exit displays the traditional costume of the Ouzguita tribe. Changes are currently being made to the gallery and some collections may not be on display.

The pool and pavilion in the Menara imperial garden

Aguedal Gardens ❷

Rue Bab Ahmar. *Reached via the outer méchouar near Bab Ighli.* ◯ *daily.*

THIS VAST ENCLOSED space, 3 km (2 miles) long and 1.5 km (1 mile) wide, contains an orchard planted with lemon, orange, apricot and olive trees.

The historic gardens were laid out in the second half of the 12th century by the Almoravids, who also installed two large irrigation pools connected by *khettaras*, or underground channels *(see pp276–7)*. Enlarged and embellished by the Almohads, and later by the Saadians, the gardens were then completely neglected until the 19th century. At that time the

Alaouite sultans Moulay Abderrahman and Sidi Mohammed ben Abdallah restored the gardens and the pavilions. So as to provide irrigation, they also diverted the course of Wadi Ourika. Gates were also built into the surrounding wall.

While the public have free access to the gardens, the pavilions, on the northern side, are for the exclusive use of the king's guests. Dar el-Hana, the largest pool, located south of the garden, dates from the Almohad period. The terrace of the small Saadian pavilion that stands next to it commands stunning views in two opposite directions: northwards across olive groves and the city rising in tiers to the hill of Jbilet, and southwards to the serene and distant snow-capped peaks of the High Atlas.

Pavilion window in Aguedal Gardens

One of the many orange trees in the Aguedal Gardens

Menara ❷

Avenue de la Ménara *(west of Hivernage).* ◯ *8am–noon & 2–6pm daily.*

A WELCOME HAVEN of coolness and shade, this imperial garden, covering almost 90 ha (220 acres) and enclosed within pisé walls, is filled mostly with olive and fruit trees. In the 12th century, an enormous pool was dug in the centre of the garden to serve as a reservoir for the Almohad sultans. In the 19th century, Moulay Abderrahman refurbished the garden and built the pavilion with a green-tiled pyramidal roof. This attractive building was used by the sultans for their romantic meetings. It is said that every morning one of them would toss into the water the concubine that he had chosen the night before. The ground floor is fronted by three arches opening onto the pool. The upper floor has a large balustered balcony on its north side.

Although the interior decoration is plain, the building's overall conception and location are remarkable, and the view from any point within, with the peaks of the Atlas as a backdrop, is quite unforgettable.

Gueliz ❷

Northwest of the medina.

ESTABLISHED DURING the Protectorate, this is the Ville Nouvelle (New Town), and it takes its name from the sandstone mined in local quarries. It was designed by Henri Prost, and its spacious layout is in line with the principles of modern town planning.

The wide avenues, municipal gardens, large hotels and cafés with shady terraces make Gueliz a pleasant quarter. Avenue Mohammed V, which runs between Gueliz and the medina, is lined with offices, banks and cinemas. The intersection of this avenue and Rue de la Liberté is the location of the **Central Market**, which offers a condensed range of the food and craft items that are on sale in the medina *(see pp228–9)*.

Despite the number of modern buildings, vestiges from the colonial period have survived. They include the **Gidel Building** (at the corner of Avenue Mohammed V and Rue de la Liberté), which is of interest for its lobby, the **Renaissance Café** (on Place Abdel Moumen ben Ali), which is decorated in typical 1950s style, and the **Société Générale** (also on Place Abdel Moumen ben Ali), a bank with a notable façade.

🏛 Central Market

Avenue Mohammed V, at the intersection with Rue de la Liberté. ◯ *daily.*

An apartment block in Gueliz, Marrakech's Ville Nouvelle

Majorelle Garden 🄬

Avenue Yacoub el-Mansour *(near the bus station).* ◯ *8am–noon & 2–6pm daily.* 🖼

THIS WONDERFUL GARDEN is like a small paradise in the heart of Ville Nouvelle (the new town). In 1923, Jacques Majorelle *(see above)* fell in love with Morocco and built himself a splendid Moorish villa, which he called Bou Safsaf, in Marrakech. He designed the patterns of the *zellij* tilework, painted the front door, and decorated the interior in tones of deep blue, green and dark red. Around the house he laid out a

Villa Majorelle, the painter's residence in Marrakech

JACQUES MAJORELLE

The painter Jacques Majorelle was born in Nancy, in northeastern France, in 1886. The son of the renowned cabinetmaker Louis Majorelle, one of the leading figures of the École de Nancy, he was raised in the artistic milieu of Art Nouveau. He seemed destined to follow in his father's footsteps. However, after studying at the École des Beaux-Arts in Paris, Majorelle decided to devote himself to painting. He travelled to Spain, Italy and Egypt. Convalescing from tuberculosis, he went to Morocco in 1917 and fell in love with its intense light. Aided by Marshal Lyautey, he settled in Marrakech, in his now-famous villa. Finding fascination in the souks, kasbahs and villages of the High Atlas, he stayed in Morocco until his death in 1962.

luxuriant garden. In 1931, at Majorelle's request, the architect Sinoir built an Art Deco studio with pergolas and bright blue walls. The garden, which is separate from the house, opened to the public in 1955.

The house was later bought by Yves Saint-Laurent, the famous couturier, and Pierre Bergé. Skilfully restored, the garden is divided by four walkways that cross each other to create parterres of brightly coloured tropical flowers. Besides yucca, bougainvillea, bamboo, laurel, geraniums, hibiscus and cypresses, the garden has over 400 varieties of palm tree and 1,800 species of cactus. Water lilies grow in a pool bordered by papyrus.

The studio has been converted into a small museum that contains a selection of Moroccan crafts such as antique carpets, Fassi ceramics and Berber doors, and some 40 engravings of the villages and kasbahs of the Atlas executed by Jacques Majorelle.

La Palmeraie 🄬

On the road to Casablanca, *22 km (14 miles) north of Marrakech. This interesting tour, 22.5 km (14 miles) long, can be made by car or horse-drawn carriage.*

LEGEND HAS IT that, after eating dates brought back from the Sahara, the soldiers of the 11th-century Almohad sultan Youssef ben Tachfine spat out the stones around their encampment. The stones are supposed to have germinated and led to the creation of La Palmeraie (Palm Grove) in Marrakech.

Covering an area of some 120 sq km (46 sq miles), the grove consists of fields, gardens and orchards irrigated by ditches and wells supplied by *khettaras*. Although it contains 150,000 trees, the agricultural function of the grove is pared away by the advance of buildings and the greed of developers who are making inroads into it by building desirable residences here.

La Palmeraie (Palm Grove) in Marrakech, with 150,000 trees

HIGH ATLAS

LITTLE-KNOWN BECAUSE *of its relative inaccessibility, the High Atlas makes up the largest massif in the Atlas chain. It is also the highest mountain range in North Africa. In this geographical isolation Berber culture and identity prospered. Over the centuries, the tribes established their own economic and social framework, and a unique collective way of life, based on blood ties and solidarity.*

Extending from the plains of the Atlantic seaboard to Morocco's border with Algeria, the High Atlas forms an impregnable barrier some 800 km (500 miles) long and, in certain places, 100 km (60 miles) wide. Consisting of great massifs rising to heights of 3,000–4,000 m (10,000–13,000 ft), and steep valleys, desolate rocky plains and deep narrow canyons, the High Atlas has played a decisive role in the history of Morocco.

From earliest times these mountains have been a place of refuge for populations fleeing from invaders. For centuries, nomads forced northwards by the desertification of the Sahara have come into conflict with the sedentary mountain-dwelling tribes, disputing possession of prized pasture. This tumultuous feudal past led to the development of a strikingly beautiful form of fortified architecture. Today, although the Berbers no longer need to guard their safety, they still live in *tighremts*, old patriarchal houses with thick walls. Hamlets built of pisé still cling to mountainsides, while every last plot of land is used to grow barley, corn, maize, turnips, lucerne and potatoes – crops that can be cultivated at high altitudes. The Berbers channel river water to irrigate small squares of land and graze their flocks of sheep and goats, which they raise for milk, butter and wool.

Sometimes isolated by snowfall in winter, the Berbers of the High Atlas live and work by the seasons, the constant round of labour punctuated by various festivals.

The kasbah in Telouet, abandoned in 1956

◁ **Muleteer with heavily laden beast in a village in the High Atlas**

Exploring the High Atlas

CROWNED WITH HIGH PEAKS, the chain of the High Atlas culminates in the west in Jbel Toubkal. At 4,167 m (13,676 ft), this is the highest peak in North Africa, with pisé villages nestling on its lower slopes. In the centre, Jbel M'Goun, at 4,068 m (13,351 ft), rises over the Tessaout, Aït Bouguemez and Aït Bou Oulli valleys. The only channels of communication between these valleys are mule trails and high passes. On the banks of the *wadi* that snakes along the valley bottoms, villages cluster around fortified houses, punctuating expanses of cultivated land. The eastern side of the High Atlas is marked by the imposing outline of Jbel Ayachi, 3,737 m (12,265 ft) high. Here high desert plateaus stretch to the horizon. From late spring to early autumn, they are filled with flocks of grazing sheep.

LOCATOR MAP

KEY

- ▬ Main road
- ═ Minor road
- ═ Track

SEE ALSO

0 km   20

0 miles   20

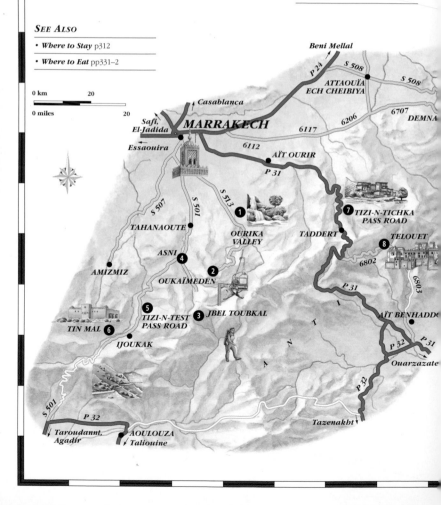

SIGHTS AT A GLANCE

Harvesting barley in the Aït Bouguemez valley

GETTING AROUND

With the High Atlas forming an insuperable east-to-west barrier, the only north-to-south route in this region is the S501, which skirts the foothills of the mountain chain. Running from Marrakech, on the western side, it crosses the Tizi-n-Test Pass and leads to Taroudannt. Another road, the P31, via the Tizi-n-Tichka Pass, leads to Ouarzazate. In the central stretch of the mountain chain, there is no road over the High Atlas for 200 km (124 miles). Only a track (1901 and 1903), which is often impassable in winter, crosses the lake-filled plateau to reach the Dadès valley. On the eastern side, a road from Fès runs along the Middle and High Atlas, leading via Midelt to the Tafilalt valley.

The village of Dar Caïd Ouriki, at the entrance to the Ourika valley

Wadi Ourika, irrigating a valley of palm tree plantations

Ourika Valley ❶

Road map C4. 68 km (42 miles) from Marrakech on road S513.
🚌 from Marrakech; alternatively, by taxi. 🛈 Marrakech; (044) 43 61 31.
🎭 Moussem of Setti Fatma (mid-Aug).

THE TRIP to the Ourika valley, 68 km (42 miles) southeast of Marrakech, offers a pleasant tour of the lower foothills of the Atlas. Beyond the village of **Tnine-de-l'Ourika**, the valley, through which flows the Ourika, becomes verdant. The largest souk in the valley takes place in the village on Mondays.

All along the road that follows the course of the *wadi*, pisé hamlets, a few isolated houses and small hotels cling to the hillside. Gardens and plots of cultivated land shaded by many fruit trees are laid out along the valley bottom. The Ourika river is occasionally subject to sudden and devastating flooding, such as in August 1995, when many houses were swept away.

Beyond Arhbalou, at an altitude of 1,500 m (4,923 ft), the valley narrows and gently rises. The road comes to an end at **Setti Fatma**, a good starting point for hikes. Seven waterfalls flow down the rocky scree above the village. The first of these is easy to reach by walking up the course of the *wadi*. The walk up to the others is over more uneven ground, and some climbing is involved, so that you will need strong walking boots. From that vantage point there is a superb view over Setti Fatma.

The village may also be used as the starting point for longer hikes to Jbel Toubkal and Jbel Yagour, whose peak is well known for the hundreds of rock engravings that can be seen here.

The tomb of Setti Fatma is the focus of a *moussem* that takes place in the village in mid-August. This religious pilgrimage is also an occasion when Berbers from a wide area can gather together.

Oukaïmeden ❷

Road map C4. 74 km (46 miles) from Marrakech on road S513 then on road 6035 A. 🚌 from Marrakech, then by taxi. 🛈 Marrakech; (044) 43 61 31.

A SKI RESORT in winter and base for mountain hikes in summer, Oukaïmeden is a haven of fresh air, just over one hour from Marrakech.

The resort is easily reached on a wide road that forks off to the right at the village of Arhbalou, with the Ourika valley on the left. Shaded by olive, oak and walnut trees, the road then winds upwards in a series of hairpin bends through stony, arid landscape.

The chalets and winter sports facilities are in the village itself, encircled by mountain peaks: Jbel Oukaïmeden, rising to a height of 3,273 m (10,742 ft), Jbel Attar, at 3,258 m (10,693 ft), and Jbel Angour, at 3,614 m (11,861 ft). The great Oukaïmeden plateau is carpeted in pasture, the grazing of which is controlled by tradition.

From November to April, if the snow is sufficiently deep, a chair lift – the highest in North Africa – runs up to the summit of Jbel Oukaïmeden, while several ski lifts allow beginners to practise on the lower slopes. The resort also offers long-distance and cross-country skiing.

Rock engravings, some in the middle of houses, can be seen in the village. Dating from the Bronze Age, they depict cattle, elephants and sun wheels.

About 2 km (1 mile) from the resort, the site of a transmission mast at an altitude of 2,740 m (8,993 ft) commands a magnificent view of the Atlas and the plain where Marrakech is located. In summer, Oukaïmeden is also the starting point for mountain hikes, particularly up to the Tizi-n-Ouaddi Pass, the beautiful village of Tacheddirt, and to Imlil and the Tizi-n-Test.

The ski resort at Oukaïmeden, built in 1950

Tour of the Jbel Toubkal Massif ❸

A S WELL AS THE OPPORTUNITY to climb to the top of Jbel Toubkal, at 4,167 m (13,676 ft) the highest peak in the Atlas, the Jbel Toubkal massif offers great scope for hikes lasting several days. Climbing Toubkal is not particularly difficult, although the fact that it is a high-altitude hike over rough terrain should be taken into account. From the Neltner hut, the summit of Jbel Toubkal can be reached in about four hours. For the finest view over the High Atlas, it is best to reach the summit in the late morning.

Tacheddirt ⑦
This pretty village, at 2314 m (7,595 ft) and set amid mountains, is reached via the Tizi-n-Tamatert Pass, east of Imlil.

Lepiney Hut ⑧
Located at the start of the hike up the Azzaden valley and across the Tazarhart plateau, at 3,000 m (9,846 ft), the hut is used by seasoned hikers and rock climbers.

Imlil ①
Surrounded by walnut and fruit trees, this little mountain village is the starting point for the ascent up Jbel Toubkal and also for many other mountain hikes.

Jbel Angour
3,616 m
(11,868 ft)

Ouaneskra ⑦

Aremd ②
The village, in the Mizane valley, lies at 1,900 m (6,236 ft). Its stone houses cling to the rocky mountainside, surrounded by cultivated terraces.

ASNI
6038

Tamatert

Tizi Oussem

Aksoual ▲
3,842 m
(12,609)

Sidi Chamharouch ③
At the end of a deep gorge, the *koubba* of Sidi Chamharouch, king of the *djinns* (genies), attracts pilgrims all year round.

Azib Tamsoult

Tichki ▲
3,753 m
(12,317 ft)

Neltner Hut ④
This is the last stopping place before the summit of Jbel Toubkal. The hut, at 3,200 m (10,502 ft), is open all year round.

Tazarhart
▲ 3,843 m
(12,613 ft)

Tizi-n-Ouanoums

Ouanoukrim
▲ 4,088 m
(13,417 ft)

Lake Ifni ⑥
The lake, five hours' walk from Neltner Hut, lies in a mineral-rich environment. Shepherds' huts stand on the lakeshore.

KEY

- - - Tour route (footpath)

- - - Track

🔆 Viewpoint

0 km   5

0 miles   5

Jbel Toubkal ⑤
You can climb to the top at the end of winter: it offers breathtaking views over the whole of the High Atlas.

TIPS FOR HIKERS

Reasonably fit hikers can climb to the summit of Jbel Toubkal without a guide, but paths in the area are not well marked.
Starting point: *Imlil, 17 km (10.5 miles) from Asni on road 6038, or 1 hour and 30 minutes from Marrakech.*
When to go: *April to October.*
Huts: *Neltner (5 hours from Imlil), Lépiney (two days' walk from the Tazarhart plateau) and Tacheddirt (2 hours and 30 minutes from Imlil).*
Information: *Detailed maps of the area can be obtained from the guides' office at Imlil. Mules can also be hired for walks lasting several days.*

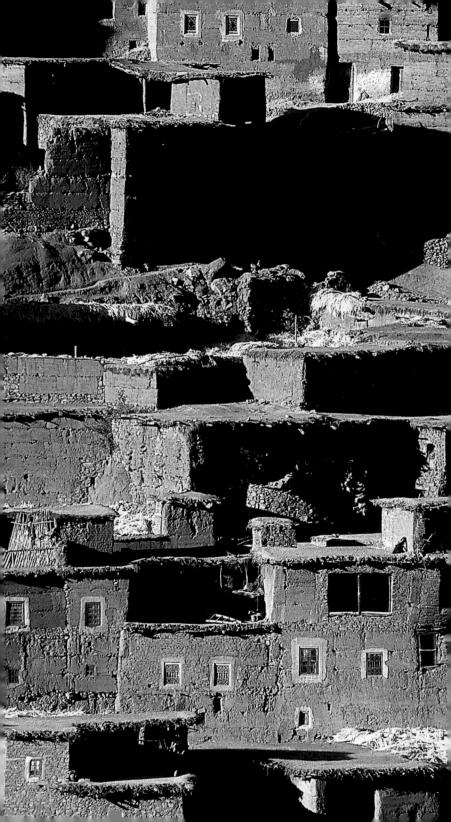

The village of Asni, encircled by the Tamaroute mountains

Asni ❹

Road map C4. 42 km (26 miles) from Marrakech on road S501. 🚌 *from Marrakech, then by taxi.* 🛒 *Sat.*

WITH AN interesting red-walled kasbah, Asni is the first large village on the road from Marrakech to the Tizi-n-Test Pass. Attractive orchards surround the village and there are many mule tracks leading up to the plateaux in its vicinity.

From this small settlement, a road that tails off into a track is the starting point for hikes to Imlil and Jbel Toubkal *(see p249)*.

ENVIRONS: The very popular *moussem* at **Moulay Brahim**, 5 km (3 miles) from Asni, takes place one to two weeks after the festival of Mouloud *(see p41)*. Moroccans ascribe to the saint Moulay Brahim the power to cure barren women. Pilgrims come to lay their gifts before his tomb and to hang small pieces of fabric from the shrubs here. When one of these fragment falls from the shrub, the woman who hung it may expect a child.

Tizi-n-Test Pass Road ❺

Road map B-C4. Accessible from Marrakech on road S501. 🚌 *from Marrakech or Taroudannt.* 🛒 *Thu in Ouirgane; Wed in Ijoukak.*

BEYOND ASNI, the road crosses the High Atlas, then runs down into the Sous plain. This road, in a good state of repair although narrow and tortuous in

places, was built by the French in the 1930s.

Just before Ouirgane, a small road to the right leads to **Amizmiz**, a pretty village with a ruined kasbah, set in the midst of olive trees. The souk here is renowned for Berber pottery made in the village itself. **Ouirgane** is a health resort whose coolness in summer makes it popular with the inhabitants of Marrakech. A few salt mines are still worked here.

As the road climbs further up to the Tizi-n-Test Pass, snaking through red, almost purple terrain, the landscape becomes more wild. Starting from **Ijoukak**, keen hikers can reach the Agoundis valley, walking in the direction of Taghbart and El-Maghzen, or make for the Jbel Toubkal massif. Beyond Ijoukak, a road on the right leads to Tin Mal *(see below)*.

Below the Tizi-n-Test Pass, imposing deserted kasbahs perch on arid outcrops. They all date from the end of the 19th century and belonged to the Goundafa, a powerful Berber tribe that controlled access to the pass. From November to April, the pass, at an altitude of 2,093 m (6,869 ft) is some-

Tizi-n-Test pottery

times blocked by snow. The descent offers a beautiful view of the Sous plain and of hills covered with argan trees, 2,000 m (6,564 ft) below.

Tin Mal ❻

Road map B4. About 25 km (15.5 miles) south of Asni on road S501. **Mosque** ⬜ *daily, except Friday for non-Muslims. To visit the mosque, ask the caretaker in the village of Tin Mal.*

IN AN ISOLATED SETTING at the foot of the Atlas, 10 km (6 miles) beyond Ijoukak on the Tizi-n-Test Pass road, the **Mosque of Tin Mal** situated uphill from the village, is the last remaining sign of the Almohad conquest in the 12th century.

Tin Mal, once a fortified holy town, was founded by the theologian Ibn Toumart in 1125. From here, he fomented a holy war against the Almoravids and was recognized as a religious leader by the Berber tribes of the High Atlas.

In 1276, the town was sacked and pillaged by the Merinids. Only the sumptuous mosque was left standing. It was built in 1153 by Abd el-Moumen, Ibn Toumart's successor and the first Almohad ruler.

The tortuous road winding up to the Tizi-n-Test Pass

◁ **The village of Magdaz, built on an outcrop of rock**

The mosque at Tin Mal, with pink brickwork and plaster stalactites

Under restoration since 1990 and declared a UNESCO World Heritage Site, it is one of the few religious buildings in Morocco that are open to non-Muslims. Its high walls and sturdy towers give it a fortress-like look.

Tizi-n-Tichka Pass Road ❼

Road map C4. From Marrakech or Ouarzazate on road P31.
🚌 *Marrakech or Ouarzazate.*
🏠 *Tue in Aït Ourir.*

BUILT BY THE FRENCH in the 1920s, this winding road runs through a landscape that is, by turn, arid, mineral-rich environments and fertile valleys. Pisé villages, in tones of red or grey, huddle at the foot of hillsides.

The first pass, **Tizi-n-Aït Imger**, at an altitude of 1,470 m (4,825 ft), offers a panoramic view of the Atlas chain. Here, the road is lined with stalls selling pottery, mineral rocks and stones whose colours are a little too bright to be natural.

From here up to the **Tizi-n-Tichka Pass** – which, at an altitude of 2,260 m (7,417 ft), is the highest road pass in Morocco – crops gradually give way to a landscape of bare red soil. The mountains become more rounded and the houses are built higher, with more decoration, anticipating those of the Moroccan south. The impressive fortified grainstore on the way out of **Igherm-n-Ougdal** is open to visitors.

Beyond Agouim, on the other side of the *wadi*, stands the restored kasbah at **El-Mdint**, its towers decorated with relief patterns. Palm trees come into view, and a wide stony desert plain with tones of pink and beige leads to Ouarzazate.

Interior of the fortified grainstore at Igherm-n-Ougdal

Telouet ❽

Road map C4. Accessible on road P31, then on road 6802. ◯ *daily; caretaker on the premises.*

ABOUT 5 KM (3 miles) along the road running down from the Tizi-n-Tichka Pass, towards Ouarzazate, a narrow metalled minor road leads off to the left. It drops down into a steep valley, and 20 km (12 miles) further on reaches the kasbah of Telouet.

This was one of the principal residences of Al-Thami el-Glaoui, pasha of Marrakech, whose fiefdom covered a large part of the High Atlas. El-Glaoui served the sultan, then switched to the employ of the French in 1912. His opposition to the king cost

him dear, for on his death his family was exiled and his possessions dispersed.

Thus it was that Telouet, a town with an illustrious past, has been the victim of neglect since 1956. The kasbah is reduced to a huddle of stone and pisé. The glazed tiles are disintegrating, the lookout towers crumbling, the walls cracking and the windows shattered. Most of the rooms are inaccessible since the roof has fallen in.

However, low-ceilinged, bare-walled corridors lead to two reception rooms that have miraculously survived the passage of time. They are vestiges of the opulence treasured by El-Glaoui. The Andalusian-style rooms have engraved stuccowork, painted cedar ceilings and doors, and colourful *zellij* tilework. Daylight entering through a glass-covered dome and a small window framed with decorative wrought iron lights the rooms from dawn to sunset.

ENVIRONS: From Telouet, a track which, outside the rainy season, can be negotiated in a four-wheel-drive vehicle, leads to **Aït Benhaddou** (*see p265*). In this fertile valley, planted with palm, fig and olive trees, and irrigated by Wadi Ounila, kasbahs signal the past importance of El-Glaoui's fiefdom. The village of **Anemiter**, 11 km (9 miles) from Telouet, is unusually well preserved.

Painted wooden ceiling in the kasbah of Telouet

Aït Bouguemez Valley 9

Wooden door from the valley

THE WIDE, FLAT Aït Bouguemez valley is flanked by a landscape of high, arid hilltops. This is the domain of the Aït Bouguemez tribe, who are settled farmers. The tribe is thought to be the oldest-established in the region. The valley is covered in meticulously tilled plots of land surrounded by ditches, and walnut trees grow in undulating fields of barley and corn. On the dry slopes, pisé hamlets cluster around *tighremts,* old fortified houses. The valley is the starting point for hikes through spectacular scenery up to the massif of Jbel M'Goun. There are 28 villages scattered along the valley between Agouti and Zaouïa Oulemsi.

Threshing the Corn
Mules attached to a post in the centre of the threshing ground circle slowly, trampling the corn. This separates the grain from the husks and straw.

★ Painted Ceilings
In the tamsriyt, *a room set aside for overnight guests, the ceilings – particularly in Agouti – are decorated with geometric motifs and thin coloured lines skilfully drawn freehand or with a compass.*

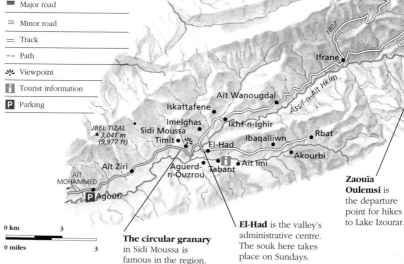

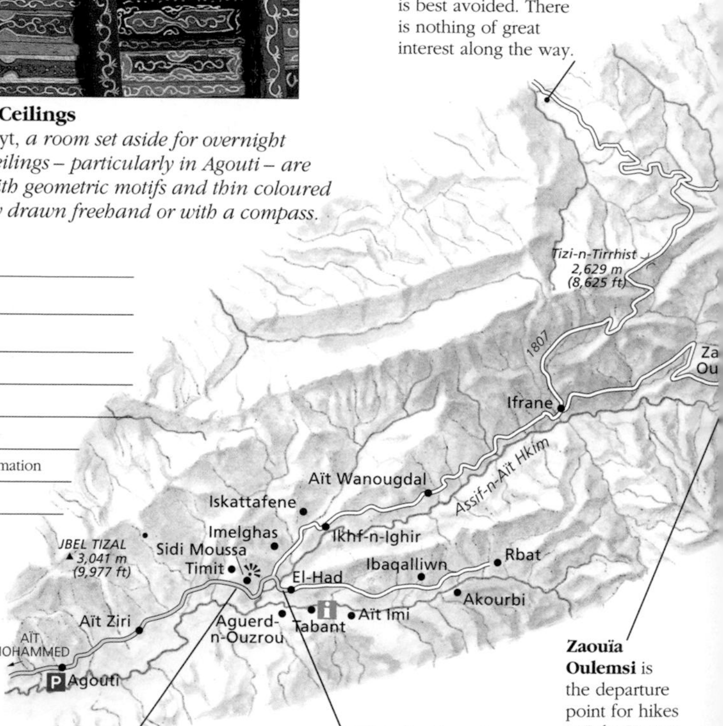
Tizi-n-Tirrhist
2,629 m
(8,625 ft)
1807
Za
Ou
Ifrane
Assif-n-Aït Hkim
Aït Wanougdal
Iskattafene
Ikhf-n-Ighir
Imelghas
JBEL TIZAL
3,041 m
(9,977 ft)
Sidi Moussa
Timit
El-Had
Ibaqalliwn
Rbat
Akourbi
Aït Ziri
Aguerd-n-Ouzrou
Tabant
Aït Imi
AÏT MOHAMMED
Agouti
0 km 3
0 miles 3

KEY

- Major road
- Minor road
- Track
- Path
- Viewpoint
- Tourist information
- Parking

The direct route to Aït Mohammed is best avoided. There is nothing of great interest along the way.

Zaouïa Oulemsi is the departure point for hikes to Lake Izourar.

The circular granary in Sidi Moussa is famous in the region.

El-Had is the valley's administrative centre. The souk here takes place on Sundays.

Maize Drying on the Rooftops
*In the autumn, maize is laid out carefully on the
tiered rooftops. When it has dried, the grain is
separated from the cob on a concrete
floor by hand.*

VISITORS' CHECKLIST

Agouti. **Road map** C3.
*Accessible on road P24 from
Marrakech, then road S508 to
Azilal, continuing south and,
before Aït Mohammed, turning
right then left to Agouti. The
road becomes a track for the last
20 km (12 miles) before Agouti.
By four-wheel-drive vehicle it is
possible to reach Zaouïa Ahanesal
then Bin el-Ouidane. Otherwise,
the valley must be followed on
foot from Agouti.* 🔲 *Guides and
mules can be hired in Tabant and
other villages. Guesthouse
accommodation is also available.*

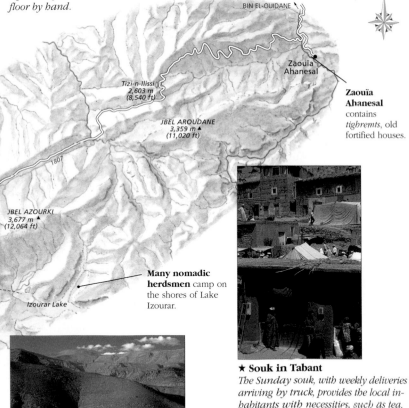

BIN EL-OUIDANE

Zaouïa
Ahanesal

Tizi-n-Ilissi
2,603 m
(8,540 ft)

JBEL AROUDANE
3,359 m ▲
(11,020 ft)

1807

JBEL AZOURKI
3,677 m ▲
(12,064 ft)

Izourar Lake

**Zaouïa
Ahanesal**
contains
tighremts, old
fortified houses.

**Many nomadic
herdsmen** camp on
the shores of Lake
Izourar.

Valley Landscape
*Drawn to the pastures in the region, the
industrious Berbers have irrigated the
land so as to extract the most from it, and
built fortified villages to ensure their safety.*

★ Souk in Tabant
*The Sunday souk, with weekly deliveries
arriving by truck, provides the local inhabitants with necessities, such as tea,
coffee, sugar, matches, oil and utensils,
that they cannot otherwise obtain.*

STAR SIGHTS

★ Painted Ceilings

★ Souk in Tabant

Exploring the Aït Bouguemez Valley

CLINGING TO THE MOUNTAINSIDE, the hamlets of the Aït Bouguemez valley blend into their setting, being almost the same colour as the landscape. The houses are stacked together like building blocks, the flat roof of the house serving as a terrace for the inhabitants of the house above. Looking down onto the river and the village's communal land, these cube-like houses catch the warmth of the rising sun and are adapted to the rigours of the climate. Houses in the valley bottom are built of pisé, raw earth dug at the spot where the house is to be built, mixed with water and sometimes straw. In villages at altitudes above 2,200 m (7,220 ft), dry stone is used, since pisé is unsuited to cold and wet conditions.

Detail of a painted ceiling, typical of the houses of the Aït Bouguemez

Setting off for the souk in a village below Jbel Ghat

Agouti
At the western extremity of the Aït Bouguemez valley.

The first of the villages that line the valley, Agouti is located at 1,800 m (5,908 ft). As an outpost of the Aït Bouguemez tribe, it once defended access to the high valley against rival tribes.

A ruined *igherm* (fortified communal granary), set on a sheer rocky promontory, towers above the village. The villagers once kept their possessions and their crops here. The houses are still without electricity and the women go down to fetch water from the river below.

In Agouti, as well as in some of the other villages in the valley, visitors can see some beautiful

Mules in the Aït Bou Oulli valley

wood ceilings in the houses of wealthier families. The painted decoration is executed by craftsmen of renown and features an infinite variety of geometric patterns.

Aït Bou Oulli Valley
West of Agouti.

From Agouti, a day trip can be made to the Aït Bou Oulli valley on mule-back or by four-wheel-drive vehicle. A sheer-sided track leads down into the valley, whose name means "the people who raise ewes". The narrow wooded valley, thickly covered with walnut trees, winds the length of the *wadi*, which irrigates small plots cultivated of land. **Jbel Ghat**, rising above the valley, is

a peak with mythical associations to which the Berbers come on a pilgrimage once a year. **Abachkou**, a high-set village at the far end of the valley, is renowned for the white capes produced by the villagers.

Sidi Moussa
East of Agouti.

Perched on the summit of a pointed hill, in the centre of the Aït Bouguemez valley, Sidi Moussa is both a granary and a shrine. It is reached by a steep path from the village of Timit. The entire Aït Bouguemez valley is visible from the top of the hill.

The **granary**, in the form of a massive sturdy, circular tower, is unique in the region. It consists of four stone-faced towers. Small look-out turrets open onto the terrace-roof. This was a place of safety for watchmen who once scoured the surroundings for enemies.

In the interior, which is lit by sparse loop-hole windows, a spiral staircase leads to the two upper floors. In the half-light, compartments arranged along the walls can be made out. This was where the inhabitants kept their possessions.

Sidi Moussa, the holy man renowned for his good deeds and his powers as a healer, is buried here. He is the object of pilgrimages. Women of the Aït Bouguemez valley and from more distant valleys go up to the shrine, where they spend the night, making a wish and sacrifing a chicken as an offering to him.

Aït Ziri, Timit, Imelghas and Iskattafène

East of Agouti. 🚌 at El-Had on Sun.
Walking around these villages, visitors will observe such details as decorated doors (either carved or painted in bright colours) and windows with interlacing wrought iron or *mashrabiyya* screens. Some very fine *tighremts* (fortified houses) dating from the early 20th century are still inhabited by village chiefs and their large families.

El-Had, the administrative centre of the valley, is well known for its Sunday souk. This is the only place in the valley where supplies can be purchased. The village is also the starting point for mountain hikes to the M'Goun or in the footsteps of dinosaurs.

Zaouïa Oulemsi

On the way from Agouti, on a narrow track on the right of track 1809.
Zaouïa Oulemsi is the last village in the Aït Bouguemez valley, which it overlooks from an altitude of 2,150 m (7,056 ft). It consists of low, red-hued dry-stone houses. Here, the snowfall comes early and tends to be heavy.

The village is the starting point for hikes to **Lake Izourar**, which lies in the heart of the mountains at an altitude of 2,500 m (8,205 ft). Many nomadic shepherds camp beside the lake, which is often dry in summer, when it turns into pasture, the use

Cultivated fields in the Aït Bouguemez valley

of which is carefully controlled to prevent over-grazing.

The shepherds include the Aït Bouguemez, who come for the summer, living in the stone-built sheepfolds, and the Aït Atta, with their flocks of sheep, goats and camels, who in summer come up to the High Atlas from Jbel Sarhro. Seeking good

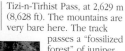
Fortified granary, Aït Bouguemez valley

pasture, they settle on the slopes of M'Goun, around Lake Izourar or on the Imilchil plateau, moving south again when the first frosts come.

Zaouïa Ahanesal

On track 1807 towards Bin el-Ouidane. 🚌 Mon.
A track running along the continuation of the Aït Bouguemez valley goes up to the

Tizi-n-Tirhist Pass, at 2,629 m (8,628 ft). The mountains are very bare here. The track passes a "fossilized forest" of juniper, with gnarled, dying trunks; the species faces extinction.

Zaouïa Ahanesal, consisting of some old *tighremts* and the tomb of its founder, Saïd Ahanesal, dates from the 14th century, when the *marabout* movement loomed large in the history of this mountain region. *Zaouias* (sanctuaries set up around the tombs of *marabouts*, holy figures and the leaders of brotherhoods) were then protected holy places, where pilgrims and the needy found refuge. In exchange for the protection given by the *marabout*, the Berbers maintained the land around the *zaouia*, were taught Arabic and received Koranic instruction.

Heedless of the power of the sultans, the leaders of some *zaouias* controlled the lives of the mountain people, settling disputes over land ownership and imposing their will. Zaouïa Ahanesal was a major influence on the local Berber populations, but the descendants of Saïd Ahanesal came into conflict with the fiefs of the *caids* of the High Atlas. They held out against the French until 1934.

The track continues for 40 km (25 miles) before reaching **La Cathédrale**, an impressive rock formation, then Lake Bin el-Ouidane.

Animals grazing around Lake Izourar, in summer

Lake Tiselit, on the Plateau des Lacs, near Imilchil

Imilchil ⑩

Road map D3. Accessible via Kasba Tadla (on road P24) and El-Ksiba (on road 1901 then 1903). ⚑ Sat.

ON ITS EASTERN SIDE, the chain of the High Atlas descends as if it had been crushed, forming a desert plateau surrounded by rolling mountains. Imilchil is at the heart of this sparsely populated region – the territory of the Aït Haddidou.

This group of semi-nomadic shepherds came originally from Boumalne du Dadès, located in the high Dadès valley, where some of them still live. They arrived in Morocco during the centuries immediately after the introduction of Islam, and there is evidence of their presence in the Boumalne du Dadès region durng the 11th century. For several years they were in conflict with the powerful Aït Atta tribe in disputes over pasture, then settled in the Assif Melloul valley in the 17th century.

The village of Imilchil is dominated by a sumptuously decorated kasbah. Its towers have a curious feature: the angles of the crenellation are set with finials resembling inverted cooking pots. This decorative device is also related to superstitious belief, as it gives protection against lightning and the "evil eye" and is a symbol of prosperity.

Chimney with "cooking pot" finial, Imilchil

Although Imilchil is remote, its claim to fame is the annual **Marriage Fair**, a *moussem* at which women may choose a fiancé and many pilgrims and traders from the mountains gather. It takes place at the end of September at a spot known as Aït Haddou Ameur, some 20 km (13 miles) from Imilchil. Arriving on foot, by truck or by mule, all the tribes of the area flock to this great yearly commercial, social and religious gathering. The pilgrims throng around the pisé walls of the shrine of Sidi Ahmed ou Mghanni, a venerated holy man, to present their offerings.

The origin of the Marriage Fair goes back to the story of two lovers, Hadda and Moha, members of rival tribes who were kept apart by their parents. Their tears created two lakes, Iseli, "the fiancé", and Tiselit, "the fiancée", on the Plateau des Lacs (see below). Ever since, young girls who come to the *moussem* with their family may converse freely with men from other tribes, although they must be accompanied by a sister or a female friend.

Young couples who wish to can visit the tent of the *adouls* (lawyers) and sign a betrothal agreement. These unions are often engineered by the respective families ahead of the *moussem*.

The event, which for some years has attracted crowds of tourists, has lost some of its authenticity. The presentation and parade of the couples and the evenings of folk dance and song are but a superficial aspect of what is a great commercial and religious gathering.

The colourful tents of the great souk spread out across the wide plateau. Traders sell basketry, cooking utensils, blankets and handwoven carpets, metalware, clothing, basic foodstuffs, and other items. On the hillside, herds of cows and camels and flocks of sheep await buyers.

The Plateau des Lacs can be reached either by following a long track that runs from El-Ksiba, crossing narrow gorges and undulating passes, or on a surfaced road via Rich, further east. This mineral-rich environment, at an altitude of 2,000–3,500 m (6,500–11,500 ft), is dotted with isolated *tighremts*, and a splash of colour is provided by the emerald waters of lakes Tiselit and Iseli. In summer, sheep are brought to the lush pasture here.

A couple at the Imilchil Marriage Fair

Berbers of the High Atlas

THE BERBERS of the High Atlas are non-nomadic peasants. Many of them have a completely self-sufficient lifestyle, and in certain valleys mule tracks are the only channel of communication with the outside world. The inhabitants of these remote valleys live by the pattern of the seasons and the round of work in the fields. In the autumn, the men till the soil with a wooden plough and buy and sell goods and produce at the weekly souk. In winter, the women collect water from the river, gather wood and weave thick woollen blankets. In spring, the men dig and maintain vital irrigation channels. In summer, the women harvest and thresh the grain, while the men winnow barley on threshing floors.

Hand painted with henna

FAMILY FESTIVALS

The daily life of the Berber women of the High Atlas is enlivened by family festivals. The women, dressed in dazzling clothes, dance the *ahwach* or the *ahidous*, according to the region, while the men intone chants as they beat out a regular rhythm on their *bendir*.

At the Marriage Fair in Imilchil, the raïs, *the dance leader of this folk troupe, beats out the rhythm on his* bendir, *a kind of tambourine, with his right hand.*

Woman carrying barley *on her back. The unripe barley will be deposited on the threshing ground.*

Berber women *from the Aït Haddidou tribe, whose differently striped cloaks signal their belonging to a certain clan.*

This weaver *from Abachkou, in the Aït Bou Oulli valley, washes, cards and spins sheep's wool. She weaves the yarn into cloth to make white capes, which are then decorated with pieces of metal.*

Men come to the souk *at Imilchil to buy and sell livestock and to stock up with vital supplies for the winter.*

OUARZAZATE
& THE SOUTHERN OASES

THIS FASCINATING REGION *begins at the southern edge of the High Atlas, where desert and mountains meet. The stony desert is broken by green oases where shade-giving date palms grow in profusion. Cut by steep canyons and studded with arid hills, it is criss-crossed by* wadis *right up to the edge of the Sahara. Here, the light is intensely bright and the colours sumptuously rich.*

The history of Morocco is closely linked to this region bordering the Sahara desert, the birthplace of the great Moroccan dynasties. In the 11th century, Almoravid warriors, who came from the Sahara, set out from the south to extend their empire from Senegal to Spain. In the 16th century, the Saadians, who came from Arabia, left the Draa valley to conquer Morocco. Lastly, the Alaouites, the dynasty that holds power in Morocco today, settled in the Tafilalt region in the 13th century.

Trade in gold, salt and slaves between black Africa and Morocco melded the local populations, so that Arabs, Berbers and Haratines, descendants of ancient black populations, lived side by side.

Life here centres on three great *wadis*, the Draa, the Dadès and the Ziz. These rivers have created stunning landscapes, carving gorges and canyons out of the sides of the High Atlas and Anti-Atlas. The date palm that brings welcome shade to small plots of corn and barley accounts for the region's wealth. The palm groves are punctuated by hundreds of kasbahs and *ksour*. These fortified villages and houses protected the sedentary populations against attack from nomadic tribes. Many of them are still inhabited today, although they are slowly crumbling. The desert begins south of the oases. Every year, aided by drought, it encroaches further on arable land.

The central patio of the kasbah at Oulad Driss, in the southern Draa valley

◁ A *marabout*, or tomb of a religious leader, with pisé walls, in the Draa valley

Exploring Ouarzazate and the Southern Oases

THE DRAA VALLEY, south of Ouarzazate, and the Tafilalt valley, south of Er-Rachidia, are the two great routes to the Sahara. The valleys are interconnected by the Dadès valley, which covers 120 km (75 miles) between Ouarzazate and Boumalne du Dadès. It cuts through a desert plateau at an average altitude of 1,000 to 1,500 m (3,282 to 4,923 ft), set between the High Atlas on its northern side and the foothills of Jbel Sarhro on its southern side. Other valleys, irrigated by *wadis* flowing down from the Atlas, impinge on the Dadès valley. Negotiable on foot or by four-wheel-drive vehicle, they give access to the interior of the High Atlas. Exploring this region, experiencing the scenic oases and visiting the most interesting *ksour*, takes at least a week.

GETTING AROUND

Roads in a good state of repair run between Ouarzazate and Zagora, Er-Rachidia and Erfoud. However, distances are great, and the mountainous terrain and passes to be negotiated must be taken into account. Although certain tracks can be followed only in a four-wheel-drive vehicle, an ordinary car is sufficient to drive major roads. Buses and *grands taxis* from Ouarzazate cover the whole region.

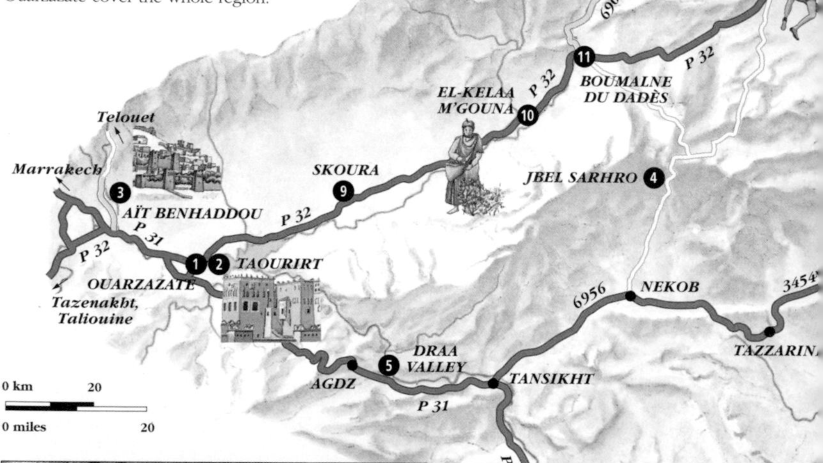

IMILCHIL

AGOUDAL

6905   3445

MSEMRIR   TAMTATTOUCHT 15

DADÈS GORGE 12   TODRA GORGE 14

6901   TINERHIR 13

11   BOUMALNE DU DADÈS   P 32

EL-KELAA M'GOUNA 10

JBEL SARHRO 4

Telouet

Marrakech

3   AÏT BENHADDOU   SKOURA 9   P 32

P 31

P 32   1 2 TAOURIRT

OUARZAZATE
Tazenakht, Taliouine

6956   NEKOB   3454

DRAA VALLEY 5   TANSIKHT   TAZZARIN

AGDZ   P 31

0 km   20

0 miles   20

P 31

ZAGORA
6   6958   7 TAMEGROU

Foum Zguid

6965

6954

MHAMID 8

Msemrir, a village at the foot of the High Atlas *(see p273)*

LOCATOR MAP

Door of the *zaouia* in Tamegroute

SIGHTS
AT A GLANCE

SEE ALSO

An austere kasbah in the Dadès Gorge

KEY

- ▬ Main road
- ═ Minor road
- ═ Track

A shop in the crafts centre opposite the Taourirt kasbah

Ouarzazate ❶

Road map C4. 🏛 *70,000.*
🚌 *Avenue Mohammed V (to Marrakech, Tinerhir, Taroudannt and Zagora) and grands taxis (Tue, Fri, Sat, Sun).* 🛈 *Avenue Mohammed V; (044) 88 24 85. Grands taxis, Land Rovers and 4x4 vehicles for hire.*
🎭 *Crafts Festival (May); Moussem of Sidi Daoud (Aug).*

A FORMER GARRISON TOWN of the French Foreign Legion, Ouarzazate was founded in 1928, having been chosen by the French as a strategic base from which to pacify the South. Located at an altitude of 1,160 m (3,807 ft) at the intersection of the Draa and Dadès valleys, with the Agadir region to the west, it is on the main route between the mountains and the desert. It is also a good base from which to visit Aït Benhaddou and the Skoura palm grove.

Ouarzazate is a peaceful provincial town with wide streets, many hotels and municipal gardens. Avenue Mohammed V, the only main street, crosses the town and leads to the Dadès valley.

About 6 km (4 miles) outside Ouarzazate, off the road to Marrakech, are the **Atlas Film Studios**, surrounded by high pisé walls that look as if they are defended by giant Hollywood-style, pseudo-Egyptian figures. The studios, which cover 30,000 sq m (322,920 sq ft) of desert, provide the livelihood of a considerable portion of the population of Ouarzazate. For a century, hundreds of films have been shot in this region, including Bernardo Bertolucci's *The Sheltering Sky* (1990) and Martin Scorsese's *Kundun* (1997). On the other side of the town, opposite the Taourirt Kasbah, are the Andromeda Italian film studios.

Atlas Film Studios
On road P31, 6 km (4 miles) northwest of Ouarzazate. ⬜ *8am–8pm daily, except when filming is going on.*

ENVIRONS: About 10 km (6 miles) to the south is the **Finnt Oasis**, with fine pisé *ksour*. A little further on is the **El-Mansour Eddahbi Dam**, filled in 1972 and fed by the Dadès and Ouarzazate rivers, which join to form the Draa. The dam provides water for the Draa's palm groves and electricity for the valley. About 7 km (4 miles) northwest of Ouarzazate is the majestic **Tiffoultoute Kasbah**, offering fine views from its terrace. It was converted into a hotel in the 1960s to provide accommodation during the shooting of David Lean's *Lawrence of Arabia*. It is now a restaurant.

Taourirt Kasbah ❷

Road map C4. Opposite the crafts centre on the road out of Ouarzazate leading to the Dadès valley. 📷

O UARZAZATE'S only historic building, the Taourirt kasbah stands as a monument to Glaoui expansionism. At the beginning of the 20th century, the Glaoui family were the lords of the South and controlled access to the High Atlas. They were the first to collaborate with the French in the expansion of the latter's rule in the South.

Begun in the 18th century and renovated in the 19th, the kasbah has been undergoing restoration since 1994. It once housed the large Glaoui family, together with their servants.

Detail of a window in the Taourirt Kasbah

The façade, consisting of high smooth earth walls, is pitted and decorated with geometric patterns in negative relief.

Inside, a bewildering maze of staircases at every level of the building leads to rooms of various sizes lit by low windows. The larger rooms have plasterwork decoration featuring floral and geometric motifs, and colourfully painted wooden ceilings. There are also some tiny rooms with low rush-matted ceilings, doorless arches, red-tiled floors and contrasting white walls.

Aït Benhaddou, which has often been chosen as a film location

Next to the kasbah is a former Berber village, which probably predates the kasbah. It is inhabited by a busy population. In the narrow winding streets of the *ksar* (fortified village), you will find an Internet café, a former synagogue that now serves as a carpet shop, and a herbalist. The crafts centre opposite the Taourirt kasbah offers carpets, stone carving, jewellery and pottery, all at relatively high prices.

geometric designs in negative relief, creating a play of light and shadow. Behind the kasbahs stand plain earth houses. Today, the *ksar* is inhabited by fewer than ten families.

Beyond Aït Benhaddou, a minor road, the 6803, peters out after a few kilometres. A track then leads to the ruined fortress of **Tamdaght**, once a kasbah inhabited by the Glaoui. Its towers are now inhabited by nesting storks.

Aït Benhaddou ❸

Road map C4. 30 km (19 miles) northwest of Ouarzazate on road P31, turning off to the right on road 6803. ℹ️ *Ouarzazate; (044) 88 24 85.*

BACKING ONTO a pinkish sandstone hill, the *ksar* of Aït Benhaddou stands on the left bank of Wadi Mellah. It is reached on foot from the newly established village on the opposite bank. The *wadi* is usually dry, except in winter and spring.

The picturesque village of Aït Benhaddou, which has often been used as a film location, can be explored without a guide. It was once fortified and has a now-ruined *igherm* (communal granary). Built near water and arable land, in a place safe from foreign attack, it contains an impressive group of ochre pisé kasbahs.

Since the village was made a UNESCO World Heritage Site, some of its kasbahs have undergone restoration to their upper sections. The kasbahs' crenellated towers are decorated with blind arches and

Jbel Sarhro ❹

Road map D4. 98 km (61 miles) south of Ouarzazate. *From Tansikht, via the Draa valley on road 6956, then to Nekob on track 6966; from Boulmane du Dadès, track 6907.* ⛺ *Sun in Nekob; Mon in Iknioun.*

STRETCHING FOR over 100 km (60 miles), Jbel Sarhro is a wild and inhospitable region that is still off the tourist track. It is separated from the Anti-Atlas by the Draa valley to the west and from the High Atlas by Wadi Dadès to the north.

Jbel Sarhro is the territory of the Aït Atta, who, from the

17th and 19th centuries, were the most important tribe in southern Morocco. This semi-nomadic people never bowed to the power of the sultans, and they were the last to resist the French at the Battle of Bou Gafer in 1933. They live in *ksour*, but take to tents for part of the year, when they drive livestock to seasonal pastures.

Jbel Sarhro is a region of sheer rockfaces, plateaux and blackish rocky escarpments. The rugged territory is crossed from north to south by tracks, which are best driven in a four-wheel-drive vehicle (routes are seldom signposted).

At the **Baha Kasbah** in Nekob guides can be hired

The Baha Kasbah in Nekob, at the foot of Jbel Sarhro

for hikes and tours in four-wheel-drive vehicles. The route from Nekob to the Tizi n'Tazazert Pass, at 2,200 m (7,220 ft), is difficult, but the spot known as Bab N'Ali is worth the visit for some striking needle-like volcanic rock formations. The track to Boulmane du Dadès crosses the **Vallée des Oiseaux** (Valley of Birds), which is home to over 150 species of birds.

Camels grazing in the rocky landscape of Jbel Sarhro

The Kasbah

KASBAHS (*tighremt* in Berber) have long fulfilled the role of fortified castles, being places of refuge from attack for people and animals, and affording protection from the cold and other threats to safety. A lordly residence or family dwelling, the kasbah is an imposing edifice built to a square plan. While kasbahs in the mountain valleys are thick-set, those in the southern oases have a taller, more slender outline. At the four corners are towers crowned with merlons rising above the height of the walls.

Fortified Citadels
High walls set at a slightly oblique angle give the kasbah a perfectly proportioned outline.

Bricks
Bricks are made from earth mixed with water, sometimes with chopped straw added. They are pressed into wooden moulds and dried in the sun.

Stepped merlons

A TYPICAL KASBAH
Their dimensions being dictated by the size of the horizontally placed beams, the rooms are often longer than they are wide. The largest room is the reception hall, which often has a painted ceiling and which is reserved for men. The stable and sheepfold are located on the ground floor.

Water Jar
Ancient pieces of pottery like this one can be seen in restored kasbahs.

Windows
Mashrabiyya *screens and wrought-iron grilles, made with no soldering, allow the inhabitants to look out without being seen.*

Defensive Walls
The upper parts of the walls are decorated with geometric patterns, incised motifs and blind arches cut into the pisé.

Fortified Granary
The interior of the igherm or agadir is divided into compartments where maize, barley, sugar and cooking vessels are stored.

The Kitchen
Circular loaves of bread, made by the women, are baked in a small igloo-like earth oven. The kitchen is often dark and badly ventilated, and cooking is done on the earth floor.

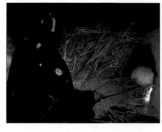

Maize drying on the roof

Painted Ceilings
Ceilings are painted with volutes, rosettes and interlacing patterns, executed freehand or with a compass. They are a feature of reception rooms of kasbahs and of wealthy houses.

Wooden Doors
They can be opened only from within.

Detail of the interior of the *ksar* at Tamnougalt, in the Draa valley

Draa Valley ❺

Road map C-D4. 200 km (124 miles) between Ouarzazate and Zagora on road P31. 🚌 *Thu in Agdz.*

ROCK ENGRAVINGS discovered near Tinzouline show that the Draa valley was inhabited by warriors from prehistoric times. The valley, where buildings are in a good state of preservation, contains a wealth of *ksour* and kasbahs.

The road between Ouarza-zate and **Agdz** crosses the desert plateaux of Jbel Tifern-ine. Beyond Aït Saoun, hills of black rock give way to steep canyons as the road climbs towards the Tizi-n-Tinififft Pass, at 1,660 m (5,448 ft). To the north appear the foothills of the High Atlas and to the east, Jbel Sarhro.

Agdz, an unassuming town on the edge of a palm grove, is convenient for a short stop.

Between Agdz and Zagora, the road follows a string of oases. Villages have grown up around the old kasbahs, on the edge of the road and in the palm grove.

About 6 km (4 miles) from Agdz, a track branching off to the left leads to the majestic *ksar* of **Tamnougalt**, which once controlled access to the trade routes of the Draa valley. The interior reveals some striking frescoes, which were painted in pale colours for the shooting of a film.

Continuing along the left bank of the *wadi*, the track leads to the pisé village of Tamnougalt, with narrow, partly covered streets. Visitors wishing to see the old kasbah may like to bring a torch, which is useful for viewing its superb painted ceilings. Tam-nougalt, which is currently undergoing restoration, also has a former mellah (Jewish quarter) with a synagogue.

Back on the Draa valley road, the elegant **Timiderte Kasbah** comes into view on the left bank of the *wadi*, backing onto Jbel Sarhro. Villages and *ksour* here are rarely signposted. In Tansikht, a narrow road turns off to the left towards Nekob, Jbel Sarhro and Rissani, 233 km (145 miles) away. The bridge over the *wadi* joins a sandy track that passes through villages in the palm grove. To rejoin the road, the river can be forded in several places. Still leading in the direction of Zagora, the road passes the **Igdaoun Kasbah**, with

towers in the shape of trun-cated pyramids. At Tinezouline, a track to the right leads to a site with rock engravings, 7 km (4 miles) away.

The valley narrows in the approaches to the Azlag gorge, to the right of which is a high, smooth cliff. Soon after, a signpost indicating "Circuit Touristique de Binzouli" leads to the palm grove, which reaches Zagora on the other side of the *wadi*. Ochre pisé *koubbas* line the valley, while cemeteries are filled with the vertical flat stones that are typical of Muslim graveyards. Between Tissergate and Zagora, the palm grove stretches away to the distant foothills of Jbel Rhart.

Zagora ❻

Road map D4. 🏠 *30,000.* 🚌 *Ouarzazate or grands taxis.* ℹ️ *Asmaa Hote;l (044) 84 72 41, and La Fibule Hotel; (044) 84 73 18.* 🚌 *Wed & Sun.* 🎪 *Moussem of Moulay Abdelkader Jilali at Mouloud.*

ESTABLISHED BY the French authorities during the Protectorate, Zagora is the most convenient base for exploring the region. The sign saying "Timbuctu, 52 Days by Camel" evokes the great age of the trans-Saharan caravans, although the illusion is spoiled by the presence of the great concrete *Préfecture* behind it.

The village of **Amazraou**, set amid lemon, almond and olive trees and gardens on the southern side of the town, is

A camel trek through the peaceful palm grove in Zagora

Green-glazed pottery vessels characteristic of Tamegroute

a haven of peace on the edge of the desert. In the former mellah, the mosque stands next to the abandoned synagogue. Amazraou is inhabited by Arabs, Haratines and Berbers, who continue the Jewish tradition of making silver jewellery. By following a footpath from the La Fibule hotel, the summit of Jbel Zagora can be reached in one hour. It is crowned by a military post and commands a breathtaking view of the valley. The remains of walls indicate the presence of the Almoravids in the 11th century.

Two hotels, the Kasba Asmaa and La Fibule, offer tours in four-wheel-drive vehicles or on camels. Lasting from a day to two weeks, the tours take in the Chigaga dunes south of Mhamid, and Foum-Zguid, west of Zagora.

Mule in the
Draa valley

Tamegroute 7

Road map D4. 🚌 Sat. 🎪 Moussem of Sidi Ahmed ben Nasser (Nov).

SURROUNDED BY RAMPARTS, the ksar at Tamegroute contains a zaouia and a library. This great centre of Islamic learning was founded in the 17th century by Mohammed Bou Nasri, and its influence extended throughout southern Morocco.

Beneath the arcades of the courtyard, near the entrance to the tomb of Mohammed Bou Nasri, invalids and

handicapped people gather, hoping to be cured.

The holy man's works laid the foundations of the **Koranic Library**. A collection of priceless manuscripts is displayed in one of the rooms. It includes an 11th-century gazelle-skin Koran, books of calligraphy with gold dust and saffron illumina-tions, and treatises on algebra, astronomy and Arabic literature. Exposed to heat and light, these works are, unfortunately, not in the best condition.

In the potters' workshop outside, members of seven families produce traditional functional pots with a green glaze typical of Tamegroute ceramics.

ENVIRONS: About 5 km (2 miles) south of Tame-groute, and off to the left, are the **Tinfou Dunes**, an isolated

ridge of sand rising up abruptly in the middle of the stony desert. From Tagounite, a difficult track leads to the foot of Jbel Tadrart and the beautiful **Nesrate Dunes**.

Mhamid 8

Road map D4. 🚶 2,000. 🚌 Mon.

THIS BORDER POST and small administrative centre is the last oasis before the great expanse of the Sahara. To the south stretches a stony desert, the Hammada du Draa. From Mhamid, Wadi Draa sinks beneath the sand to reappear on the Atlantic coast 540 km (338 miles) to the west.

The ruins of a ksar indicate the former existence of a great caravan centre, from which Ahmed el-Mansour's army set out in the 16th century to take Timbuctu.

ENVIRONS: Coming from Zagora, the Tizi-Beni-Selmane Pass, at an altitude of 747 m (2,451 ft), offers a stunning view of Jbel Bani and the desert, which looks black since it is covered with volcanic stone. A little further on, a track to the left leads to **Foum-Rjam**, one of the largest prehistoric necro-polies in the Maghreb. Tumuli mark thousands of family graves. About 45 km (28 miles) south of Mhamid, the **Chigaga dunes**, which can be reached only by four-wheel-drive vehicle, stretch to the horizon.

Camel and rider on the Tinfou Dunes, south of Tamegroute

The palm grove at Skoura

Skoura **9**

Road map C4. 🚃 *from Ouarzazate and Tinerhir.* 🚌 *Mon.*

THE SMALL SLEEPY TOWN of Skoura is surrounded by an impressive palm grove, which was laid out in the 12th century by the Almohad sultan Yacoub el-Mansour. The most beautiful kasbahs in southern Morocco are to be found here. Some of these are still partially inhabited, and some are attached to private houses. Many of Skoura's inhabitants, however, have moved into the breeze-block villages that line the road.

The **Ben Morro Kasbah** stands on the left of the road above Skoura. It was built in the 17th century and, now completely restored, has been converted into a guesthouse. The entrance to the palm grove is on the other side of Wadi Amerhidil. The grove can be explored only on foot, by bicycle or on mule-back. The grove is irrigated by *khettaras* (underground

pipes) and wells dug at regular intervals. Ruined kasbahs stand among palm trees, fig trees, birch and tamarisk – whose tannin-rich flowers are used in the processing of skins. The most imposing is **Amerhidil Kasbah**, which was once owned by the Glaoui family and which dominates the *wadi*. The restored interior is now open to visitors. The kasbahs of Aït Sidi el-Mati, Aït Souss, El-Kebbaba and Dar Aïchil are also worth a visit.

Further east, **Aït Abou**, built in 1863 and the oldest kasbah in the palm grove, has six storeys and walls 25 m (82 ft) high. Its outbuildings have been turned into a small short-stay *gîte*. An orchard with pomegranate, apple, pear, fig, quince and olive trees provides the necessary shade for growing crops.

From Skoura, road 6831 leads northeast to the village of **Toundout**, 25 km (15 miles) away, where there are some highly decorated kasbahs. The **Marabout of Sidi M'Barek** served as a stronghold where the semi-nomadic people stored their crops, under the protection of the saint.

A little way beyond Skoura, towards El-Kelaa M'Gouna, unexpected plantations of grasses imported from Australia in the 1990s help to preserve a little moisture in the arid ground.

El-Kelaa M'Gouna **10**

Road map D4. 🛈 *guides office;* *(044) 83 63 11.* 🚌 *Wed.* 🌹 *Rose Festival (May).*

THIS TOWN, whose name means "fortress", is located at an altitude of 1,450 m (4,759 ft), in the heart of rose country. In the 10th century, pilgrims returning from Mecca brought *Rosa damascena* back with them to Morocco. These peppery-scented flowers have developed a resistance to the cold and dry conditions in which they are now grown.

Spectacular landscape at the approach to the M'Goun valley

Each spring, rose-picking produces 3,000 to 4,000 tonnes of petals. The harvest is taken to two local distillation factories. One of them, in El-Kelaa M'Gouna, is laid out in a kasbah, and it is open to visitors in April and May. While a proportion of the roses is used to make rosewater for local distribution, the rest is processed and exported for use in the perfume industry.

The Rose Festival takes place after the harvest and is attended by all the inhabitants of the valleys of the Dadès. Accompanied by a *bendir* (a tambourine), young girls from El-Kelaa M'Gouna perform a sinuous dance, their long hair braided with coloured wool.

On the road out of the town is a craft cooperative with about 30 workshops. Daggers are made here, the craftsmen continuing a Jewish tradition of making sheaths and dagger handles out of cedar or camel bone. The steel blades are made in the mountain village of Azlague, not far from El-Kelaa M'Gouna.

The Amerhidil Kasbah, in the palm grove at Skoura

◁ **The Aït Benhaddou *ksar*, ar sunrise**

The Rose Festival in El-Kelaa M'Gouna

ENVIRONS: Between Skoura and El-Kelaa M'Gouna, kasbahs are set among greenery throughout the Dadès valley. The modern concrete houses that line the roads here are an artless imitation of these fine traditional buildings. Ruined kasbahs are now part of the local landscape. From offices on the way out of El-Kelaa M'Gouna, many hikes and tours by four-wheel-drive vehicle are organized, particularly to the **Vallée des Roses** and to the *ksar* at **Bou Thrarar**, a breathtaking mountain tour.

Further into the interior of the High Atlas some impressive gorges lead to the remote M'Goun valley. It is best to hire a guide because the tracks are not signposted.

Boumalne du Dadès ⓫

Road map D4. 🏠 *13,000.*
ℹ️ *Tizzarouine kasbah; (044) 83 06 90.* 🛒 *Wed.*

Tᴴɪꜱ ᴘʟᴇᴀꜱᴀɴᴛ stopping place at the beginning of the Dadès gorge is a regional administrative centre. From the edge of the plateau above the town, the view stretches over the fertile Dadès Oasis. At Tizzarouine Kasbah, from where there are fine views, guides offer tours and camping trips in the High Atlas and Jbel Sarhro.

Dadès Gorge ⓬

Road map D3. Grand taxi *from Boumalne du Dadès.* 🛒 *Sat in Msemrir.*

Bᴏʀᴅᴇʀᴇᴅ ʙʏ greenery, the course of Wadi Dadès stands out against the rocky landscape. Cultivated land on the banks of the *wadi* is

The Aït Mouted Kasbah, in the Dadès Gorge

surrounded by fig, almond and walnut trees and poplars.

About 2 km (1 mile) from Boumalne, in a bend in the road, stands the **Aït Mouted Kasbah**, which once belonged to the Glaoui. Here and there, large constructions in brown breeze-block, built by emigrants who have returned to Morocco, stand out as unfortunate blots on the landscape.

As it rises, the road passes some dramatic geological folds covered with limestone rock that has been shaped by erosion. At the foot of these natural formations stand the ruins of the **Aït Arbi Kasbah**. Further on are the stone and pisé **Tamnalt Kasbahs**, whose slender towers rise up against a backdrop of rocks that seem to be pressed together sideways like the fingers of a human hand. Beyond Aït Oudinar, the road crosses Wadi Dadès, following

Tamnalt Kasbah in the Dadès Gorge with a dramatic backdrop of rocks

the bottom of the gorge between sheer cliffs. It then runs along the edge of deep canyons, home to Royal Eagles and Vultures. On the plateau, the valley widens again, and attractive stone and pisé villages overlook the opposite riverbank.

The road running up the gorge from Boumalne du Dadès is metalled as far as Msemrir, 60 km (37 miles) to the north. The final stretch before Msemrir passes through much wilder country than in the lower part of the gorge. Beyond Msemrir, a track that is passable only by four-wheel-drive vehicle leads east to the Todra gorge and north to the High Atlas and Imilchil.

The Tinerhir oasis, stretching out along the banks of Wadi Todra

Tinerhir ⑬

Road map D3-4. 🏠 *40,000.* 🚌 *from Er-Rachidia and Ouarzazate, and grands taxis.* 🛈 *Hôtel Tombouctou; (044) 83 46 04.* 🗓 *Mon.*

THIS LIVELY TOWN, the region's administrative centre, lies midway between the Draa valley and the Tafilalt. Built on a rocky outcrop, it has an elongated layout. On its northern and southern sides it is bordered by a lush palm grove laid out at the foot of arid hills and containing dozens of *ksour* and kasbahs.

With several silver mines in the vicinity, Tinerhir is a wealthy town known for its silver jewellery. To the west stands a kasbah once owned by the Glaoui and now in a state of disrepair. To the southeast is Aït el-Haj Ali, the former mellah (Jewish quarter), whose houses make an interesting architectural ensemble. North of the town stretches a palm grove irrigated by Wadi Todra.

About 2 km (1 mile) from the bridge across the *wadi*, on the road to the **Todra Gorge**, a viewing platform commands a stunning view. Here, guides with camels offer their services. However, visitors need no assistance to walk down into the palm grove and follow the network of

shady paths that lead through orchards and run along irrigation ditches. This is a wonderful walk, as the Todra palm grove stretches for 12 km (7.5 miles).

On the other side of the *wadi* are many semi-ruined *ksour*, where 50 to 100 families once lived. The most interesting and most easily reached are the **Aït Boujane Ksar** and **Asfalou Ksar**.

Further north, about 5 km (3 miles) before the start of the gorge, there is an alternative route to the palm grove; this is via the Imarighen spring, the "Spring of the Sacred Fish".

ENVIRONS: At **El-Hart-n-Igou-ramene**, south of Tinerhir,

Detail of the walls of Tinerhir Kasbah

craftsmen produce a bronze-coloured local pottery that is sold in the souk. The sweep of road taking in El-Hart, Tadafalt and Agoudim offers the opportunity to see many *ksour*, some of which are still inhabited.

Todra Gorge ⑭

Road map D3.

SHEER CLIFFS 300 m (985 ft) high rise up dramatically each side of the narrow corridor that forms the Todra gorge. These are the most impressive cliffs in southern Morocco, and they

are well known to experienced mountaineers.

Wadi Todra flows through this great geological fault and on into the Tinerhir palm grove *(see above)*. Two hotels make possible an overnight stop in the Todra gorge. The best time of day to view the gorge is in the morning, when the rays of the sun break through between the high cliffs on either side.

The cliffs soon widen and a stony track leads to the village of Tamtattouchte, 22 km (14 miles) further on.

The Todra gorge, sandwiched between sheer cliffs

Tamtattouchte ⑮

Road map D3. 36 km (22 miles) north of Tinerhir on road 6902.

THE PICTURESQUE VILLAGE of Tamtattouchte is located at the other extremity of the Todra gorge, its earth houses blending into the red-ochre tones of the mountains. Here, small plots of land that stand out from their arid, rocky surroundings are irrigated by Wadi Todra.

Tamtattouchte is the starting point of tracks to the Dadès gorge to the west and Imilchil to the north, leading over passes, through gorges, across plateaux and over mountains. Ask a local for information about the state of tracks

The village of Tamtattouchte, at the northern end of the Todra gorge, with several fine *ksour*

negotiable by four-wheel-drive vehicles, particularly after periods of rainfall. Visitors should also be aware that no destinations are signposted.

Goulmima ⓰

Road map D3. 🚌 *from Er-Rachidia and Tinejdad.* 🏠 *Mon & Thu.*

ALTHOUGH IT IS SET in the heart of the Rheris oasis, where about 20 *ksour* stand on the banks of Wadi Rheris, the modern village of Goulmima is of no great interest to visitors. The inhabitants of neighbouring *ksour* come to the village to buy supplies.

The sturdiness of their fortifications make the *ksour* here unusual. Their towers are remarkably high and, when tribal feuds were rife, they protected the inhabitants against the incursions of the

The *ksar* at Goulmima, a labyrinth of narrow streets and alleys

Aït Atta, who came to pillage their harvests.

The old fortified village of Goulmima, 2 km (1 mile) east on the road to Erfoud, is worth the detour. Still inhabited, the **Goulmima ksar**, which exemplifies southern Moroccan defensive architecture, is surrounded by walls set with two massive towers. Cows and

sheep are enclosed within small corrals outside. A gate set at an angle opens onto a second gate. On a small square within the walls stand a mosque and the well that provides the *ksar* with water. The upper floors of some of the houses span the narrow streets, providing a strange contrast of light and shadow.

MOROCCO'S ARCHITECTURAL HERITAGE

The vestiges of a past age and of unique ways of life, kasbahs, *ksour* and granaries – all of them built of earth – are the victims of neglect. The kasbahs are crumbling, the ruins of once-luxurious residences are abandoned and clay walls slowly disappear into the ground. The Moroccan government seems indifferent to the unique value and interest of these buildings. Aside from sparse and sporadic activity, action to protect Morocco's architectural heritage goes little further than listing its

Detail of the Taourirt kasbah in Ouarzazate

monuments and drawing up conservation programmes that produce no concrete results. The only active conservation in Morocco is that resulting from European initiatives. Besides the uncompleted restoration of the *ksar* at Aït Benhaddou, funded by UNESCO, that of the granary at Igherm-n-Ougdal, on the road to the Tizi-n-Tichka Pass, and of the Taourirt kasbah in Ouarzazate, the small number of kasbahs in the Dadès valley that have been restored were saved by private funding. Private initiative is also responsible for the skilful restoration of the Ben Morro kasbah and Aït Abou kasbah in Skoura and the Hôtel Tombouctou in Tinerhir. Unfortunately, most of the Glaoui fortresses in the valleys of the Atlas are being left to their fate.

The Southern and Eastern Oases

Jerboa, or
desert rat

SOUTHERN AND EASTERN MOROCCO has
many oases. Their existence
depends on the presence of water,
which is either supplied by rivers
flowing down from the mountains or
provided by an underground water
table. Underground water rises naturally
at the foot of dunes or is pumped by artesian wells
or along underground channels known as *khettaras*,
some of them covering considerable distances. This
accounts for the fact that the oases are strung out in
a line along the arid Dadès, Draa and Ziz valleys.

Seguias *are channels that criss-cross
the oasis, bringing water to the
various crops and trees. Clay plugs
are sometimes used to divert the
water along particular routes.*

IRRIGATION IN THE OASES

Set in particularly hostile surroundings, oases
are a very fragile ecological environment that
survives thanks only to ceaseless human
intervention. Many dams are built to control
the flow of water in the *wadis*, which, when
they are in flood, can devastate the plantations
in the oases in a few hours. *Khettaras* and
seguias must be regularly cleared.

Clay plugs are used to
direct the flow of water to
other parts of the oasis.

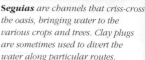

Date palms, *of which
there are many varieties,
produce abundant fruit.
A single tree can provide
30 to 100 kg (66 to 220 lb)
of dates a year. They are
harvested in autumn.*

**Animal-skin
container**

Barley

Crops *such as tomatoes,
carrots and lettuce, as well as
fruit trees such as olive, fig
and apricot, thrive in the shade
provided by the palm trees.*

Irrigation *is produced by* khettaras,
*underground channels that bring
water to the oasis. Here, the water is
either drawn from a well or is simply
forced to the surface by gravity.
The exact amount of water needed
for each crop is provided by* seguias.

Work in the fields *is done by women, who carry out all stages in the cultivation of cereals and various kinds of vegetables.*

Water is channelled as it flows from the *khettara*.

Well

Arid zone

The tops of the shafts *that are sunk to dig and then maintain the* khettara *are visible on the surface.*

Underground water gently flows into the oasis.

Porous layer

Clay

Spring

Temporary wadi

Dam across the *wadi*

Main canal (seguia)

Temporary wadis, *across which dams are built, feed water to the various* seguias *in the oasis.*

ANIMALS OF THE OASIS

The common bulbul, rufous bush robin, house bunting and doves are some of the more familiar birds seen in the oases. Toads frequent the banks of the water-courses, geckos and lizards cling to stone walls and the trunks of trees, and scorpions hide under stones. During the night, hyenas and jackals approach places of human habitation. The fennec, horned viper and herbivorous lizard rarely venture beyond the dunes and rocks where they were born.

At Tinerhir, *many* seguias *channel water from Wadi Todra, bringing it to the beautiful palm grove nearby.*

Herbivorous lizard

Horned viper

Fennec

Majestic Jbel Ayachi, rising over extensive and sparesely populated desert plateaux

Midelt ⑰

Road map D3. 👥 *20,000.* 🚌 *from Meknès, Rabat, Erfoud, Er-Rachidia and Azrou.* ℹ️ *Timnaï Cultural Centre, 20 km (12 miles) north of Midelt; (055) 36 01 88.* 🏪 *Wed & Sun.* 🎭 *Apple Festival (Oct).*

ON THE BORDER between the High and Middle Atlas, Midelt is considered to be part of southern Morocco. The small villages on each side of the road leading out of the town consist of traditional buildings that are very similar to those typical of southern Morocco. While, at the beginning of the 20th century, Midelt was no more than a modest *ksar*, under the Protectorate it became a French garrison town.

Located at the foot of **Jbel Ayachi**, which rises to a height of 3,737 m (12,264 ft), Midelt is the starting point for tours. At an altitude of 1,500 m (4,923 ft), the town enjoys a continental climate – very cold in winter and very hot in summer.

Beautiful Middle Atlas carpets, as well as fossils and mineral stones, are on sale in Souk Jedid. There is also a workshop where carpets and blankets are woven and high-quality embroidery is produced. It is run by Franciscan sisters, who teach Berber women these handicrafts. The convent (Kasbah Myriem) is located on the road to Tattiouine.

ENVIRONS: The **Cirque de Jaffar**, a limestone gorge on the way out of Midelt, makes for the most interesting tour here. However, tracks 3424 and 3426, which go there and back, covering 79 km (49 miles), are tough going, being passable only from May to October and only by four-wheel-drive vehicle.

The track along the hillside is overshadowed by the imposing outline of Jbel Ayachi, which can be climbed without much difficulty. The Cirque de Jaffar is set in a wild landscape of cedar, oak and juniper growing in stony ground. The winding track

passes through remote Berber hamlets. A turning off to the left, at the Mit Kane forestry hut, leads back to Midelt. The track that continues west leads eventually to Imilchil.

Disused lead and silver mines in the impressive **Aouli Gorge**, 25 km (15 miles) northeast of Midelt (on roads S317 and 3419), are sunk into the mountainside. Although they were abandoned in the 1980s, the machinery is still in place.

Ziz Gorge ⑱

Road map D-E3. 88 km (55 miles) south of Midelt on road P21.

WADI ZIZ, which springs near Agoudal, in the heart of the High Atlas, runs in an easterly direction, then obliquely south, level with the village of Rich. It then carves a gorge in the mountains, irrigates the Tafilalt then disappears into the Saharan sands.

South of Midelt, beyond the Tizi-n-Talrhemt Pass, at an altitude of 1,907 m (6,259 ft), forests give way to arid plains. The fortified villages of the Aït Idzerg tribe, as well as a few old forts of the French Foreign Legion, line the road. The **Tunnel de Foum-Zabel**, or Tunnel du Légionnaire, was driven through the limestone rock here by the French Foreign Legion in 1927, thus opening a route to

Berber women learning embroidery with the Franciscan sisters of Midelt

Dates drying after the autumn harvest in the Ziz Gorge

the south. The tunnel opens on to the Ziz Gorge, whose impressive red cliffs jut into the Atlas. Two fine *ksour*, Ifri and Amzrouf, both surrounded by palm trees, stand here.

The Hassan-Addakhil dam, contained by a thick dyke of red earth, demarcates the lower foothills of the Atlas. Built in 1970, it irrigates the Tafilalt and Ziz valleys and provides electricity for Er-Rachidia.

Er-Rachidia ⑲

Road map D3. 🏛 62,000. 🚌 *from Erfoud, Midelt, Ouarzazate and Figuig.* ℹ *Tourist office; (055) 57 09 44.* 🛒 *Tue, Thu & Sun.*

As a result of its strategic location between northern and southern Morocco, and between the Atlantic seaboard and Figuig and the Algerian border, Er-Rachidia became

KSOUR IN THE OASES

The Ziz valley is *ksar* country. The *ksar* (plural *ksour*) was developed originally as a communal stronghold for sedentary populations, to protect them against the incursions of bandits and nomadic tribes that raided the oases when the harvests had been brought in. The defensive design of these fortified villages is connected to this warlike past. The *ksar* usually overlooks the oasis. Originally, the *ksar* consisted of no more than a central alley with family houses on each side. Over time, it expanded to become a village, with a mosque, a medersa and granaries. Built of pisé and earth bricks in its upper part, every *ksar* bears the individual stamp of its builders, who devised elaborate incised geometric patterns.

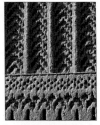

Detail of the *ksar* of Oulad Abdelhalim in Rissani

the main town in the province. Here the palm groves of the Ziz and Tafilalt begin, and the town also stands at the start of the road to the south. Er-Rachidia, also an administrative and military centre, was built by the French in the early 20th century, when it was known as Ksar es-Souk. Its present name was bestowed in 1979 in memory of Moulay Rachid, the first of the Alaouites to overthrow Saadian rule in 1666. Many *ksour* here were abandoned after 1960, when the Ziz broke its banks, causing serious floods and washing land away.

Although they are busy, the town's perfectly straight, grid-like streets hold scant appeal. A craft centre offers locally made pottery, carved wooden objects and rush baskets.

Source Bleue de Meski ⑳

Road map E3. 23 km (14 miles) south of Er-Rachidia on road P21.

THE SPRING, located 1 km (0.6 mile) off the main road, is a reappearance of Wadi Ziz, which runs underground for part of its course. The blue spring waters flow from a cave at the foot of a cliff into a pool built by the Foreign Legion. The water provides a natural swimming pool for the campsite in the palm grove.

The clifftop offers a view of the oasis and the ruined *ksar* of Meski. The road to Erfoud (*see p280*) also offers fine views of the Ziz valley and the oases of Oulad Chaker and Aourfous.

Er-Rachidia, a town at the junction of roads leading south

Shop in Erfoud, selling fossils – a local speciality – and a range of craft items

Erfoud ㉑

Road map E4. 🏠 *10,000.* 🚌 *from Fès, Er-Rachidia, Midelt, Rissani and Tinejdad, and grands taxis.* 🛍 *daily.* 🎪 *Date Festival (Oct).*

Before the development of the town began in 1930, the French had set up a military post here to watch over the Tafilalt valley. The Berber tribes put up a long-drawn-out resistance to the establishment of French rule, and the valley was one of the last parts of southern Morocco to surrender.

Erfoud's checkerboard layout is a vestige of this military past. This peaceful town, with an extensive palm grove, is the base for tours of the dunes of the Erg Chebbi. From the top of the eastern *borj,* a small bastion 3 km (2 miles) southeast of Erfoud, the view takes in a wide swathe of desert and palm groves.

In October, the souk at Erfoud overflows with dates of every variety. This is also when the three-day Date Festival, at the end of the date harvest, takes place. Both a religious and a secular event, the festival attracts local tribes. It begins with prayers at the mausoleum of Moulay Ali Cherif in Rissani, 17 km (11 miles) to the south, and continues with processions of people dressed in traditional costume and with folk dances.

Polished marble containing fossils is Erfoud's other main source of income. The cutting workshops, the **Usine de Marmar**, is open to visitors.

The road is also bordered with many small craters – the tops of shafts down to *khettaras.*

Usine de Marmar
On road 3451 to Tinejdad.
⬤ *8am–noon & 2–4pm Mon–Sat.*

Tafilalt Palm Grove ㉒

Road map E4. *South of Erfoud on road P21.*

Stretching out along the bends of Wadi Rheris and Wadi Ziz, which run from Erfoud, the Tafilalt oasis nestles in a stretch of greenery, extending beyond Rissani. The oasis was once a welcome stopping-place for caravans, as they arrived exhausted after weeks in the desert.

Today, the inhabitants of the Tafilalt rely on it for their livelihood: the 800,000 date palms that grow here are

Date harvest in the Tafilalt Palm Grove

renowned for their fruit. Unfortunately, and despite care, for a century the trees have suffered from Bayoud palm sickness – caused by a microscopic fungus – and the effects of excessive drought, both of which can kill them.

The October date harvest in the palm grove is a spectacular sight. Each owner climbs to the top of his tree and, as the grove resonates to the sound of machetes, bunches of dates crash to the ground, falling in large orange heaps (they turn brown as they ripen).

Symbols of happiness and prosperity, dates figure many rituals, and in birth, weddings and burial ceremonies.

Rissani ㉓

Road map E4. 🏠 *15,000.* 🚌 *from Meknès, Erfoud and Er-Rachidia, and grands taxis.* 🛍 *Tue, Thu & Sun.*

This small town on the edge of the Sahara marks the end of the metalled road and the start of tracks into the desert. To the east is the Hammada du Guir, a stony desert notorious for its violent sandstorms.

Rissani, built on the ruins of Sijilmassa, was once the capital of the Tafilalt. The origins of Sijilmassa are as mysterious as the reasons for its decline. The city was probably established by Zenet tribes in the 7th century, as a major stopping place on the trans-Saharan caravan routes and an independent kingdom. Over the centuries, it became prosperous from trade in gold, slaves, salt, weapons, ivory and spices, reaching its peak in the 13th and 14th centuries. However, religious dissent and the instability of the rival tribes that regularly launched raids on the city led to its destruction. The first Muslim city, Sijilmassa contained hundreds of kasbahs and palaces; just west of Rissani, on the road to Erfoud, a few vestiges of these, including the scant remains of walls, emerge from the sand.

The **Rissani Souk** is one of the most famous in the area. Donkeys, mules, sheep and goats are enclosed in corrals. Stalls are piled with shining pyramids of dates, as well as with vegetables and spices. Beneath roofs made of palm-matting and narrow pisé alleyways, jewellery, daggers, carpets, woven palm fibre baskets and pottery are laid out for sale.

South of Rissani, a 20-km (13-mile) route marked by many *ksour* crosses the palm grove. After 2.5 km (1.5 miles) stands the **Mausoleum of Moulay Ali Cherif**, where the father of Moulay er-Rachid, founder of the Alaouite dynasty, is laid to rest. The mausoleum was rebuilt in 1955, after it was damaged by a serious flooding of Wadi Ziz. A courtyard leads to the burial chamber, to which non-Muslims are not admitted. Behind the mausoleum are the ruins of the 19th-century **Abbar Ksar**. This former residence once housed exiled

Erg Chebbi, and the small rain-filled lake, Dayet Srji

Alaouite princes, the widows of sultans and, protected by a double earth wall, part of the royal treasury.

About 2 km (1 mile) from the mausoleum stands the **Oulad Abdelhalim Ksar**. It

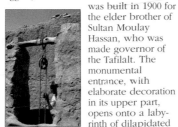

Well in the Oulad-Abdelhalim *ksar*

was built in 1900 for the elder brother of Sultan Moulay Hassan, who was made governor of the Tafilalt. The monumental entrance, with elaborate decoration in its upper part, opens onto a labyrinth of dilapidated rooms. Two rooms still have their painted ceilings.

The route takes in many other *ksour*, including those of Assererhine, Zaouïa el-Maati, Irara, Gaouz, Tabassamt and Ouirhlane. The *ksar* of Tinrheras, set on a promontory, also comes into view.

The road leading to the Draa valley via Tazzarine and Tansikht starts from Rissani.

Merzouga ㉔

Road map E4. 53 km (33 miles) southeast of Erfoud on road 3461.
🏠 *Sat.*

THE SMALL SAHARAN OASIS of Merzouga is famous for its location at the foot of the **Erg Chebbi Dunes**. These amazing dunes, which rise up out of the stony, sandy desert extend for 30 km (19 miles), and reach a maximum height of 250 m (820 ft). At sunrise or dusk, the half-light gives the sand a fascinating range of subtle colours.

Although they are nearer to Rissani, Merzouga and the Erg Chebbi dunes are easier to reach from Erfoud. The services of a guide are not necessary, except when high winds whip up the sand. From Erfoud, going in the direction of Taouz, the metalled road degenerates into a track after 16 km (10 miles). Beyond the Auberge Derkaoua, visitors should follow the line of telegraph poles. The dunes come into view on the left. At Merzouga, camel drivers offer one-hour to two-day tours of the dunes.

Dayet Srji, a small lake west of the village, sometimes fills with water during the winter, after sudden rainfall. It attracts hundreds of pink flamingoes, storks and other migratory birds.

Procession at the foot of the Erg Chebbi Dunes, during the Date Festival

SOUTHERN MOROCCO AND WESTERN SAHARA

THE VAST SOUTHWESTERN REGION *of Morocco embraces a variety of spectacular landscapes. The fertile Souss plain, an area dotted with oases and extensive stony deserts, is bordered by the rugged mountains of the Anti-Atlas. On the southern Atlantic coast, sheer cliffs give way to large areas of dunes linking Morocco to the Sahara and the republic of Mauritania.*

Six thousand years ago, hunters forced northwards by the desertification of the Sahara moved into southwestern Morocco, as shown by the thousands of rock engravings that have been discovered in the Anti-Atlas. The Arab conquest in the 7th century inaugurated the age of the independent kingdoms. An important point for trans-Saharan trade between Morocco and Timbuctu, the Atlantic coast was coveted from the 15th century by the Portuguese and the Spaniards, who eventually colonized it in the late 19th century, re-naming it Río de Oro (Golden River).

When Spain withdrew from western Sahara in 1975, King Hassan II initiated the Green March during which 350,000 civilians reasserted Morocco's claim to the region *(see p58)*.

The great Souss plain, east of Agadir, lies at the heart of this isolated region. The commercially grown fruit and vegetables here are irrigated by the underground waters of Wadi Souss, and the surrounding argan trees provide food for herds of black goats. To the south, the Anti-Atlas is the final mountainous barrier before the Sahara. Its almost surreal geological folds, shaped by erosion, alternate with verdant oases. Stone-built villages, often with an *agadir* (fortified granary), cluster along *wadis* or at the foot of mountains. Further south, the wide deserted beaches are sometimes cut off by lagoons that attract thousands of migratory birds.

Camel in the Sahara desert, southern Morocco

◁ **Spectacular cacti in the gardens of the Musée Municipal du Patrimoine Amazighe in Agadir**

Exploring the South and the Saharan Provinces

LOCATOR MAP

ALL ROADS HEADING into the deep South begin at
Agadir, Morocco's foremost coastal resort. To the
east lies the great Souss plain, which stretches north
as far as the High Atlas and south as far as the Anti-
Atlas. This mountain chain of rocky peaks and stony
plateaux culminates on its eastern side in Jbel Siroua,
a remarkable volcanic massif that reaches a height of
3,304 m (10,844 ft), and whose western side, pitted
with isolated valleys, slopes down towards the
Atlantic. The resort of Agadir is linked to Tafraoute,
to the southeast, and to the numerous oases on the
Saharan slopes of the Anti-Atlas. The road south links
Agadir with the Saharan provinces, which start at the
coastal town of Tarfaya. The focal points of human
life in the Sahara are a few large towns, surrounded
by banks of dunes stretching to infinity.

SIGHTS AT A GLANCE

**Sand dunes along the coast between
Tan Tan Plage and Tarfaya**

ATLANTIC

OCEAN

TAN TAN
PLAGE ❿

TAN TAN

M'SIED

P 41

ABETTEH

P 44

TARFAYA ⓫

P 41

EL-HAGOUNIA

LAAYOUNE

S 906

P 41

P 42

⓬

Galtat
Zemmour

El-Mahbas,
Tindouf

El-Mahbas

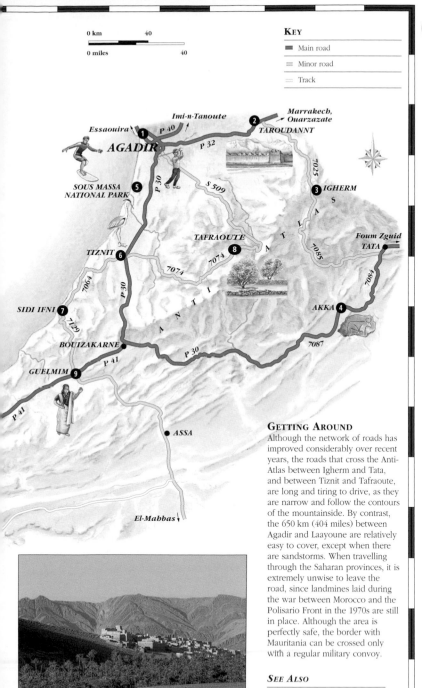

KEY

■ Main road

▬ Minor road

═ Track

0 km   40

0 miles   40

Essaouira

Imi-n-Tanoute

AGADIR

Marrakech, Ouarzazate

TAROUDANNT

P 40

P 32

S 509

P 30

SOUS MASSA NATIONAL PARK

7025

IGHERM

TAFRAOUTE

Foum Zguid

TATA

7085

TIZNIT

7074

7074

A N T I   A T L A S

AKKA

7064

7084

SIDI IFNI

P 30

7129

BOUIZAKARNE

7087

P 41

P 30

GUELMIM

P 41

ASSA

El-Mahbas

GETTING AROUND

Although the network of roads has improved considerably over recent years, the roads that cross the Anti-Atlas between Igherm and Tata, and between Tiznit and Tafraoute, are long and tiring to drive, as they are narrow and follow the contours of the mountainside. By contrast, the 650 km (404 miles) between Agadir and Laayoune are relatively easy to cover, except when there are sandstorms. When travelling through the Saharan provinces, it is extremely unwise to leave the road, since landmines laid during the war between Morocco and the Polisario Front in the 1970s are still in place. Although the area is perfectly safe, the border with Mauritania can be crossed only with a regular military convoy.

SEE ALSO

• *Where to Stay* p315

• *Where to Eat* pp334–5

Tata, with many kasbahs and a palm grove

Agadir ❶

AGADIR, THE REGIONAL CAPITAL of the South beyond the Atlas, draws thousands of visitors a year. Its gentle climate – temperatures range from 7 to 20 °C (45 to 68 °F) in January, the coolest month – together with its sheltered beach and hotels make it Morocco's second tourist city after Marrakech. Having been completely rebuilt in the 1960s after the terrible earthquake that destroyed the city, Agadir has none of the charm of traditional Moroccan towns, although its wide-open spaces and its modernity appeal to many holiday-makers. The industrial quarter consists of oil storage tanks and cement works, as well as factories where fish is canned – Agadir is Morocco's foremost fishing port – and where fruit from the fertile Souss plain is processed.

Nouveau Talborj

Agadir's modern centre, the Nouveau Talborj, was built south of the old city, which was completely razed as the result of the earthquake of 1960.

The main streets of the city centre run parallel to the beach. Pedestrian areas, lined with restaurants, shops and crafts outlets are concentrated around Boulevard Hassan II and Avenue du Prince Moulay Abdallah.

There are some fine modern buildings, including the post office, the town hall and the stately law courts. The city's bright white buildings are interspersed by many gardens.

Traditional doorway

🏛 Musée Municipal du Patrimoine Amazighe

Avenue Hassan II, passage Ait Souss.
🕿 (048) 82 16 32.
🕐 10am–7pm daily. 🌐
This museum was opened on 29 February 2000, on the day of the commemoration of the reconstruction of Agadir, forty years after the violent earthquake that destroyed the city. The museum exhibits everyday objects derived from the peoples of the Souss plains and the pre-Saharan regions.

Among the exhibits is a rich collection of magnificent Berber jewellery, superbly displayed alongside information on how the jewellery was made.

🎭 Open-Air Theatre

Boulevard Mohammed V.
🕿 (048) 84 07 48.
Concerts and shows take place here.

🌳 Vallée des Oiseaux

Avenue Hassan II.
🕐 9am–noon & 3–6pm Tue pm–Sun.
This open space in the heart of the city, laid out on a narrow strip of greenery, contains aviaries with a multitude of exotic birds. A small zoo features mouflons (wild mountain sheep) and macaques. There is also a play area for children.

Polizzi Medina

Ben-Sergaou. 10 km (6 miles) south of Agadir, towards Inezgane. 🕿 (048) 28 07 06. 🕐 8am–5:30pm daily. 🌐
This medina was restored by Coco Polizzi, an Italian architect, who used traditional Moroccan building methods. Houses, restaurants and craft workshops are to be built in the medina.

Riding on the beach at Agadir

🏖 Beach

South of the city, the sheltered beach, in a bay with 9 km (6 miles) of fine sand, is Agadir's main attraction, offering some of the safest swimming off Morocco's Atlantic coast. However, although the city enjoys 300 day of sunshine a year, it is often shrouded in mist in the morning. Sailboards, jet-skis and water scooters can be hired on the beach, and rides, on horses or camels, are also on offer. Many cafés, hotels and restaurants line the beach.

🏯 Old Kasbah

At an altitude of 236 m (775 ft), the hilltop ruins of the kasbah, within restored ramparts, offer a stunning view of Agadir and the bay. The kasbah was built in 1540 by Mohammed ech-Cheikh, to keep the Portuguese fortress under surveillance. It was restored in 1752 by Moulay Abdallah and accommodated a garrison of renegade Christians and Turkish mercenaries.

White houses in Agadir, a city completely rebuilt in the 1960s

AGADIR'S HISTORY

The origins of Agadir are not fully known. In 1505, a Portuguese merchant built a fortress north of the present city. It was later acquired by Manuel I, king of Portugal, who converted it into a garrison. By this time, Agadir had became a port of call on the sea routes to the Sudan and Guinea, and a century of prosperity began in 1541, when the Portuguese were expelled by the Saadians. Although the Sous fell under the control of a Berber kingdom in the 17th century, Moulay Ismaïl later reconquered the region. In 1760, however, Sidi Mohammed ben Abdallah sealed the city's fate when he closed its harbour and opened a new port in Essaouira. In 1911, Agadir was the object of a dispute between the French and the Germans relating to its strategic location. On 29 February 1960, an earthquake destroyed the city in a few minutes.

The German cruiser *Berlin* off Agadir in 1911

VISITORS' CHECKLIST

110,000. Agadir El-Massira, 22 km (13.5 miles) on the road to Taroudannt. from Casablanca, Essaouira, Marrakech & Tiznit. Avenue du Prince Moulay Abdallah; (048) 84 63 77. Tue–Sun.

Port

Located on the edge of the city, the port consists of a large complex with about 20 canning and freezing factories where the produce of the sea is processed. An auction takes place in the fish market here every afternoon. Agadir also exports citrus fruit, fresh vegetables, canned food and ore.

The port at Agadir, the second-largest sardine port in Morocco

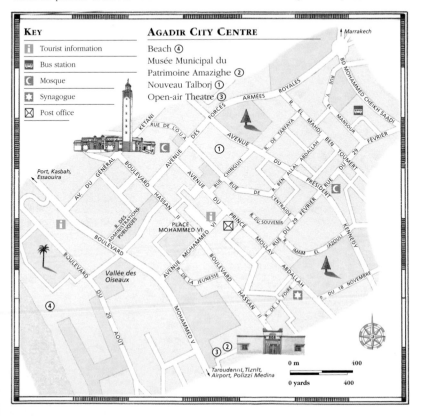

KEY

- Tourist information
- Bus station
- Mosque
- Synagogue
- Post office

AGADIR CITY CENTRE

Beach ④
Musée Municipal du Patrimoine Amazighe ②
Nouveau Talborj ①
Open-air Theatre ③

The imposing ramparts of Taroudannt

Taroudannt ❷

80 km (50 miles) east of Agadir.
🏛 36,000. 🚌 from Casablanca,
Agadir, Marrakech & Ouarzazate, or
grands taxis; Thu & Sun. 🅰 Berber
souk daily. 📷 Moussem (Aug).

ENCLOSED WITHIN red-ochre
ramparts and encircled
by orchards, orange groves
and olive trees, Taroudannt
has all the appeal of an old
Moroccan fortified town. It
was occupied by the
Almoravids in 1056 and in
the 16th century became the
capital of the Saadians, who
used it as a base from which
to attack the Portuguese in
Agadir. Although the Saadians
eventually chose Marrakech
as their capital, they made
Taroudannt wealthy through
the riches of the Sous plain,
which included sugar cane,
cotton, rice and indigo.
  Under the Alaouites, the
town resisted royal control,

The daily Berber market in
Taroudannt

forming an alliance with
Ahmed ibn Mahrez, the dissident nephew of Moulay
Ismaïl. The latter regained
control of the region by
massacring the inhabitants.
  Taroudannt is a generally
peaceful town, except during
the annual olive harvest when
it is enlivened by itinerant
pickers. On its two main
squares, Place Assarag and
Place Talmoklate, horse-
drawn carriages can be hired
for a tour of the **ramparts**,
which are 7 km (4 miles)
long. Set with bastions and
pierced by five gates, they are
in a remarkably good state of
preservation, a part of them
dating from the 18th century.
  The **souks**, between the
two squares, are the town's
main attraction. The daily
Berber market sells spices,
vegetables, clothing, household goods, pottery and other
items. In the Arab souk the
emphasis is on handicrafts:
terracotta, wrought iron, brass
and copper, pottery, leather
goods, carpets and Berber
jewellery of a type once made
by Jews can be seen. Carvings
in chalky white stone are a
speciality of Taroudannt.
  Outside the ramparts is a
small tannery, which is open
to visitors. Its shop sells goatskin and camel-hide sandals,
lambskin rugs, soft leather
bags, belts and slippers.

ENVIRONS: The peaks of the
western High Atlas – particularly Jbel Aoulime, at a height
of 3,555 m (11,667 ft) – can
be reached via road 7020,
north of the town. About
37 km (23 miles) southeast of
Taroudannt, the imposing

Tioute Kasbah dominates
the palm grove. This was the
location for the film *Ali Baba
and the Forty Thieves,* made
by Jacques Becker in 1954.
A restaurant adjacent to the
kasbah rather spoils the site.
On the banks of Wadi Souss,
which attracts migratory birds,
stands the older Freija kasbah,
now uninhabited.
  Between Taroudannt and
Ouarzazate, the road (P32)
passes through landscape of
wild beauty. Plains covered
with argan trees give way to
the volcanic massif of Jbel
Siroua, which bristles with
peaks and where soft geological folds alternate with
rocky plateaus.
  Taliouine, a town between
two mountain chains at an
altitude of 1,180 m (3,873 ft),
has a stately kasbah once
owned by the Glaoui *(see p57)*.
Though dilapidated, it is still
inhabited. The town is the
centre of the world's biggest
saffron-growing area. In
Tazenakht, 85 km (53 miles)
east of Taliouine, beneath
Jbel Siroua, carpets with an
orange weft are woven by the
Ouaouzguite tribe.

Desert landscape in the Anti-Atlas

Igherm to Tata ❸

Road P32 east from Taroudannt,
then roads 7025 and 7085 to Tata.
🚌 Taroudannt, Tiznit, Agadir &
Bouizarkane. 🅰 Souk Wed in Igherm,
Thu in Tata.

A RELATIVELY NEW road (built
in 1988), the P32 crosses
the Anti-Atlas, passing through
some remarkable landscapes.
Between Taroudannt and
Igherm, argan fields alternate
with dry-stone villages overlooking terraced plantations.

Saffron flowers, harvested for their stigmas

SAFFRON FROM TALIOUINE

Saffron *(Crocus sativus)* is a bulbed herbaceous plant that belongs to the iris family. It grows at altitudes of 1,200 to 2,000 m (4,000 to 6,600 ft), in slightly chalky soil. Almost 6 sq km (2.3 sq miles) of saffron fields around Taliouine are cultivated by families, each of which tends its own plot of land. The bulbs are planted in September at a density of 7,500 per 1,000 sq m (10,760 sq ft), and the mauve flowers appear at the end of October. Harvesting takes place before sunrise and goes on for 15 to 20 days. It is a delicate process, involving the separation of the red stigmas that contain the colorant from the plant. After drying, 100,000 flowers produce 1 kg (2.2 lb) of saffron, and just 1 gram (a tiny pinch) is enough to colour 7 litres (12 pints) of liquid. The precious powder is then poured into airtight boxes and stored away from daylight to preserve its flavour. Good-quality saffron is sold in the form of whole filaments. Saffron is used in food, as a dye for carpets and pottery, and for dyeing the hair and hands of brides. It is also a medicinal plant that is thought to aid digestion and calm toothache.

Igherm, 94 km (58 miles) southeast of Taroudannt, is a large mountain village at an altitude of 1,800 m (5,908 ft). It is the base of the Ida Oukensous tribe, renowned for the daggers and guns that they make. The houses here are built of pink stone, their windows outlined in blue. Women dressed in black and wearing coloured headbands fetch water in tall copper jars *(situle)* which they carry on their head.

Between Igherm and Tata the road crosses a rugged desert plain, with mountains of folded strata in hues of ochre, yellow and violet. The Tizi-Touzlimt Pass, at 1,692 m (5,553 ft), is followed by a succession of oases. In the Souk-Khemis-d'Issafen palm grove women dressed in indigo can be seen walking around the well-watered gardens, except when the Thursday souk is on. Some 30 *ksour* stand in the great **Tata Palm Grove**, where Berber and Arabic are spoken.

Crossing Wadi Tata, which irrigates the grove, the road leads to Agadir-Lehne, where a stone *koubba* stands below a spring. Some 4 km (2.5 miles) further on are the Messalite caves, which are inhabited sporadically by shepherds.

Akka ❹

62 km (39 miles) southwest of Tata on road 7084. 🏃 *6,500.* 🏠 *Souk Thu & Sun.*

THE AKKA PALM GROVE lies north of the village. A dozen *ksour* are interspersed among the date palms and the pomegranate, fig, peach, apricot and nut trees. On a hill is Tagadirt, a mellah, now in ruins, where the rabbi Mardoch was born in 1883. He discovered ancient rock engravings in the area and accompanied the French ascetic Charles de Foucauld, disguised as a Jew, on his peregrinations *(see 217).*

The troglodytic granary at Aït-Herbil, still in use

The Aït-Rahhal springs in the palm grove supply the oasis. A strange brick-built minaret dating from the Almohad period can also be seen here.

ENVIRONS: Many rock engravings can be seen in the area, notably at **Foum-el-Hassan**, 90 km (56 miles) southwest of Akka on the road to Bouizarkane *(road 7087 then road P30),* and at **Aït-Herbil**. To visit them, you need to hire a guide (details from Café-Hôtel Tamdoult in Akka). There are also many *igherm* (granaries), some dug into the cliff face.

The *koubba* at Agadir-Lehne, in the Tata Palm Grove

Greater flamingoes flying in the Sous Massa National Park

Sous Massa National Park **5**

65 km (40 miles) south of Agadir on road P30; 50 km (31 miles) north of Tiznit on road P30.

CREATED IN 1991, the Sous Massa National Park extends along the banks of Wadi Massa, which, en route to the Atlantic, irrigates a large palm grove. This nature reserve, where river and sea water meet, where tides ebb and flow, and where winter temperatures are mild, attracts hundreds of migratory birds.

The reed beds on the banks of the *wadi* are inhabited by greater flamingoes from the Camargue, in southern France, and from Spain, as well as godwit, turnstone, snipe, dunlin, coots, grey heron and many other species. The primary purpose of creating the park was to preserve the bald ibis, a species threatened with extinction. Morocco is home to half the world's population of this curious bird, which has a pink featherless head.

Only certain areas of the park are open to the public. Visitors should approach the *wadi* from Sidi Rbat. The best time to see the birds is early in the morning, from March to April and October to November.

Tiznit **6**

91 km (57 miles) south of Agadir on road P30. ♦ 45,000. ▭ from Agadir, Safi, Guelmim and Tafraoute, or grands taxis. ⓘ ONMT Agadir. ⓐ Souk Wed & Thu. ◈ Moussem of Sidi Ahmed ou Moussa (Aug), 35 km (22 miles) east of Tiznit.

LOCATED slightly inland from the coast, Tiznit is a small town where the proximity of both the Atlantic and the desert can be felt. In 1881, Sultan Moulay Hassan settled here in order to exert greater control over the dissident Berber tribes of the Souss.

The town came to fame in 1912, when El-Hiba, a populist rebel leader, was proclaimed sultan of Tiznit in the mosque. Opposed to the establishment of the French

Protectorate in Morocco, El-Hiba conquered the Sous by rallying the tribes of the Anti-Atlas and the Tuareg to his cause. He launched an attack on Marrakech, where he was repulsed by French troops.

It is possible to walk round the 5-km (3-mile) pink pisé ramparts that encircle the town. The *méchouar*, a rectangular parade ground that functioned as the pasha's reception courtyard, is lined with arcades beneath which are cafés and shops. The renowned craftsmen of Tiznit still work with silver here, as the Jews once did, producing chunky Berber jewellery, daggers and sabres with inlaid handles.

The vertical poles on the clay walls of the minaret of the Grand Mosque are put there to help the souls of the departed enter paradise.

ENVIRONS: Sidi Moussa Aglou, 15 km (9 miles) northwest of Tiznit, is a fine beach used by surfers. Caves in the cliffs are used by local fishermen.

Sidi Ifni **7**

75 km (47 miles) south of Tiznit on road 7064. ♦ 20,000. ⓘ ONMT Agadir. ▭ Tiznit or grands taxis. ⓐ Souk Sun. ◈ Moussem (end of Jun).

FROM TIZNIT, a scenic minor road leads to the coast, which it follows until Sidi Ifni. Formerly a Spanish coastal enclave, the town, on the crest of a rocky plateau overlooking the ocean, is buffeted by wind and is often shrouded in sea mist. The colonial style

Women spreading washing out to dry on the banks of Wadi Massa

◁ Cube-like houses rendered with pink plaster in Tafraoute, in the Anti-Atlas

of some of the buildings –
such as the former Spanish
Consulate and the Hispano-
Berber Art Deco church that
is now the law courts – gives
the town an unusual aspect.

Tafraoute ⑧

143 km (89 miles) southeast of
Agadir. Road P30 from Agadir then
road S509; road 7074 from Tiznit.
🏠 1,700. 🚌 Tiznit and Agadir, or
grands taxis. 🛈 ONMT Agadir.
🛒 Souk Tue & Wed.
Mountain bikes can be hired in
the town centre.

AT AN ALTITUDE of 1,200 m
(3,938 ft), Tafraoute
stands in the heart of a
stunning valley of the Anti-
Atlas. It is surrounded by a
cirque of granite whose
colours at the end
of the day change
from ochre to
pink. The palm
groves here are
lush and, for the
brief period of
their flowering –
two weeks in
February – the
almond trees are
covered with
clouds of pink and
white blossom.
    The square
dry-stone houses
consist of a central courtyard
and a tower. They are
rendered with pastel pink
plaster and their windows are
outlined with white limewash.
    Tafraoute is the territory of
the Ameln, the best known of
the six tribes of the Anti-Atlas.

The fortified village of Tioulit

their homeland, so that their
villages are today inhabited
only by children, elderly
people and women shrouded
in black. However, as soon as
they can, the émigrés return
to build comfortable houses.
    Tafraoute is also a centre

MONK SEALS

The largest colony of monk seals (monachus monachus)
in the Mediterranean area is found along the Atlantic coast,
in the very south of Morocco. In 1995, 200 seals still
existed here but half the colony was destroyed by disease
in 1998, and it faces a very uncertain future. This brown
seal can grow to a length of 3 m (10 ft) and weigh up to
300 kg (660 lb). During the 20th
century it has disappeared from
the Canary Islands archipelago,
Madeira and most of the islands
of the Mediterranean. Today, it is
still to be found in the Black Sea
and on the Bulgarian and Turkish
coasts, and it may still survive in
Sicily and Sardinia.

The monk seal, facing an
uncertain future in Morocco

They are renowned for their
acumen as traders. As spice
merchants, they have spread
throughout Morocco and also
abroad. Limited local resources
have forced them to leave

for the manufacture of round-
toed slippers, in natural, red,
yellow or embroidered leather.

ENVIRONS: Jean Vérame's
painted rocks can be seen
3 km (2 miles) north of Tafraoute. The smooth, rounded
rocks, painted by the Belgian
artist in 1984, rise chaotically
from a lunar landscape.
Although their colours – red,
purple and blue – have faded,
the effect is still surreal.
    About 4 km (2.5 miles)
further north is the fertile
Ameln Valley, carpeted with
orchards and with olive and
almond trees. It is dotted with
26 Berber villages perching on
the mountain side, above which
runs a precipitous mountain
chain culminating in Jbel
Lekst, at 2,359 m (7,743 ft).
Taghdichte, the highest
village, is the starting point
for the ascent of Jbel Lekst.
    North of Tafraoute, on the
road to Agadir, is the igherm
(communal granary) of Ida ou
Gnidif, on the top of a hill. A
little further on is the fortified
village of **Tioulit**, perching on
another outcrop and looks
down into the valley.
    About 3 km (2 miles) south
of Tafraoute a cluster of huge,
strangely shaped rocks known
as Napoleon's Hat overlooks
the village of Agard Oudad. A
one-day detour from Tafraoute
leads to the **Afella Ighir Oasis**.
Laid out along the wadi, it is
filled with tiny gardens, palm
trees and almond trees clinging
to the cliffs. Beyond the point
where the road becomes a
rough track, a four-wheel-
drive vehicle is needed.

Houses in Tafraoute, covered in pink plaster

Angling from the cliff-top near Tan Tan Plage

Guelmim ❾

56 km (35 miles) south of Sidi Ifni on road 7129. 🏚 38,000. 🛈 (048) 87 29 11. 🚌 from Agadir, Marrakech, Laayoune and Tan Tan, or grands taxis. 🛒 Camel souk (Sat). 🎭 Moussem of Asrir (Jul).

Aلso known as Goulimine, this small settlement of red houses with blue shutters was an important centre on the caravan route from the 11th to the 19th centuries. Today, it is known chiefly for its camel souk. The *moussem* of Asrir, 6 km (4 miles) southeast, is attended by the Sahraouis, known as the "blue men" because of their indigo clothing.

ENVIRONS: 14 km (9 miles) to the north are the **Abeino** thermal springs with bathing pools for men and women. The vast **Plage Blanche** (White Beach), 60 km (37 miles) west of Guelmim, can

A trader at the camel souk in Guelmim

be reached along tracks. The beautiful **Aït Bekkou Oasis**, 17 km (11 miles) to the southeast, is the largest in the area.

Tan Tan and Tan Tan Plage ❿

125 km (78 miles) southwest of Guelmim on road P41. 🏚 50,000. 🚌 Agadir, Tarfaya and Laayoune, or grands taxis. 🎭 Moussem of Sheikh Ma el-Ainin (May/Jun).

The province of Tan Tan is sparsely populated by pastoral nomads and fishermen. The road from Guelmim is good but police checks are frequent since the region remains a military zone.

Tan Tan has a certain raffish charm, with everything from shops and mosques to the *petits taxis* painted in blue or mustard. In the medina, Saharan-style bric-a-brac is for sale and there is a colourful Sunday souk. A *moussem* held in May or June, honouring local resistance hero Sheikh Ma el-Ainin, is the occasion of a huge camel market. At night women dance the *guedra* in tribal tents.

On the coast, 25 km (15 miles) away, is Tan Tan Plage where low-key tourism development has begun.

ENVIRONS: About 245 km (152 miles) south of Tan Tan, via road P44, a route leads across the desert to **Smara**. Today no more than a garrison base, this historic and legendary town put up fierce resistance to the expansion of French rule,

Tarfaya ⓫

235 km (146 miles) south of Tan Tan. 🚌 from Tan Tan or grands taxis.

The spectacularly scenic route between Tan Tan and Tarfaya follows the coastline, where cliffs give way to dunes of white sand.

Tarfaya, today an expanding fishing port, was a stop on the Service Aéropostale, the French airmail service, in the 1920s and 1930s. There is a statue of writer and airman Saint-Exupéry who has left vivid descriptions of flying over this desolate region in terrible sandstorms. It was also the rallying point for the Green March of 1975 (see p58).

Boundless expanses of desert near Laayoune

Laayoune ⓬

117 km (73 miles) south of Tarfaya. 🏚 100,000. ✈ from Agadir, Dakhla and Tan Tan. 🚌 from Agadir, Dakhla and Tan Tan. 🛈 Avenue de l'Islam; (048) 89 16 94 or 89 22 33.

A large oasis on Wadi Sagia el-Hamra, Laayoune is today the economic capital of the Saharan provinces. Since Spain relinquished the territory in 1976 (see p58), Morocco has invested in making Laayoune a modern town.

Dakhla, 540 km (335 km) further south, stands on the tip of an attractive peninsula extending 40 km (25 miles). The bay is one of the most beautiful places in the country. Dakhla is the last town before the border with Mauritania, 350 km (217 miles) away. The area is safe but the border can be crossed only if you are escorted by a military convoy.

The Nomad's Tent

THE *KHAÏMA*, or nomad's tent, seen on the desert plateaux of the High Atlas, outside the towns of Zagora and Guelmim, is the moveable home of shepherds who travel to provide their flocks with seasonal grazing. The sturdy tent is easy to set up and gives protection against the heat. The brown fabric is woven from goat or camel hair.

Detail of a carpet

It consists of *flijs*, strips 40 to 60 cm (16 to 24 in) wide, sewn together edge to edge. It rests on a ridgepole supported on two vertical wooden poles. The interior of the tent is divided into two. One side, with basic cooking equipment and a loom, is for the women. The other side, separated by a screen, is reserved for the men and for visitors.

Nomads are rarely seen because they mostly frequent mountain or desert environments that are remote from civilization. However, for a few weeks of the year, some of them settle in an oasis. Their tents are very simply furnished, with little more than thick, heavy carpets and wooden chests where the women keep their most prized possessions. The hospitality of the nomads is legendary.

The nomad's tent is set up on level ground. In summer, the covering is laid over the poles in such a way as to allow air to circulate freely. In winter, the sides are drawn together and are insulated with long woollen blankets and carpets.

Nomadic Berber women card wool before spinning it into yarn. Using a loom unchanged since ancient times, they weave blankets and lengths of cloth.

These nomads, portrayed in a century-old photograph, lived in a way which hasn't changed much to this day. Nomads still travel from one source of water to another.

Driving animals to seasonal pastures occurs in Morocco's more arid regions. In summer, the nomads take their herds and flocks up to the high pastures of the Atlas, returning to the south in winter.

RAVELLERS
NEEDS

WHERE TO STAY

I N MOROCCO, choosing a hotel depends primarily on its location and on the services that you require during your stay. Hotels are graded according to an official system of classification that is now usually much more reliable than it once was, although at the cheaper end of the spectrum standards may be somewhat below European expectations. There are hotels in a wide range of price bands, so that visitors will have no difficulty in finding accommodation to suit their budget. Luxury

Hotel porter

hotels are becoming increasingly numerous, as are guesthouses, many of which are in *riads* (houses with patios). In the low season, prices are often negotiable, even in the smartest establishments. Beware of travelling without having made prior reservations, however, since at certain times of the year accommodation is almost impossible to find. For those with smaller budgets, youth hostels and guest rooms are attractive alternatives so long as visitors observe the ground rules.

Le Méridien Mérinides *(see p308)*, a hotel with a splendid view of Fès

CHOOSING A HOTEL

T HE LOCATION of your hotel, especially in large towns and cities, is an important criterion. It is usually best to stay somewhere near the old town, where the main tourist sites are often found. The disadvantage of such a location, however, is that the hotel is noisy and unlikely to offer parking. If you would like more space, especially a garden – and many gardens also have a swimming pool – it is best to choose a hotel on the edge of the old town or in a modern quarter.

Smaller towns rarely offer high-class accommodation, especially in the South. Here, your choice of hotel should be governed by your itinerary. In the South, most places of interest to tourists are not in the towns themselves but along the roads between them, so that rather

than planning your route according to the desirability of a hotel, it is best to choose where to stay in relation to the distance you intend to cover each day.

CLASSIFICATION OF HOTELS AND SERVICES

T HE MOROCCAN MINISTRY of Tourism has devised an official system of classification for hotels. Accordingly, hotels are graded on a scale of one to five stars, with two subcategories, A and B. In principle, each grade corresponds to certain standards of comfort, as well as criteria such as the size of the establishment.

Once bearing little relation to reality, the system by which stars are awarded was recently overhauled. Although some hotels may still be over-ambitiously graded, many have been downgraded to reflect more accurately the

standard of accommodation that they offer.

As a general rule, four- and five-star hotels are well equipped, with satellite television, telephone, en-suite bathrooms and room service, as well as many other features such as a restaurant, swimming pool, sports centre and hammam. Two- and three-star hotels are comfortable and clean, with private bath or shower. The small one-star hotels, or hotels without classification, are often quite basic and may not be very clean. It is advisable to ask to see the room before you decide.

Although most ungraded hotels do not deserve to be listed, some are, in fact, very comfortable etablishments. It is only reluctance on the part of the necessary paperwork that prevents them from being listed.

**The Anezi Hotel in Agadir,
overlooking the bay**

◁ **Multicoloured slippers laid out for sale**

The Kasbah Darkaoua Hotel, a haven of coolness on the track to Merzouga

PRICES

BY LAW, prices for accommodation must be shown in the reception area as well as in the rooms, and this requirement is widely fulfilled. Be aware, however, that advertised prices rarely include tax (ranging from 1 to 25 dirhams, according to the town and the hotel) and that they do not include breakfast.

The average price of a single room in a small one-star or unlisted hotel is 100 dirhams. A two- or three-star establishment will charge 200 to 300 dirhams, and a three-star category-A hotel or a four-star hotel 300 to 450 dirhams. The numerous five-star hotels charge 600 dirhams, and some of them over 2,000 dirhams. There is no official upper limit.

Prices vary according to the season, and it is not unusual to see prices double around the holiday periods at the end of the year and in spring, and during the summer in the coastal resorts. Prices also vary according to the number of people renting the room. For example, for a child or a third adult sharing a room, a supplement will be charged, though usually with a reduction of 5 to 50 per cent.

The reliable **Kenzi** hotel chain, which has hotels all over Morocco, gives discounts when reservations are made in several of their establishments, and also in the low season. Information about hotels is available from the **Fédération Nationale de l'Industrie Hôtelière** in Casablanca.

NEGOTIATING A LOWER PRICE

NEGOTIATING a lower price for a hotel room is quite common practice, and it bears results. At slack times, it is possible to obtain reductions of up to 30 per cent. However, it is a waste of time trying to negotiate at the peak of the high season, or in the very smart hotels, such as the La Mamounia in Marrakech.

RESERVATIONS

DURING THE high seasons, and particularly over the spring and end-of-year holiday periods, the crowds of holiday-makers can be unexpectedly large. This is also true of coastal resorts during the summer. At such times, in small towns that have a limited number of hotels (particularly in the South) it can be quite impossible to find a room. This can also happen in towns with a much larger choice of hotels, such as Marrakech or Fès.

At these busy times, it is essential to make a reservation in advance. This can be done at a travel agency, through a tour operator covering Morocco or by contacting hotels directly. When making a direct booking, you will be asked to quote the number of your credit card so as to confirm the reservation. Doing this is usually quite safe, even though it is best to deal only with large establishments or with hotels belonging to a reputable chain.

One consequence of the European-style hotel management that has taken root in Morocco is the practice of overbooking. Put simply, the hotel accepts more reservations than it has rooms so as to compensate for any cancellations. Unfortunately, if you happen to be a victim of this practice, there is little that you can do. The best way to try to avoid this happening is to pay for your stay in full at the time of booking and check in at the hotel earlier than rather than later in the day.

The Kasba Asmaa Hotel in Zagora (*see p314*), with a pleasant swimming pool and palm trees giving welcome shade

Swimming pool at La Mamounia, the famous hotel in Marrakech, in a luxuriant garden

CHAIN AND LUXURY HOTELS

SUCH LEADING international hotel chains as Hilton, Hyatt and Le Méridien have many establishments in Morocco. The **Ibis** group manages six hotels belonging to the **Moussafir** chain. The **Salam** chain owns hotels throughout the country built in the traditonal Moroccan architectural style. Discounts are available when you book in advance through the Salam chain and also through the **Kenzi** chain in Paris.

There is a large number of luxury hotels in Morocco. Although many of them are modern, the country also boasts a few old legendary establishments, such as La Mamounia in Marrakech *(see p310)*, which, although it has lost some of its appeal as a result of the most recent phase of renovation, still has a great atmosphere. The Palais Jamaï in Fès *(see p309)*, converted from a former palace, is not only an architectural marvel but has a unique location above the medina. The El-Minzah in Tangier *(see p307)* looks like something from a film set and, although it is showing its age, is still one of Morocco's great hotels.

CAMPSITES

CAMPSITES can be found in every large town, and they are very numerous on the Atlantic and Mediterranean coasts. As a general rule, standards of cleanliness in campsites leave much to be desired, and it is not safe to leave property unattended in tents. Staying in a campsite in Morocco is also something that best suits those who are not too fussy about hygiene and facilities.

Finding your own place to set up camp outside official sites is not officially unlawful, but it is definitely not recommended for reasons of personal safety and because the authorities do not like tourists camping anywhere they please.

GUESTHOUSES

IN SMALL SEASIDE villages, where it is sometimes very difficult to find accommodation, many Moroccans offer rooms to let in their own houses. Comforts are often basic and, before accepting the room, it is wise to check the cleanliness of the bedclothes and that toilets and washing facilities are in working order.

Guesthouse accommodation can be a useful option when you are staying for a few days away from the large tourist coastal resorts.

Often, when travelling in the Atlas, visitors will be offered accommodation, rather than be left to camp in the open. In such cases, you may be offered space in a living room, or on the roof of a pisé house, which can be a magical experience. The owner of the house (often the village chief) will steadfastly refuse money, and will even invite you to share a meal. You can always offer a gift, or deal with the women of the house, who will often accept remuneration or a present for their children.

YOUTH HOSTELS

THERE ARE several youth hostels in Morocco, and these make it possible to stay in the country for a minimal cost. However, most youth hostels are not centrally located and are quite basic, although they are usually clean. If you do not have an international Youth Hostel Association membership card, you may be asked to pay a little extra. The easiest way to obtain a card is to join your country's youth hostel association, such as the YHA in Britain or the HI-AYH in the United States. Information in Morocco is available from the **Fédération Royale Marocaine des Auberges de Jeunesse** in Casablanca.

UNMARRIED COUPLES

IT IS AS WELL to know that in Morocco strict rules apply to the accommodation of couples. A Muslim cannot sleep with a woman if the couple are not married. Some hoteliers respect scrupulously

The restaurant at the Kasba Asmaa hotel in Zagora *(see p314)*

this ruling. Allowances are normally made for Western couples, however, except by particularly strict hotel keepers.

DISABLED VISITORS

APART FROM certain recently built hotels, no establishment in Morocco is equipped for disabled visitors. Nevertheless, Moroccans are very well disposed to anyone needing help, so that people with disabilities will be pleasantly surprised at the thoughtfulness and helpfulness that they encounter in Morocco.

RIADS

THE LITERAL TRANSLATION of the Arabic word *riad* is "garden". Thus a *riad* should consist, theoretically, of a garden planted with trees. By extension, the word *riad* is applied to all old houses that have at least a patio or courtyard. These old-style Moroccan houses can be found in the medinas, and very many have become available to visitors over recent years, especially in Marrakech, Fès and Essaouira. These traditional residences each have their own particular architectural design and

One of the many *riads* in Essaouira that are now guesthouses

have usually been very well restored. Converted into guesthouse accommodation, they are very pleasant places to stay in, particularly because they are quiet and because of their often excellent location. By contrast to a large international hotel, staying in a *riad* is usually an experience that will transport you to another age.

Either individual rooms or the whole *riad* can be rented, and many also offer breakfast and an evening meal. No official grading applies to this type of accommodation, and standards, service and prices vary widely according to the individual *riad*.

While some *riads* are run by people who have only a vague idea of the hotel business, others are out of the ordinary. Into this category come La Villa des Orangers and La Maison Arabe, both in Marrakech *(see p310–11)*. These *riads* will delight those who love old buildings as well as visitors who expect a high standard of service.

Riads can be booked through **Riads au Maroc**, **Marrakech-Medina** and **Fès Medina Morocco** (US based). Of the agencies that handle the booking of *riads*, however, not all are reputable, some of them merely making the most of the popularity of this type of accommodation.

Choosing a Hotel

THE HOTELS LISTED BELOW have been selected across a wide range of price categories for the excellence of their facilities, location or character. They are listed by area, starting with Rabat, and the colour-coded thumb tabs correspond to those by which the regions of Morocco are identifed throughout this guide.

	NUMBER OF ROOMS	RESTAURANT	ROOMS WITH A VIEW	GARDEN OR TERRACE	SWIMMING POOL

RABAT

AGDAL: *Ibis Moussafir* (Dh) (Dh) — **94**
Boulevard Abderrahmane Rhafiki. 🄲 *(037) 77 49 19.*
A recently built and very clean hotel located opposite Rabat Agdal railway station, in a quiet but relatively central area. 🗗

CITY CENTRE: *Hôtel Balima* (Dh) — **71** ● | | ●
Avenue Mohammed V. 🄲 *(037) 70 86 25 & (037) 70 79 67.* 🄵🄰🄷 *(037) 70 74 50.*
Although it is very clean, this hotel has a rather old-fashioned character. The terrace bar, a popular meeting place, is surrounded by palm trees and faces the Moroccan parliament building. 🔳 🈔 📺 🗗

CITY CENTRE: *Kenzi Belère* (Dh) — **110** | | ●
Avenue Moulay Youssef. 🄲 *(037) 70 96 89/70 98 01.* 🄵🄰🄷 *(037) 70 98 01.*
Recently incorporated into the Kenzi chain, this hotel has undergone thorough renovation. It offers some of the best value for money in Rabat. 🔳 🈔 📺 📋 📖

CITY CENTRE: *Hôtel Royal* (Dh) — **67** ●
1 Rue Amman. 🄲 *(037) 72 11 72.* 🄵🄰🄷 *(037) 72 54 91.* 🄰 royalhotel@mtds.com
A hotel with a lot of cachet, in a fine old residential building. Ask for one of the renovated rooms on the highest floors. 🔳 🈔

CITY CENTRE: *Hôtel Terminus* (Dh) — **130** ●
384 Avenue Mohammed V. 🄲 *(037) 70 52 67/70 06 16.* 🄵🄰🄷 *(037) 70 19 26.*
A stone's throw from the Rabat-Ville railway station, this is an ideal hotel for tourists making a brief visit to Rabat. Avoid the rooms looking onto the noisy avenue. 🔳 🈔 📺 📋 📖

CITY CENTRE: *Hôtel Chellah* (Dh) (Dh) — **116** ●
2 Rue d'Ifni. 🄲 *(037) 70 10 51.* 🄵🄰🄷 *(037) 70 63 54.*
A hotel with a relatively high standard of comfort Some of the rooms have an excellent view of the Grand Mosque. 🔳 🈔 📺 📋 📖

CITY CENTRE: *Hôtel Safir* (Dh) (Dh) (Dh) — **197** ● ■ ● ■
Place Sidi Makhlouf. 🄲 *(037) 73 47 47.* 🄵🄰🄷 *(037) 72 21 55.*
🅆 www.hotelsiaha-rabat.com
Very near the Hassan Tower, the hotel offers a view of the Bou Regreg estuary. The terrace bar, with rooftop swimming pool, commands a panoramic view. 🔳 🈔 📺 📋 📖

CITY CENTRE: *La Tour Hassan* (Dh) (Dh) (Dh) — **139** ● ■ ● ■
26 Rue Chellah, BP 14. 🄲 & 🄵🄰🄷 *(037) 72 54 08.* 🄰 thassan@menara.ma
Midway between the city and the Hassan Tower, this is a very quiet, very comfortable establishment. Ask for a room with a view of the lovely Andalusian garden. 🔳 🈔 📺 📋 ★ 📖

HASSAN TOWER: *Hôtel Shéhérazade* (Dh) (Dh) — **77** ● | | ●
21 Rue de Tunis. 🄲 *(037) 72 22 26/27/28.* 🄵🄰🄷 *(037) 72 45 27.*
A small, welcoming hotel in the quiet ambassadorial district of Rabat, two streets from the Mausoleum of Mohammed V. 🔳 🈔 📺 📋 📖

SALÉ: *Le Dawliz* (Dh) (Dh) — **45** ● ■ ● ■
Avenue du Prince Héritier. 🄲 *(037) 88 32 77.* 🄵🄰🄷 *(037) 88 32 79.*
🄰 ledawliz@iam.net.ma
A luxurious complex is set on the riverbank opposite Rabat. With its pleasant swimming pool, the hotel is ideal for a relaxing stay. 🔳 🈔 📺 📋 📖

SOUISSI: *Hôtel Hilton* (Dh) (Dh) (Dh) (Dh) — **269** ● ■ ● ■
Aviation Souissi. 🄲 *(037) 67 56 56.* 🄵🄰🄷 *(037) 67 14 92.* 🅆 www.hilton.com
This very comfortable hotel, in the almost exclusively residential quarter of Souissi, is used mostly by businessmen and diplomats. 🔳 🈔 📺 📋 📖

Price categories are per night for two people occupying a standard double room in the high season, with service and tax included:

(Dh) under 500 dirhams
(Dh)(Dh) 500–1,000 dirhams
(Dh)(Dh)(Dh) 1,000–2,000 dirhams
(Dh)(Dh)(Dh)(Dh) over 2,000 dirhams

RESTAURANT
This is not necessarily recommended. Very good hotel restaurants are listed in Where to Eat *(pp322–34)*.

ROOMS WITH A VIEW
The hotel has an excellent location and some rooms have a fine view.

GARDEN OR TERRACE
The hotel has a garden, interior courtyard or terrace, and meals may be served outdoors.

SWIMMING POOL
Outdoor swimming pool unless otherwise indicated.

NORTHERN ATLANTIC COAST

	Price	Number of Rooms	Restaurant	Rooms with a View	Garden or Terrace	Swimming Pool
ASILAH: *Hôtel Mansour* (& FAX *(039) 41 73 90.* @ elmansourhotel@yahoo.fr Comfortable and well maintained, this hotel offers excellent value for money. Slightly unfriendly reception. 🔲 24 TV 🔲 P 🔲	(Dh)	47				
ASILAH: *Hôtel El-Khaima* (*(039) 41 74 28.* FAX *(039) 41 75 66.* A large hotel complex offering a range of sports and leisure facilities, including tennis court and swimming pool. It is the best hotel in Asilah, although it is slightly lacking in character. 🔲 24 P 🔲	(Dh)(Dh)	113	●	■	●	■
ASILAH: *Hôtel Zelis* 10 Avenue Mansour-Eddhabi. (*(039) 41 70 69.* FAX *(039) 41 70 98.* Despite its rather austere external appearance, this is a hotel with a lot of character. Recently opened, it offers all modern comforts. Some of the rooms have a sea view. 🔲 24 TV 🔲 ★ 🔲	(Dh)(Dh)	55	●	■		■
KENITRA: *Hôtel Mamora* Place de l'Hôtel de Ville. (*(037) 37 17 75/37 13 10.* FAX *(037) 37 14 46.* @ mamora@yahoo.fr The best hotel in Kenitra. Modern, with excellent facilities. 🔲 🔲 P ★ 🔲	(Dh)	70	●	■	●	■
KENITRA: *Hôtel Safir* Place Administrative. (*(037) 37 30 30.* FAX *(037) 37 19 26* A well-kept though somewhat old-fashioned hotel. The quietest rooms are those looking onto the garden and swimming pool. 🔲 P 🔲	(Dh)	87	●	■	■	■
LARACHE: *Hôtel España* 2 Avenue Hassan II. (*(039) 91 31 95.* FAX *(039) 91 56 28.* The best choice for a short stay in Larache. Some of the rooms look onto the town's lively central square. 🔲 TV 🔲	(Dh)	45				
LARACHE: *Hôtel Riad* Avenue Mohammed Ben-Abdellah. (*(039) 91 26 26.* FAX *(039) 91 26 29.* This welcoming, very central hotel is set in extensive parkland. Bungalows for four people are also available. 🔲 24 P 🔲	(Dh)(Dh)	22	●	■	●	■
MOHAMMEDIA: *Hôtel Hager* Avenue Ferhat-Hachad. (*(023) 32 59 21.* FAX *(023) 32 59 29.* W www.hotelhager.com The rooms in this welcoming and particularly well-kept establishment are not large but are very pleasantly furnished. The rooms on the upper floor offer a sea view. 🔲 24 P 🔲	(Dh)	18	●	■		
MOHAMMEDIA: *Complexe Skoura* 10 km (6 miles) N of town, towards Rabat. (*(023) 31 19 93* FAX *(023) 31 19 95.* @ kouhli@iam.net.ma The complex consists of ten maisonette apartments, each sleeping eight. Attentive staff. In summer, a minimum stay sometimes applies. 🔲 TV P 🔲	(Dh)(Dh)(Dh)	10	●	■	●	

CASABLANCA

	Price	Number of Rooms	Restaurant	Rooms with a View	Garden or Terrace	Swimming Pool
CITY CENTRE: *Hôtel Majestic* 55 Boulevard Lalla Yacout. (*(022) 31 09 51.* FAX *(022) 44 62 85.* The hotel, in a very fine residential building, provides excellent value for money. The rooms are simply furnished but comfortable. It is best to avoid those that look onto the street. 🔲 P 🔲	(Dh)	105	●		●	
CITY CENTRE: *Hôtel Plaza* 18 Boulevard Félix Houphouët-Boigny. (*(022) 29 76 98/29 78 22.* FAX *(022) 27 64 39.* In a fine, typically Casablancan residential building, this appealing hotel is ideally located for exploring the city on foot. 🔲	(Dh)	27		■		

Price categories are per night for two people occupying a standard double room in the high season, with service and tax included:

(Dh) under 500 dirhams
(Dh)(Dh) 500–1,000 dirhams
(Dh)(Dh)(Dh) 1,000–2,000 dirhams
(Dh)(Dh)(Dh)(Dh) over 2,000 dirhams

RESTAURANT
This is not necessarily recommended. Very good hotel restaurants are listed in Where to Eat (pp322–34).

ROOMS WITH A VIEW
The hotel has an excellent location and some rooms have a fine view.

GARDEN OR TERRACE
The hotel has a garden, interior courtyard or terrace, and meals may be served outdoors.

SWIMMING POOL
Outdoor swimming pool unless otherwise indicated.

	NUMBER OF ROOMS	RESTAURANT	ROOMS WITH A VIEW	GARDEN OR TERRACE	SWIMMING POOL
CITY CENTRE: *Hôtel Ibis Moussafir* (Dh)(Dh) Place de la Gare Casablanca Voyageurs. (*(022) 40 19 84.* FAX *(022) 40 07 99.* Located opposite the Casablanca Voyageurs railway station, this small hotel has a family atmosphere and is very clean. It has an attractive garden with a small swimming pool.	97	●		●	
CITY CENTRE: *Hôtel Safir* (Dh)(Dh) 160 Avenue des F.A.R. (*(022) 31 12 12.* FAX *(022) 31 65 44.* @ hotelsafir@resotel.net.ma Like all the hotels in the Safir chain, this is a good establishment. The rooms are large and well equipped.	312	●	■		■
CITY CENTRE: *Hôtel El-Kandara* (Dh)(Dh)(Dh) 44 Boulevard d'Anfa. (*(022) 26 15 60.* FAX *(022) 22 28 90.* W www.elkandara.com Conveniently located in the city centre, this hotel offers everything that one would expect from a large hotel. Good value for money and facilities for children.	213	●	■		■
CITY CENTRE: *Hôtel Kenzi Basma* (Dh)(Dh)(Dh) 35 Avenue Moulay Hassan I. (*(022) 22 33 23/20 39 26.* FAX *(022) 26 89 36.* While some of the rooms of this recently renovated hotel offer a view of the Mosque of Hassan II, others have a sea view. A very warm reception.	115	●	■		
CITY CENTRE: *Hôtel Suisse* (Dh)(Dh)(Dh) 1 Boulevard de la Corniche. (*(022) 39 60 62/3.* FAX *(022) 36 77 58.* Good-quality accommodation for minimal cost in the centre of Casablanca. The service is excellent and the bar is located in a large, very quiet courtyard.	192	●	■	●	■
CITY CENTRE: *Hôtel Hyatt Regency* (Dh)(Dh)(Dh)(Dh) Place des Nations Unies. (*(022) 26 12 34.* FAX *(022) 22 01 80.* W www.hyatt.com A central hotel used almost exclusively by businessmen. Unobtrusive and attentive service.	253	●	■		■
CITY CENTRE: *Le Royal Mansour Méridien* (Dh)(Dh)(Dh)(Dh) 27 Avenue des F.A.R. (*(022) 31 30 11.* FAX *(022) 31 48 18.* W www.lemeridien.com The smartest hotel in Casablanca, offering the most modern comforts amid superb Moorish architecture. Top-quality service.	182	●	■	●	
CORNICHE: *Bellerive* (Dh) 38 Boulevard de la Corniche. (*(022) 79 75 16.* FAX *(022) 79 76 39.* @ sonia@plvplus.net.ma A recently renovated hotel offering a good standard of comfort. Most of the rooms have a sea view. It is one of the least expensive places to stay along the coast.	33	●	■		■
CORNICHE: *Riad Salam* (Dh)(Dh)(Dh)(Dh) Boulevard de la Corniche. (*(022) 39 13 13* FAX *(022) 39 66 39.* This hotel, at a remove from the lively city centre, has restaurants and a park, and is a restful place to stay. It also has a thalassotherapy centre.	196	●	■		■
SOUTHERN ATLANTIC COAST					
AGADIR: *Hôtel Ibis Moussafir* (Dh) Corner of Avenue Abderrahim Bouabid and Rue Oued-Ziz (the road to Marrakech). (*(048) 23 28 42–43.* FAX *(048) 23 28 49.* W www.accorhotels.com A very pleasant hotel in the city centre. It is ideal for visitors staying just one night in Agadir or for those preferring to keep away from the crowds of tourists. The garden within has a small swimming pool. Ask for a quiet room.	114	●	■	●	■

AGADIR: *Anezi* ⓓⓗ   386
Boulevard Mohammed V. 〖 (048) 84 09 40. 𝗙𝗔𝗫 (048) 84 07 13.
🆆 www.hotel-anezi.com
A classic, slightly ageing hotel, with a very friendly reception.
Conveniently located in the tourist area of the city. Some rooms offer
a spectacular view of the Bay of Agadir. 🛏 24 📺 🍽 🅿 ★ 🏊

AGADIR: *Sud Bahia* ⓓⓗ   246
Avenue des Administrations Publiques. 〖 (048) 84 63 87. 𝗙𝗔𝗫 (048) 84 63 86.
A well-maintained establishment with comfortable rooms and a large
swimming pool. It faces onto the sea and is ideal for families.
🛏 24 🅿 🏊 🛗

AGADIR: *Oasis* ⓓⓗ ⓓⓗ   149
Boulevard Mohammed V. 〖 (048) 84 33 13. 𝗙𝗔𝗫 (048) 84 42 60.
A hotel in the city centre, though within a few minutes of the beach.
Simple décor and unobtrusive reception. 🛏 📺 🍽 🅿 🏊

AGADIR: *Hôtel Melia el-Madina Salam* ⓓⓗ ⓓⓗ ⓓⓗ   206
Boulevard du 20 Août. 〖 (048) 84 53 53. 𝗙𝗔𝗫 (048) 84 53 08.
＠ ltielmadina@agadirnet.net.ma
A hotel in the Moorish style, laid out almost like a small town with narrow
streets. It has seven restaurants and a superb swimming pool. The rooms
are comfortable and attractively decorated. 🛏 24 📺 🍽 🅿 ★ 🏊 🏋

AGADIR: *Tikida Beach* ⓓⓗ ⓓⓗ ⓓⓗ   232
Chemin des Dunes, BP 901. 〖 (048) 84 54 00. 𝗙𝗔𝗫 (048) 84 58 62.
🆆 www.agadir-tikida.com
The hotel complex consists of low buildings set in luxuriant gardens
on the edge of the beach. Excellent service and all comforts.
🛏 24 📺 🍽 🅿 ★ 🏊 🏋

AGADIR: *Beach Club* ⓓⓗ ⓓⓗ ⓓⓗ ⓓⓗ   450
Chemin des Dunes, BP 310. 〖 & 𝗙𝗔𝗫 (048) 84 43 24.
＠ abcmaroc@marocnet.net.ma & zagora@wanadoo.net.ma
One of the finest and most comfortable hotels in Agadir. Located on the
edge of the beach, though a little away from the crowds, it offers
everything that one would expect from a five-star establishment. Several
restaurants and large, comfortable rooms. 🛏 24 📺 🍽 🅿 ★ 🏊

AGADIR: *Dorint* ⓓⓗ ⓓⓗ ⓓⓗ ⓓⓗ   332
In the tourist district. 〖 (048) 82 41 46. 𝗙𝗔𝗫 (048) 84 43 92.
＠ info.agapal@dorint.com & atlanticpalace@agadirnet.net.ma
The most luxurious hotel in Agadir, opened in 2000, with several
drawing rooms, stately gardens and a well-equipped thalassotherapy
centre. Top-quality, unobtrusive service. 🛏 24 📺 🍽 🅿 ★ 🏊 🏋

EL-JADIDA: *Le Palais Andalou* ⓓⓗ   28
Boulevard Docteur-de-Lanoë. 〖 (023) 34 37 45. 𝗙𝗔𝗫 (023) 35 16 90.
This hotel, in a former palace, has small drawing rooms with typically
Moroccan décor, and an attractive courtyard. Comfortable rooms. 🛏 🅿 🏊

EL-JADIDA: *Royal Golf Hotel* ⓓⓗ ⓓⓗ ⓓⓗ   116
7 km (4 miles) along the road to Casablanca. 〖 (023) 35 41 41.
𝗙𝗔𝗫 (023) 35 34 73. 🆆 www.accorhotels.com
Set in the middle of an 18-hole golf course, this is essentially a hotel
designed for golfers. It is relatively unknown, but its standard and facilities
are those of a large hotel. Many sports activities. 🛏 24 📺 🍽 🅿 🏊

ESSAOUIRA: *Palazzo Desdemona* ⓓⓗ ⓓⓗ   14
Avenue Oqba Ben Nafi. 〖 (044) 47 22 27. 𝗙𝗔𝗫 (044) 78 57 35.
The most recent of the *riads* to open in Essaouira. It consists, in fact, of two
combined *riads*. Delightful décor. 🛏 24 🏊

ESSAOUIRA: *Riad Al-Madina* ⓓⓗ ⓓⓗ   49
9 Rue El-Attarine. 〖 (044) 47 57 27. 𝗙𝗔𝗫 (044) 47 66 95. 🆆 www.riadalmadina.com
Guests in this 19th-century *riad* have included Jimi Hendrix and
Tennessee Williams. Excellent restaurant. 🛏 📺 🏊

ESSAOUIRA: *Riad Mogador* ⓓⓗ ⓓⓗ   156
On the road to Marrakech. 〖 (044) 78 35 55. 𝗙𝗔𝗫 (044) 78 35 56.
Recently built and near the city centre, this comfortable hotel offers a
range of facilities, a hamman and a pleasant garden. 🛏 24 🍽 📺 🅿 🏊

Price categories are per night for two people occupying a standard double room in the high season, with service and tax included:

(Dh) under 500 dirhams
(Dh)(Dh) 500–1,000 dirhams
(Dh)(Dh)(Dh) 1,000–2,000 dirhams
(Dh)(Dh)(Dh)(Dh) over 2,000 dirhams

RESTAURANT
This is not necessarily recommended. Very good hotel restaurants are listed in Where to Eat (pp322–34).

ROOMS WITH A VIEW
The hotel has an excellent location and some rooms have a fine view.

GARDEN OR TERRACE
The hotel has a garden, interior courtyard or terrace, and meals may be served outdoors.

SWIMMING POOL
Outdoor swimming pool unless otherwise indicated.

	NUMBER OF ROOMS	RESTAURANT	ROOMS WITH A VIEW	GARDEN OR TERRACE	SWIMMING POOL
ESSAOUIRA: *Villa Quieta* (Dh)(Dh) 89 Boulevard Mohammed V. [(044) 78 50 04 & 78 50 05. FAX (044) 78 50 06. @ villa.quieta@iam.net.ma W www.villa-quieta.com This hotel, a recently converted private residence, is decorated in the Moroccan style. It includes two suites and an apartment.	14		■	●	
ESSAOUIRA: *Sofitel Mogador* (Dh)(Dh)(Dh) Boulevard Mohammed V. [(044) 47 90 00. FAX (044) 47 90 80. W www.sofitel.com Opened in December 2000, this luxurious complex offers the full range of thalassotherapy treatments. A very well-appointed establishment, with high-quality service.	117	●	■	●	■
ESSAOUIRA: *Terrasses d'Essaouira* (Dh)(Dh)(Dh) 2 Rue Mohammed-Douri. [(044) 47 51 14. FAX (044) 47 51 23. W www.les terrasses-essaouira.com Close to Moulay el Hassan square, this up-market, charming hotel is set in an ancient riad. Comfortable, well-decorated rooms.	15	●		●	
ESSAOUIRA: *Villa Maroc* (Dh)(Dh)(Dh) 10 Rue Abdellah ben Yassin. [(044) 47 61 47. FAX (044) 47 58 06. W www.villa-maroc.com A superb hotel converted from two 18th-century *riads* in the heart of the medina. Friendly, attentive staff. Breakfast is served on the terrace and table d'hôte meals are available for guests.	22	●	■	●	
NEAR ESSAOUIRA: *Auberge Tangaro* (Dh)(Dh)(Dh) 5 km (3 miles) in the direction of Agadir. [(044) 78 47 84. FAX (044) 78 57 35. This auberge, with white limewashed walls, overlooks the sea from a hilltop location. Comforts are rudimentary but the reception is friendly and the atmosphere relaxed. Half-board compulsory. ★	18	●	■	●	
IMOUZZER DES IDA OUATANANE: *Hôtel des Cascades* (Dh)(Dh) [(048) 82 60 16 & 82 60 23. FAX (048) 82 60 24. W www.cascades-hotel.com Some 42 km (26 miles) from Agadir, this characterful hotel has 27 rustic though comfortable rooms, and relaxing gardens and communal areas. Many tours are organized from the hotel.	72	●	■	●	■
OUALIDIA: *Hôtel le Chems* (Dh) [(067) 16 10 42. This complex on the edge of a lagoon was recently renovated and enlarged. Most of the rooms and bungalows have a view of the lagoon.	31		■	●	
OUALIDIA: *Hôtel L'Hippocampe* (Dh)(Dh)(Dh) Route du Palais. [(023) 36 61 08. FAX (023) 36 64 61. The terrace of this hotel offers the best view of the lagoon anywhere in Oualidia. Very comfortable rooms in small bungalows set in a beautiful garden. Direct access to the beach.	24	●	■	●	■
SAFI: *Hôtel Assif* (Dh) Avenue de la Liberté. [(044) 62 29 40. FAX (044) 62 18 62. A very clean and comfortable hotel. The décor and atmosphere are a little cold but the staff are friendly and helpful.	62	●	■		
SAFI: *Hôtel Atlantide* (Dh) Rue Chaouki. [(044) 46 21 60. FAX (044) 46 45 95. A hotel of distinction. The terrace overlooks the medina. The surroundings are quiet and the staff very friendly. Excellent restaurant.	40	●	■	●	■
SAFI: *Hôtel Safir* (Dh)(Dh) Avenue Zerktouni. [(044) 46 42 99. FAX (044) 46 45 73. In a residential quarter, this luxurious modern hotel overlooks the town. It is very well run but is somewhat lacking in character.	90	●	■	●	■

TANGIER

CITY CENTRE: *Hôtel Rembrandt* (Dh) — 65
Corner of Boulevard Mohammed V and Avenue Pasteur.
(039) 33 33 14/15/16. FAX (039) 93 04 43.
One of Tangier's legendary hotels. It is favourably located and very comfortable. Some of the rooms have a sea view. 🛏 24 TV ▤ 🗹

CITY CENTRE: *Hôtel Tanjah Flandria* (Dh)(Dh) — 150
6 Boulevard Mohammed V. (039) 93 44 67/93 32 79 /93 31 64. FAX (039) 93 43 47.
A modern, well-equipped hotel with a high level of comfort, although the rooms looking onto the noisy boulevard are best avoided. 🛏 24 TV ▤ 🗹

CITY CENTRE: *Hôtel El-Minzah* (Dh)(Dh)(Dh) — 140
85 Rue de la liberté. (039) 93 58 85. FAX (039) 93 45 46. @ minzah@iam.net.ma
Very near to the Grand Socco, this is the best hotel in Tangier. The rooms in this splendid building are comfortable and the swimming pool, set in a luxuriant garden, is exceptional. Excellent service. It also has an excellent restaurant, El Korsan (see p326). 🛏 24 TV ▤ ★ 🗹

PARC BROOKS: *Hôtel Inter-Continental* (Dh)(Dh) — 120
Parc Brooks. (039) 93 60 53. FAX (039) 93 01 51. @ inter@wanadoo.net.ma
About 10 minutes' walk from the city centre, this hotel is a little out of the way. However, it is modern, quiet and spacious, with a superb setting in the middle of a huge park. 🛏 24 TV ▤ P 🗹

ENVIRONS OF TANGIER: *Hôtel Tarik* (Dh) — 150
Just outside the city, on the road to Malabata. (039) 34 09 49/34 19 18.
A hotel-club catering for families and offering a range of activities. The rooms are spacious and very pleasant. 🛏 🗹

ENVIRONS OF TANGIER: *Ibis Moussafir Tanger* (Dh) — 104
12 km from city centre, on Route National 1, (039) 39 39 30. FAX (039) 39 39 31.
W www.bestlodging.com
Within easy access of Boukhalef airport, this hotel offers good facilities and comfortable rooms at affordable rates. 🛏 24 TV ▤ P 🗹

MEDITERRANEAN COAST & THE RIF

AL-HOCEIMA: *Hôtel National* (Dh) — 16
23 Rue de Tétouan. (039) 98 21 41. FAX (039) 98 86 81.
A charming hotel run by cheerful, highly professional staff. The rooms are light and airy and extremely clean. An ideal, inexpensive place for a short stop. 🛏 P 🗹

AL-HOCEIMA: *Hôtel Mohammed V* (Dh)(Dh) — 26
Place de la Marche Verte. (039) 98 22 33/34. FAX (039) 98 33 14.
@ naim2@iam.net.ma
A classic hotel with comfortable, clean rooms offering a superb view of the sea and surrounding cliffs. 🛏 24 ▤ P ★ 🗹

AL-HOCEIMA: *Hôtel Quemado* (Dh)(Dh) — 102
On Quemado Beach. (039) 98 33 15. FAX (039) 98 33 14.
This hotel, one of the most recently built in the town, is located right on the beach. The rooms are comfortable, and beach bungalows can be rented. 🛏 24 TV ▤ P ★ 🗹

CABO NEGRO: *Le Petit Mérou* (Dh) — 23
On the beach. (039) 97 81 15. FAX (039) 97 80 65.
This small hotel, set right on the beach, is an ideal base from which to explore the Mediterranean coast. The plainly furnished rooms are clean and airy. Friendly atmosphere. 🛏 ▤ P 🗹

CAP SPARTEL: *Le Mirage* (Dh)(Dh)(Dh) — 30
(039) 33 33 32. FAX (039) 33 33 92. W www.lemirage-tanger.com
About 15 km (9 miles) from Tangier, 22 luxury bungalows with a breathtaking view of the extensive beach at Cap Spartel, where the Atlantic Ocean and Mediterranean Sea meet. Excellent service. 🛏 24 TV P ★ 🗹

CHEFCHAOUEN: *Hôtel Asma* (Dh) — 94
2 km (1.2 miles) from the centre. (039) 98 60 02. FAX (039) 98 71 78.
A hotel with average comforts, its main advantages being the view of Chefchaouen and its quiet location, on a rocky outcrop overlooking the town. 🛏 P ★ 🗹

For key to symbols see back flap

	Price categories / Restaurant info	NUMBER OF ROOMS	RESTAURANT	ROOMS WITH A VIEW	GARDEN OR TERRACE	SWIMMING POOL

Price categories are per night for two people occupying a standard double room in the high season, with service and tax included:

(Dh) under 500 dirhams
(Dh)(Dh) 500–1,000 dirhams
(Dh)(Dh)(Dh) 1,000–2,000 dirhams
(Dh)(Dh)(Dh)(Dh) over2,000 dirhams

RESTAURANT
This is not necessarily recommended. Very good hotel restaurants are listed in Where to Eat (pp322–34).

ROOMS WITH A VIEW
The hotel has an excellent location and some rooms have a fine view.

GARDEN OR TERRACE
The hotel has a garden, interior courtyard or terrace, and meals may be served outdoors.

SWIMMING POOL
Outdoor swimming pool unless otherwise indicated.

Hotel	Dh	Rooms	Rest.	View	Garden	Pool
CHEFCHAOUEN: *Hôtel Parador* Place El Mahzien. (039) 98 63 24/98 61 36. FAX (039) 98 70 33. At the entrance to the medina, this characterful hotel has simple but comfortable rooms. The swimming pool offers a view of the mountains. 📶 TV P ★ 🖃	(Dh)	35	●	■	●	■
CHEFCHAOUEN: *Casa Hassan* 22 Rue Targui. (039) 98 61 53. FAX (039) 98 81 96. In the heart of the medina, this hotel feels more like a guesthouse. Superb Moroccan architecture and a very warm reception. 📶 ★	(Dh)(Dh)	7	●	■	●	
OUJDA: *El-Manar* 50 Boulevard Zerktouni. (056) 68 83 15. FAX (056) 68 16 70. The best hotel in Oujda. The relatively large rooms are light, airy and comfortable. High-quality, unobtrusive service. 📶 24 TV P 🖃	(Dh)	44			●	
OUJDA: *Ibis Moussafir* Place de la Gare. (056) 68 82 01. FAX (056) 68 82 08. W www.ibishotel.com This hotel offers comfortable, well-equipped rooms. The swimming pool can be very crowded. 📶 TV 🟰 P 🖃	(Dh)(Dh)(Dh)	73	●		●	■
TETOUAN: *Hôtel Oumaima* Avenue du 10 Mai. (039) 96 34 73. This recently built, functional hotel is somewhat lacking in character but it is very suitable for a short, inexpensive stay in Tetouan. 📶 P 🖃	(Dh)	33			●	
TETOUAN: *Hôtel Chams* Avenue Abdeljalak-Torres. (039) 99 09 01. FAX (039) 99 09 07. Since it was renovated, this has become the best hotel in Tetouan. Comfortable, well-equipped rooms and a very pleasant swimming pool. 📶 🟰 ★ 🖃	(Dh)(Dh)	78	●	■	●	■
TETOUAN: *Hôtel Safir* Avenue Kennedy. (039) 97 01 44. FAX (039) 97 06 92. Although it is slightly old-fashioned and not very central, this is still one of the best hotels in Tetouan. The rooms are clean and comfortable, and the hotel's parkland setting makes for a peaceful atmosphere. 📶 TV P 🖃	(Dh)(Dh)	100	●		●	■
FÈS						
MEDINA: *Hôtel Batha* Place de l'Istiqlal Batha. (055) 74 10 77. FAX (055) 74 10 78. A very pleasant small hotel with an attractive courtyard. Despite its central location at the entrance to the medina, it is surprisingly quiet. There is a small swimming pool on the first floor. 📶 24 TV 🟰 ★ 🖃	(Dh)	62	●	■	●	■
MEDINA: *Dar el-Ghalia* 15 Ross-Rhi. (055) 63 41 67. FAX (055) 63 63 93. W www.maisondhotes.co.ma This 17th-century royal palace converted into a guesthouse is run by a couple who have lavished much attention on it. Staying here is like stepping back several centuries into the past. 📶 P ★ 🖃	(Dh)(Dh)(Dh)	13	●		●	
MEDINA: *La Maison Bleue* 2 Place de l'Istiqlal-Batha (055) 74 06 86/63 60 52. FAX (055) 74 18 43. W www.maisonbleue.com This sumptuous, typically Fassi residence is primarily a restaurant with rooms that can sometimes be rented. Atmospheric and redolent of old Fès. 📶 ★ 🖃	(Dh)(Dh)(Dh)(Dh)	5	●	■	●	

MEDINA: *Le Méridien Mérinides*   (Dh)(Dh)(Dh)(Dh)   **106**
Bordj Nord. **C** *(055) 64 52 26/64 62 18/64 60 99.*
FAX *(055) 75 16 59.* **@** *merinides-hotelfes@iam.net.ma*
Overlooking the medina, the hotel commands a splendid view of the old
city. Recently built, it offers standards of comfort and service in line with
the Méridien chain. Discreet, attentive service. 🛏 24 📺 🍽 P ★ 🏊

MEDINA: *Sofitel Palais Jamaï*   (Dh)(Dh)(Dh)(Dh)   **143**
Bab el-Guissa. **C** *(055) 63 43 31.* **C** *(055) 63 50 96.* **W** *www.sofitel.com*
This hotel, a former 19th-century palace, overlooking the medina of Fès,
is one of the most beautiful in Morocco. 🛏 24 📺 🍽 P ★ 🏊

VILLE NOUVELLE: *Hôtel Wassim*   (Dh)(Dh)   **104**
9 Rue du Liban. **C** *(055) 65 49 39.* **FAX** *(055) 93 02 20.*
Despite a fairly austere exterior, this modern hotel offers an excellent
standard of comfort. Panoramic rooftop terrace. 🛏 24 📺 🍽 P ★ 🏊

VILLE NOUVELLE: *Ryad Sheberazade*   (Dh)(Dh)(Dh)   **13**
23 Arssat Bennis Douh, Medina **C** *(055) 74 16 42.* **FAX** *(055) 74 16 45.*
W *www.sheheraz.com*
In a lovingly restored, late 19th Century building you will find yourself in a
real *One Thousand and One Nights* setting. Refinement, luxury and comfort
are all guaranteed in this hotel where all the rooms differ. 🛏 📺 🍽 P ★ 🏊

VILLE NOUVELLE: *Hôtel Jnan Palace*   (Dh)(Dh)(Dh)(Dh)   **243**
Avenue Ahmed Chaouki. **C** *(055) 65 22 30/65 39 65.*
FAX *(055) 62 35 10.* **W** *www.moroccoweb.com/fes/jnan-palace*
This is an oasis of calm, set in an extensive park. Very comfortable,
with faultless service. Excellent swimming pool. 🛏 24 📺 🍽 P ★ 🏊

MEKNÈS & VOLUBILIS

MEKNÈS: *Hôtel Rif*   (Dh)(Dh)   **120**
Rue d'Accra. **C** *(055) 52 25 91–94.* **FAX** *(055) 52 44 28.*
A hotel with a good location in the heart of the town. It is well equipped,
which compensates for its rather old-fashioned character. Friendly reception.
Some of the rooms are not very quiet. 🛏 24 📺 🍽 P 🏊

MEKNÈS: *Hôtel Transatlantique*   (Dh)(Dh)   **120**
Rue el-Mriniyne. **C** *(055) 52 50 50 –55.* **FAX** *(055) 52 00 57.* **@** *Transat@iam.net.ma*
Although it is in need of a little refurbishment, this is easily the best
hotel in Meknès, with a lovely garden. There are two types of rooms: in
Moroccan style and with a more modern décor. 🛏 24 📺 🍽 P 🏊

MEKNÈS: *Hôtel Zaki*   (Dh)(Dh)   **155**
Boulevard al-Massira. **C** *(055) 51 41 47.* **FAX** *(055) 52 48 36.*
W *www.zakihotel.ifrance.com/zakihotel*
Located in the southeast of the town, this large hotel complex overlooks
the Wadi Boufekrane valley. With quite a high standard of comfort, it is
one of the most recently built establishments in Meknès. 🛏 24 📺 🍽 P 🏊

VOLUBILIS: *Hôtel Volubilis*   (Dh)(Dh)   **54**
In Fertessa, the village opposite the ruins. **C** *(055) 54 43 69 /54 44 06 to 08.*
FAX *(055) 54 43 69.*
Overlooking the valley and the ruins of Volubilis, this charming hotel
provides a welcome respite from the bustle of nearby Fès and Meknès.
Excellent terrace swimming pool, overlooking the ruins. 🛏 24 📺 🍽 ★ 🏊

MIDDLE ATLAS

AFOURER: *Hôtel Le Tazarkount*   (Dh)(Dh)   **135**
Province d'Azilal. **C** *(023) 44 01 01.* **FAX** *(023) 44 00 84.* **W** *www.tazarkount.com*
20 km (12 miles) from Beni Mellal, this hotel makes for a good pit-stop
between Marrakech and Fez. Gardens and two pools, one heated. 🛏 📺 P 🏊

AZROU: *Hôtel du Panorama*   (Dh)   **38**
Near main post office. **C** *(055) 56 20 10.* **FAX** *(055) 56 18 04.*
On the site of an ancient inn, this hotel has the appeal of a quiet and
comfortable alpine chalet. Friendly, welcoming staff. 🛏 📺 P 🏊

BENI MELLAL: *Hôtel Ouzoud*   (Dh)(Dh)   **58**
On the road to Marrakech. **C** *(023) 48 37 52.* **FAX** *(023) 48 85 30.*
A slightly old-fashioned though pleasant establishment, with a very attractive
restaurant. Lovely garden with swimming pool. 🛏 24 📺 🍽 P 🏊

For key to symbols see back flap

<table>
<tr><td colspan="2">

Price categories are per night for two people occupying a standard double room in the high season, with service and tax included:

Dh under 500 dirhams
Dh Dh 500–1,000 dirhams
Dh Dh Dh 1,000–2,000 dirhams
Dh Dh Dh Dh over 2,000 dirhams

</td><td colspan="2">

RESTAURANT
This is not necessarily recommended. Very good hotel restaurants are listed in Where to Eat (pp322–34).

ROOMS WITH A VIEW
The hotel has an excellent location and some rooms have a fine view.

GARDEN OR TERRACE
The hotel has a garden, interior courtyard or terrace, and meals may be served outdoors.

SWIMMING POOL
Outdoor swimming pool unless otherwise indicated.

</td></tr>
</table>

	NUMBER OF ROOMS	RESTAURANT	ROOMS WITH A VIEW	GARDEN OR TERRACE	SWIMMING POOL
IFRANE: *Hôtel des Perce-Neige* — Dh Dh Rue des Asphodèles. (055) 56 63 50/56 62 10. FAX (055) 56 71 16. A small congenial hotel, the best place to stay in Ifrane. The excellent restaurant is well known in the area.	27	●		●	■
IFRANE: *Hôtel Mischliffen* — Dh Dh (055) 56 66 08. FAX (055) 56 66 23. The largest hotel in Ifrane, well equipped and with an excellent view of the town. Very comfortable but a little below its five-star rating.	80	●	■	●	■
KHENIFRA: *Moha Hammou Zayani* — Dh Cité Amal, BP 94. (055) 58 60 20. FAX (055) 58 65 32. The main advantage of this rather decrepit hotel is its open location.	60	●	●		
MIDELT: *Hotel Kasbah Asmaa* — Dh Km 3, on road from Errachidia. (055) 58 04 08. FAX (055) 58 39 45. Situated on the long road between Fèz and the great South, this essential stop-off point has typical local architecture and décor. Large rooms and friendly welcome.	34	●	●	●	
OUZOUD: *Hôtel Les Cascades* — Dh Dh (023) 45 96 58. FAX (023) 45 88 60. @ riad@ouzoud.com This small, recently renovated hotel has a lot of character and is an excellent base for various excursions. The French hoteliers are welcoming.	6	●	●		
MARRAKECH					
CITY CENTRE: *Hôtel La Mamounia* — Dh Dh Dh Dh Avenue Bab el-Jedid. (044) 38 86 00. FAX (044) 44 44 09. W www.mamounia.com One of Morocco's most legendary hotels, set in a huge park in the heart of Marrakech. Recently renovated. Several excellent restaurants. Exceptional service.	236	●	●	●	■
HIVERNAGE: *Hôtel Es-Saadi* — Dh Dh Dh Dh Avenue el-Quadissia. (044) 44 88 11. FAX (044) 44 76 44. W www.essadi.com This slightly antiquated, though very characterful, luxury hotel is located in the heart of Hivernage, the residential quarter, a few minutes from the medina. It is set in a large park and has a casino.	147	■	●	●	■
HIVERNAGE: *Le Sofitel* — Dh Dh Dh Dh Rue Harroun Errachid. (044) 42 56 00. FAX (044) 42 56 50. A few hundred metres from the medina, this luxury hotel richly deserves its five-star status. The sense of comfort is excellent in this haven of peace and greenery and the service is fautless.	270	●	■	●	■
MEDINA: *Hôtel Gallia* — Dh 30 Rue de la Recette. (044) 44 59 13. FAX (044) 44 48 53. Located in a lovely building right at the foot of the Koutoubia. Excellent value for money.	19	●	■	●	
MEDINA: *Les Almoravides* — Dh Dh Arset Djebel Lakhdar, Koutoubia. (044) 38 69 42. FAX (044) 38 69 33. Rather old-fashioned, but homely and welcoming. The excellent location, very near the Koutoubia, is its main advantage.	106			●	
MEDINA: *Les Jardins de la Medina* — Dh Dh 21 Rue Derb Chtouka. (044) 38 18 51. FAX (044) 38 53 85. W www.lesjardinsdelamedina.com This hotel is situated in the Kasbah and is hidden behind high walls and vegetation. The gardens make for a peaceful setting and the hotel's traditional architecture and modern comfort combine to make it an exceptional place to stay.	36	●		●	■

MEDINA: *Dar Les Cigognes* ⓓⓗ ⓓⓗ ⓓⓗ — 9
108 Rue de Berima. 〖 *(044) 38 27 40.* FAX *(044) 38 47 67.* Ⓦ www.lescigognes.com
Housed in a traditional *riad*, this boutique hotel boasts individually
decorated rooms and excellent service. 🖥 24 🅿 ★ 🗎

MEDINA: *Riad Kaiss* ⓓⓗ ⓓⓗ ⓓⓗ — 8
65 Derb Jdid, Riad Zitoune Kedim. 〖 & FAX *(044) 44 01 41.* Ⓦ www.riadkaiss.com
This historic *riad* is beautifully decorated with *zellijs* and lit at night by lanterns
and candles. The rooms are tastefully adorned with textiles and traditional
furniture. Meals, made on request, are taken in either of the two leafy courtyards
or on the roof terrace with views of the medina and the Atlas. 🖥 ★ 🗎

MEDINA: *La Maison Arabe* ⓓⓗ ⓓⓗ ⓓⓗ ⓓⓗ — 13
1 Derb Assehbe. 〖 *(044) 38 70 10.* FAX *(044) 38 72 21.* Ⓦ www.lamaisonarabe.com
Once a renowned restaurant, this establishment was renovated and
converted into a hotel in 1997. Refined furnishings and decoration.
Unobtrusive, elegant service and intimate atmosphere. 🖥 TV 🗎 🅿 🗎

LA PALMERAIE: *Dar Ayniwen* ⓓⓗ ⓓⓗ ⓓⓗ ⓓⓗ — 14
Tafrata, in La Palmeraie. 〖 *(044) 32 96 84.* FAX *(044) 32 96 86.* Ⓦ www.ayniwen.com
A luxuriously appointed guesthouse in parkland in La Palmeraie. It has lovely
rooms and very comfortable communal areas. Impeccable service and top-
quality restaurant. 🖥 24 TV 🗎 🅿 ★ 🗎

LA PALMERAIE: *Hôtel Les Deux Tours* ⓓⓗ ⓓⓗ ⓓⓗ ⓓⓗ — 24
Douar Abiad. 〖 *(044) 32 95 27.* FAX *(044) 32 95 23.* Ⓦ www.deux-tours.com
A characterful hotel complex in the heart of La Palmeraie, consisting of
six villas with a total of 18 rooms. The maze-like layout evokes a past age.
Heated swimming pool and hammam. 🖥 24 🗎 🅿 ★ 🗎

LA PALMERAIE: *Jnane Tamsna* ⓓⓗ ⓓⓗ ⓓⓗ ⓓⓗ — 17
Douar Abiad. 〖 *(044) 38 52 72.* FAX *(044) 38 52 71.* Ⓦ www.tamsna.com
This Moorish-style guest house offers luxurious accommodation in the heart of
the Palmeraie. Facilities include tennis courts. 🖥 24 TV 🗎 🅿 ★ 🗎

LA PALMERAIE: *Palmeraie Golf Palace* ⓓⓗ ⓓⓗ ⓓⓗ ⓓⓗ — 314
In La Palmeraie, BP 1488. 〖 *(044) 30 10 10.* FAX *(044) 30 50 50.* Ⓦ www.pgpmarrakech.com
This huge complex features an 18-hole golf course, nine swimming pools
(two of them heated), an equestrian centre and facilities for children. The
rooms are very large and the staff friendly. 🖥 24 TV 🗎 🅿 ★ 🗎

VILLE NOUVELLE: *Ibis Moussafir* ⓓⓗ — 103
Avenue Hassan II. 〖 *(044) 43 59 29 to 33.* FAX *(044) 43 59 36.* @ 2034@accor-hotels.com
A modern, very clean hotel just 50 m (55 yds) from Marrakech railway
station. Good value for money. The rooms overlooking the noisy avenue
are best avoided. Friendly reception. 🖥 24 TV 🗎 🅿

VILLE NOUVELLE: *Oudayas* ⓓⓗ ⓓⓗ — 92
147 Rue Mohammed el-Bequal. 〖 *(044) 44 71 09.* FAX *(044) 43 54 00.* Ⓦ www.oudaya.ma
A small, comfortable hotel ideal for a short stay in Marrakech. Small
swimming pool. 🖥 24 TV 🗎 ★ 🗎

VILLE NOUVELLE: *Hôtel Melia Tichka Salam* ⓓⓗ ⓓⓗ ⓓⓗ — 138
Semlalia, BP 894. 〖 *(044) 44 87 10.* FAX *(044) 44 86 91.* Ⓦ www.groupesalam.com
A well-designed modern hotel with tasteful décor. The hotel boasts two good
restaurants, French and Moroccan and a lovely pool. 🖥 24 TV 🗎 🅿 ★ 🗎

VILLE NOUVELLE: *Villa Hélène* ⓓⓗ ⓓⓗ ⓓⓗ — 3
89 Boulevard Moulay Rachid. 〖 & FAX *(044) 43 16 81.* Ⓦ www.villahelene.com
In the heart of the colonial quarter of Marrakech, the hotel occupies a superb
1930s building. Bruno, the friendly hotel manager, and the culinary skills of
Fatima, the chef, are guaranteed to make this a pleasurable stay. 🖥 🅿 ★

VILLE NOUVELLE: *Le Méridien N'Fis* ⓓⓗ ⓓⓗ ⓓⓗ ⓓⓗ — 277
Avenue de France. 〖 *(044) 33 94 00.* FAX *(044) 44 74 46.* Ⓦ www.lemeridienhotels.com
Recently renovated, this five-star hotel has a large swimming pool
with a view of the Atlas. Attentive service. 🖥 24 TV 🗎 🅿 ★ 🗎

VILLE NOUVELLE: *Villa des Orangers* ⓓⓗ ⓓⓗ ⓓⓗ ⓓⓗ — 16
6 Rue Sidi Mimoun. 〖 *(044) 38 46 38.* FAX *(044) 38 51 23.* Ⓦ www.villadesorangers.com
One of the few *riads* to be run by a professional hotelier, this is a luxurious,
sophisticated establishment. Car pick-up from the airport, outdoor bar (soft
drinks only) and small rooftop swimming pool with a spectacular view.
🖥 24 TV 🗎 🅿 ★ 🗎

For key to symbols see back flap

Price categories are per night for two people occupying a standard double room in the high season, withservice and tax included:

Dh under 500 dirhams

Dh Dh 500–1,000 dirhams

Dh Dh Dh 1,000–2,000 dirhams

Dh Dh Dh Dh over 2,000 dirhams

RESTAURANT
This is not necessarily recommended. Very good hotel restaurants are listed in Where to Eat *(pp322–34)*.

ROOMS WITH A VIEW
The hotel has an excellent location and some rooms havea fine view.

GARDEN OR TERRACE
The hotel has a garden, interior courtyard or terrace, and meals may be served outdoors.

SWIMMING POOL
Outdoor swimming pool unless otherwise indicated.

	NUMBER OF ROOMS	RESTAURANT	ROOMS WITH A VIEW	GARDEN OR TERRACE	SWIMMING POOL
ENVIRONS OF MARRAKECH: *Caravan Sérail* Dh Dh Dh Dh Ouled ben-Rahmoune, 10 km (6 miles) from Marrakech on the road to Casablanca. 📞 *(044) 30 03 02.* 📠 *(044) 33 14 80.* @ caravanserai@iam.net.ma A recently opened hotel in a traditional pisé village 15 minutes by car from the centre of Marrakech. Splendid views of Wadi Tensift, the palm grove and the Atlas. 🛏 24 📋 **P** ★ 🍴	17	●		●	▪

HIGH ATLAS

	NUMBER OF ROOMS	RESTAURANT	ROOMS WITH A VIEW	GARDEN OR TERRACE	SWIMMING POOL
AÏT BENHADDOU: *Auberge Étoile Filante* Dh In the village of Aït Benhaddou. 📞 *(044) 89 03 22.* 📠 *(044) 88 61 13.* Newly built, though in keeping with the local architectural style, this small establishment has nine beautiful rooms. Several terraces offer a fine view of the *ksar*. 🛏 **P** ★	26	●		●	
AÏT BENHADDOU: *Hôtel de la Kasba* Dh In the village of Aït Benhaddou. 📞 *(044) 89 03 02.* 📠 *(044) 89 03 08.* Located near the old part of the village, this is a café that gradually became a hotel. The rooms are comfortable and the price includes half-board. 🛏 **P** ★	82	●	▪	●	▪
IMLIL: *Atlas Gîte* Dh 📞 *(044) 48 56 09.* 📠 *(022) 48 56 09.* This small gîte offers basic comforts and a warm reception. Wonderful food made with fresh local produce. Ideal as an overnight stopping-place for hikers.	4	●	●		
OUIRGANE: *La Bergerie* Dh Dh BP64, 2150 Asni. 📞 *(044) 48 57 18.* 🌐 www.passionmaroc.com On the road to Marrakech, a few metres before the entrance to Ouirgane, a trail leads to this beautiful little inn, lovingly maintained by its owner. The idyllic setting guarantees a great start-off point for walks. 🛏 **P** ★	12	●	▪	●	
OUIRGANE: *La Roseraie* Dh Dh Dh Ouirgane valley, BP 769 Marrakech. 📞 *(044) 43 91 30.* A characterful establishment with 40 well-equipped bungalows set in luxuriant vegetation. Three swimming pools, one of which is indoors. 🛏 24 **P** ★ 🍴 🍽	45	●	▪	●	▪
OUKAÏMEDEN: *Kenzi Louka* Dh Dh 📞 *(044) 31 90 80.* 📠 *(044) 43 23 71.* A large, modern hotel. Indoor heated swimming pool, with glass walls affording a view of the mountains. Comfortable rooms and fine communal areas for après-ski relaxation. 🛏 24 📺 📋 **P** ★ 🍴	101	●	▪	●	▪
OURIKA VALLEY: *Auberge de Ramuntcho* Dh BP 13, Ourika. 📞 *(044) 48 45 21.* 📠 *(044) 48 45 22.* 🌐 www.ramuntcho.ma In the heart of the Ourika valley, an ideal base for tours starting from Marrakech. Excellent food served in a very pleasant restaurant. 🛏 **P** ★ 🍴	14	●	▪	●	
OURIKA VALLEY: *Dar Piano* Dh 5 Km (3 miles) from Aghbalou village. 📞 *(044) 48 48 42.* A tiny, welcoming guesthouse offering a good place to stop before heading off to explore the mountainous surroundings. In summer, dine on the terrace with fine views or around the live fire in winter. 🛏 **P**	4	●	▪	●	
OURIKA VALLEY: *Auberge Le Maquis* Dh Dh 📞 *(044) 48 45 31.* 📠 *(044) 48 45 61.* 🌐 www.le-maquis.com A small *auberge* (inn) with a lot of character. Comforts are basic but the welcome very friendly. The location offers a wide range of possibilities for walks and drives in the vicinity. Four-wheel-drive vehicles can be hired on the premises. The hotel also has a dormitory for six people. 🛏 **P** 🍴 👤	6	●	▪	●	

OUARZAZATE & THE SOUTHERN OASES

OUARZAZATE: *Hanane Club* (Dh) (Dh) 120
Avenue Erraha. (044) 88 25 55. FAX (044) 88 57 37.
This well-designed hotel with efficient staff is a good place to stay in
Ouarzazate, and costs less than others in its class. The rooms are large and
there is a lovely swimming pool.

OUARZAZATE: *Karam Palace* (Dh) (Dh) 147
Avenue Moulay Rachid. (044) 88 22 25/88 25 22. FAX (044) 88 26 42.
@ solkaranona@solmelia.com
A high-standard, value for money tourist hotel. Welcoming with comfortable
rooms, good swimming pool and well-kept gardens.

OUARZAZATE: *Hôtel Kenzi Azghor* (Dh) (Dh) 113
Avenue Moulay Rachid. (044) 88 65 01–5. FAX (044) 88 63 53.
One of the most pleasant hotels in the town, not least because of the
swimming pool with a stunning view of the surroundings. It belongs
to a major tour operator, which brings the hotel most of its custom.

OUARZAZATE: *Hôtel Kenzi Bélère* (Dh) (Dh) 250
Avenue Moulay Rachid. (044) 88 28 03/88 29 37/88 30 04.
FAX (044) 88 31 45.
A very comfortable hotel, well designed in the Moroccan style. The
huge swimming pool and the quality of the food make this an ideal
place for relaxation.

OUARZAZATE: *Le Méridien Berbère Palace* (Dh) (Dh) (Dh) 240
El-Mansour Eddahbi Quarter. (044) 88 31 05/88 21 39/88 29 67.
FAX (044) 88 30 71/ 88 20 20. W www.ouarzazate.com/leberberepalace
The most luxurious hotel in Ouarzazate, and the most comfortable in
the entire South. Its design is influenced by local kasbahs, giving it a
very congenial atmosphere.

OUARZAZATE: *Hôtel Riad Salam* (Dh) (Dh) 160
Avenue Mohammed V. (044) 88 33 35. FAX (044) 88 27 66.
A little nearer the centre of the town than most of the other large hotels.
While its main appeal is its strong family atmosphere, the services are well
up to the standard of a hotel in this bracket. Highly recommended.

BOUMALNE DU DADÈS: *Hôtel Chems* (Dh) 30
On the road to Er-Rachidia. (044) 83 00 41. FAX (044) 83 13 08.
A small and straightforward, though not spartan, establishment with a lot of
character. Most of the rooms have a beautiful view. Good restaurant.
Prices include half-board.

BOUMALNE DU DADÈS: *Kasba Tizzarouine* (Dh) (Dh) 50
On the road to Er-Rachidia. (044) 83 06 90. FAX (044) 83 02 56.
@ tizzarouine@atlanet.net.ma
Located a short distance outside the town, this hotel offers different types
of accommodation. The 13 rooms cut into the rockface are wonderfully
cool in summer. Very friendly and attentive staff.

ERFOUD: *Kasba Hotel Xaluca Maadid* (Dh) 48
Route d'Er-Rachida. (055) 57 84 50. FAX (055) 57 84 49.
This hotel, constructed using traditional methods, is a veritable palace
in the desert. Elegantly decorated rooms and extensive grounds surrounding
a central swimming pool. Good value for money.

ERFOUD: *Kasba Tizimi* (Dh) (Dh) 70
On the road to Tineghir. (055) 57 61 79 /57 73 74. FAX (055) 57 73 75.
@ ktizimi@iam.net.ma
A simple yet unusual establishment of modest size. Well designed and
decorated. Pleasant swimming pool.

ERFOUD: *Hôtel Salam* (Dh) (Dh) 156
On the road to Rissani. (055) 57 66 65/57 64 25. FAX (055) 57 64 26.
@ salamers@iam.net.ma
Used mostly by groups, this hotel offers a good standard of comfort
and all the usual services. The evening meal is served as a buffet. A
good starting point for exploring the region, particularly Rissani.

For key to symbols see back flap

<table>
<tr><td colspan="2">

Price categories are per night for two people occupying a standard double room in the high season, with service and tax included:

(Dh) under 500 dirhams
(Dh)(Dh) 500–1,000 dirhams
(Dh)(Dh)(Dh) 1,000–2,000 dirhams
(Dh)(Dh)(Dh)(Dh) over 2,000 dirhams

</td></tr>
</table>

RESTAURANT
This is not necessarily recommended. Very good hotel restaurants are listed in Where to Eat (pp322–34).

ROOMS WITH A VIEW
The hotel has an excellent location and some rooms have a fine view.

GARDEN OR TERRACE
The hotel has a garden, interior courtyard or terrace, and meals may be served outdoors.

SWIMMING POOL
Outdoor swimming pool unless otherwise indicated.

	NUMBER OF ROOMS	RESTAURANT	ROOMS WITH A VIEW	GARDEN OR TERRACE	SWIMMING POOL
ER-RACHIDIA: *Hôtel Kenzi Rissani* (Dh)(Dh) Avenue Moulay Ali Cherif. (055) 57 25 84/57 21 86. FAX (055) 57 25 85. www.kenzihotel.com A very well maintained establishment set in a garden with swimming pool. By far the best hotel in Er-Rachidia.	62	●	●	●	●
MERZOUGA: *Kasba Darkaoua* (Dh)(Dh) Km 23, on the track to Merzouga. & FAX (055) 57 71 40. This small kasbah in the middle of the desert is run by French people who have a thorough knowledge of the area. Full of character and a haven of peace. Newly built swimming pool. Compulsory half-board, with some mouthwatering specialities.	10	●	●	●	●
SKOURA: *Hôtel Ben Moro* (Dh) & FAX (044) 85 21 16. @ hotelbenmoro@yahoo.fr A hotel in a recently restored, evocative 17th-century kasbah. Breathtaking view from the terrace, over the valley and the kasbahs in the vicinity. A wonderful place to stop off the main tourist trail.	13	●	●	●	
TINERHIR: *Hôtel Kenzi Bougafer* (Dh)(Dh) Boulevard Mohammed V. (044) 83 32 00/83 32 80. FAX (044) 83 32 82. A surprisingly large hotel for a small town like Tinerhir. Comfortable rooms and a very friendly reception.	108	●	●	●	●
TINERHIR: *Hôtel Tombouctou* (Dh)(Dh) Avenue Bir Anzarane. (044) 83 46 04. FAX (044) 83 35 05. @ tombctu@iam.net.ma Run by a Spaniard with detailed knowledge of the area, this well-restored kasbah is an attractive establishment.	20	●	●	●	●
ZAGORA: *Hôtel Kasba Asmaa* (Dh)(Dh) 1.5 km (1 mile) from the town centre, beyond the bridge over Wadi Draa. (044) 84 72 41/ 84 75 99. FAX (044) 84 75 27. A reasonably priced hotel in a well-designed pisé building. Great dining by the pool or in Berber tents and friendly, professional staff. The hotel organizes tours in four-wheel-drive vehicles.	33	●		●	●
ZAGORA: *La Fibule du Draa* (Dh)(Dh) 1.5 km (1 mile) from the town centre, beyond the bridge over Wadi Draa. (044) 84 73 18. FAX (044) 84 72 71. @ fibule@atlasnet.net.ma A relatively old hotel with a lot of character. Relatively small, it has a lovely flower-filled courtyard, a swimming pool and plainly furnished rooms. The pleasant bar, in the garden, serves alcoholic drinks. Tours in four-wheel-drive vehicles are organized from the hotel.	24	●	●	●	●
ZAGORA: *Hôtel Riad Salam* (Dh)(Dh) On the road to M'Hamid. (044) 84 74 00. FAX (044) 84 75 51. One of Zagora's two top hotels (see also *Hôtel Reda, below*). It has 113 comfortable, well-equipped rooms, a swimming pool, garden and two restaurants. A pleasant place to stay.	120	●	●	●	●
ZAGORA: *Hôtel Ksar Tinzouline* (Dh)(Dh) Avenue Hassan II. (044) 84 72 52. FAX (044) 84 70 42. @ tinsouli@iam.net.ma Very clean, comfortable and unpretentious. The tastefully decorated rooms are fully equipped with all modern conveniences.	96	●	●	●	●
ZAGORA: *Hôtel Reda* (Dh)(Dh) On the road to M'hamid, BP 88. (044) 84 70 79. FAX (044) 84 70 12. One of the two best hotels in Zagora, built in the local style. Comfortable rooms and a lovely swimming pool.	144			●	●

SOUTHERN MOROCCO & WESTERN SAHARA

GUELMIM: *Hôtel Babich*	(Dh)	30	●	■	●	
31 Avenue Abaynou. (048) 77 21 78. A recently opened hotel, with basic comforts and remarkable standards of cleanliness. Pleasant staff.						
GUELMIM: *Hôtel Salam*	(Dh)	30			●	
On the road to Tan Tan. *no telephone*. This hotel, one of the most comfortable in Guelmim, is often used by United Nations delegates concerned with the western Sahara. Advance booking advisable.						
SIDI IFNI: *Hôtel Bellevue*	(Dh)	40	●	■	●	■
Place Hassan II. (048) 87 50 72. FAX (048) 78 04 99. This relatively old hotel is clean and well-maintained. Cliff-top settng with a fine view of the sea. The restaurant specializes in fish.						
TAFRAOUTE: *Hôtel des Amandiers*	(Dh)(Dh)	60	●	■	●	■
On the top of the hill in the town. (048) 80 00 08/80 00 88 FAX (048) 80 03 43. This hotel, an imposing hill-top building, has simply furnished but large and comfortable rooms. It also has the only swimming pool in Tafraoute, and a fine view of the surrounding countryside.						
TALIOUINE: *Hôtel Ibn Toumert*	(Dh)(Dh)	100	●	■	●	■
Next to the Glaoui kasbah. (048) 53 43 33. FAX (048) 80 03 43. A classic hotel with pleasant, simply furnished rooms, some of which look onto the kasbah. Somewhat impersonal since the establishment's trade consists mainly of groups.						
TAN TAN: *Hôtel Les Sables d'Or*	(Dh)	32			●	
Boulevard Hassan II. (048) 87 80 69. FAX (048) 87 80 69. The only hotel in Tan Tan with a reasonable standard. Being newly built, it is clean and quite comfortable.						
TAROUDANNT: *Hôtel Tiout*	(Dh)	38	●			
Avenue du Prince Héritier Sidi Mohammed. (048) 85 03 41/85 44 78. FAX (048) 85 44 80. A relatively basic hotel, though for those on a limited budget it is ideal for a short stay in Taroudannt.						
TAROUDANNT: *Palais Salam*	(Dh)(Dh)	142	●	■	●	■
Along the ramparts. (048) 85 25 01/85 21 30/85 23 12. FAX (048) 85 26 54. W www.groupesalam.com One of the most pleasant hotels in Morocco. The best rooms are those in the two new wings, built as a pair of mazes. There is a garden within the town walls and a lovely swimming pool in a fine setting.						
TAROUDANNT: *La Gazelle d'Or*	(Dh)(Dh)(Dh)(Dh)	30	●	■	●	■
1 km (0.5 mile) from the town centre, on the road to Agadir. (048) 85 20 39/85 20 48. FAX (048) 85 27 37. @ gazelle@marocnet.net.ma This legendary hotel, used by the rich and famous, also has two comfortably appointed and well-equipped bungalows. Sophisticated, unobtrusive service. Expensive and very luxurious.						
TATA: *Le Relais des Sables*	(Dh)	56	●	■	●	■
1 km (0.5 mile) from the town centre, on the road to Akka. (048) 80 23 01/02. FAX (048) 80 23 00. For a short stay, a hotel slightly above the average in a town that is not well endowed with good hotels. The 18 largest rooms have air-conditioning, for which a supplement is charged.						
TIZNIT: *Hôtel Tiznit*	(Dh)	38	●	■	●	■
Rue Bir Inzaran. (048) 86 24 11/86 38 86. FAX (048) 86 21 19. A classic hotel, clean and well maintained though a little antiquated. Adequate for a short stop in Tiznit.						
TIZNIT: *Hôtel Kerdous*	(Dh)(Dh)	35	●	■	●	■
Kerdous Pass, at Km 54 between Tiznit and Tafraoute. (048) 86 20 63. FAX (048) 60 03 15. A spectacularly isolated hotel in the style of a kasbah set on a rocky outcrop. Breathtaking view of the valley, pleasant swimming pool and two restaurants.						

WHERE TO EAT

IN MOROCCO, cooking is an integral part of the art of living. Since this is also a country with a large number of restaurants, the choice of what and where to eat is boundless. Prices vary widely from one place to the next and from one town to the next, and tipping is still a well-entrenched custom. Although restaurant opening hours are similar to those of Western Europe, they may change during

Oysters, a speciality of Oualidia *(see p115)*

Ramadan. Religious strictures also mean that establishments serving alcohol are relatively rare and tightly regulated.

Restaurants span the full range, from the smartest, with international cuisine, to the more modest, which offer delicious Moroccan dishes. Finally, there are the little stalls that are found on every street corner or on the quay in harbours, which serve freshly cooked fish and other succulent treats.

Le Chalet de la Plage, a beach restaurant at Essaouira *(see p325)*

TYPES OF RESTAURANT

IN LARGE TOWNS and cities in Morocco you will find every kind of restaurant. At one end of the scale are modest street stalls and small bistros; at the other are classic restaurants and prestigious gastronomic establishments. Athough, in this bracket, French and Italian establishments predominate, these restaurants enable you to sample specialities from all over the world. Fast-food outlets are also becoming ubiquitous, particularly in city centres.

In medium-sized towns, the choice is more limited, with relatively basic establishments offering mostly local specialities. In small seaside towns, fish restaurants are particularly numerous.

Restaurants serving typically Moroccan food are, in fact, comparatively rare. They can be roughly divided into two types: "tourist" restaurants, which cater for groups and

which sometimes put on shows such as fantasias *(see pp34–5),* and higher-class restaurants, such as those in Fès or Marrakech. These are more like tables d'hôte in old traditional residences. The prices that they charge are higher (400 to 600 dirhams in the most renowned establishments), but you will enjoy a more refined cuisine and a more authentic atmosphere.

Given the pleasantly warm climate in Morocco, most

restaurants like to serve their customers outdoors, setting out tables in a quiet and pleasantly shaded courtyard, in the corner of a garden or even on the pavement outside the restaurant.

MOROCCAN SPECIALITIES

ALTHOUGH MOROCCO is well provided with restaurants offering international specialities, it is essential to sample Moroccan cuisine *(see pp318–19),* which is by far the best food that is served in the country.

A traditional Moroccan meal begins with a large number of starters, consisting of salad, or vegetables flavoured with different kinds of spices. Then follows the main course, often couscous or *tajine (see p319).*

Tajine is a kind of stew made with fish, chicken or lamb, and including prunes or almonds. There is a great variety of *tajines,* which differ according to the region, and it is hardly an exaggeration to say

A restaurant and shop on the Tizi-n-Test Pass road

Food stalls on Place Jemaa el-Fna in Marrakech at nightfall

that there are almost as many variations as there are cooks. All, however, are prepared and served in a terracotta dish with a conical lid; this cooking vessel is called a *tajine*, hence the dish's name.

Moroccan desserts, especially milk *pastilla*, are mouth-watering. Meals are usually eaten with mint tea, although more and more restaurants now offer wine.

OPENING HOURS AND RESERVATIONS

IN MOST RESTAURANTS, lunch is served between noon and 3pm and dinner between 7pm and 10.30pm. However, during the fast of Ramadan *(see p41)*, some restaurants, especially the less expensive ones, will not open at lunchtime.

In very fashionable restaurants, particularly those in the centre of the largest towns and cities, it is advisable for large parties to make a reservation, especially on Thursdays, Fridays and on Saturday evenings.

Reservation is absolutely essential for the tables d'hôte in Marrakech and Fès. Here it is often necessary to reserve several days in advance, since space can be limited, as can the number of sittings each evening.

PRICES AND TIPPING

PRICES VARY widely according to a restaurant's quality. They may range from 40 dirhams for a basic meal to about 150 dirhams for a meal with wine in a classic establishment, and between 250 and 600 dirhams in a high-class restaurant. Prices

are higher in large towns and cities and in places that attract many foreign visitors, such as Casablanca, Agadir and Marrakech. Prices given on menus usually include service and tax, so that unpleasant surprises are rare.

Tipping is a widely accepted custom in Morocco. It is customary to give 5 to 10 per cent of the bill. The tip should be in cash, and should be left on the table when you leave the restaurant. Do not add it to the total when you pay by cheque or bankers' card since the waiters will not receive it.

ALCOHOLIC DRINKS

MOROCCO IS A Muslim country where stringent laws apply to the sale of alcohol. However, most restaurants from a certain level upwards has a license to serve alcohol, as do Moroccan restaurants with a largely Western clientele.

Unlicensed restaurants may sometimes serve wine discreetly. Visitors should not, however, insist on being

served alcohol in an unlicensed restaurant since not serving alcohol may be the manager's deliberate policy. During Ramadan, some restaurants that normally serve alcohol close or stop serving it.

DRESS

EVEN THOUGH it is the custom to eat out of doors, Moroccans usually dress quite smartly when they go out to eat. Restaurants never insist on a particular type of dress. The only exception is in a few very high-class establishments, where gentlemen will be expected to wear a tie, or where ties will be lent. It is best to avoid too relaxed a style of dress, and very revealing clothes, such as beachwear, are likely to be considered offensive.

STREET STALLS

STALLS SELLING cheap food are seen everywhere in Morocco. Typical dishes are soup, skewered meat or fish and sandwiches.

At dusk, Place Jemaa el-Fna in Marrakech *(see p234)* turns into a huge open-air restaurant. In coastal towns and villages, usually on the quays of harbours where fishing boats come in, trestle tables serving freshly cooked seafood are often set up.

Although the food served from stalls is usually fresh, it is best to single out those that are the most popular with Moroccans. This is the best indication of good quality.

Traditional dining room in a restaurant in Agadir

What to Eat in Morocco

Olive oil

RICHLY FLAVOURED, Moroccan cuisine is a mixture of Berber, Arabic and Andalusian traditions. Couscous is a ubiquitous dish on Muslim dining tables on Fridays, and *tajine*, made with lamb, poultry or fish, is the national dish. Various salads, soups, *keftas* (meatballs) and the salt-and-sweet *bstilla* are also among the classic dishes of the Moroccan repertoire. Round loaves of bread are eaten at every meal. In the country, bread dipped in olive oil also constitutes the main dish. It is in a guesthouse that visitors are likely to taste the best Moroccan cooking.

Kesra, *flat bread, is often still baked at home. Bread has an almost sacred status and is freely offered. It symbolizes sharing and conviviality.*

STARTERS

According to the season, starters consist of refreshing raw vegetable salads, cooked vegetable purées or thick soups.

Tomato, onion and cucumber salad *is very popular as an accompaniment to skewered meat.*

Chick-pea salad, *with onion and cumin, is eaten warm or cold.*

Carrot and orange salad *is sprinkled with cinnamon and flavoured with orange-flower water.*

Harira *is a thick soup of vegetables, meat, rice and spices. It is eaten at the end of each day during Ramadan.*

Grilled sardines *may be stuffed with chermoula (garlic, coriander, lemon, oil, cumin and red pepper).*

Bstilla *is stuffed with chicken or pigeon, and with eggs, almonds, onions and spices, all layered with sheets of filo pastry.*

SPICES

Spices are an essential part of Moroccan cooking. They are sold unpackaged, their warm colours and subtle aromas adding a magical dimension to marketplaces. Used in moderation, spices bring out the full flavour of meat and vegetables. They are also used to flavour cakes. Cumin, saffron, ginger, turmeric, cloves and cinnamon are the most commonly used spices. The most highly prized is *ras el hanout*, "top of the shop", a carefully prepared blend of more than 20 different spices.

Coriander   Turmeric   Red pepper

Saffron   Saffron threads   Cumin

MAIN DISHES

Ordinary meals feature a single dish. On feast days there may be many, and everyone takes a little from each.

Pickled lemons

Chicken

Onions

Olives

Herbs

Kefta tajine *consists of meatballs cooked in tomato sauce with onions, cumin and saffron.*

Chicken tajine *with olives and pickled lemons, flavoured with coriander, cumin and saffron, should simmer for a long time on a low flame.*

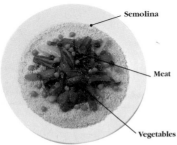

Semolina

Meat

Vegetables

Seven-vegetable couscous *is made with meat or fish, and there are endless variations. Steaming the grains is an art in itself.*

Skewered lamb, *macerated in onion, parsley and pepper and smeared with cumin, is enjoyed with salad and mint tea.*

SWEETS AND PASTRIES

Home-made pastries can be enjoyed at any time of day, usually washed down with mint tea.

Kaab Ghzahl *(gazelle's horns) are pastry stuffed with almonds, sugar, butter, orange-flower water and gum arabic.*

Sfenj *are delicious doughnuts, which are sold on street corners in every town.*

Oranges with cinnamon *are sliced, flavoured with orange flowers and sprinkled with cinnamon and icing sugar.*

Chebakyas *are whirls of fried pastry coated in honey and flavoured with sesame seeds, cinnamon and saffron.*

Briouats *are filo pastry triangles stuffed with almonds, sugar, orange flowers and cinnamon.*

Beghrirs *are distinctive honeycomb pancakes. They are eaten hot, spread with honey and butter.*

What to Drink in Morocco

GREEN MINT TEA is the national drink in Morocco. It is served several times a day at home, in the office, in shops and on café terraces. Moroccans are also very fond of coffee, which is usually served with milk but may sometimes be flavoured with cinnamon, orange-flower water or a few grains of pepper. Freshly squeezed orange juice is delicious, as are all fruit juices – cherry, grape and pomegranate being the most widely available choices. Although the Koran forbids the consumption of alcohol, fairly good-quality wines are produced in Morocco, and these can be bought in certain shops.

The tea ceremony, performed in front of guests

TEA

KNOWN FOR 3,000 years in China, green tea, with long fine leaves, reached Morocco in 1854. It was introduced by the British, and immediately became popular in every Moroccan home. All over Morocco, from the sophisticated town house to the simple nomad's tent, green mint tea has become the national drink. This thirst-quenching drink, which is made with varying amounts of sugar and mint, is a symbol of hospitality, and it is considered very ill-mannered to refuse it.

Glass of mint tea

The tea ceremony is almost always performed in front of guests and according to immutable rules. Mint tea is always served in small, slender glasses decorated with a gold or coloured filigree pattern. The tea leaves are rinsed in the scalded teapot so as to remove their excessive bitterness. Whole mint leaves, complete with stems, are then added, together with large lumps of sugar, which prevent the leaves from rising to the surface. After being left for a few minutes to infuse, a little tea is poured into a glass and returned to the pot. This is repeated several times. The host finally tastes the tea, which will not be served to guests until it is deemed to be perfect.

Traditionally served mint tea

COFFEE

ALTHOUGH IT IS less widely drunk than tea, Moroccans are also fond of coffee, which they like to drink very strong. It is accceptable to ask for a little boiling water with which to dilute it. Unless you request otherwise, your coffee will automatically be served with milk. A black coffee is a *qahwa kahla*; a *noss noss* is half coffee and half milk; and *café cassé* consists of more coffee than milk.

Coffee with milk (noss noss)   **Black coffee (qahwa kahla)**

COLD DRINKS

ALTHOUGH LEMONADE and cola are sold on every street corner, freshly squeezed orange juice is the real Moroccan speciality. It is absolutely delicious, so long as it is served undiluted. The sweet, juicy and famously flavoursome Moroccan oranges can be seen laid out for sale everywhere, piled up in glossy pyramids on barrows and on market stalls. On Place Jemaa el-Fna in Marrakech *(see p234)*, they are almost a sideshow in themselves. Almond milk, banana milk, apple juice and pomegranate juice are also popular drinks.

Orange juice

Almond milk

BEER AND SPIRITS

ALL KINDS OF IMPORTED alcoholic drinks can be purchased in supermarkets. Flag Spéciale is a light ale brewed in Tangier and Casablanca. Stork is brewed in Casablanca. *Mahia* is a Moroccan fig distillation, 40 per cent proof. The sale of wine and other alcohol is forbidden to Muslims during Ramadan and after 7.30pm.

Casablanca beer

Flag Spéciale, from Tangier

MINERAL WATER

ALTHOUGH THE TAP WATER in towns is safe to drink, it tastes strongly of chlorine. Mineral water – such as Sidi Ali and Sidi Harazem, which are still, and Oulmès and San Pellegrino, which are sparkling – is much more palatable.

Sidi Ali mineral water **Sidi Harazem mineral water** **Oulmès mineral water**

MOROCCAN WINES

WINE HAS BEEN produced in Morocco since Roman times, and local wine production was encouraged during the Protectorate. The country has three major wine-producing areas: around Oujda, in the northeast, in the Fès and Meknès area, and in the west between Rabat and Casablanca.

The most popular wines include red and white Médaillon, red, white and rosé Siroua, and the higher-quality wines produced by the winemakers Celliers de Meknès: Merlot and Cabernet Sauvignon; Sémillant, a fruity, dry white wine, and two rosé wines – Gris de Guerouane and Gris de Boulaouane. Also produced are Aït Soual, Vieux-Papes, Oustalet, Valpierre, Chaud-Soleil and Spécial

Vineyard near Boulaouane

Coquillages, which is best drunk with fish and seafood. Note that the quality of Moroccan wines can differ widely from year to year and sometimes even from bottle to bottle.

Red Amazir **Red Cabernet** **Red Siroua** **Red Guerrouane** **Red Oustalet** **Rosé Guerrouane** **Rosé Cabernet**

Choosing a Restaurant

THE RESTAURANTS LISTED BELOW have been selected across a wide range of price categories, for their good food, good value and interesting location. They are listed by area, starting with Rabat, and the colour-coded thumb tabs correspond to those by which the regions of Morocco are identifed throughout this guide.

	SET MENU	CHILDREN'S MENU	OPEN LATE	VEGETARIAN CUISINE	OUTSIDE DINING

RABAT

AGDAL: *L'Entrecôte* (Dh)(Dh)
74 Charia Al-Amir-Fal-Ould-Oumeir. (037) 67 11 08.
A French-style restaurant offering a good selection of meat and fish dishes. Attracts a fairly smart clientele. A very good establishment with efficient, accomplished service.

| | | ● | ■ | |

KASBA DES OUDAÏA: *Restaurant de la Plage* (Dh)(Dh)(Dh)
On the beach, below the Kasba des Oudaïa. (037) 72 31 48.
This beach restaurant specializes in fresh, high-quality fish and seafood. Its appeal lies largely in its peaceful setting with a view of the beach.

| | | | ■ | ■ |

MEDINA: *Dinarjat* (Dh)(Dh)(Dh)(Dh)
6 Rue Belgnaoui. (037) 70 42 39 & (037) 72 23 42.
A restaurant in a 17th-century résidence serving good-quality Moroccan food. A traditional show is performed after the meal. It is essential to make a reservation since you must be taken here by a guide from the entrance to the medina. 🍴

| ■ | | ■ | ● | |

RIVE DY BOU REGREG: *Chez Jean-Pierre* (Dh)(Dh)
Tarik el Marsa, Bou Regreg. (037) 20 13 65.
This typically Rababat restaurant is frequented by buisness people during the week and has a family atmosphere at weekends. Fish - dried, baked or grilled - is the order of the day.

VILLE NOUVELLE: *La Mamma* (Dh)(Dh)
6 Rue Tanta. (037) 70 73 29.
Justly renowned for many years, this family-run Italian restaurant with informal, friendly décor is always well patronized. Very good Italian dishes and excellent meat dishes.

| | ■ | | ■ | ● |

VILLE NOUVELLE: *Zerda* (Dh)(Dh)
7 Rue Patrice Lumumba. (037) 73 09 12.
A tiny restaurant offering excellent Moroccan-Jewish specialities. It is run by Michel, a famous singer in the Jewish community. There is always a musician playing, and, on a good night, Michel may go on singing until late.

| | | ■ | ● | ■ |

VILLE NOUVELLE: *Le Goéland* (Dh)(Dh)(Dh)
9 Rue Moulay Ali-Cherif. (037) 76 88 85.
A restaurant in a superb setting, with high-quality service, specializing mainly in fish and seafood, all of it excellent. Lovely courtyard with flowers in spring and summer.

| | | | | ■ |

NORTHERN ATLANTIC COAST

ASILAH: *Miramar* (Dh)
Below the ramparts. No telephone.
A restaurant in a pleasant setting, with a friendly welcome and good food. Prices are very reasonable, which is rare in Asilah.

| | ■ | | ■ | ● |

ASILAH: *Sevilla* (Dh)(Dh)
18 Avenue Iman al-Assili. No telephone.
A restaurant with pleasant décor, charming staff and a tempting menu that changes daily according to the catch of fish. An establishment above the average for Asilah.

| | | | | ■ |

Price categories are for a three-course meal for one person, including tax and service but without wine:

(Dh) under 100 dirhams
(Dh)(Dh) 100–200 dirhams
(Dh)(Dh)(Dh) 200–300 dirhams
(Dh)(Dh)(Dh)(Dh) 300–400 dirhams
(Dh)(Dh)(Dh)(Dh)(Dh) over 400 dirhams

SET MENU
Set menu usually consisting of three courses.
CHILDREN'S MENU
Simple food adapted to suit children's tastes.
OPEN LATE
Restaurant serves meals until 10pm.
VEGETARIAN CUISINE
Good selection of vegetarian dishes available.
OUTSIDE DINING
Tables outside, on a terrace, in a courtyard or on a quayside.

Restaurant	Price	SET MENU	CHILDREN'S MENU	OPEN LATE	VEGETARIAN DISHES	OUTSIDE DINING
KENITRA: *Restaurant of the Hôtel Mamora*	(Dh)(Dh)	■	●		●	■
LARACHE: *Cara Bonifa*	(Dh)				■	■
LARACHE: *Estrella del Mar*	(Dh)(Dh)	■			■	
MOHAMMEDIA: *La Frégate*	(Dh)	■	●	■		■
MOHAMMEDIA: *Restaurant du Port*	(Dh)(Dh)(Dh)(Dh)	■	●	■	●	■
CASABLANCA						
ANFA: *Ryad Zitoun*	(Dh)(Dh)	■			●	■
CITY CENTRE: *Au Petit Poucet*	(Dh)	■		■		■
CITY CENTRE: *Le Point du Jour*	(Dh)	■				
CITY CENTRE: *El-Mounia*	(Dh)(Dh)	■		■	●	■
CITY CENTRE: *Taverne du Dauphin*	(Dh)(Dh)			■		

KENITRA: *Restaurant of the Hôtel Mamora*
Avenue Hassan II, Place Administrative. **(** *(037) 37 17 75/37 13 10.*
One of the few pleasant restaurants in Kenitra, serving well-presented European cuisine in an inviting setting. Tables on the terrace in summer. Friendly staff.

LARACHE: *Cara Bonifa*
Place de la Libération. **(** *No telephone.*
A small, unpretentious restaurant offering good, freshly caught fish. Very central and ideal for a quick stop in Larache.

LARACHE: *Estrella del Mar*
68 Rue Zerktouni. **(** *(039) 91 22 43/91 33 25.*
One of the best restaurants in Larache, specializing in fish dishes served by friendly, professional staff. Delicious paella made to order.

MOHAMMEDIA: *La Frégate*
Rue Oued Zem. **(** *(023) 32 44 47.*
A family-run restaurant with Mediterranean-style décor of limewashed walls, serving good-quality fish dishes and succulent paella. Attractive terrace.

MOHAMMEDIA: *Restaurant du Port*
1 Rue du Port. **(** *(023) 32 24 66.*
A restaurant decorated like the interior of a boat, serving excellent fish dishes, such as cream of sea-bream soup, fish cooked in a salt crust and salmon in tartar sauce. A sophisticated establishment. 🍷 🍸

CASABLANCA

ANFA: *Ryad Zitoun*
31 Boulevard Rachidi. **(** *(022) 22 39 27.*
A restaurant serving Moroccan specialities, including classic dishes, in a pleasantly decorated dining room. Excellent fish *tajine.*
● *Sat and Sun lunchtime.*

CITY CENTRE: *Au Petit Poucet*
86 Boulevard Mohammed V. **(** *(022) 27 54 20.*
A historic establishment, set up in the 1920s. Good-quality French cuisine and a friendly welcome.

CITY CENTRE: *Le Point du Jour*
27 Rue Belloul Mohammed. **(** *No telephone.*
One of the more convenient restaurants in Casablanca, serving plain, good-quality French cuisine. Relaxed family atmosphere and very reasonable prices.

CITY CENTRE: *El-Mounia*
95 Rue du Prince Moulay Abdellah. **(** *(022) 22 26 69.*
A high-quality Moroccan restaurant offering very refined dishes. The pleasant courtyard fills quickly. Reservation advised. 🍷

CITY CENTRE: *Taverne du Dauphin*
115 Boulevard Houphouët Boigny. **(** *(022) 22 12 00.*
For many years this restaurant has attracted a large and heterogeneous clientele. A relaxed atmosphere and good seafood specialities. 🍸

Price categories are for a three-course meal for one person, including tax and service but without wine:

(Dh) under 100 dirhams
(Dh)(Dh) 100–200 dirhams
(Dh)(Dh)(Dh) 200–300 dirhams
(Dh)(Dh)(Dh)(Dh) 300–400 dirhams
(Dh)(Dh)(Dh)(Dh)(Dh) over 400 dirhams

Set Menu
Set menu usually consisting of three courses
Children's Menu
Simple food adapted to suit children's tastes.
Open Late
Restaurant serves meals until 10pm.
Vegetarian Cuisine
Good selection of vegetarian dishes available.
Outside Dining
Tables outside, on a terrace, in a courtyard or on a quayside.

	Set Menu	Children's Menu	Open Late	Vegetarian Dishes	Outside Dining
City Centre: *La Brasserie Bavaroise* — (Dh)(Dh)(Dh) 129 Rue Allal Ben Abdallah. *(022) 31 17 60.* Run by a Frenchwoman, this excellent brasserie right in the centre of Casablanca offers a very attractive menu. The meat dishes are particularly good.	■		■	●	
City Centre: *Retro 1900* — (Dh)(Dh)(Dh)(Dh) Centre 2000, Boulevard Houphouët Boigny. *(022) 27 60 73.* Run by Jacky Rollings, a renowned French chef, this establishment offers excellent gastronomic dishes in tastefully decorated surroundings.	■		■	●	■
Corniche: *Dawliz* — (Dh)(Dh) Boulevard de la Corniche. *(022) 39 12 25.* The terrace of this small, unpretentious restaurant commands a superb view of the ocean. A fairly conservative menu and very professional service.			■	●	■
Port Quarter: *Le Port de Pêche* — (Dh)(Dh) In the port, next to the customs house. *(022) 31 85 61.* This restaurant in the heart of the port is always full, a good indication of quality. It serves the full range of fish dishes, and the food is always fresh and well presented. A real treat. Reservation advised.			■		
Port Quarter: *Ostrea* — (Dh)(Dh)(Dh) In the fishing harbour. *(022) 44 13 90.* Located right in the harbour, this restaurant uses one of the most modern oyster farms in Morocco. Besides oysters, some other, unusual dishes are served. Friendly service.	■	●	■	●	
Racine: *Toscana* — (Dh)(Dh) 7 Rue Yaala Elifrani. *(022) 36 95 92.* A fashionable restaurant patronized by the privileged young people of Casablanca and the European community. Recommended for its cheerful décor and its delicious Italian specialities.			■	●	■
Outside Casablanca: *À Ma Bretagne* — (Dh)(Dh)(Dh) Boulevard de l'Atlantique, Sidi Abderrahman. *(022) 39 79 79.* An excellent gastronomic restaurant under French management. It offers refined cuisine and some excellent wines. The many fish dishes include: fillet of sole with sorrel, perch in red wine, roast turbot and lobster salad. Impeccable service. Reservation advised.	■		■	●	■

SOUTHERN ATLANTIC COAST

	Set Menu	Children's Menu	Open Late	Vegetarian Dishes	Outside Dining
El-Jadida: *Ali Baba* — (Dh)(Dh) Avenue El-Jamia el-Arabia. *No telephone.* On the way out of the town, towards Casablanca. A restaurant serving Moroccan and international dishes. Fine ocean views.	■	●	■		
El-Jadida: *Restaurant de l'Hôtel de Provence* — (Dh)(Dh) 42 Avenue Fquih Mohammed Errafii. *(023) 34 41 12/34 23 47.* One of the best restaurants in El-Jadida, serving good though unadventurous cuisine. The terrace, which is very pleasant when the weather is warm, creates a relaxing atmosphere.	■	●	■	●	■

ESSAOUIRA: *Les Alizés* ⓓ
26 Rue de la Sqala. **[** *(044) 47 68 19.*
A restaurant in a traditional 19th-century house, serving high-quality
but inexpensive cuisine. Candle-lit tables and wine available. One of the
best establishments in Essaouira.

ESSAOUIRA: *Grilled fish served in the harbour* ⓓ
Essaouira harbour. **[** *No telephone.*
Small stalls in the harbour serving tasty grilled fish at lunchtime.
Bargaining is essential. Standards of hygiene may not be the highest but
it is well worth experiencing the atmosphere.

ESSAOUIRA: *La Licorne* ⓓ ⓓ
26 Rue de la Sqala. **[** *(044) 47 36 26.*
A restaurant with a festive atmosphere, and fairly regular shows.
It is run by two French people and offers excellent fish and
seafood dishes.

ESSAOUIRA: *Chalet de la Plage* ⓓ ⓓ
Boulevard Mohammed V. **[** *(044) 47 59 72.*
The reputation of this establishment as the best in Essaouira
no longer seems entirely justified, although it is still one of
the smartest in the town. Friendly welcome and very pleasant
beach setting. **Ⓣ**

ESSAOUIRA: *Chez Sam* ⓓ ⓓ
At the end of the fishing harbour. **[** *(044) 47 65 13.*
A slightly old-fashioned restaurant with a lot of character. The
conservative though good-quality menu features, among other
things, crayfish and lobsters. Good views of fishing port.

ESSAOUIRA: *Dar Loubnane* ⓓ ⓓ
24 Rue du Rif. **[** *(044) 47 62 96.*
A very smart restaurant in a beautiful *riad* in the heart of
the medina. The candle-lit tables and sophisticated décor
create an intimate atmosphere.

ESSAOUIRA: *Riad Bleu Mogador* ⓓ ⓓ
23 Rue Bouchentouf. **[** *(044) 78 41 28/47 40 10.*
Good-quality European and Moroccan cuisine served in a very
tastefully decorated house in the medina. Recommended for
its original menu. Guests may telephone in advance and ask
to be taken here. **Ⓣ**

ESSAOUIRA: *Taros Café* ⓓ ⓓ ⓓ
2 Rue de la Sqala. **[** *(044) 47 64 07.*
This café-restaurant offers simple, tasty dishes in well-kept surroundings.
The library of books on art and the quality of the music make having a
meal here an interesting stop. **Ⓣ ●** *Sun.*

IMMOUZER DES IDA OUTANANE: *Restaurant de Tifrit*
3 km (1 mile) before Askri. **[** *(061) 65 42 31 or (048) 82 60 44.*
This restaurant serves excellent Moroccan cuisine. All the standard fare
such as couscous, tagines and brochettes can be enjoyed in a wonderful
poolside setting. Owners are friendly and welcoming. Home-made honey
is available to taste and to purchase.

OUALIDIA: *L'Araignée Gourmande* ⓓ ⓓ
On the beach. **[** *(023) 36 61 44.*
A restaurant offering various set meals, all featuring fish and seafood.
Oualidia's beautiful lagoon can be seen from the terrace.

OUALIDIA: *Ostrea II* ⓓ ⓓ
At the Ostrea oyster farm *(parc à huîtres)*, on the edge of the lagoon.
[*(023) 36 64 51.*
A smaller branch of the restaurant of the same name in Casablanca
(see p324). Some excellent, and sometimes unusual, oyster dishes are
on offer. In a stunning setting on the edge of the lagoon. **Ⓣ**

For key to symbols see back flap

	SET MENU	CHILDREN'S MENU	OPEN LATE	VEGETARIAN DISHES	OUTSIDE DINING

Price categories are for a three-course meal for one person, including tax and service but without wine:

Dh under 100 dirhams
Dh Dh 100–200 dirhams
Dh Dh Dh 200–300 dirhams
Dh Dh Dh Dh 300–400 dirhams
Dh Dh Dh Dh Dh over 400 dirhams

SET MENU
Set menu usually consisting of three courses.

CHILDREN'S MENU
Simple food adapted to suit children's tastes.

OPEN LATE
Restaurant serves meals until 10pm.

VEGETARIAN CUISINE
Good selection of vegetarian dishes available.

OUTSIDE DINING
Tables outside, on a terrace, in a courtyard or on a quayside.

OUALIDIA: *Restaurant of the Hôtel Hippocampe* — Dh Dh
Off to the right of the road leading down to the beach.
(023) 36 61 08.
High-quality cuisine served by friendly staff. Delicious fish soup. The terrace commands the best view of the lagoon in Oualidia. ▮
OPEN LATE ■; OUTSIDE DINING ■

SAFI: *Le Refuge* — Dh Dh
On the road to El-Jadida, 3.5 km (2 miles) outside Safi. (044) 66 80 86.
A very good fish restaurant on the seafront a little way outside the town. The tempting menu offers a wide choice. Crayfish is a speciality. ● *Mon.*
SET MENU ■; OUTSIDE DINING ■

TANGIER

CITY CENTRE: *Negresco* — Dh
20 Rue du Mexique. (039) 93 80 97.
A restaurant evocative of the legendary Tangier of the 1920s. Good, traditional food served in a delectably antiquated atmosphere.
OPEN LATE ■

CITY CENTRE: *The Pub* — Dh
4 Rue Sorolla. (039) 93 47 89.
The atmosphere here can be very lively, since the restaurant also doubles as a bar. Good international dishes are served and meals can be ordered until 1.30am. ▮ ▮
SET MENU ■; OPEN LATE ■

CITY CENTRE: *El Korsan* — Dh Dh
85 Rue de la Liberté. (039) 93 58 85.
The restaurant of the beautiful Hôtel El-Minzah (see p307) serves high-quality traditional Moroccan food, with dishes from different regions. Guests can also get a glimpse of the hotel. ▮
SET MENU ■; CHILDREN'S MENU ●; OPEN LATE ■; VEGETARIAN DISHES ●; OUTSIDE DINING ■

CITY CENTRE: *L'Eldorado* — Dh Dh
21 Avenue Allal Ben Abdallah. (039) 94 33 53.
A very small, well patronized restaurant. Fresh skewered fish is always available. A pleasant, inexpensive establishment with friendly staff.
OPEN LATE ■; VEGETARIAN DISHES ●; OUTSIDE DINING ■

CITY CENTRE: *Restaurant San Remo* — Dh Dh
15 Rue Ahmed Chaouki. (039) 93 84 51.
One of the best-known restaurants in Tangier, offering refined Italian dishes. The fresh pasta is particularly good. A pleasant atmosphere.
SET MENU ■; OPEN LATE ■; VEGETARIAN DISHES ●

CITY CENTRE: *London's Pub* — Dh Dh Dh
15 Rue Mansour Eddhabi. (039) 94 20 94.
Choice international cuisine served in the setting of a traditional English pub. An intimate atmosphere and distinguished service. Strongly British in character. ▮ ▮
SET MENU ■; OPEN LATE ■

MEDITERRANEAN COAST & THE RIF

AL-HOCEIMA: *Café-Restaurant Paris* — Dh Dh
21 Avenue Mohammed V. No telephone.
This restaurant, on an upper floor, offers a varied range of dishes, served in very pleasant surroundings enhanced by the manager's friendliness. No alcohol available.
SET MENU ■

CAP SPARTEL: *Le Mirage*   ⓓ ⓓ ⓓ
At Cap Spartel, above the Grottes d'Hercule.
🍴 *(039) 33 33 32.*
An exceptionally fine setting, at the point where the Atlantic and
the Mediterranean meet. Fish is, of course, the speciality here, and
it is cooked to perfection by the chef. 🍷

CHEFCHAOUEN: *Aladin*   ⓓ
17 Rue Targui. 🍴 *No telephone.*
A little haven of peace in quite a bustling town. Simple
but excellent Moroccan cuisine. Very inexpensive, with
good service.

CHEFCHAOUEN: *Zouar*   ⓓ
Rue Tarik El Wahda. 🍴 *(039) 98 66 70.*
A small Spanish inn serving a range of uncomplicated dishes,
mostly featuring fish and seafood. Run by a very friendly
Spanish-Moroccan couple.

MARTIL: *Granada*   ⓓ
58 Avenue de Tétouan. 🍴 *No telephone.*
In comfortable, warm and welcoming Moorish surroundings, this
restaurant offers a menu featuring fish and also some typical
Moroccan dishes, all for very reasonable prices.

OUJDA: *Comme Chez Soi*   ⓓ ⓓ
Rue Sijilmassa. 🍴 *(055) 68 60 79.*
The menu here offers a wide choice of dishes of European and
Moroccan inspiration, all of them exquisitely prepared. One of
the few establishments in Oujda that serves alcohol.

OUJDA: *Le Dauphin*   ⓓ ⓓ
38 Rue Berkane. 🍴 *(055) 68 61 45.*
An unpretentious Moroccan restaurant that is easily one of the best
places to eat in Oujda. The various *tajines* are always good. The
décor and welcome are uninspiring.

TETOUAN: *La Restinga*   ⓓ
21 Rue Mohammed V. 🍴 *No telephone.*
A small Moroccan restaurant in the very centre of Tetouan. The
dishes are tasty and the portions generous. Relatively unusually,
alcohol is served.

TETOUAN: *Saïgon*   ⓓ
Boulevard Mohammed ben-Larbi Torres. 🍴 *No telephone.*
Contrary to what its name might suggest, this restaurant serves Spanish
food. The surroundings are cosy and prices very reasonable.

FÈS

FÈS EL-BALI: *Zobra*   ⓓ
3 Derb Aïn Nass Blida. 🍴 *(055) 63 76 99.*
This small unpretentious restaurant offers good Moroccan specialities
at reasonable prices. A rarity in a medina.

FÈS EL-BALI: *Le Palais des Mérinides*   ⓓ ⓓ
36 Chrablyne Medina-Fès. 🍴 *(055) 63 40 28.*
One of many Moroccan restaurants in Fès, in the setting of a
sumptuous 14th-century palace. The cuisine is unremarkable
but nevertheless refined and prices are reasonable. 🍷

FÈS EL-BALI: *Le Palais de Fès*   ⓓ ⓓ ⓓ ⓓ
15 Rue Makhfia. 🍴 *(055) 76 15 90.*
In an old residence, where succulent Moroccan specialities are served
on the terrace. The upper floors are reserved for groups, and also
accommodate a carpet shop. The view of the medina of Fès is
breathtaking. 🍷

Price categories are for a three-course meal for one person, including tax and service but without wine:

Dh under 100 dirhams
Dh Dh 100–200 dirhams
Dh Dh Dh 200–300 dirhams
Dh Dh Dh Dh 300–400 dirhams
Dh Dh Dh Dh Dh over 400 dirhams

SET MENU
Set menu usually consisting of three courses.
CHILDREN'S MENU
Simple food adapted to suit children's tastes.
OPEN LATE
Restaurant serves meals until 10pm.
VEGETARIAN CUISINE
Good selection of vegetarian dishes available.
OUTSIDE DINING
Tables outside, on a terrace, in a courtyard or on a quayside.

Restaurant	Price	Fixed Menu	Children's Menu	Open Late	Vegetarian Dishes	Outside Dining
FÈS EL-BALI: *El-Fassia* Place Bapha. *The Moroccan restaurant of the Palais Jamaï Hotel.* (055) 63 73 14. Besides offering the chance to taste traditional Moroccan cuisine that is often prepared to perfection, a meal in this restaurant also provides the opportunity to step inside a legendary Fassi hotel. There is a magical view over the rooftops of Fès from the terrace. ▼	Dh Dh Dh Dh Dh	■		■	●	■
VILLE NOUVELLE: *Chamonix* 5 Rue Mokhtar Soussi. (055) 62 66 38. A simple establishment offering light meals, such as salad, *tajine* and a dessert for reasonable prices. The great cordiality of the manager gives this restaurant its special character.	Dh	■	●	■	●	■
VILLE NOUVELLE: *Sicilia* 4 Avenue Chefchaouni. (055) 62 52 65. Ideal for a light snack at lunchtime, this buffet is always well patronized, which is a good indication of the freshness of what is served here. Cheerful, friendly waiters.	Dh					
VILLE NOUVELLE: *La Cheminée* 6 Avenue Lalla Asmaa, near the railway station. (055) 62 49 02. This fairly traditional restaurant offers four different menus featuring French and Moroccan dishes. Excellent service. Good wine list. ▼	Dh Dh	■		■	●	

MEKNÈS & VOLUBILIS

Restaurant	Price	Fixed Menu	Children's Menu	Open Late	Vegetarian Dishes	Outside Dining
MEDINA: *Zitouna* 44 Rue Jamaa Zitouna. (055) 53 20 83. A restaurant offering classic cuisine. Located in the heart of the old town, it is therefore quite difficult to find (ask for directions at your hotel). The rather undistinguished former residence in which the restaurant has been laid out has been very well converted.	Dh Dh	■		■		
MEDINA: *L'Arabesque* 20 Derb el-Miter, Quartier Zenjfour. (055) 63 53 21. Not far from the Jamai Palace is this superb riad which also has guest rooms. The restaurant offers traditional Moroccan cuisine of the highest quality.	Dh Dh Dh Dh					■
VILLE NOUVELLE: *Annexe du Métropole* 11 Rue Cherif Idrissi. (055) 52 56 68. This restaurant offers two good-quality Moroccan menus. Meals are served in exquisitely decorated surroundings, which include some magnificent ceilings.	Dh	■	●	■	●	■
VILLE NOUVELLE: *Gambrinus* Avenue Omar Ibn el-Has. (055) 52 02 58. Despite its Baroque, almost giddy décor, this is a lifeless restaurant. The menu is quite wide-ranging, however, and includes international dishes. Competent waiters and reasonable prices.	Dh	■		■	●	
VILLE NOUVELLE: *Marhaba* 23 Avenue Mohammed V. No telephone. A small informal restaurant serving skewered meat, simple *tajines* and *harira*. Both the décor and the thronging clientele make for an authentically Moroccan atmosphere.	Dh					

VILLE NOUVELLE: *Le Dauphin* Ⓓⓗ Ⓓⓗ
5 Avenue Mohammed V. ☎ *(055) 52 34 23.*
A popular restaurant offering a varied fish menu. The room looking
out over the avenue is reserved for group bookings only.

VILLE NOUVELLE: *Le Collier de la Colombe* Ⓓⓗ Ⓓⓗ Ⓓⓗ
67 Rue Driba. ☎ *(055) 55 50 41.*
A fine establishment from which there is a panoramic view of the
valley. Carefully prepared Moroccan and international dishes are
served by attentive staff.

MOULAY IDRISS: *Baraka* Ⓓⓗ
22 Aïn Smen (the main street), Khiber quarter. ☎ *(055) 54 41 84.*
The only restaurant in Moulay Idriss that rises above the average.
It is a little expensive for its grade, but the cuisine is of a good
standard and the welcome friendly.

VOLUBILIS: *La Corbeille Fleurie* Ⓓⓗ
At the entrance to the archaeological site. ☎ *No telephone.*
Very simple meals featuring *tajines*. Its main virtue is its location.

MIDDLE ATLAS

BENI MELLAL: *SAT Agadir* Ⓓⓗ
155 Boulevard el-Hansali. ☎ *(023) 48 14 48.*
Very often packed, this small restaurant offers such simple dishes
as *tajines*, skewered meat and soup for next to nothing. The dining
room on the upper floor commands a fine view of the square.

IFRANE: *La Paix* Ⓓⓗ Ⓓⓗ
Avenue de la Marche Verte. ☎ *(055) 93 17 97.*
The very pleasant terrace and the cheerfulness of the restaurateurs go
some way to making up for rather a limited menu. The quality of the
European and Moroccan cuisine here is, however, good.

IFRANE: *Restaurant of the Hôtel des Perce-Neige* Ⓓⓗ Ⓓⓗ
Rue des Asphodèles. ☎ *(055) 56 63 50.*
Quite highly esteemed in Ifrane, this restaurant holds some pleasant
surprises. The menu is wide-ranging and the waiters' recommendations
are usually reliable.

KHENIFRA: *Restaurant de France* Ⓓⓗ
Quartier des Forces Armées Royales. ☎ *(055) 58 61 14.*
A restaurant forming part of a small hotel and serving tasty
Moroccan dishes. A good place to stop on the long road between
Fès and Marrakech.

OUZOUD: *Dar Es-Salam* Ⓓⓗ
Oppposite the parking area. ☎ *(023) 45 96 57.*
A small hotel-restaurant whose classic menu offers such items
as *crudités* and *tajines*, washed down with good mint tea,
all for about 70 dirhams.

OUZOUD: *Restaurant of the Hôtel Les Cascades* Ⓓⓗ Ⓓⓗ
Near the parking area, on the road above the waterfall.
☎ *(023) 45 96 58.* FAX *(023) 45 88 60.*
Good cuisine that varies daily, together with reasonable prices, make this
one of the best restaurants in Ouzoud. Simple but good-quality.

MARRAKECH

GUELIZ: *Grillades* Ⓓⓗ
On the corner of Avenue Mohammed V and Rue Ibn Iacha. ☎ *No telephone.*
Three restaurants in a row. Choose the one in the middle, which is
always full. An informal clientele and ordinary fare, such as *tajines*,
skewered meat and sandwiches made to order. Food is served until
midnight. Ideal for a quick snack.

Price categories are for a three course meal for one person, including tax and service but without wine:

Dh under 100 dirhams
Dh Dh 100–200 dirhams
Dh Dh Dh 200–300 dirhams
Dh Dh Dh Dh 300–400 dirhams
Dh Dh Dh Dh Dh over 400 dirhams

SET MENU
Set menu usually consisting of three courses.

CHILDREN'S MENU
Simple food adapted to suit children's tastes.

OPEN LATE
Restaurant serves meals until 10pm.

VEGETARIAN CUISINE
Good selection of vegetarian dishes available.

OUTSIDE DINING
Tables outside, on a terrace, in a courtyard or on a quayside.

	Price	FIXED MENU	CHILDREN'S MENU	OPEN LATE	VEGETARIAN DISHES	OUTSIDE DINING
GUELIZ: *El-Fassia*	Dh Dh			■		■
GUELIZ: *Bagatelle*	Dh Dh			■		■
GUELIZ: *Le Catanzaro*	Dh Dh			■	●	
GUELIZ: *Villa Rosa*	Dh Dh Dh	■		■	●	●
GUELIZ: *Le Jardin des Arts*	Dh Dh Dh Dh					
GUELIZ: *La Trattoria*	Dh Dh Dh Dh			■	●	■
HIVERNAGE: *Le Comptoir Paris-Marrakech*	Dh Dh Dh					
MEDINA: *Pizzeria Venezia*	Dh		●	■	●	■
MEDINA: *Échoppes*	Dh			■	●	■

GUELIZ: *El-Fassia*
232 Avenue Mohammed V. *(044) 43 40 60.*
A Moroccan restaurant in Ville Nouvelle. The décor may a little too new for some tastes (though still authentically Moroccan) but the quality of the food on offer and the friendly staff completely make up for it. Many groups come here in the high season, although the fact that there are several dining rooms allows smaller parties some intimacy.

GUELIZ: *Bagatelle*
101 Rue de Yougoslavie. *(044) 43 02 74.*
This delectably old-fashioned restaurant gives the impression of having remained unchanged for years. Run by a French couple, it offers good European dishes. In fine weather, meals are served in the garden.

GUELIZ: *Le Catanzaro*
Rue Tarik Ben Ziad. *(044) 43 37 31.*
A restaurant that is a real institution in Marrakech, and that has attracted a large clientele for 15 years. Italian specialities and the best meat dishes in the city. The friendly, thoughtful waiters add to the already enjoyable experience.

GUELIZ: *Villa Rosa*
64 Avenue Hassan II. *(044) 43 08 32.*
This restaurant, with cosy and cheerful décor, offers choice European cuisine. There is a very good wine list. In warm weather meals are served in the garden.

GUELIZ: *Le Jardin des Arts*
6-7, Rue Sakia el Hamra, Semalalia. *(044) 44 66 34.*
A lovely restaurant with an innovative menu that features camel and ostrich meat. The décor is tasteful and the pictures on the walls are for sale. ● *Monday lunchtime.*

GUELIZ: *La Trattoria*
179 Rue Mohammed el-Beqal. *(044) 43 26 41.*
This up-market Italian restaurant is located in a very fine colonial house, whose eclectic style of decoration is the result of the owner's extensive travels. The excellence of the cuisine is equalled by the outgoing, friendly character of the restaurateur himself. ● *lunchtime.*

HIVERNAGE: *Le Comptoir Paris-Marrakech*
Avenue Echouada. *(044) 43 77 02.*
In just a few years, this restaurant has become one of the musts of the Ville Rouge. Along with its Parisian twin, Comptoir, it seeks to be a place of cultural exchange against a background of good food and world music.

MEDINA: *Pizzeria Venezia*
279 Avenue Mohammed V. *(044) 44 00 81.*
Situated in front of the Koutoubia Mosque this friendly restaurant offers all the standard Italian fare including pizzas and a good choice of salad.

MEDINA: *Échoppes*
Place Jemaa el-Fna. *No telephone.*
From 8pm onwards, the atmosphere here is unbeatable. Small stalls geared to the tourist trade and offering skewered meat and grilled fish stand alongside other, more authentically Moroccan stalls serving snails, traditional Moroccan soup and sheep's head, the latter being a delicacy. Bargaining is essential. ● *lunchtime.*

MEDINA: *Les Terrasses de l'Alhambra* (Dh)(Dh)
Place Jemaa el-Fna. (044) 42 75 77.
Centrally located, this restaurant offers all the standard Italian
fare - pasta, pizza, salad - at reasonable prices.

MEDINA: *Dar Moha* (Dh)(Dh)(Dh)(Dh)
81 Rue Dar el-Bacha. (044) 38 64 00.
One of the few *riads* in the medina that opens at lunchtime. Good
Moroccan cuisine, including some rarely seen dishes, served by
accomplished staff in a very attractive setting.

MEDINA: *Le Foundouk* (Dh)(Dh)(Dh)(Dh)
55 Souk Hal Fassi, Kat Bennahïd. (044) 37 81 90.
Set in a converted caravanserai building, this restaurant serves excellent
Moroccan and Mediterranean-style cuisine. The restaurant is structured
on two levels around an interior central courtyard. Multicoloured lanterns
create a magical atmosphere.

MEDINA: *L'Mimouna* (Dh)(Dh)(Dh)(Dh)
47 Place des Ferblantiers. (44) 38 68 68.
Set in an old medina residence, this restaurant offers good
quality, traditional Moroccan cuisine. Dine outside on the large
terrace with views of the town or inside by the fire in one of
the many dining rooms.

MEDINA: *Dar El-Yacout* (Dh)(Dh)(Dh)(Dh)(Dh)
79 Rue Sidi Ahmed Soussi. (044) 38 29 00. FAX (044) 38 25 38.
This *riad*, an exquisitely restored palace, is the very best in Marrakech.
The menu features succulent Moroccan specialities in generous portions.
Excellent service. A pre-dinner drink on the terrace overlooking the
medina is an unforgettable experience. Reservation compulsory.
lunchtime.

MEDINA: *Dar Marjana* (Dh)(Dh)(Dh)(Dh)(Dh)
15 Derb Sidi Ali Taïr. (044) 38 51 10/38 57 73. FAX (044) 38 51 52.
A restaurant in a former palace in the medina, serving top-quality
Moroccan cuisine. Inspired menu and wine list. A brief
show is performed after the meal. Reservation compulsory.
lunchtime.

MEDINA: *Le Pavillon* (Dh)(Dh)(Dh)(Dh)(Dh)
47 Derb Zaouia. (044) 38 70 40.
This French gastronomic restaurant, located in a palace in the
medina, has quickly become one of the best in Marrakech. Recently
acquired by the Maison Arabe hotel nearby, it has lost none of its
character nor any of its quality. Reservation advised since space is
very limited. *Thu; lunchtime.*

MEDINA: *Le Tobsil* (Dh)(Dh)(Dh)(Dh)(Dh)
22 Derb Abdallah ben Hessaien Ksour.
(044) 44 40 52/44 15 23. FAX (044) 44 35 15.
This restaurant, whose name means "plate" in Arabic, serves some
of the best food in the medina. This is an opportunity to sample a
wide range of very refined dishes. The décor is superb and the staff
professional. Reservation compulsory. *lunchtime.*

HIGH ATLAS

OUIRGANE: *Le Sanglier qui Fume* (Dh)(Dh)
At the lower end of the village. (044) 48 57 07/08.
An inn offering a relaxing pause on the Tizi-n-Test Pass road. Classic
international cuisine is served in a lush setting. Very friendly staff. The
inn also organizes tours.

OUKAÏMEDEN: *L'Angour (Chez Juju)* (Dh)(Dh)
Below the ski pistes. (044) 31 90 05.
A restaurant decorated in the manner of a French chalet, serving simple
but generous dishes. Located beneath the pistes, it is also an ideal place
to enjoy a glass of mulled wine after a day's skiing.

Price categories are for a three-course meal for one person, including tax and service but without wine:

Dh under 100 dirhams
Dh Dh 100–200 dirhams
Dh Dh Dh 200–300 dirhams
Dh Dh Dh Dh 300–400 dirhams
Dh Dh Dh Dh Dh over 400 dirhams

SET MENU
Set menu usually consisting of three courses.
CHILDREN'S MENU
Simple food adapted to suit children's tastes.
OPEN LATE
Restaurant serves meals until 10pm.
VEGETARIAN CUISINE
Good selection of vegetarian dishes available.
OUTSIDE DINING
Tables outside, on a terrace, in a courtyard or on a quayside.

Restaurant	Price	FIXED MENU	CHILDREN'S MENU	OPEN LATE	VEGETARIAN SPECIALITIES	OUTSIDE EATING
OUKAÏMEDEN: *Restaurant of the Kenzi Louka hotel*	Dh Dh	■			●	
OURIKA VALLEY: *Dar piano*	Dh Dh	■				■
OURIKA VALLEY: *Ramuntcho*	Dh Dh Dh	■	●	■	●	■
TELOUET: *Auberge de Télouèt: Dar Piano*	Dh	■	●		●	■
TIZI-N-TEST PASS ROAD: *La Belle Vue*	Dh	■				
AÏT BENHADDOU: *L'Étoile Filante*	Dh	■	●	■	●	■
ERFOUD: *Erg Chebbi*	Dh	●	■		■	●
ERFOUD: *Restaurant des Dunes*	Dh	●	■	●	■	●
ER-RACHIDIA: *Hôtel Oasis*	Dh	●	■		■	
ER-RACHIDIA: *Imilchil*	Dh			■		■

OUKAÏMEDEN: *Restaurant of the Kenzi Louka hotel*
In the centre of the village. (044)31 90 80.
The only restaurant really worthy of the name in this small winter-sports resort. International and Moroccan cuisine served in a modern, pleasant and well-heated setting.

OURIKA VALLEY: *Dar piano*
Ighref, Km 53. no telephone.
An attractive guesthouse run by French people serving Moroccan and international specialities. The pleasant terrace looks onto a pretty garden.

OURIKA VALLEY: *Ramuntcho*
At Km 50. (044) 48 45 21.
A restaurant that is a favourite with people from Marrakech. Genuinely international and authentically Moroccan cuisine is served in a verdant setting. Ask for a table on the terrace.

TELOUET: *Auberge de Télouèt: Dar Piano*
Opposite the Glaoui kasbah. (044) 89 07 17.
A small inn serving excellent *tajines*. The owner is also the caretaker of the kasbah, about which he has many tales to tell.

TIZI-N-TEST PASS ROAD: *La Belle Vue*
About 1 km (0.5 mile) beyond the pass. no telephone.
A small hut tucked away up on the pass. The simple food – such as omelettes and salads – is in keeping with the basic décor but the view over the Sous plain is breathtaking. lunchtime.

OUARZAZATE & THE SOUTHERN OASES

AÏT BENHADDOU: *L'Étoile Filante*
In the centre of the village. (044) 89 03 22.
A traditional restaurant very near the ksar offering simple but tasty *tajines* and salads. A friendly establishment that is a world away from the tourist traps that are so much in evidence here.

ERFOUD: *Erg Chebbi*
142 Avenue Moulay Ismaïl. (055) 57 75 27.
This small restaurant on the upper floor has a varied menu featuring very good Moroccan and international specialities. Friendly welcome. The terrace is pleasantly quiet.

ERFOUD: *Restaurant des Dunes*
Avenue Moulay-Ismaïl. (055) 57 67 93.
A small, very basic establishment situated on the outskirts of Erfoud. The restaurant offers good local meat specialities and is convenient for its swift, friendly service.

ER-RACHIDIA: *Hôtel Oasis*
10 Rue Sidi Bou Abdallah. (055) 57 25 19.
A restaurant serving adequate set meals for around 80 dirhams, consisting of traditional Moroccan dishes. A convenient, relaxing place for a short stop.

ER-RACHIDIA: *Imilchil*
Avenue Moulay Ali Cherif. (055) 57 21 23.
This small restaurant offers a pleasant terrace and simple à la carte food. The staff are friendly and efficient.

MHAHMID: *Iriqui*
On the main square. (044) 84 80 23.
In a small town where choice is limited, this unpretentious restaurant is perfectly adequate. Simple food prepared and served with care.

MIDELT: *Restaurant de Fès*
2 Rue Lalla Aicha. No telephone.
A well-maintained restaurant with a family atmosphere and offering a varied range of choice Moroccan dishes. Satisfying food that is excellent value for money.

OUARZAZATE: *Restaurant Er-Raha*
11 Avenue al-Mouahidine. (044) 88 40 41.
An excellent restaurant for a good meal and generous servings at a reasonable price. The varied menu offers very generous Moroccan dishes. Pleasant terrace.

OUARZAZATE: *Restaurant Es-Salam*
Avenue du Prince Héritier Sidi Mohammed. (044) 88 23 76.
A small, unpretentious restaurant in the town centre, with several set meals and an inexpensive wine list. It is always full, and is patronized both by Moroccans and tourists.

OUARZAZATE: *Chez Dimitri*
22 Avenue Mohammed V. (044) 88 76 76.
The first good restaurant to open in Ouarzazate and one that has gained an illustrious reputation. Authentic international cuisine and a wide choice of alcoholic drinks. The décor relates to the building's interesting history.

OUARZAZATE: *Ouarzazate Tourist Complex*
On the outskirts of the town, on the road to Tineghir. (044) 88 31 10.
Do not be put off by the fact that the tourist complex outside the town has all the outward appearances of a tourist trap, This is a very fine building with large tents, tasteful décor and a superb pool. Moroccan cuisine is served here.

SKOURA: *La Kasba*
Rue Principale. (044) 85 20 78.
A basic restaurant for a quick stop where good skewered meat and refreshing salads are served. A short distance outside the town, it is quiet and very relaxing.

TAMEGROUTE: *Jnane Dar*
Opposite the library. (044) 84 86 22.
This small, family-run establishment is located opposite the Koranic Library, the focal point of interest in Tamegroute. Simple, typically Moroccan dishes are served in the dining room and in Berber tents.

TAOURIRT: *La Kasba.*
Opposite the Taourirt kasbah. (044) 88 20 33.
A restaurant laid out in a traditional building with a suite of small dining rooms and terraces with a view of the Taourirt kasbah. Excellent Moroccan dishes are served.

TINERHIR: *Restaurant of the Tombouctou hotel*
Avenue Bir Anzarane. (044) 83 46 04.
The restaurant is owned by a Spaniard, and Spanish specialities, including excellent paella, are served here along with classic Moroccan cuisine. Very friendly welcome.

TINERHIR: *Restaurant of the Hôtel de l'Avenir*
Rue Zaid Ouhamed. (044) 83 45 99.
This ordinary restaurant in the heart of the town offers a choice of two set meals for very reasonable prices. Salads, simple but tasty *tajines* and classic desserts are on the menu.

DADÈS VALLEY: *Auberge Chez Pierre*
Km 25, Dadès valley. At the head of the Dadès gorge. (044) 83 02 67.
A small guesthouse with a good reputation. Besides a small number of rooms, it also offers delectable international food with a local flavour. The Dadès valley setting is also impressive.

Price categories are for a three-course meal for one person, including tax and service but without wine:

- ⓓ under 100 dirhams
- ⓓⓓ 100–200 dirhams
- ⓓⓓⓓ 200–300 dirhams
- ⓓⓓⓓⓓ 300–400 dirhams
- ⓓⓓⓓⓓⓓ over 400 dirhams

SET MENU
Set menu usually consisting of three courses.

CHILDREN'S MENU
Simple food adapted to suit children's tastes.

OPEN LATE
Restaurant serves meals until 10pm.

VEGETARIAN CUISINE
Good selection of vegetarian dishes available.

OUTSIDE DINING
Tables outside, on a terrace, in a courtyard or on a quayside.

	Price	FIXED MENU	CHILDREN'S MENU	OPEN LATE	VEGETARIAN DISHES	OUTSIDE DINING
ZAGORA: *Restaurant of the Fibule du Draa hotel* 2 km (1 mile) outside the town, beyond the bridge over Wadi Draa. ◖ *(044) 84 73 18.* Succulent Moroccan dishes including *tajines, bstillas* and *méchoui* (cooked to order) are served in a large dining room. There is also a magnificent garden for pre-dinner drinks. Typically Moroccan surroundings and very friendly staff.	ⓓ	■		■	●	■
ZAGORA: *Restaurant of the Ksar Tinsouline hotel* Avenue Hassan II. ◖ *(044) 84 72 52.* This hotel restaurant has a fine architectural and natural setting, in the middle of a beautiful palm grove. The varied menu features both international and Moroccan dishes. Swift, efficient service.	ⓓⓓ	■	●		●	■

SOUTHERN MOROCCO & WESTERN SAHARA

	Price	FIXED MENU	CHILDREN'S MENU	OPEN LATE	VEGETARIAN DISHES	OUTSIDE DINING
AGADIR: *Grilled fish in the harbour* In the fishing harbour. ◖ *No telephone.* Dozens of little eateries, patronized by many tourists and quite a few Moroccans. Bargaining essential.	ⓓ					
AGADIR: *Jour et Nuit* Promenade de la Plage. ◖ *(048) 84 06 10.* A good range of dishes at fair prices is served continuously throughout the day. Well patronized at all times, with a buzzing atmosphere.	ⓓ	■		■	●	■
AGADIR: *Mimi la Brochette* Promenade de la Plage. ◖ *(048) 84 03 87.* A restaurant well known for its skewered meat and fish, in a very pleasant setting near the sea.	ⓓ			■	●	■
AGADIR: *Via Venneto* Avenue Hassan II. ◖ *(048) 84 14 67.* A good Italian restaurant near the Vallée des Oiseaux. Quite a classic menu. Warm welcome.	ⓓ				●	■
AGADIR: *Restaurant of the Shems casino* Boulevard Mohammed V, in the direction of Promenade de la Plage. ◖ *(048) 82 11 11.* A restaurant offering a constantly changing and innovative menu. Refined European cuisine with prices to match. 🍴 🍷	ⓓⓓ	■	●	■	●	
AGADIR: *Jazz Restaurant* Boulevard du 20 Août, Complexe Igoudar. ◖ *(048) 84 02 08.* A fashionable restaurant in a very pleasant setting. The wide-ranging menu features a range of European dishes. Prices are lower at lunchtime. Live music in the evenings. 🍴 🍷	ⓓⓓⓓ	■	●	■	●	■
AGADIR: *Le Miramar* Boulevard Mohammed V. ◖ *(048) 84 07 70.* A family-run Italian restaurant with a very good varied menu. Intimate atmosphere, with candles round the hearth. 🍴 🍷	ⓓⓓⓓ			■	●	
DAKHLA: *Le Samarkan* On the beach. ◖ *No telephone.* A small establishment serving good fish dishes. Simple food but very friendly service.	ⓓⓓ					■

GUELMIM: *El-Manara*
232 Place Anzarane. █ *No telephone.*
A stall selling roast chicken and chips, to eat in or take away. Ideal for a
snack or quick lunch stop.

GUELMIM: *Restaurant in the Complexe Touristique*
Route d'Assa. █ *(048) 77 20 10.*
The campsite on the outskirts of the town has a fine, comfortable
restaurant offering carefully prepared Moroccan dishes. Prices are
reasonable.

SIDI IFNI: *Restaurant of the Bellevue hotel*
Place Hassan II. █ *(048) 87 50 72.*
A splendid view of the sea from the terrace and some excellent
fish specialities make this the best restaurant in Ifni. Friendly,
cheerful staff.

TAFRAOUTE: *L'Étoile d'Agadir*
Place de la Marche Verte. █ *(048) 80 02 68.*
Very popular with the inhabitants of Tafraoute, this restaurant serves
excellent almond *tajine*, a local speciality, and other Moroccan dishes.

TALIOUINE: *Le Safran*
Rue Principale. █ *(048) 53 40 46.*
A good restaurant where simple meals are served inside Berber
tents. The friendly owners also organize some excellent tours in
the Atlas mountains.

TAN TAN PLAGE: *Equinoxe*
On the beach. █ *(048) 87 96 25.*
Run by a Frenchman, this beach restaurant serves *tajines* and freshly caught
fish. The view from the terrace is magnificent.

TAROUDANNT: *Restaurant of the Saadien hotel*
Borj Oumansour. █ *(048) 85 25 89.*
This quiet, intimate restaurant on an upper floor offers a Moroccan menu
with a few French dishes. The Moroccan salad is excellent. Discreet
service and a fine view of the town.

TAROUDANNT: *Jnane Soussia*
On the road to Marrakech. █ *(048) 85 49 80.*
A Moroccan restaurant a little way outside the town, where meals
are served in tents. Although the establishment caters for parties,
individuals are also welcome.

TAROUDANNT: *Restaurant of the Palais Salam hotel*
At the entrance of the town, beneath the ramparts.
█ *(048) 85 25 01/85 21 30.*
Excellent international and Moroccan cuisine served in a fine dining
room or in the luxuriant garden. Guests can enjoy pre-dinner drinks in
the bar or beside the swimming pool.

TIZNIT: *Café-restaurant du Carrefour*
Avenue Hassan II. █ *(048) 60 08 36.*
A small air-conditioned restaurant offering classic Moroccan dishes at
very reasonable prices. Very friendly staff. A pleasant stop and provides
a respite from the heat.

TIZNIT: *Restaurant of the Hôtel de Paris*
Avenue Hassan II. █ *(048) 86 28 65.*
A pleasant restaurant in a small hotel. The menu features international
and Moroccan dishes. Portions are generous and the service very
professional.

TIZNIT: *Restaurant of the Kerdous hotel*
On the road to Tafraoute, at the Kerdous Pass.
█ *(048) 86 20 63.*
This small hotel built on a rocky outcrop in a remote location
has a restaurant with a panoramic view. It is worth making a
detour for the stunning view.

For key to symbols see back flap

SHOPPING IN MOROCCO

EVERY VILLAGE in Morocco has its weekly souk. Lasting for a few hours, souks are busy, colourful places where agricultural produce and craft items brought by country people are sold alongside a range of other essential everyday items.

Large towns have several souks. These take place in the medinas and are laid

Ceramic box

out according to the type of goods that they sell. Traders are friendly and always ready to please their customers. The rich and diverse range of Moroccan crafts can be found in the country's souks and markets, as well as at cooperative craft outlets and specialist shops, and are also offered for sale by the roadside along tourist routes.

Slipper merchant with a colourful range of footwear in Tafraoute

OPENING HOURS

COUNTRY SOUKS take place only in the morning. Grocers' shops, local supermarkets and butchers' shops are open every weekday from 8am to 9pm, although they close for about two hours in the middle of the day. Some may also open on Sundays, when different opening hours apply. Friday is theoretically a day of rest for Muslims; however, business goes on as

normal, although some larger shops close in the middle of the day. During Ramadan, grocers' shops open late in the morning, close for part of the day and then open from the evening until very late. Shops run by Jews close on Saturdays (the Sabbath). In large towns and cities, clothes shops and fabric shops open from 9am to noon and from 3pm to 7pm. They do not open on Sundays. The hypermarkets that have sprung up in some large towns are open from 9am to 9pm seven days a week.

METHODS OF PAYMENT

CREDIT CARDS are accepted only in large towns and cities and in modern shops. Some shopkeepers will add a percentage as tax onto the total automatically if you choose this form of payment. Also, credit card slips can be pre-dated or printed twice without your knowing. It is best, therefore, to carry sufficient amounts of cash before setting off on a shopping spree.

FOOD STORES

ALL TOWNS are very well provided with grocers' shops. In villages, the grocer's is the only place, apart from the weekly souk, where people can buy provisions and essential items.

These shops are usually no bigger than a large cupboard. They are fitted with shelves from floor to ceiling, and offer all kinds of foods and household goods. It is wise to

Dates for sale, Ziz Gorge

avoid buying perishable items such as yoghurt and milk, since there is no guarantee that they are fresh. In butchers' shops, what is on offer is neither labelled nor priced. Fruit and vegetable shops, dairies and bakers are found only in large towns. Although French bread was introduced during the Protectorate, Moroccans prefer *kesra (see p318)*, a round loaf baked at home or in the local communal oven.

A few *charcuteries*, selling cooked meats, have appeared in Casablanca, Rabat and Marrakech but they are geared to an exclusively Western clientele, pork being forbidden to Muslims. By using a local supermarket, you can check the sell-by dates of fresh produce (when

Semi-precious stones laid out for sale at the roadside, Middle Atlas

marked, that is). Imported foods can also be bought in supermarkets.

Hypermarket chains were set up in Morocco several years ago. There are branches of Marjane, a subsidiary of the French hypermarket Continent, in Casablanca, Rabat, Marrakech and Agadir.

MARKETS

A LL LARGE TOWNS have several markets that supply fresh fruit and vegetables to the population every day of the year. In every market there is a fresh herb stall and a spice and olive stall. Household utensils, basketry and craft items are also on sale.

In the harbours along the Atlantic coast, particularly in the towns of Oualidia, Safi, Essaouira and Agadir, the fruits of the daily catch – such as sole, sardines, perch, shrimps, squid and oysters – can be eaten on the spot.

SOUKS

F OR FOREIGN VISITORS, souks are lively and authentic expressions of rural life in Morocco *(see p201)*, offering the opportunity to see a fascinating and genuine aspect of the country. Taking place once a week, souks are the focus of economic, social and administrative life in Morocco's rural areas. Country people come from miles around to stock up on supplies or to exchange agricultural produce (such as fruit, vegetables, eggs, butter and cereals) or craft items (such as pottery and carpets) for tea, oil, sugar and spices. Also on offer are plastic

A brassware and copperware shop in the Quartier Habbous, Casablanca

utensils and clothing made of synthetic fabrics, along with chickens, sheep and sometimes mules.

In the medinas of Rabat, Fès, Marrakech and Tarou-dannt, souks take place almost daily. Their location and layout are dictated by the nature of what they offer. More oriented towards tourists than are the country souks, they offer a huge range of craft items from all over Morocco. Fassi glazed pottery is by no means identical to that made in Salé or Safi, and it differs from the Berber pottery of the Rif or that made in Tamegroute. Thuya wood *(see p122)* is a speciality of Essaouira; Ouaouzguite carpets are renowned in Tazenakht; and El-Kelaa M'Goun is famous for its daggers.

HOW TO BARGAIN

I N MOROCCO, bargaining is not so much a custom as a duty. Every self-respecting Moroccan uses this method, even when buying vegetables in the souk or renting a hotel room. In craft shops, no prices are marked and the shopkeeper considers it quite natural that potential clients should bargain over the price. When a potential customer shows an interest, the shop-owner will quote an initial price, which often bears no relation to the real price of the object in question but which tests the buyer's willingness to make a counter-offer.

In order to bargain effectively, it is

important to know the value of what you wish to buy or at least to have a price in mind beyond which you will not go. By contrast, if you refuse to raise your offer sufficiently to allow the seller to make a profit, he will not pursue the transaction. The real purpose of bargaining is to obtain the

A bellows merchant in the souk in Marrakech

desired object while feigning indifference. This is why bargaining takes time and should be a subtle game between buyer and seller.

FORGERIES

S OUKS IN medinas and in Morocco's major tourist centres offer "authentic" goods of dubious quality and origin, and for very inflated prices. You are advised to be on your guard against goods that, contrary to what the seller may assure you, are often no more than skilfully concocted and very convincing forgeries.

Vegetables for sale at the Tahar el-Alaoui market in Casablanca

What to Buy in Morocco

Straw basket

Souks in morocco present the visitor with a vast choice of jewellery, leather goods, wrought-iron work, brass and copper, pottery, carpets, basketry and fabrics. But the quantity, colours and sheer diversity of the items on offer can be bewildering and it can be difficult to distinguish quality pieces from inferior ones. Before deciding to buy, it is best to take some time to compare what is on offer in different shops. Country craft items offered for sale in markets are genuine and utilitarian, ranging from the baskets carried by donkeys and combs for carding wool to terracotta coolers for keeping milk or dried meat fresh.

Pouffe
Like other leather goods, this pouffe is made of good-quality goatskin or sheepskin, which, after tanning, is dyed and embroidered.

Ceramics

The place of origin of ceramics can be identified by their colours and decoration. Pottery from Fès is the most refined, that from Salé is glazed in pale colours, and that from Safi features polychrome colours and Berber motifs. Recently, potters have been devising new designs, such as that on the vase shown on the left.

Vase from Safi

Vase

Ashtray
This is an example of Fès blue-glazed ware. The Fassi potting industry goes back to the 10th or 11th centuries.

Decorated *tajine* dish

Plate with a modern design

Wood and Stone Carving

Fès, Tetouan and Azrou are renowned for their carved cedar. In Essaouira, craftsmen work with thuya wood *(see p122)*, making boxes in various shapes, statues, trays, frames and other pieces. In Taroudannt, objects are carved from soft stone, and in Erfoud trinkets and other small items are fashioned from marble.

Inlaid Wood
Boxes and other objects made of thuya are decoratively inlaid with yellow citron wood and ebony or cedar.

Duck carved in stone

Thuya Camel
Small pieces like this figure of a camel are easier to make than larger items, since thuya wood tends to split as it dries out.

METALWARE

Wrought iron, brown-hued copper, bright yellow brass (a mixture of copper and zinc) and nickel silver (a mixture of copper, zinc and nickel) are the main materials used in Moroccan metalware. The finest pieces are engraved or damascened (inlaid with contrasting metal).

Brass tray

Teapot
A squat teapot with tapering lid, made of stainless steel or silver, is an essential piece of equipment for making mint tea.

Lantern

TERRACOTTA

Berber pottery features a combination of simple, sturdy shapes, ochre and brown colours and geometric motifs.

Terracotta kasbah

Berber pottery

SILVER

Silver is the predominant material of Berber jewellery. The most common items are brooches, which Berber women wear in pairs, to secure their veils at each shoulder. The shape and decoration of brooches varies according to the region.

Hand of Fatima, a lucky charm

Anklet

Koumiya dagger

Silver and Coral Necklace
Berber women traditionally wear a lot of jewellery. Today, jewellery is made increasingly often of synthetic resin that mimics the colour of coral.

CLOTHING

Jellabas, loose-fitting hooded cloaks with long sleeves, and *gandouras*, tunics with short sleeves, can be purchased in souks Burnouses, hooded woollen cloaks, are seen in rural areas. Embroidered silk belts, traditionally made in Fès, are highly sought-after but are increasingly difficult to find.

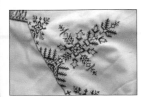

Embroidery
Each city has its own traditions and styles of embroidery. It adorns tablecloths, table napkins, cushions and other items, in a variety of stitches.

A child's *gandoura*

Babouches

Moroccan Carpets

Carpet knot

THERE ARE AS MANY different types of carpets in Morocco as there are tribal traditions. Moroccan carpets can, however, be divided into two main groups: Berber carpets and city carpets. The former are either knotted or woven; they are pleasingly unrefined and each one is unique. Their wool, which the women weave into simple or complex patterns, their harmonious colours, their shape and size, and also their patterns, vary from one region to another. City carpets, influenced by Oriental traditions, are finer. Symbols of luxury, they grace the living rooms of wealthy houses.

The fringe, at one end of the carpet, is part of the warp.

BERBER CARPETS
Most of the carpets made in Tazenaght and Taliouine, in the High Atlas, are made by the Ouaouzguite tribe. These carpets are typically long, narrow and supple, and thus well suited to use in the interiors of kasbahs in the Atlas.

CARPET WEAVING

Carding wool

After the men have sheared the sheep in the spring, the women wash the wool and carefully pick over it. It is then carded, a process by which the strands are untangled by brushing with comb-like implements. Next, the wool is spun into yarn with a small spindle. Either in its natural colour or after it has been dyed, the wool is then ready to be woven. Berber women knot carpets on large, rudimentary looms consisting of two wooden vertical and two horizontal planks. The warp is set up by threading vertical strands vertically on the loom. These determine the length and thickness of the carpet. The weft (the horizontal threads) are threaded by hand between the strands of the warp, the weaver working row by row, pressing the weave together with an iron comb.

Carpet from the High Atlas, in which woven bands alternate with knotted bands. The well ordered geometric motifs feature lozenges, triangles and broken lines.

A weaver in Abachkou

Carpet made by the Zaïane of the Middle Atlas, featuring a combination of strict geometric and random motifs. These carpets are well suited to use in tents or for covering the beaten earth floors of houses.

CITY CARPETS

Woven in Rabat, Salé and Casablanca, city carpets are perfectly symmetrical. They feature floral and geometric motifs and are edged with borders of differing widths.

A carpet seller in the Rue des Consuls in Rabat

BUYING A CARPET

Colour and pattern are the primary considerations when buying a carpet. Then come the material, the carpet's softness, the density of the weave or knotting, and condition. A good-quality carpet has clearly defined motifs and perfectly straight edges. The value of a carpet is based on the number of knots per row and the density of the warp and weft. Some carpets have up to 380 knots per square metre (11 sq ft) and official price bands per square metre apply. Carpets checked by the Ministry of Crafts are hallmarked with the date that they were checked, their provenance and their quality. An orange label indicates extra-superior quality; a blue label, superior quality; a yellow label, medium quality, and green label, ordinary quality. Once the carpet has been unrolled in front of you, you can start to bargain (see p337).

Carpet shop in a crafts complex

Mediouna carpets, made in Casablanca, feature shades of brick red or soft pink, and always have a lozenge-shaped or star-shaped central motif.

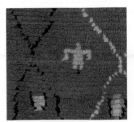

Haouz carpets, made in Marrakech, are knotted. They are characterized by a background scattered with naive motifs.

Middle Atlas carpets have a woollen pile. The exact outlines of the pattern can be seen only on their smooth side.

Dyes are traditionally obtained from vegetable extracts but are now very often supplemented by synthetic dyes.

ENTERTAINMENT IN MOROCCO

MOST NIGHTLIFE in Morocco takes place in the large towns and cities. International tourism and the desire for modernity on the part of the younger generation have both contributed to the development of centres of culture and entertainment. These are often the best places to meet young Moroccans. The number of fashionable

The Rialto, one of Casablanca's cinemas

bars and nightclubs is increasing, too, while Morocco's thriving cultural life ensures a wide variety of entertainment. Certain private art galleries showcase the country's artistic talent. The many feast days and *moussems* (pilgrimage festivals) provide opportunities to watch shows that are more authentically Moroccan than those aimed at tourists.

The Institut Français de Casablanca, a good source of cultural information

INFORMATION SOURCES

SCANNING the entertainment section of various newspapers (entitled *"Spectacles"* in Francophone publications) is the best way of checking what's on, even though they give such information only very irregularly.

The main daily newspapers are *El-Bayane, Le Matin du Sahara* and *Libération.* Weeklies include *Le Magazine* and *Les Nouvelles du Nord.* Monthly magazines, such as *Femmes du Maroc* and *Citadine,* or the fortnightly *Medina,* carry listings of cultural events. These publications are available from kiosks as well as in most tobacconists.

There are no good sources of entertainment information available in English.

CINEMAS

TAKING UP the threads of the movie culture that the country enjoyed in the 1950s, when Moroccans had the privilege of seeing early screenings of many American productions, Moroccan cinemas are enjoying a new lease of life as is, to a certain extent, the new Moroccan film industry *(see p29).* Authentically restored auditoriums dating from the 1940s have reopened, particularly in Casablanca. The main cinemas in Rabat are the **Renaissance** and the **Dawliz**, a complex located on the outskirts of the city and comprising three auditoriums, a bar and restaurant. In Casablanca there is the **Rialto**, the **Dawliz**, the **Lynx** and the new **Megarama** in Fès the **Empire** and the **Rex**; and, in Marrakech, the **Colisée.** In Tangier, the leading cinemas are the

Dawliz, **Le Paris** and the **Rif**. But if you don't understand French or Arabic, this might not be your first choice of entertainment since almost all films are dubbed in French, or are in Arabic.

Daily local newspapers provide information on what is showing, or you can phone the cinemas themselves. The cultural institutes in various cities *(see p344)* are also good sources of information.

THEATRES

MOROCCO IS not well endowed with theatres. They are found only in the cities, and productions are usually limited and irregular. Nevertheless, foreign theatrical companies perform in Morocco, and efforts are being made to launch the Moroccan theatre, which is still in its infancy.

Although theatre listings are usually given in the daily press, it is best to obtain information directly from the theatres or from cultural institutions.

The Feast of the Throne, a highly colourful and popular event

FEAST DAYS AND FESTIVALS

PROMINENT AMONG the many feast days that punctuate the year *(see pp38–41)* are the *moussems*. These large popular gatherings usually focus on the tomb of a saint *(see pp198–9)*, and are spectacular shows with traditional dance performances.

Certain festivals, such as the Marrakech Folk Festival in June, draw dancers and musicians from all over Morocco, and the Gnaoua Music Festival in Essaouira, also in June, offers high-quality performances. Other festivals include the Sacred World Music Festival held in Fès in June and the Rabat Cultural Festival in July. Fantasias *(pp34–5)* are typically high-spirited Moroccan shows. They are performed most famously at the *moussem* of Moulay Abdallah, which takes place near El-Jadida in August.

The types of dances vary between the different Berber and rural tribes. Often performed are the *abouach* of the High Atlas and Ouarzazate, and the *ahidou* of the Middle Atlas, in which men and women take part. The *guedra*, a dance from the Guelmim and Sahara, is performed by one woman within a circle of musicians.

A group performing at the Festival of Andalusian Music in Fès

SHOWS AND CONCERTS

LARGE HOTELS often organize Moroccan evenings giving visitors a chance to see authentic popular performances of music and dance.

Certain restaurants also put on performances of folk dance in the evenings. At **Chez Ali** in Marrakech, on certain evenings guests are served their meal in a tent while a fantasia is performed.

Those interested in hearing Moroccan music *(see p26)* can choose between *raï*, which has roots in Bedouin music and whose star performer is Cheb Amrou; Gnaoua music *(see p27)*, which Mustapha Baqbou has taken to many European jazz festivals; and the nostalgic chants of Andalusian music. Many such concerts are organized by various cultural institutes. Ask the local tourist office for information.

DIRECTORY

CINEMAS

AGADIR

Rialto
Avenue des F.A.R.
((048) 84 10 12.

CASABLANCA

Dawliz
Boulevard de la Corniche.
((022) 39 54 76.

Lynx
150 Avenue Mers Sultan.
((022) 22 02 29.

Megarama
Boulevard de la Corniche.
((022) 79 88 88.

Rialto
35 Rue Med Qorri.
((022) 26 26 32.

FÈS

Empire
60 Avenue Hassan II.
((055) 62 28 64.

Rex
Corner of Avenue Mohammed Es-Slaoui and Boulevard Mohammed V.
((055) 62 24 96.

MARRAKECH

Colisée
Boulevard M. Zerktouni.
((044) 44 88 93.

RABAT

Dawliz
Bd du Bou Regreg, Salé.
((037) 88 15 98.

Renaissance
266 Avenue Mohammed V.
((037) 72 21 68.

TANGIER

Dawliz
42 Rue de Hollande.
((039) 33 33 77.

Le Paris
11 Rue de Fès.
((039) 93 58 16.

Rif
Place du 9 Avril 1947.
((039) 93 46 83.

THEATRES

AGADIR

Théâtre Municipal de Plein Air
Avenue Mohammed V.
((048) 84 07 84.

CASABLANCA

Complexe Culturel du Maarif
Rue Oussama Ibn Zaid.
((022) 25 10 07.

Complex Culturel de Sidi-Belyout
28 Rue Léon l'Africain.
((022) 30 44 49.

Théâtre Municipal
140 Avenue des F.A.R.
((022) 31 12 64.

RABAT

Théâtre Mohammed V
Charia al Mansour Eddahbi.
((037) 70 73 00.

Salle Haj Mohammed Bahnini
1 Rue Gandhi.
((037) 70 80 37.

SHOWS

Chez Ali
After Pont de Tensift.
((022) 44 30 77 30.

The Villa des Arts in Casablanca, which opened in 1999

CULTURAL CENTRES

AMONG THE MOST dynamic cultural centres in Morocco are the **French Cultural Institutes**, which are found in major cities. These organize a wide-ranging programme, including exhibitions, film festivals highlighting the work of particular directors, as well as concerts and theatrical performances. The remarkably well laid-out **Institut Français de Marrakech** even has an amphitheatre for open-air performances. The Spanish **Instituto Cervantes** and the German **Goethe Institüt** also contribute to the promotion of the artistic activity of the multiple cultures that coexist in Morocco.

These centres are good places to meet Moroccans who have an interest in Europe. Programmes in the form of a bimonthly pamphlet are available on the premises. The **British Council** in Rabat also organizes an interesting range of events.

ART GALLERIES

SINCE THE DANE **Frederic Damgaard** *(see p124)*, opened an art gallery in Essaouira in 1988, the artistic world in Morocco has enjoyed a new dynamism. Galleries, for example **L'Orange Bleue**, exhibit the work of painters from far and wide, including, for example, that of the well-known "free artists of Essaouira" *(see p125)*. Galleries in Casablanca include the **Villa des Arts**, an extensive showcase of Moroccan artistic creativity

over the last 50 years, and in Marrakech the **Matisse Arts Gallery** and **Dar Bellarj**.

PIANO BARS

PLACES WHERE traditional Moroccan music can be heard are relatively few. However, piano bars in large hotels

Painting by Mohammed Tabal, one of Essaouira's "free artists"

and jazz clubs offer the opportunity of hearing European and North American bands.

The **Amstrong Jazz Bar** and the **Villa Fandango** in Casablanca, for example, are very fashionable. Marrakech has several modish venues such as the huge **A l'Anbar**, whose restaurant contains several hundred tables and has live orchestras, and the **Montecristo**, which is more intimate and is located in one

of Gueliz's villas. In Essaouira, Fès, Ouarzazate, Rabat and Tangier, it is mostly in hotel bars that music can be heard. The best approach is to obtain information directly from the various bars and hotels themselves.

NIGHTCLUBS

EXCEPT IN CASABLANCA and Rabat, most nightclubs in Morocco are located within hotels. In Rabat, one of the most fashionable discos is **L'Amnesia**. In Casablanca, night clubs are concentrated around Aïn-Diab. They include **La Notte**, the **Vanity Lounge** and the **Barosa Club**. **Le Diamant Noir** in Marrakech has a good reputation, as does **Le Flamingo** in Agadir.

While discos and nightclubs are relatively empty on weekday nights, all are filled to capacity at weekends and during school holidays.

Some close at about 3am or 4am. Others stay open until dawn, particularly in Marrakech, Agadir and other large tourist centres.

CASINOS

GAMBLING IS severely frowned on by Islam, so that there are very few casinos in Morocco. The casino in **La Mamounia**, the famous hotel in Marrakech *(see p310)*, is easily the most prestigious.

If you decide to spend the evening in a casino, dress smartly. A jacket is essential, and jeans, tracksuits and trainers are definitely not acceptable.

Night club in Agadir, with dancing beneath a replica of the Eiffel Tower

DIRECTORY

CULTURAL CENTRES

AGADIR

Institut Français d'Agadir
Rue Cheinguit,
Nouveau Talborjt.
(048) 82 59 95.

CASABLANCA

Dante Alighieri
4 Rue d'Aquitaine.
(022) 26 01 45.

Goethe Institüt
11 Place du 16 Novembre.
(022) 26 30 75.

Instituto Cervantes
31 Rue d'Alger.
(022) 26 73 37.

Institut Français de Casablanca
121 Boulevard Zerktouni.
(022) 25 21 21.

FÈS

Institut Français de Fès
33 Rue Loukili.
(055) 62 39 21.

MARRAKECH

Institut Français de Marrakech
Route de Targa,
Jbel Gueliz.
(044) 44 71 15.

RABAT

British Council
36 Rue de Tanger.
(037) 76 08 36.

Instituto Cervantes
5 Rue Madnine.
(037) 70 87 38.

Institut Français de Rabat
2 Rue el-Yanboua.
(037) 70 11 38.

TANGIER

Instituto Cervantes
9 Rue de Belgique.
(039) 94 76 30.

Institut Français de Tanger
41 Rue Hassan Ibn Ouazzan
(039) 94 10 54.

ART GALLERIES

AGADIR

Artomagnia
El-Faïs Brahim estate
(next to the Ecole Pigier),
industrial quarter.
(048) 82 26 77.

CASABLANCA

Almanar
Rue 204, No.19,
Boulevard de la Corniche.
(022) 39 54 76.

Venise Cadre
65 Rue Allal Ben Abdallah.
(022) 31 05 76.

Villa des Arts
ℹ *(022) 29 50 87.*

ESSAOUIRA

Galerie Frederic Damgaard
Avenue Oqba Ibn Nafiaa.
(044) 78 44 46.

L'Orange Bleue
18, Rue de Zayan.
(062) 60 73 13.

MARRAKECH

Dar Bellarj
9 Toualate Zaouite Lahdar.
(044) 44 45 55.

Matisse Arts Gallery
61 Rue de Yougoslavie.
(044) 44 83 26.

RABAT

Le Manoir,
7 Rue Baitlahm.
(037) 70 80 31.

TANGIER

Lawrence Arnott Art Gallery
68 Rue Amr Ibn Ass
(039) 33 34 82.

PIANO BARS

CASABLANCA

Amstrong Jazz Bar
41 Boulevard de la Corniche.
(022) 39 76 56.

Villa Fandango
Rue de la Mer Egée,
Boulevard de la Corniche.
(022) 79 85 08.

ESSAOUIRA

L'Orson Welles
Hôtel Les Îles, Boulevard
Mohammed V.
(044) 78 36 36.

FÈS

Le Birdy
Jnan Palace hotel, Avenue
Ahmed Chaouki.
(055) 65 22 30.

Le Lobby
Sheraton, Av. des F.A.R.
(055) 93 19 34 /37.

MARRAKECH

A l'Anbar
47 Rue Jbel Lakhadar
(044) 38 07 62.

Le Churchill
La Mamounia Hotel,
Bab el-Jedid.
(044) 40 59 50.

Le Monecristo
20 Rue Ibn Aïcha.
(044) 43 90 31.

OUARZAZATE

Le Piano-Bar
Hôtel Kenzi Bélère, Avenue
du Prince Moulay Rachid.
(044) 88 28 03.

Zagora Bar
Hôtel Karam Palace,
(044) 88 22 25.

RABAT

Club Five
Hôtel Safir,
Place Sidi Makhlouf.
(037) 73 47 47.

Hamilton Travel Bar
Hilton, Souissi quarter.
(037) 67 56 56.

Le Puzzle
79 Avenue Ibn Sina.
(037) 67 00 30.

TANGIER

Le Blue Dahlia
42 Rue de Hollande.
(039) 33 18 20.

Le Caïd's
Hôtel El-Minzah
85 Rue de la Liberté.
(039) 93 58 85.

Le Palace
Hôtel Tanjah-Flandria1.
Boulevard Med V.
(039) 93 30 00.

NIGHTCLUBS

AGADIR

Le Flamingo
Hôtel Beach Club.
(048) 84 43 24.

CASABLANCA

La Notte
25 Boulevard de la Corniche.
(022) 36 73 61.

Le Barosa
Hotel Riad Salam, Boulevard
de Corniche.
(022) 39 12 28.

Le Vanity Lounge
41 Boulevard de la Corniche.
(022) 79 76 57.

MARRAKECH

Le Diamant Noir
Hôtel Le Marrakech,
Place de la Liberté.
(044) 43 43 51.

RABAT

L'Amnesia
18 Rue Monastir.
(037) 70 18 60.

CASINO

MARRAKECH

La Mamounia Hotel
Bab el-Jedid.
(044) 40 59 50/51.

SPORT AND OUTDOOR ACTIVITIES

OROCCO'S MOSTLY WARM climate and great topographical diversity make it suitable for all sorts of sports and outdoor activities. The natural environment, often on a majestic scale, readily lends itself to horseback riding, trekking, birdwatching and, in winter, skiing. In areas suitably developed for the purpose, the Moroccan landscape is also a paradise for golfers.

The Atlantic coast is internationally renowned for surfing and sailboarding. More recently, thalassotherapy (therapeutic treatment using sea water and marine products) has also developed, and thalassotherapy centres continue to burgeon in the major tourist centres.

The beach at Agadir, where horseback rides are available

HORSEBACK RIDING

THANKS TO the impulse provided by King Hassan II, horseback riding has become very popular in Morocco. Many equestrian centres have been established, and an International Equestrian Week takes place every year in Dar es-Salam, near Rabat, where the **Fédération Royale Marocaine des Sports Equestres** is based.

Most horseback riding is organized by clubs and large hotels, mainly those in Agadir, Marrakech and Ouarzazate. All equestrian centres are staffed by instructors with state-approved qualifications.

SKIING

ALTHOUGH MOROCCO is not primarily a winter sports destination, the country has several high-altitude resorts, including Ifrane *(see p212),* near Fès, and Oukaïmeden *(see p248),* 60 km (37 miles) from Marrakech. Oukaïmeden can be reached by *grand taxi* for a one-way fare of about 300 to 400 dirhams.

Although the resort is small, it is equipped with all the necessary facilities, including ski-lifts located near where ski equipment is hired. Hiring equipment for a day costs about 250 dirhams. Skiers can sleep in one of several gîtes. These elegant rest-houses are built in a combined European and traditional Moroccan style.

There are not many areas of the country that are suitable for skiing, so this remains a marginal activity in Morocco. Mountain resorts offer a diverse range of activities, however, including hang gliding, hiking and trekking *(see pp348–9).*

GOLF

AN INCREASING NUMBER of overseas travel agents offer packaged golfing holidays. Over the last ten years, 14 golf links have been created in Morocco. Many are very pleasant, and popular with golfers. In addition, there are the royal golf courses (which are open to the public) and numerous private courses, the latter often forming part of hotel complexes, particularly in Agadir and Marrakech.

In April, the height of the holiday season, visitors are advised to book in advance so as to avoid a long wait. A handicap is theoretically required although in practice this is always overlooked.

Oukaïmeden *(see p248),* renowned for its pistes

One of the many fine golf courses in Morocco

There are some excellent golf coaches in Morocco, and their services can be hired for much less than in Europe and the US. The low cost of tuition, combined with an often outstanding natural environment, are ideal conditions for an introduction to the sport.

TENNIS

ALMOST ALL the large hotels have tennis courts. The major towns and cities are also well provided with tennis clubs. Most of them have beaten earth courts, of which the condition can vary. Around the courts it is not unusual to see young Moroccans, who readily offer their services as ball boys or tennis partners. Many are good players.

BIRD-WATCHING

MOROCCO OFFERS many excellent opportunities for bird-watching, and many travellers, particularly Britons and Americans, tailor their visit around this interest.

Morocco has a small number of bird sanctuaries, the most important of them being at Sous Massa, south of Agadir (see p292), and at Moulay Bousselham, north of Rabat (see p90). The latter attracts large numbers of migratory birds, including some rare species.

Unfortunately, these areas are being threatened by the massive urban development that is spreading along the Moroccan coastline, despite the efforts of associations for the protection of birds.

OFF-ROAD DRIVING

MOROCCO IS an excellent country for off-road activities, either in a four-wheel-drive vehicle or on a motorbike. The good network of tracks, even near large towns, means that the hinterland is always within easy reach.

It is, however, advisable to check your route thoroughly and preferable to travel in groups of two or more vehicles, since breaking down in a remote spot can be a real problem. Some areas, particularly in southern Morocco, near the border with Mauritania, are patrolled by the army and may be set with land mines. It is unwise to venture into this territory without the help of a reliable guide.

In Marrakech and Ouarzazate quad bikes and go-karts can be hired and **Wilderness Wheels** (see p349) organises all-inclusive motorcycle excursions into the High Atlas mountains and the desert .

WATERSPORTS

FOR WINDSURFERS, certain spots along Morocco's Atlantic coast are among the best in the world. Essaouira and its environs are the best-known locations, and these are Morocco's windsurfing centres, particularly in

Sailing, a popular sport off the Atlantic and Mediterranean coasts

DIRECTORY

HORSEBACK RIDING

Fédération Royale Marocaine des Sports Equestres
📞 (037) 75 44 24 (Rabat).

SKIING

Fédération Royale Marocaine de Ski et Montagne
📞 (022) 47 49 79 (Casablanca).

GOLF

Fédération Royale Marocaine de Golf
📞 (022) 36 53 55 (Casablanca).
📞 (037) 75 59 60 (Rabat).

WATERSPORTS

Windsurfing Centre
📞 (044) 47 34 05. (Essaouira).

Fédération Royale Marocaine de Ski Nautique
📞 (037) 67 09 56 (Rabat).

summer. Most of these places are, however, suitable only for experienced windsurfers. Strong winds, currents and the high Atlantic waves are not safe for beginners.

The best surfing beaches are also on the Atlantic coast. In summer, the beaches between Agadir and Essaouira are overrun by surfers from all over the world. A particularly popular beach is La Madrague, near Taghazout, 20 km (12 miles) north of Agadir. There is also a **Windsurfing Centre** in Essaouira.

For less strenuous watersports, there are also some very fine beaches all along the Atlantic and Mediterranean coasts. On the Mediterranean coast, sailing boats and jet-skis can be hired.

Information on water-skiing, which is also available, can be obtained from the **Fédération Royale Marocaine de Ski Nautique**.

Hiking and Trekking

Cotton
sun hat

IN THE SPACE of a few years, Morocco has become a paradise for hikers. The country's spectacular and varied landscape offers great scope for hikers and trekkers of all abilities. However, any hiking or trekking expedition requires preparation. It is essential to take proper equipment, and basic safety precautions must be observed. Options are many – whether to go on an organized or an independent trek, and whether or not to have porters: luggage carried by mule, camel or vehicle. The most important decision is the choice of route through Morocco's numerous and highly diverse geographical regions.

A hike in the South, with luggage carried by camels

Mountain biking, an increasingly popular activity in Morocco

BASIC SAFETY PRECAUTIONS

THE FIRST CONSIDERATION is your physical condition. You must be able to withstand the sometimes arduous demands of a long trek. Do not venture even a little way off the beaten track without a reliable guide, or unless you are on a well-organized trek. Never set off alone, and if you are not part of an organized party, inform your next of kin or your country's embassy of your intended date of return so that emergency aid can be sent if necessary. The cost of mountain rescue in the more remote regions of Morocco is very high. Check your personal insurance to see whether it will cover you for this type of risk.

By far the best option is to let a specialist agency arrange your hike or trek. This may be a Western tour operator or one of the specialist agencies

in Morocco. Using their infrastructure and logistics will give you peace of mind.

EQUIPMENT

THE MOST IMPORTANT piece of equipment is a good pair of walking boots. Even though ordinary trainers may be quite adequate for a short walk on even ground, a strong pair of walking boots is essential for longer and more demanding walking over rough ground.

As for clothing, strong, lightweight fabrics are the best choice. Although it rarely rains in Morocco, it is prudent to pack a rainproof garment as well as a few warm clothes, since temperatures drop quickly at high altitudes. Finally, even for a short walk, always take enough water, and something to eat.

A first-aid kit is also necessary. The minimum that it should contain is treatment for minor cuts and blisters. More adequate first-aid equipment will also include anti-venom treatment, insect repellent, antihistamine for allergies, aspirins and sunblock cream.

For nights in a tent or in the open air, a good-quality body-hugging sleeping bag is recommended. Check carefully its insulating properties, but bear in mind that you will still need a light mattress

to insulate you from cold or wet ground.

Finally, it is the small things that can be the most useful. Head lamps, for example, give you light while also leaving your hands free. Also remember to pack water-purifying tablets, so that you can drink from springs and refreshing mountain streams along the way.

TYPES OF HIKING

SOME HIKES are organized with the advantage of using animals to carry equipment. Hikes with mules take place in the Atlas, a region where this animal is particularly at home. Further south, camels are used to carry luggage and food supplies. Caravans of camels are a common sight here, particularly south of Zagora.

It is also possible to go on combined treks, alternating walking with mountain biking, or with canoeing or rafting. Vehicle-assisted treks allow greater distances to be

Participants in the Marathon des Sables

Four-wheel-drive vehicles, essential for negotiating rough tracks

covered. More luggage can also be carried, which means that camping can be much more comfortable.

POPULAR ROUTES

THE MAIN REGIONS of Morocco that are most suitable for trekking and hiking are the Atlantic coast; the Middle Atlas, High Atlas and Atlantic slopes of the Atlas; Jbel Sirwa and Jbel Sarhro; the valleys of Wadi Draa, Wadi Dadès and Wadi Tafilalet; and the Saharan provinces of the South.

In the High Atlas, Jbel Toubkal, which reaches a height of 4,167 m (13,676 ft), is the highest point in North Africa *(see p249)*. The mountain offers great scope for hikes. The summit can be reached in two days and climbing it does not require a high level of experience as a mountaineer. The only disadvantage is the fact that this is where most hikers come in the high season, so you will not be alone. The **Club Alpin Français** manages five refuges on Jbel Toubkal.

In the central High Atlas, the Aït Bouguemez valley *(see pp254–7)* offers a very fine itinerary. The route is not very demanding and passes through a striking variety of different landscapes. This expedition to the deep heart of Berber country takes five to six days, and the starting point is Demnate, four hours' drive from Marrakech.

On the other side of the Atlas, there are hikes that combine Jbel Sarhro, the foothills at the edge of the Sahara, and the sublime Dadès gorge *(see p273)*, one of the great attractions of the Moroccan South.

Many camel treks take place southwest of Zagora, their ultimate destination being Mhamid and Iriki, where the first dunes of the immense Sahara can be seen. Further east, towards Erfoud *(see p280)*, the spectacular Merzouga dunes *(see p281)* offer many possibilities for hikes and camel rides through unforgettable scenery.

MARATHON DES SABLES

THIS LONG-DISTANCE race takes place in the Ouarzazate region every year. About 700 competitors from all over the world take part. The route covers 230 km (143 miles) and the race lasts seven days. Each competitor carries his or her own food and equipment. The Marathon des Sables is considered to be the most demanding race of its kind in the world.

Jbel Toubkal, to which large numbers of hikers are drawn

DIRECTORY

SPECIALIST TOUR OPERATORS

Backroads
801 Cedar Street, Berkeley, CA 94710-1800, USA.
☎ 1-800 228 8747.

Discover
Timbers, Oxted Road, Godstone, Surrey RH9 8AD, UK.
☎ 01883 744 392.
W www.kasbahdutoubkal.com

Exodus
9 Weir Rd, London SW12 0LT, UK.
☎ 020 8675 5550.
W www.exodus.co.uk

Morocco Travel International
5146 Leesburgh Pike, Alexandria, VA 22302, USA.
☎ 1-800 428 5550.

Overseas Adventure Travel
625 Mount Auburn St, Cambridge, MA 02138, USA.
☎ 1-800 221 0814.

Ramblers Holidays
Box 34, Welwyn Garden City, Herts, AL8 6PQ, UK.
☎ 01707 331 133.
W www.ramblersholidays.co.uk

Sherpa Expeditions
131a Heston Road, Hounslow, Middlesex TW5 0RD, UK.
☎ 020 8577 2717.
W www.sherpaexpeditions.com

AGENCIES IN MOROCCO

Atlas Sahara Trek
6 bis Rue HoudHoud, Majorelle Quarter, Marrakech.
☎ (044) 31 39 01.

Club Alpin Français
BP 6178, Casablanca.
☎ (022) 27 00 90.

Sport Travel
Third floor, 154 Boulevard Mohammed V, Gueliz, Marrakech.
☎ (044) 43 05 59.

Wilderness Wheels
☎ (044) 96 08 69 (Ouarzazate).
W www.wildernesswheels.com

SURVIVAL
GUIDE

PRACTICAL INFORMATION

OROCCO, A COUNTRY with a wide range of attractions, receives a large number of visitors. Much of its economic success is due to tourism. The country has a good tourism infra-structure and tourist offices, both at home and abroad. Moroccan hotels have undergone major restructuring and many regions have significantly increased their capacity to

**Berber
from the Sahara**

accommodate visitors. The major museums and historic monuments have been reorganized so as to be seen to their best advantage by the maximum number of visitors. Customs formalities are minimal and while French is the most widely spoken foreign lan-guage, at least the bigger hotels and restaurants and all tourist offices have English-speaking staff.

Summer crowds on the beach at Casablanca

WHEN TO GO

MOROCCO IS a relatively large country with a varied climate, ranging from the arid, desert conditions of the south to the Mediterranean climate of the north *(see pp42–3)*.

The peak of the tourist season in the South, is in spring, from March to mid-May, and, to a lesser extent, in the early autumn, in September and October. At those times, visitors can enjoy many hours of sunshine and almost no rain.

Summer is the best time to visit the Mediterranean and Atlantic coasts. The South and the Centre, where the heat is then intense, are best avoided. Even when the winters are mild they are still very cold, and snowfall at high altitude, which can close passes, may interfere with your itinerary.

RESERVATIONS

MOROCCO IS a fashionable tourist destination, and the publicity campaigns that are mounted to advertise its attractions are effective in

attracting large numbers of visitors. Some 3 million tourists visit Morocco each year.

Most months are busy and hotel reservations have become essential. It is best to arrange your visit several months in advance, so as to be able to use the most direct flights and the most convenient schedules, and particularly if you want to reserve a room in smaller hotels and guesthouses, which have more character and which get booked up quickly.

Tourist brochure

TOURIST INFORMATION

ALL THE MAJOR tourist centres in Morocco have a branch of the Office National Marocain du Tourisme (ONMT), which often goes under the name "Délégation Générale du Tourisme". Smaller towns have a Syndicat d'Initiative (tourist bureau). These bureaux provide information on the town's principal features of interest, and the addresses of hotels

and restaurants. Official guides are also usually available. The Délégations Générales and Syndicats d'Initiative are open from 8.30am to noon and from 2.30pm to 6.30pm. During Ramadan and in summer, in the busiest towns and cities they are open continuously from 9am to 5pm. Before leaving home, you may also wish to contact the Moroccan tourist office in your own country.

ENTRY CHARGES AND OPENING HOURS

AN ENTRY CHARGE (usually about 10 to 20 dirhams) is made for museums and historic sites and buildings. When entry is free, it is customary to give the caretaker a tip equal to the average value of an entry ticket. Opening hours can be irregular. Tourist sites are generally open from 9am to noon and from 3 to 6pm. However, these times may change during Ramadan and at times of the year when the heat is very intense. The opening of smaller sites sometimes depends on the goodwill of the caretaker.

PASSPORTS AND VISAS

CITIZENS OF the European Union, Swiss nationals and citizens of the United States, Canada, Australia and New Zealand need a valid passport to visit Morocco. A passport, which should be valid for at least six months after the date of your arrival,

Entrance to the Dar Si Saïd Museum in Marrakech

allows you to stay in Morocco for three months. If this period is exceeded, the authorities react strictly and at the very least will escort you back to the frontier.

If you intend to stay in Morocco for more than three months, you will need to obtain a visa. Information on entry formalities is available from the Moroccan Consulate in your home country.

The border with Algeria is closed and no-one can cross over into Mauritania without authorization from the Ministry of the Interior.

Customs

DURING YOUR FLIGHT to Morocco, or when you arrive at the border, you will

be handed a customs declaration form which you should fill in and hand over at passport control. You are legally entitled to bring into the country 200 cigarettes, 75 cl of alcohol and small quantities of photographic material and video equipment.

Drugs, firearms and pornographic material are strictly prohibited. Permission must be obtained to bring in hunting weapons.

Importing a vehicle for a limited period is possible but the formalities are very lengthy. The vehicle should be registered in your exact first name and surname.

Language

THE OFFICIAL LANGUAGE is Arabic, which is spoken by almost all Moroccans. French, a vestige of the Protectorate, is also very widely used, at least in large towns. It is less current in country areas, except among older people. In the South, Berber is widely spoken, especially in rural areas.

Sign in a town, in French and Arabic

Because of the city's proximity to Spain, Spanish is widely understood in Tangier, and is spoken in the Spanish enclaves. German is most often heard in Agadir, which attracts large numbers of Germans. English is spoken only by those closely involved in the tourist industry, such as guides and certain staff in the larger hotels.

Trekkers following a high mountain trail in an arid region of Morocco

EMBASSIES IN MOROCCO

Canada
13 Bis, Rue Jaafar As-Sadik, Rabat.
(037) 68 74 00.

United Kingdom
17 Boulevard Hassan, Rabat.
(037) 72 96 96.

United States
2 Avenue Mohamed el-Fassi, Rabat. (037) 62 22 65.

CONSULATES IN MOROCCO

United Kingdom
9 Rue Amérique du Sud, Tangier.
(09) 93 58 95.
British Commercial Consulate, 60 Boulevard d'Anfa, Casablanca.
(02) 22 16 53.

United States
8 Boulevard Moulay Youssef, Casablanca.
(02) 36 15 88.

Citizens of Australia and Eire may use the United Kingdom embassy and consulate. Citizens of New Zealand may use the Canadian embassy.

USEFUL WEBSITES

Adventures of Morocco
W www.lexicorient.com/morocco
General information, maps, encyclopedia of Arabic words and useful links.

Arab.net
W www.arab.net/morocco
Background information on Moroccan history and culture.

Moroccan Links
W www.maroc.net/ipm/maroc.html
Wide-ranging directory of websites on Morocco.

Tourism in Morocco
W www.tourism-in-Morocco.com
IOn tourist attractions and leisure activities.

US Consular Travel Advisory
W travel.state.gov/morocco/html
Strictly practical matters, such as entry requirements for US citizens, personal safety, etc.

Etiquette

MOROCCANS ARE very friendly people. You will have many opportunities to talk to them, and may even be invited into their homes. However, Morocco is a Muslim country and certain conventions must be observed to avoid inadvertently causing offence. It is especially important to dress appropriately, not to take photographs of Moroccans without their permission, and to avoid certain sensitive subjects in conversation. If you are invited into the home of a Moroccan family, it is as well to be aware of certain points of etiquette. Respecting a few simple rules will be appreciated by your naturally hospitable hosts.

Mint tea served to guests, one aspect of Moroccan hospitality

HOSPITALITY

AMONG MOROCCANS, hospitality is more than a tradition; it is an honour. After just a few minutes of conversation, traders in the souks and country people in the remotest regions of the Atlas may well invite you into their homes to drink a glass of tea or share a meal. It is difficult to decline these invitations, and a refusal may be interpreted as an offence.

When you enter a house, take your shoes off if shoes have already been left near the door; this is a sign of respect towards your host. It is often the men who will invite you in, although you are sure to see the women of the house as well, in which case avoid being over-familiar. Accepting an invitation from a trader in a souk puts you under no obligation to buy anything from him. Finally, even if you are invited in by Moroccans of very modest means, never offer to pay for your meal. Offering a small gift is a far better and more acceptable way of thanking your hosts.

SHARING A MEAL

IIF YOU ARE INVITED to share a meal in the home of a Moroccan family, be prepared

Moroccans customarily eat with their right hand

to be plied with copious helpings of food. As with other invitations, it is difficult to refuse first let alone second helpings of food.

People usually eat with their fingers, with the additional aid of a piece of bread. If you cannot master the technique, you will be given eating implements. When eating, you should use your right hand since the left hand, used for personal hygiene, is traditionally considered to be impure.

A Moroccan meal invariably ends with mint tea. It is not unusual to drink three or four glasses of this very sweet infusion. Again, the offer is very hard to refuse.

PHOTOGRAPHY

YOU CAN TAKE photographs almost anywhere in Morocco. In some museums, a supplementary fee is charged if you want to take photographs, and in others photography is forbidden.

Avoid taking pictures of military or official buildings since this may result in your film being confiscated and your being questioned at length about what you were trying to photograph.

Before turning the lens on anyone, always ask the person's permission, since Moroccans have an ingrained suspicion of any type of image. Bear in mind that anyone who agrees to your photographing them may ask you for a little money, especially in the major tourist spots.

MUSLIM CUSTOMS

ISLAM IS A state religion and the king of Morocco is the leader of the faithful. It is thus considered very bad form to criticize religion. It is also ill-mannered to disturb someone while they are at prayer, whether by speaking to them or by taking a photograph of them.

It is above all during Ramadan that certain rules must be obeyed. The fast of Ramadan is strictly observed in Morocco. Although non-Muslims may eat, drink and

The Grand Mosque in Casablanca, open to non-Muslims

smoke whenever they please, they should avoid doing so in public. Lastly, couples in the street must behave with decorum; they should not kiss in public, for example.

VISITING MOSQUES

ALL MOSQUES, except the Grand Mosque in Casablanca and the old Tin Mal Mosque, are closed to non-Muslims. When visiting these mosques, remove your shoes and behave in a respectful manner, appropriate to the holy nature of the building.

Never insist on being admitted to a mosque and do not try to see inside it by peeping through the door. Acting like this is likely to be considered sacrilegious.

DRESS

ATTITUDES TOWARDS dress have changed significantly in Morocco, so that, in large towns and cities, it is far from unusual to see Moroccan women in Western-style dress. Even so, scanty clothing should not be worn when exploring traditional quarters of towns or venturing into the country. Very short skirts, shorts and clothes that leave the shoulders or chest bare are likely to cause deep offence to Moroccans. For women, wearing a headscarf may help avoid unwanted attention. Women going topless, on the beach or in the swimming pool, is severely frowned on. Nudity is strictly forbidden in Morocco, and nudists run the risk of being arrested.

THE MONARCHY

SINCE THE ACCESSION of Mohammed VI, attitudes towards the monarchy are now much more relaxed. You may even hear Moroccans openly criticizing the king. Even so, the subject of the monarchy is surrounded by a great deal of taboo in Morocco. As a general rule, do not express too trenchant an opinion on the subject and never show disrespect towards the king's image,

which can be seen hanging in all shops and public places. Lastly, be aware that the Moroccans are very patriotic and that any discussion of their country can quickly become heated.

BARGAINING

YOU MAY BITTERLY disappoint a trader if you do not show a willingness to indulge in the ritual of bargaining, another Moroccan custom.

Bargaining revolves around the considerable difference between the price quoted by the buyer and that offered by the seller and the slow process by which both sides arrive at a mutually fair figure.

When bargaining, you should keep smiling since the whole process is treated as a game.

Moroccan women, customarily fully dressed, on the beach

SMOKING

PUBLIC PLACES very rarely have no-smoking areas. However, smoking is now prohibited in most buses and modern cinemas.

Except in large towns and cities, where attitudes have changed, it may still be considered shocking for women to smoke in public. Smoking *kif* (marijuana) is technically illegal, and it is best to avoid any contact with dealers.

Tourist negotiating the price of a camel ride

Health and Security

Mosquito repellent

CRIME IN MOROCCO is no worse than elsewhere and most visitors will experience no serious problems. The fact that the police have a high-profile presence contributes to this degree of personal safety. As in any other country, a few basic precautions should be taken so as to avoid the attentions of pickpockets. Visitors should also be aware that drug-taking, especially in the north of the country, is one of the prime threats to personal safety. The best policy is to have nothing whatsoever to do with drugs, however mild. While the standard of Morocco's public hospitals is uneven, private clinics are very expensive. It is advisable to take out health insurance in your own country before you leave.

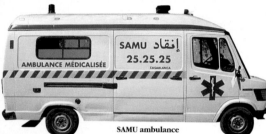

SAMU ambulance

VACCINATIONS AND MINOR HEALTH RISKS

NO VACCINATIONS are required for visitors entering Morocco, except for those coming from a country where yellow fever exists. However, vaccination against hepatitis A and B and typhoid is advised. Visiting certain regions of southern Morocco in summer carries a slight risk of exposure to malaria; anti-malaria pills are available locally.

However long you plan to stay in Morocco, and wherever you intend to go, take a first-aid kit with you. It should include gauze, bandages, antiseptic and syringes, particularly if you intend to spend any time in sparsely inhabited rural areas.

To prevent sunstroke, drink plenty of water, wear a hat and use a sunblock with a high UV-protection factor.

MEDICAL CARE

ALTHOUGH MOST public hospitals in Morocco have excellent specialist doctors,

they are underfunded and lacking in equipment. Standards of hygiene are also unsatisfactory.

If you have the option, choose a private clinic. Although these are expensive, standards of care are close to European ones. Your country's embassy or consulate will provide a list of approved doctors and hospitals.

EMERGENCIES

IN THE CASE OF accidents that occur in the home or on the public highway, the fire brigade is the first to attend the scene. Its ambulances are usually run by the Moroccan Red Crescent and they are marked "ambulance".

In the case of medical emergencies that occur in the street, SAMU ambulances will take you to the nearest hospital. Tell the ambulance or taxi driver to which (private)

hospital or clinic you wish to go, otherwise you will be taken automatically to the nearest public hospital. In remote regions, the only way of reaching a hospital is to hire a taxi.

PHARMACIES

ALL PHARMACIES in Morocco are denoted by a sign in the form of a crescant. Duty pharmacies are open on Sundays, and their address is posted in the window of pharmacies that are closed. In large towns and cities, duty pharmacies stay open round the clock.

Pharmacies have helpful, knowledgeable staff who are able to give advice on minor health problems. Certain medicines that can only be obtained on prescription in Europe are available over the counter in Morocco.

FOOD AND WATER

MANY VISITORS to Morocco suffer from stomach upsets, which are often caused by the change of diet. Avoid drinking tap water, especially in rural areas, and keep to bottled mineral water (see *p321*). Make sure that the bottle is opened in front of you. Do not add ice to any drink and avoid diluted fruit juices.

On hikes and treks take water-purifying tablets to make spring water safe to drink. Alternatively, boil the water for 20 minutes.

Pharmacy sign

Be wary of salads and raw vegetables, and of unpeeled fruit and vegetables. They should be washed carefully. Food prepared at street stalls is another potential hazard. Although it is usually safe, as

A fire brigade vehicle

A pharmacy in Essaouira

long as it is freshly cooked, people with delicate stomachs are advised to resist it.

Fortunately, Moroccans like their meat well cooked. This destroys such parasites as tapeworms, which are rampant in Morocco.

INSECTS

THERE ARE NO particularly harmful insects in Morocco, but scorpions, snakes, cockroaches and spiders are common in the countryside. Check your clothes and shoes before dressing, particularly when camping in rural areas.

If you are bitten by a snake or spider or stung by a scorpion, apply a suction pump to the wound. These devices are sold in pharmacies all over the country.

Mosquitoes can be very bad in desert oases. An effective mosquito repellent is essential, especially in summer.

SERIOUS ILLNESS

BEING CAREFUL about what you eat should stop you contracting cholera. In case of

serious diarrhoea that persists after taking ordinary medication, consult a doctor without delay.

Stray animals – especially dogs, which roam the streets of large towns during the night – may carry rabies. If you are bitten, it is essential to seek first aid immediately.

Although the authorities deny it, sexually transmitted diseases such as AIDS are spreading in Morocco. The use of condoms (which are available in all pharmacies) is strongly advised.

PERSONAL SAFETY

VIOLENCE IS RARE throughout Morocco, and it is safe to go anywhere with no great risk to personal safety. Serious theft and burglary are not a widespread problem; this is because of the large number of caretakers who supplement the work of the police and act as an effective deterrent.

However, pickpockets with finely honed techniques are likely to patrol the souks, and unwary tourists are the most likely targets. If you are the victim of theft, report it

immediately at the nearest police station. If you intend to make an insurance claim, ask to be given a copy of the police record of the incident; this should be written in French rather than Arabic.

POLICE

POLICEMEN ARE omnipresent both in towns and cities and on the roads in Morocco, and they have considerable powers. Uniformed police officers, traffic police on the roads and numerous plain-clothes officers are present everywhere.

The Moroccan police, who once had a reputation for corruption, have adopted a very courteous attitude in their dealings with tourists.

In the case of more serious problems, you should contact your country's consulate (see p353) as soon as possible. The consulate will give you advice and assistance in dealing with the finer details of the Moroccan legal system.

Entrance to the Hôpital Ibn Rochd in Casablanca

Banking and Currency

Logo of Banque Centrale Populaire

MOROCCAN CURRENCY cannot be obtained abroad. On your arrival in the country, you will find many exchange offices where you can easily obtain dirhams. With an international banker's card you will also be able to draw money from automatic cash dispensers, as well as over the counter in banks that do not have ATMs. In country areas it can sometimes be difficult to change foreign currency, and shopkeepers and traders are seldom able to give change for high-denomination banknotes. It is also useful to keep a collection of coins for small purchases.

A branch of the French bank Société Générale

BANKS

MOROCCO'S MAIN BANKS are Banque Marocaine du Commerce Extérieur (**BMCE**), Banque Marocaine du Commerce et de l'Industrie (**BMCI**), Banque Commerciale du Maroc (**BCM**) and **Crédit du Maroc**. Most of them either have agreements with certain large international banks, such as **Citibank**, **ABN** and the French bank **Société Générale**, or are their subsidiaries. There are branches throughout the country. Small towns usually have only one bank, and there are no banks at all in rural areas.

Banks are open from 8.30am to noon and from 2pm to 4pm Monday to Thursday. On Friday, the day of prayer, they close a little earlier in the morning and open a little later in the afternoon. During Ramadan banks are often open continuously from about 8.30am to about 3pm.

AUTOMATIC CASH DISPENSERS

IN LARGE TOWNS, automatic cash dispensers (ATMs) are becoming increasingly easy to find. Most have instructions in several languages, and a notice or sticker lists those cards – Visa, Eurocard and MasterCard – that are accepted.

Some dispensers give cash only against accounts that are held in Morocco and may swallow your international card if you insert it by mistake. Cash dispensers give out dirhams, and there is often an upper limit to individual withdrawals. The machines do not always work properly, and it is advisable to withdraw money during bank opening hours so that you can retrieve your card immediately in the event of any problems arising.

Banks charge commission for foreign cash withdrawals, usually between 4.50 and 7 dirhams, regardless of how much is withdrawn. Obtain information on charges from your bank and avoid making frequent withdrawals of small amounts.

Automatic cash dispenser

DIRECTORY

MOROCCAN BANKS

BCM
2 Bd My-Youssef, Casablanca.
((022) 22 41 69.

BMCE
140 Avenue Hassan II, Casablanca.
((022) 26 50 76/62.

BMCI
26 Place des Nations Unies, Casablanca.
((022) 47 13 18/26.

Crédit du Maroc
48/58 Boulevard Mohammed V, Casablanca.
((022) 47 70 00.

FOREIGN BANKS

BMCI
47 Rue Allal Ben-Abdallah, Casablanca.
((022) 20 88 00.

Citibank
Zinit Millennium, Immeuble A, Attaoufik, Casablanca.
((022) 97 41 48.

Société Générale
84 Bd Mohammed V, Casablanca.
((022) 27 74 86.

If the cash dispenser fails to work, most banks will issue cash over the counter to holders of a banker's card.

BUREAUX DE CHANGE

BUREAUX DE CHANGE can be found in almost all banks, in hotels with a grading of three stars and upwards, and at airports. The exchange rate is uniform and variations in the commission charged are unusual. To avoid queueing, it is often best to change money at a hotel. While exchange offices in hotels and airports are open almost permanently, those attached to a bank have the same opening hours as the bank's.

When changing money, you will usually be asked to show your passport. All foreign currencies are accepted, but the euro and the dollar are the preferred currencies. Worn and torn banknotes are not accepted

as a matter of policy. In the major tourist centres, money-changers may offer you their services in the street at a preferential rate, but it is best to decline the offer.

You can change back any dirhams that you have over at the end of your stay, although the exchange rate will be poor and, unlike dollars and euros, pounds sterling are not always available.

CREDIT CARDS

MOST REASONABLY comfortable hotels (usually those with a rating of three stars and above), as well as mainstream restaurants in large towns, and certain stores (usually those in the most upmarket bracket) accept credit cards for payments.

TRAVELLER'S CHEQUES

THE SAFEST WAY OF carrying money when travelling is still in the form of traveller's cheques (in sterling, euros or dollars). Traveller's cheques are accepted at almost all exchange offices and in most large hotels.

CURRENCY

THE MOROCCAN UNIT of currency is the dirham (Dh in its abbreviated form), which is divided into 100 centimes. Banknotes are issued in the following denominations: 20, 50, 100 and 200 dirhams. Coins are issued in denominations of 5, 10, 20 and 50 centimes, and of 1, 5 and 10 dirhams.

Notes and coins are inscribed in French and Arabic. In country areas and in souks it is very difficult to obtain change for large-denomination notes. Always carry some small change to cover ordinary purchases.

Both banknotes and coins bear the likeness of King Hassan II or, less commonly, of his father Mohammed V. It is therefore considered sacrilegious to tear or damage them. Any coin or banknote where the sovereign's portrait is defaced in any way may even be refused.

In some parts of Morocco, especially rural areas, prices are given in riales (or reales) as well as, or instead of, in centimes. One rial equals 5 centimes, but it is a purely conceptual unit: there are no rial coins.

Coins
Coins come in denominatons of 5, 10, 20 and 50 centimes and of 1, 5 and 10 dirhams. While centime coins are not widely used, 1 dirham pieces are extremely handy, especially for paying someone to guard your car and for occasional tips.

10 dirhams   **5 dirhams**

1 dirham   **50 centimes**   **20 centimes**   **10 centimes**   **5 centimes**

Banknotes
Banknotes are issued in denominations of 20 dirhams, 50 dirhams, 100 dirhams and 200 dirhams.

20-dirham note

50-dirham note

100-dirham note

200-dirham note

Communications

**Logo of a
television channel**

Morocco's TELEPHONE NETWORK is run by Maroc Télécom, the national operator (formerly known as Itissalat El-Maghrib). It has developed significantly and provides an efficient service, despite occasional problems. The use of mobile telephones is now widespread. Postal services are generally reliable, although deliveries can be subject to long delays. Moroccan television is fighting a losing battle against satellite channels and foreign programmes. Newspapers, many of which are in French, cover current affairs both in Morocco and on the international stage.

A "téléboutique", where telephone calls can be made and faxes sent

Typical yellow postbox

PUBLIC TELEPHONES

PUBLIC PHONE BOXES, which are relatively rare, are usually located outside post offices, markets and bus stations. Coin-operated telephones are still relatively common, and they take coins up to a denomination of 5 dirhams. Because of the number of coins needed, it is not practical to make international calls from a coin-operated telephone. Such calls are best made from a card-operated telephone. Phonecards are available at post offices and in tobacconists, which are indicated by a blue and white sign with three interlinked rings.

With some telephones, an illegal card rental system applies. The cardholder inserts the phonecard for you, noting the number of existing

Moroccan phonecard

units on the card. You make the call, and then pay the cost (based on the difference between the number of units on the card before and after your call). Calls made by this method are more expensive but obviate the need to buy a whole card.

PUBLIC TELEPHONE CENTRES

THE NUMBER OF small public telephone centres, known as *téléboutiques*, has mush-roomed in Morocco. These centres, located at the intersection of streets, are run either by private operators or by Maroc Télécom, the national operator. They house plastic phone boxes or kiosks (which are usually a sandy colour) with card-operated, coin-operated or metered telephones. The cards that are sold here often only work in telephones in the centre from which the card was bought or in telephones owned by the relevant operator. Faxes can also usually be sent and received in these public telephone centres.

MOBILE PHONES

ALMOST EVERYONE, it seems, has a mobile phone in Morocco. The two competing network operators, Méditel and Maroc Télécom, are locked in a fierce price war.

The network is excellent and mobile phones can be used in even the most remote regions of the country.

Most European network operators have arrangements with one or other of the two Moroccan network operators, so that visitors can use their mobile phones in Morocco (but bear in mind that calls will be expensive).

Mobile-phone users may also buy a prepaid SIM card from either of the Moroccan network operators. For a modest charge (no more than about 200 dirhams), you are provided with a Moroccan number through which national and international calls can be made at a more favourable rates.

USEFUL DIALLING CODES

• Telephone numbers consist of nine digits, and the country is divided into four zones.
– Casablanca zone: 022 + 6 digits
– Rabat zone: 037 + 6 digits
– Marrakech zone: 044 + 6 digits
– Fès zone: 055 + 6 digits.
• Mobile telephones: 06 + 7 digits
• Always dial nine digits, whether calling from one zone to another or within a single zone.
• To call Morocco from abroad: dial 00 212 + eight digits (the nine-digit number minus the initial 0).
• To dial internationally: dial 00 + country code + telephone number.

An Internet café in a large town in Morocco

INTERNET CAFÉS

IN LARGE TOWNS, it is increasingly common to find Internet cafés. Here, you can pick up and send e-mail and surf the Internet. Charges vary widely between different cybercafés, and are calculated according to the time spent on line.

POSTAL SERVICE

MOROCCO'S POSTAL SERVICE has a reputation for being very slow. This is often borne out by reality, especially in the case of international mail.

There are post offices in all sizeable towns. Here, you can buy stamps, send letters and parcels and cash, or send

Moroccan postage stamps

postal orders. Stamps are also available in tobacconists and at the reception desk of large hotels. Central post offices are open from 8.30am to 6.30pm. Sub-post offices close at lunchtime; precise times vary according to location.

Post offices also provide an

Newspaper vendor's display

express mail delivery service. However, if you have something urgent to send, it is better to use a private company such as **DHL Worldwide Express** or **Globex (Federal Express)**. It is also best to post letters at a central post office rather than use one of the yellow street postboxes as collections can be unreliable.

POSTE RESTANTE

MOST POST OFFICES provide a poste restante service, and this system works well in Morocco. Mail should bear the first name and surname of the recipient, as well as the name of the town. You will need some form of identification when collecting mail from a poste restante. The service is free of charge.

NEWSPAPERS

MOROCCO HAS MANY daily newspapers in Arabic and in French. The major leading newspapers in French are *Le Matin du Sahara*, *L'Opinion*, *Maroc Soir*, *Libération* and *El-Bayane*. Several weekly magazines, such as *Le Journal* and *Demain*, or the quarterly publications such as *Medina*, *Femmes du Maroc* and *Citadine* were launched in recent years. They have given a new voice to the Moroccan press, which is usually quite conservative.

French newspapers like *Le Monde* and *Le Figaro* are printed in Casablanca at the same time as in France. English language newspapers are available in Tangier, Agadir and Marrakech. Outside large towns you often find outdated daily newspapers on sale.

Medina, the quarterly magazine

TELEVISION AND RADIO

MOROCCO HAS two television channels: Radio Télévision Marocaine (RTM),

the public national channel that broadcasts in Arabic and in French, and 2M, a privately run pay channel that also broadcasts in both languages, although programmes in French predominate.

Both the Moroccan television channels are, however, severely rivalled by the spread of satellite dishes, which provide access to a huge number of international channels. Most households, as well as upmarket hotels, have satellite dishes.

Broadcasts in English are obtainable only via satellite (mostly CNN). Around Tangier, it is also possible to tune in to broadcasts in English from Gibraltar.

Moroccan radio is dominated by the omnipresent RTM, which broadcasts in French and Arabic, and Médi 1, which broadcasts mostly in French. It is also possible to tune into some European stations, including BBC World Service (on MHz 15,070) and Voice of America.

TRAVEL INFORMATION

THE EASIEST WAY to reach Morocco is by air. The country is served by many regular flights from most major European cities and less frequent flights from North America. Internal flights link Morocco's major cities. During the high tourist season, many charter flights are also available. Getting to Morocco by

Logo of Royal Air Maroc

train or bus can be cheaper than travelling by air, but for most visitors the journey overland by these means is far too long to be practicable. It is also possible to reach Morocco by car and ship. Using your own car also saves the cost of hiring one on arrival in Morocco, which can be quite expensive.

A Royal Air Maroc aircraft taking off from Ouarzazate airport

ARRIVING BY AIR

MOROCCO HAS eight international airports. The busiest are those at Casablanca, Marrakech and Agadir. **Royal Air Maroc** (RAM), the national carrier, provides many links between Morocco and Europe, including departures from provincial cities, and a less frequent service between North America and Casablanca.

RAM provides flights from London Heathrow to Casablanca, Marrakech, Ouarzazate and Agadir, and from London Stansted to Marrakech. **GB Airways**, a British Airways franchise, also serves Casablanca, Tangier and Marrakech from London Heathrow, and Agadir and Marrakech from London Gatwick.

From North America, RAM flies three times a week from Montreal and New York JFK to Casablanca. From other North American cities, the best links are via London or Paris.

There are no direct flights to Morocco from Australia or New Zealand. Connections can be made either via

Singapore to Casablanca or via Dubai to Casablanca, or by flying to London. During the high tourist season, many charter flights supplement the regular scheduled services. Most charter flights serve Marrakech, Agadir and Ouarzazate.

Many tour operators offer economical package deals including flights and accommodation in hotels, villas or resorts. The deals may also include guided tours, desert trips, activity and sporting holidays, and trekking. Specialist tour operators offer all this and can also provide tailor-made arrangements.

CASABLANCA AIRPORT

MOHAMMED V airport in Casablanca is Morocco's main airport both in terms of its size and of the volume of traffic that it handles. Most international flights arrive in and depart from Casablanca, and many flights serving other cities in Morocco

touch down here. Internal flights to smaller airports – at Agadir, Marrakech, Ouarzazate, Fès, Oujda and Essaouira, also depart from Mohammed V Airport. The airport is located about 30 km (19 miles) south of the city centre, and is served by efficient bus and train services.

MARRAKECH AIRPORT

RECENTLY REBUILT and considerably enlarged, Marrakech-Ménara Airport is now able to handle a large volume of flights and passengers. Located not more than a few kilometres from the city centre, it is very easy to reach. Charter flights make up most of its traffic, although it also handles many scheduled flights.

AIRPORT LINKS

MOHAMMED V AIRPORT, outside Casablanca, is served by bus and train links (there is one train service every hour). By contrast, the only-way of reaching certain other airports is by taxi from the town centre.

Only the *grands taxis* are permitted to wait for passengers at airports. The fact that they hold a monopoly allows them

Ferry in the Straits of Gibraltar

to charge relatively high fares, and they are unwilling to bargain. Airports are well provided with car-hire companies, and if you plan to travel around during your stay, hiring a car from the airport means, of course, that you will not need to use a taxi.

To reach an airport from a city centre, you can hire a *petit taxi*. Fares are reasonable, but ask the driver to switch on his meter, assuming that it actually works, of course.

ARRIVING BY CAR AND FERRY

SEVERAL FERRY companies provide various sea links between Spain and Morocco, including the Spanish Transmediterrànea and the Moroccan Comarit. Their UK agent **Southern Ferries** has schedules and prices. The crossing from Algeciras, in Spain, to Tangier or Ceuta (the Spanish enclave in Morocco) takes about two hours but boarding can be very slow, especially in summer, when Moroccans working abroad return home.

Ferry tickets can be purchased in advance or at the time of travel. In either case, the time spent queuing is the same. The adult fare is about 24 euros (£15). Taking a car across costs between about 90 and 180 euros (£56 and £112), depending on its size. Most travellers take the ferry from Algeciras to

Sign for Casablanca's Mohammed V Airport

Tangier, since services from here are more frequent, but there are also ferry links to Tangier and to Melilla from Málaga and Almería; to Ceuta from Málaga; and to Tangier from Gibraltar.

In Spain, you need to collect an exit form before boarding. On leaving Morocco, you need to fill in an embarkation form and have this and your passport stamped before boarding the ferry.

ARRIVING BY TRAIN

TRAVELLING BY TRAIN means a long but scenic journey. From London, take the Eurostar to Paris, from where there is a daily TGV service to Algeciras, in Spain, changing at Irún, on the Spanish border. This is run by the French SNCF, but tickets (including Eurostar) can be bought at **European Rail Ltd** and **Rail Europe**. Holders of an InterRail card, which allows travel in 29 European countries (Spain, Portugal and Morocco are treated as a single zone), can break their journey anywhere they wish.

The fare from Paris to Algeciras is about 155 euros (£97). Avoid train services that go via Barcelona, as links between Catalonia and Algeciras are poor. It is far better to use a service that goes via Madrid. From Algeciras, there are ferry services to Tangier and to Ceuta *(see Arriving by Car and Ferry, left)*.

(see Arriving by Car and Ferry, left).

DIRECTORY

AIRLINES

Royal Air Maroc (RAM)
[(020) 7439 4361/8854 (UK).
[(800) 344 6726 (US).
w www.royalairmaroc.com

GB Airways
[(0845) 773 3377 (UK).
w www.gbairways.com

FERRY COMPANIES

Southern Ferries
179 Piccadilly, London W1V 9DB.
[(020) 7491 4968.

RAILWAYS

European Rail Ltd.
[(020) 7387 0444.
w www.europeanrail.com

Rail Europe
179 Piccadilly, London W1V 9DB.
[(0870) 584 8848.
w www.raileurope.co.uk
www.raileurope.com/us

TOUR OPERATORS

Best of Morocco
Seend Park, Wiltshire SN12 6NZ.
[(01380) 828 533.
w www.morocco-travel.com

Cagodan Holidays
9–10 Portland Street,
Southampton SO14 7EB.
[(023) 8082 8304.
w www.cadoganholidays.com

Morocco Made to Measure
69 Knightsbridge,
London SW1X 7RA.
[(020) 7235 0123.
w www.clmleisure.co.uk

The interior of Agadir's airport

Travelling by Car in Morocco

Caution, camels on road

THE BEST WAY of travelling around Morocco, and of exploring the country's historic sites and natural environment in areas not served by local public transport, is by car. The imperfect road network is constantly being improved, and the number of metalled roads means that a four-wheel-drive vehicle is not essential, even in the South. A greater hazard is Moroccan driving standards, even though visitors will soon become used to them. There are a large number of car-hire companies in Morocco. Do not, however, assume that they all offer an identical service.

Traffic in town, where other cars are not the only obstacles

RULES OF THE ROAD

THE MOROCCAN highway code is based on that of France, so you must usually give way to the right. At roundabouts, you should give way to cars already on the roundabout.

In general, Moroccan drivers obey traffic lights, perhaps because most junctions are patrolled by a gendarme or policeman.

The speed limits are 40 or 60 kmh (25 or 37 mph) in built-up areas, 100 kmh (60 mph) on the open road and 120 kmh (74 mph) on the motorway. In the approach to towns, drivers will sometimes see signs giving different speed limits; when in doubt, keep to 40 kmh (25 mph), since speed traps are common on these stretches of road. Fines for speeding and other traffic offences were recently raised, and are now set at 300 to 600 dirhams.

ROAD SIGNS

THE INTERNATIONAL system applies to road signs in Morocco, most of which have wording in Arabic and French. In large towns, direction signs are sparse, so that it is inadvisable to set out without a map or reliable instructions.

Signage on motorways and major roads is usually good. Lighting, however, is normally non-existent, except on the approaches to large towns.

Road sign in French and Arabic

TRAFFIC HAZARDS

NEGOTIATING LOCAL traffic is difficult mainly because of the great variety of vehicles that use the roads. As a general rule, avoid driving at night, when carts and bicycles with no lights are a real

hazard. In towns, the rules of the road are not meticulously observed at night. Be particularly careful about pedestrians crossing roads and even motorways.

Indicator lights are rarely used, and you will find that you must try to anticipate changes of direction of vehicles in your vicinity. Many major roads often have two carriageways, which can make overtaking hazardous. On mountain roads, taxis and buses are often driven somewhat dangerously. Sound your horn when driving into a blind bend.

ROADS AND TRACKS

MOROCCO'S RELATIVELY dense road network is undergoing constant improvements. So as to reap the benefit of the latest new stretches of road, buy the most up-to-date road map.

The well-developed road network in northern Morocco is gradually being supplemented by motorways, which are very pleasant to use as they do not carry many trucks. The road network in southern Morocco is less dense and the few minor roads in the region are often in a bad state of repair.

In the South and in the Atlas mountains, metalled roads serve most places of interest to tourists, and they are complemented by a relatively good network of tracks. A four-wheel-drive vehicle is essential for journeys in these regions.

DRIVING IN TOWNS

THE VOLUME OF traffic in large towns and cities can be considerable, and the increasing number of vehicles on the roads leads to multiple jams and bottlenecks, which are aggravated by the flotilla of bicycles and mopeds that also impede traffic flow.

Although it is possible to drive into most medinas (the old areas of towns), their

Parking attendant

narrow streets and many dead ends can make circulation difficult. It is usually far more pleasurable to explore them on foot.

DRIVING IN THE COUNTRY

WHEN DRIVING on minor roads in rural areas, you should look out for animals, such as donkeys and flocks of sheep or goats. Wandering freely without human supervision, they may step into the road without warning.

The many trucks and buses that use the roads may slow your progress considerably, and overtaking, particularly in the mountains, is difficult. Passing on narrow roads is often hazardous. Slow down and hug the hard shoulder so as to reduce the risk of collision.

A "Stop" sign in Arabic

FUEL

SERVICE STATIONS are found at fairly frequent intervals along roads in Morocco, even in the most remote areas. Although four-star petrol (gas) and diesel are widely available, unleaded petrol is rarely sold outside large towns. Irregular deliveries to service stations in rural areas may mean that they run out of fuel. Wherever you are, you should fill up before starting a long journey.

Self-service is uncommon; you should wait for the attendant to arrive and then pay him in cash, including a tip.

PARKING

IN LARGE TOWNS and cities (except for Casablanca), an attendant wearing a small brass badge is assigned to every pavement. He will help you to park, will watch your car in your absence and will help you manoeuvre out of your parking place when you leave.

Payment for this service varies according to how long the car is parked, and is at the driver's discretion; allow

1 to 2 dirhams for a short stay (even lasting no more than a few minutes) and 5 dirhams for several hours' parking. If you want to park for a longer period (overnight, for example), it is advisable to come to an agreement with the attendant before leaving your vehicle. The advantage of this system is that car theft and break-ins are virtually non-existent.

CAR HIRE

LARGE TOWNS and airports are well provided with car-hire companies, not all of which offer the same service. When hiring a car for an extended period, it is best to use an international car-hire company (such as **Hertz**, **Avis** or Europcar) or a Moroccan firm (such as Thrifty or First-Car) with an extensive network and reliable insurance and breakdown assistance. On payment of a supplement, the hire vehicle may be dropped off at a different place from where it was picked up. Check the terms of the agreement, especially clauses relating to insurance and cover in case of accident or theft. Also check the state of the vehicle and ask for any damage to be noted before you drive off.

Car hire in Morocco is quite expensive. Charges (excluding collision damage waiver) are about 300 dirhams per day for a Class A car (such as a Fiat Uno) and 1,800 dirhams

for a four-wheel-drive vehicle. There is usually a wide range of cars to choose from.

IN CASE OF ACCIDENT

IF YOU ARE involved in a road accident, you should wait for the police to arrive. They will usually arrive quickly and will arbitrate in case of any disagreement. Official statement forms similar to those used in Europe are available at tobacconists.

Driving in the desert, where a four-wheel-drive is essential

Getting Around in Towns

**Bilingual
street sign**

THE MOST IMPORTANT historic sites in
Morocco's towns and cities are
often located in the medinas, where, in
a maze of narrow streets and frequent
dead-ends, the only practical way of
getting around is on foot. But because
many hotels are located in the modern
quarters of towns, visitors will
frequently need to takes buses or taxis. Although buses
are an inexpensive means of getting around in a town,
visitors may be baffled by the way that they work and
the routes that they follow. *Petits taxis* offer a greater
degree of flexibility at relatively little cost. In some towns
the services of a guide are virtually indispensable to save
spending too much time working out a route, but others
are much more straightforward to navigate.

A *petit taxi*,
for short journeys in towns

By Bus

ALL LARGE TOWNS in Morocco
are served by a wide
network of bus lines linking
their various districts. It can,
however, be difficult to find
the bus that you need since
the destination is often given
only in Arabic. For visitors,
the most useful routes are
those running between the
new town (*ville nouvelle*) and
the medina. Bus fares are
cheap (3 to 4 dirhams) and
tickets are purchased on
board from the driver. Be sure
to carry some small change.

By Grand Taxi

THE MOST FREQUENT journeys
made by *grands taxis*,
many of which are Mercedes
and which seat up to six passengers, are those between
towns and cities (*see p369*).
They are also useful if you
are a large party, are weighed
down with luggage or want to
explore the countryside beyond the town, although they
won't leave until they are full.

Grands taxis are not fitted
with meters, so the fare for
your journey must be agreed
according to mileage and the
length of time that you hire it.
The charge for hiring a *grand
taxi* for a whole day will be
about 500 dirhams.

Grands taxis often wait
outside large hotels, and
they should not be mistaken
for *petits taxis*, which are
cheaper and which are used
for shorter runs.

By Petit Taxi

THESE VEHICLES are identifiable by their colour,
which is different in every
town, and by the words *"petit
taxi"* on the roof. They are
prohibited by law from going
beyond built-up areas and can
only be hired for short trips.

The use of meters is
becoming more common.
You should always ask for
the meter to be switched on,
and be prepared to round up
the usually modest amount
that is shown at the end of
your journey. The usual fare
for a short journey by *petit
taxi* during the day is about
10 dirhams. At night a 50 per
cent surcharge is added to the
amount shown on the meter.
Taxi fares are paid in cash,
and it is important to have a
good supply of small change
as drivers are rarely able to
give change for a 100- or
200-dirham banknote.

Petits taxis usually take up
to four people (three in the
back and one in front). They
make frequent stops along
the way to pick up other
passengers going in the same
direction. This usually reduces
the cost of the journey.

It is better to ask to be
taken to a specific restaurant,
hotel or historic building,
rather than name the relevant
street. Although most drivers
have a good knowledge of
the town in which they work,
they navigate by landmarks
rather than street names.

Local bus, a cheap but not always easy way of getting around in towns

The medina in Oujda, easily explored on foot

Taxi ranks are marked by white rectangular signs saying "taxi". You can also hail a taxi in the street by waving your hand. Because of the large number of taxis circulating in towns, it is unusual to wait for very long. There are no radio taxi firms, but some drivers have mobile phones and will give you their card.

If your journey entails driving along a track, the fare will automatically increase. In this case, the full amount should be agreed with the driver beforehand.

On Foot

MOROCCAN TOWNS, and their medinas in particular, are typically very poorly sign-posted for pedestrians. A street map is therefore useful. You can also ask your way, in return for a few words of thanks in French or, if the person takes you there, a few dirhams. Town centres are easy to explore on foot and best appreciated at a relaxed pace, especially if you have time to enjoy the maze of narrow streets. Cars, mopeds and bicycles take little heed of pedestrians, and you should take special care when crossing the street.

Streets in towns throughout Morocco are very safe. There are, of course, insalubrious quarters, although these are rarely frequented by tourists. In tourist spots, an obvious police presence together with large numbers of people (both Moroccans and visitors) is the best guarantee of safety. In small crowded streets where pickpockets may operate, take special care of personal possessions.

By Bicycle or Moped

IN THE MAJOR tourist centres, particularly Marrakech and Agadir, bicycles and mopeds can be hired. The level terrain in these two cities makes cycling here quite easy. Mopeds and bicycles are an ideal means of getting around the old quarters, where the streets are narrow. However, a degree of caution is called for, since car drivers show little consideration to other road-users.

Bicycle attendants, who can be found where there is a concentration of parked cycles and mopeds, are worth using. Charges range from 1 to 2 dirhams for a few hours to 10 dirhams for a night. Lock your bicycle or moped even if an attendant is guarding it.

By Carriage

HORSE-DRAWN CARRIAGES are found mainly in Marrakech. Hiring one costs

Bus stop in a town

more than a *petit taxi*, but they can be a fun way of getting around towns. In Marrakech, the largest carriage "rank" is at the foot of the Koutoubia Mosque.

Guides

THE BOGUS GUIDES who were once so ubiquitous in tourist spots have become more discreet since measures were taken to clamp down on anyone without an official card acting as a guide.

Even if you have a street map, you will find some towns very confusing to explore. The services of a guide may be necessary on your first day in a certain town or city, particularly in the largest medinas, like that of Fès.

Official guides are identifiable by the cards that they carry, almost always pinned to their clothing. These cards are issued by the Ministry of Tourism and bear an identity photograph of the holder.

Official guides can be requested at tourist information offices, and also by hotels (in which case make sure they carry the card). They also often wait near hotels and major historic buildings. Specify which buildings and other features you wish to see, and whether or not you wish to be taken into shops. The fees are fixed by the government, but always agree the fee with the guide beforehand.

A horse-drawn carriage, a popular form of transport in Marrakech

Travelling Around in Morocco

**Sign indicating
a bus station**

THE MOROCCAN RAIL network (ONCF) links the towns and cities of northern Morocco, the southernmost town with a rail link being Marrakech. Trains are clean and reliable, and journey times depend on the number of stops along the route. The rail network is complemented by long-distance bus services, which are run either by public or by private companies, and which are cheaper than the train. Whatever your chosen means of transport, you should check beforehand the various timetables and any stops that may seriously lengthen your journey. *Grands taxis (see p366)* are a swift means of travelling from one town to another, but their fares are not fixed and bargaining is a matter of course. The best way to travel between principal cities is often on a domestic flight.

**Regional Air Lines, operating
domestic flights in Morocco**

An aircraft on a domestic flight arriving in Ouarzazate

THE RAIL NETWORK

RUN BY THE Office National des Chemins de Fer (**ONCF**), the Moroccan rail network, while very good, is not very extensive. It covers just 1,700 km (1,056 miles) and serves mainly the northern part of the country, linking Tangier, Oujda, Rabat, Casablanca, Fès and Marrakech. Plans to extend the railways southwards, particularly to Agadir, are under way. The Atlas, however, is an insuperable barrier.

Services are frequent, since trains are the preferred means of transport for ordinary people. A separate rail network is used for transporting phosphates, of which Morocco is the world's largest producer.

Casablanca and Rabat have several railway stations, located in different districts but served by the same line.

TRAINS

WITH A FEW exceptions, Moroccan trains are relatively modern. Those known as Trains Navettes Rapides, or TNR (express shuttles), and referred to as "Aouita" after a famous Moroccan marathon runner, link Casablanca and Rabat in 50 minutes, Mohammed V Airport and Casablanca in 40 minutes, and Rabat and Kenitra in 30 minutes. The service is frequent at peak times. Trains known as Trains Rapides Climatisés (air-

conditioned express trains) cover the longer distances between Casablanca, Fès, Oujda, Tangier and Marrakech, and are identified by names such as Koutoubia and Hassan. They are air-conditioned and soundproofed and have proper toilets. On the most heavily used route (from Casablanca to Marrakech, Fès and Tangier), there is a service at least every two hours, and it is possible to make the round trip from Casablanca to Tangier and back again in a single day.

For long journeys, the compartments on night trains can be converted into couchettes. Second class, which is air-conditioned, is very comfortable. The toilets are located at the end of the coach and are reasonably clean. On-board catering services are rather basic. Vendors walk up and down the coaches offering cakes, confectionery, drinks and sometimes sandwiches.

Some older trains, which often have wooden seats, are used for shorter journeys and stop at the smallest stations.

TRAIN TICKETS AND FARES

THE CHEAPEST WAY to buy a train ticket is at a railway station. Passengers must have a ticket valid for the relevant class of seat and type of train. If you reserve a couchette or a bed in a sleeper, you must be able to show the ticket for the relevant supplement. You can purchase a ticket without booking a seat six days in advance, a combined

A *grand taxi*, used for longer journeys

train and bus ticket one month in advance, and a ticket with a bed booked on a sleeper two months in advance. You can break your journey so long as you collect a form *(bulletin d'arrêt)* at the station where you alighted. This form makes your ticket valid for an extra five days.

If you have to board a train without having bought a ticket at the station ticket office, ask for a boarding ticket *(ticket d'accès)*, which is issued free of charge at the entrance to the platform, or tell the inspector before you board the train. A ticket bought on the train is always more expensive than one bought from a station ticket office before boarding.

The train is a relatively inexpensive means of getting around. A second-class ticket on an express train from Casablanca to Marrakech or Fès costs about 100 dirhams, and from Marrakech to Tangier about 250 dirhams. There are various concessions for families, young people and groups, and season tickets are also available, although these are economical only for regular travel on a particular route.

COACHES

MANY COACH (bus) companies operate in Morocco. The best known is **CTM**, the national company that runs services between towns in Morocco and also abroad. Two private companies, **SATAS** and **Supratours**, also cover long-distance routes. Coaches are comfortable and air-conditioned, and are very convenient, especially in the South. They depart from bus stations, which are usually well signposted.

It is advisable to buy your ticket, and thus reserve a seat, at least 24 hours in advance since coaches are often fully booked at time of departure. Luggage is checked in ahead of departure and is carried in the hold. Make sure that yours has been loaded.

Many small local coach companies also operate in Morocco, although the

comfort of their buses is often minimal and journey times painfully long.

GRANDS TAXIS

THIS IS THE MOST flexible way of travelling from one town to another. *Grands taxis* are mostly found at bus stations, parked according to their destination.

Grands taxis are not fitted with meters, and fares must be agreed by bargaining. The main factors involved are the length of the journey and how many people are to be carried. If the taxi is full (with seven or perhaps eight people), each person's fare will be only slightly higher than for the same journey made by bus.

If you do not wish to share the taxi, expect to pay the equivalent that the driver would receive for a fully loaded car. This allows you the option of a tailor-made route. Any stops along the way, to visit places of interest, should be agreed beforehand, since they will lengthen the journey time and add to the fare.

DOMESTIC FLIGHTS

THE MOST ECONOMICAL way of making longer journeys between Morocco's largest cities is often on one of the internal flights provided by **Royal Air Maroc**, especially to Agadir or Ouarzazate, neither of which has a rail

DIRECTORY

RAILWAY COMPANY

ONCF
8 bis Rue Abderrahmane El-Ghafiki, Agdal, Rabat.
📞 *(037) 77 47 47.*
FAX *(037) 77 44 80.*
W www.oncf.org.ma

BUS COMPANIES

CTM
📞 *(022) 54 10 10 or 43 82 82.*
(for travel in Morocco).

SATAS
185 Boulevard Moulay Ismaïl, Casablanca.
📞 *(022) 40 45 60 or 40 29 08.*

Supratours
📞 *(037) 77 65 20 or 77 93 27.*
(for travel in Morocco).

AIRLINES

Regional Airlines
Mohammed V Airport, Casablanca.
📞 *(022) 53 85 92.*

Royal Air Maroc
44 Avenue des F.A.R., Casablanca.
📞 *(022) 31 11 22 or 0900 0800.*
(for travel in Morocco).
W www.royalairmaroc.com

link. The one-way fare to either place is about 700 dirhams, although prices may vary according to the time of year. **Regional Airlines** also operates internal flights.

Train drawing into the station at Mohammedia, near Casablanca

Index

Ferries 363
Fès 63, **163–83**
  Bou Inania Medersa
  172–3
  cinemas 343
  climate 43
  cultural centres 345
  festivals 38, 40
  hotels 308–9
  Karaouiyine Mosque
  176–7
  map 164–5
  Musée Dar el-Batha
  168–9
  piano bars 345
  restaurants 327–8
  Tanneries of Fès **174**
Fès, Treaty of (1912) 56
Fès el-Bali 163, 164
Fès el-Jedid 163, 164,
  180–83
  map 181
Festival of Folk Music
  (Al-Hoceima) 39
Festival of Volubilis
  (Meknès) 40
Festivals **38–41**, 343
  Holy Men and Mystics
  198–9
  religious festivals 31, **41**
Fig Festival (Bouhouda)
  39
Figuig **161**
Film **342**, 343
  Atlas Film Studios
  (Ouarzazate) 264
  Moroccan cinema **29**
Finnt Oasis 264
Fire brigade 356,
  357
Fishing
  Sea fishing in Morocco
  119
Le Flamingo (Agadir) 345
Flint, Bert 235
  Bert Flint Museum
  (Marrakech) 235
Flynn, Errol 139
Fondation Lorin (Tangier)
  134
Fondouk (Chefchaouen)
  150

Fondouk Chejra (Tangier)
  138
Fondouk el-Nejjarine (Fès)
  167
Food and drink
  Olives and olive oil **217**
  safety 356–7
  sharing a meal 354
  shopping 336–7
  What to Drink in
  Morocco **320–21**
  What to Eat in Morocco
  318–19
  see also Restaurants
Forbes, Malcolm 139
Foreign Legion
  Ouarzazate 264
  Source Bleue de Meski
  279
  Tunnel de Foum-Zabel
  278–9
Forest of Mamora **87**
Forêt de Cèdres 212
Forgeries 337
Former Mellah (Essaouira)
  123
Fortresses **266–7**
Forum, Basilica and
  Capitol (Volubilis) 205
Foucauld, Charles de 217,
  289
Foucault, Michel 141
Foum el-Anser 220
Foum-el-Hassan 289
Foum-Rjam 269
Fountains
  Chrob ou Chouf
  Fountain (Marrakech) **226**
Franco, General Francisco
  56
François, Marcel 86
French Protectorate **56–7**
  architecture 21
  Casablanca 95, 99, 106
  El-Jadida 114
  Er-Rachidia 279
  Erfoud 280
  Fès 163
  Kenitra 87
  Rabat 77
  Zagora 268
  see also Foreign Legion

Friday prayers 31
Funerary architecture
  Musée Dar el-Batha
  (Fès) 169

G

Galerie Abderrahim
  Harabida (Essaouira) 345
Galerie Bazar Kasba
  (Essaouira) 345
Galerie Bouafia
  Mohammed (Essaouira)
  345
Galerie Damgaard
  (Essaouira) 124
Galerie Delacroix
  (Tangier) 138, 139
Galerie Frédéric
  Damgaard (Essaouira)
  345
Galerie du Musée de
  Marrakech (Marrakech)
  345
Galerie Seddik Saddiki
  (Essaouira) 345
Galleries see
  Museums and galleries
Gardens see
  Parks and gardens
GB Airways 363
Genet, Jean 135
  Café de Paris (Tangier)
  139
  Hôtel el-Minzah
  (Tangier) 139
  tomb of 90
Genseric, King of the
  Vandals 45
Geography **51**
Gibraltar 147
Gibraltar, Straits of 129
Gidel Building
  (Marrakech) 243
Glaoui family
  Aït Benhaddou 265
  Aït Mouted Kasbah
  (Dadès Gorge) 273
  Amerhidil Kasbah
  (Skoura) 272
  Taliouine 288
  Taourirt Kasbah 264

Further Reading

HISTORY AND SOCIETY
David Hart, *Tribe and Society in Rural Morocco*, Frank Cass, UK and US. Essays on Moroccan tribes and the Berbers.

Donna Lee Bowen and Evelyn A. Early (eds), *Everyday Life in the Muslim Middle East*, Indiana University Press, US. Focusing on Morocco.

Peter Mansfield, *The Arabs*, Penguin, UK and US. General history, with a section on Morocco.

Gavin Maxwell, *Lords of the Atlas, The Rise and Fall of the House of Glaoui 1893–1956*, Cassell, UK.

Susan Raven, *Rome in Africa*, Routledge, US and UK. North Africa in Roman times.

Barnaby Rogerson, *A Traveller's History of North Africa*, Windrush, UK; Interlink, US. Readable general history, from the Roman period to the present day.

NATURAL AND URBAN LANDSCAPES
Ann and Yan Arthus-Bertrand, *Morocco Seen from the Air*, Vendome Press, UK and US, 1994. A fascinating literal overview.

Jean-Marc Tingaud and Tahar Ben Jelloun, *Medinas: Morocco's Hidden Cities*, Thames & Hudson, UK and US. An intimate glimpse into the palaces of the imperial cities.

Hugues Demeude, Jacques Bravo and Xavier Richer, *Morocco*, Taschen, Germany. Lavish photographic survey.

ART AND ARCHITECTURE
Titus Burkhardt, *Art of Islam, Language and Meaning*.

Lisl and Landt Dennis, *Living in Morocco*, Thames & Hudson, UK. Lavishly illustrated portrait of the domestic environment.

James F. Jereb, *Arts and Crafts of Morocco*, Thames & Hudson, UK; Chronicle Books, US. Well-illustrated survey, including a guide to major museums in Morocco.

A. Khatabi and M. Sigilmassa, *The Splendours of Islamic Calligraphy*, Thames & Hudson, UK.

Richard Parker, *A Practical Guide to Islamic Monuments in Morocco*, Baraka Press, US.

FLORA AND FAUNA
T. Haltenorth and H. Diller, Heinzel, BA, *Field Guide to the Mammals of Africa*, Collins, UK.

Fitter and Parslow, *The Birds of Britain and Europe with North Africa and the Middle East*, Collins, UK.

COOKING
Robert Carrier, *Taste of Morocco*, Arrow, London.

Anissa Helou, *Café Morocco*, Conran Octopus, UK and US.

Paula Wolfert, *Couscous and Other Good Foods from Morocco*, HarperCollins, US.

TRAVEL, BIOGRAPHY AND FICTION
Paul Bowles, *The Sheltering Sky*, Penguin, UK; Ecco Press, US. *Let It Come Down*, Penguin, UK; Black Sparrow Press, US. *Collected Stories of Paul Bowles 1939–76*, Black Sparrow Press, US. *Midnight Mass*, Peter Owen, UK; Black Sparrow Press, US. On the theme of Westerners in a foreign land, from the best-known writer on Morocco. *Their Heads are Green*, Peter Owen, UK. Travel essays. *Without Stopping*, Peter Owen, UK; Ecco Press, US. Bowles' autobiography.

William Burroughs, *Naked Lunch*, Flamingo, UK; Grove Press, US. Revolutionary novel of sexuality and drug addiction, set in Tangier.

Anthony Burgess, *Earthly Powers*, Penguin, UK; Carroll & Graf, US. *The Complete Enderby*, Carroll & Graf, US. Tangier in the 1950s.

Elias Canetti, *The Voices of Marrakesh*, Marion Boyars, UK. Marrakech near the end of the Protectorate.

Esther Freud, *Hideous Kinky*, Penguin UK, WW Norton, US. An English hippy in Marrakech.

Walter Harris, *Morocco That Was*, Eland Books, UK. Observations by *The Times* correspondent, 1890s–1933.

Richard Hughes, *In the Lap of Atlas*, Chatto, UK. Moroccan tales.

Amin Malouf, *Leo the African*, Abacus, UK; *Leo Africanus*, New Amsterdam, US. Historical novel about the 15th-century geographer.

MOROCCAN WRITING IN ENGLISH
Tahar Ben Jalloun, *The Sand Child*, Hamish Hamilton UK, Johns Hopkins UP, US. Novel of childhood in southern Morocco.

Mohammed Choukri, *For Bread Alone*, I.B. Tauris, UK. Volume I of the Rif-born Choukri's autobiography.

Five Eyes, Black Sparrow Press, US. Stories by five Moroccan writers.

Driss Chraibi, *Heirs to the Past*, Heinemann, UK and US. Semi-autobiographical novel set in post-colonial times.

See also pages 28–9.

Glossary

adrar: mountain.

agadir: collective granary in the western Atlas.

agdal: large garden, orchard.

aguelmane: permanent natural lake.

ahidou: collective dance performed by the Berber tribes of the Middle Atlas and eastern High Atlas.

ahwach: collective dance performed by villagers of the western High Atlas and the Anti-Atlas.

aïd: festival.

aït: "son of", referring to a tribe or the region occupied by this tribe.

Ammeln: Berber tribe of the Anti-Atlas whose language is Chleuh (qv).

assif: river or watercourse.

bab: city gate.

baraka: divine blessing, which is passed down from parent to child. *Baraka* is also obtained by making a pilgrimage to a holy shrine.

bendir: drum consisting of a goatskin stretched over a frame.

bled: countryside, village.

borj: bastion or tower set at the corners of the defensive walls of fortified houses.

burnous: voluminous woollen hooded cloak worn by men.

cadi: religious judge, once having the power to impose *sharia* law.

caid: chief of a defined territory, subordinate to the governor of a province.

caliph: title held by a Muslim chief, designating Mohammed's successor.

chergui: hot, dry south-easterly wind.

Chikhate: female dancer from the Middle Atlas.

Chleuh: Berber tribe of the Atlas and Anti-Atlas. Also the language spoken by the tribes of these regions.

dahir: decree having the force of law in Morocco.

dar: house.

dayet: natural lake formed by underground water.

diffa: feast-day meal.

dirham: Moroccan unit of currency.

douar: hamlet.

emir: personal title meaning "he who commands".

erg: expanse of sand or ridge of dunes.

Fassi: inhabitant of Fès.

fiqh: Islamic legal code.

fondouk: in the past, hostelry for travelling merchants, their beasts of burden and their merchandise.

gebs: plaster that can be decoratively carved. Also known as stucco.

gurbi: house of semi-nomadic people, built with mud and branches.

Gnaoua: religious brotherhood of popular belief originating in black Africa. Followers consider themselves to be the spiritual descendants of Bilal, an Ethiopian slave, whom the Prophet Mohammed set free before making him his muezzin (qv).

guedra: dance characteristic of the Goulimine region of Morocco, performed by kneeling women. Also the large drum that is played to accompany the dancers.

Hadith: collection of legends relating to the life, words and deeds of the Prophet Mohammed.

Hadj: pilgrimage to Mecca.

haik: long woman's wrap made from a single piece of fabric, worn draped around the body.

hamada: stony, arid plateau in the Sahara.

hammam: Turkish bath.

hanbel: carpet or blanket woven by Berbers.

Hegira: starting point of the Muslim era, on 16 July 622.

henna: shrub grown for its leaves, which, among other things, are used in the manufacture of cosmetics.

igherm: communal fortified granary typical of the central High Atlas.

imam: Islamic leader of congregational prayer.

jbel: mountain.

jellaba: wide-sleeved, hooded garment worn by both men and women.

jemaa: village assembly of the heads of families in Berber tribes.

kaftan: long woman's garment secured at the front and decorated with passementerie and embroidery.

kasbah: fortified house with a single crenellated tower, or four crenellated towers, one at each corner of the walls.

khoubz: bread (usually a circular loaf).

khaima: tent made of woven goat-hair or camel-hair, used by the nomads of the Sahara and the semi-nomadic people of the Atlas.

khettara: underground channels for the provision of water, along whose course wells are sunk. Synonymous with *foggara*.

koubba: cube-like building crowned by a dome and